HIGH-SPEED SOCIETY

HIGH-SPEED SOCIETY

SOCIAL ACCELERATION, POWER, AND MODERNITY

EDITED BY HARTMUT ROSA AND
WILLIAM E. SCHEUERMAN

THE PENNSYLVANIA STATE UNIVERSITY PRESS
UNIVERSITY PARK, PENNSYLVANIA

LIBRARY OF CONGRESS CATALOGING-IN-PUBLICATION DATA

High-speed society : social acceleration, power, and modernity /
    edited by Hartmut Rosa and William E. Scheuerman.
        p.   cm.
Includes bibliographical references and index.
Summary: "Examines the processes of acceleration in
politics, economic, culture, and society at large. Focuses
on why and how the high-speed contours of crucial forms
of social activity now shape so many facets of human
existence, and suggests possible responses"— Provided by
publisher.
ISBN 978-0-271-03416-4 (cloth : alk. paper)
ISBN 978-0-271-03417-1 (pbk. : alk. paper)
1. Speed—Social aspects.
2. Time—Social aspects.
3. Time pressure.
I. Rosa, Hartmut, 1965– .
II. Scheuerman, William E., 1965– .

HM656.H54 2008
304.2'37—dc22
2008021775

CONTENTS

ILLUSTRATIONS

ACKNOWLEDGMENTS

The editors are grateful to Sandy Thatcher, Patricia Mitchell, John Morris, as well as the entire staff at Penn State Press, for helping to make this book a reality. James Ingram, now in the Political Science Department at McMaster University, did a superb job translating a series of difficult texts.

Chapter 1 reprints Chapter 34 of *The Education of Henry Adams,* by Henry Adams (Boston: Houghton Mifflin, 1918). Chapter 2 is from *The Philosophy of Money,* by Georg Simmel, translated by Tom Bottomore and David Frisby, copyright © 1978 [1907] by Routledge and Kegan Paul. Reproduced by permission of Taylor and Francis Books UK. Chapter 3, "The New Religion-Morality of Speed," [1916] is from *Marinetti: Selected Writings,* by F. T. Marinetti, edited by R. W. Flint, translated by R. W. Flint and Arthur A. Coppotelli. Translation copyright © by Farrar, Straus and Giroux, Inc. Reprinted by permission of Farrar, Straus and Giroux, LLC. Chapter 4 is from *The Public and Its Problems* [1927], by John Dewey. Reprinted with the permission of Swallow Press, Ohio University Press, Athens, Ohio. Chapter 5 is a translation of an excerpt from *Lage der europäischen Rechtswissenschaft,* by Carl Schmitt (Tübingen: Internationale Universitätsverlag, 1950). Used by permission of George Schwab. An earlier version of Chapter 6 appeared in *Constellations* 10, no. 1 (2003). Chapter 7 is a translation of "Gibt es eine Beschleunigung der Geschichte?" in *Zeitschichten: Studien zur Historik,* by Reinhart Koselleck, © Suhrkamp Verlag, Frankfurt am Main, 2000. Chapter 9 is a translation of "Gegenwartsschrumpfung," by Hermann Lübbe, in *Die Beschleunigungsfalle oder der Triumph der Schildkröte,* edited by Klaus Backhaus and Holger Bonus, 3rd ed. (Stuttgart: Schäfer-Pöschel, 1998). Chapter 11 is from *Speed and Politics,* by Paul Virilio, translated by Mark Polizzotti (Los Angeles: Semiotext(e), 2006). Reproduced by permission of Semiotext(e) USA. Chapter 14 reprints William Connolly, "Speed, Concentric Cultures, and Cosmopolitanism," *Political Theory* 28, no. 5 (2000): 596–618, copyright 2000 by Sage Publications, Inc. Reprinted by permission of Sage Publications, Inc. An earlier version of Chapter 15 appeared as "Busyness and Citizenship," by William E. Scheuerman, *Social Research* 72, no. 2 (2005).

INTRODUCTION

Hartmut Rosa and William E. Scheuerman

Acceleration, Deceleration, and Critical Social Theory

What does its mean for society to accelerate? We all notice that events around us seem to take place faster all the time. Our computers process huge sums of information at ever more impressive velocities. What was experienced as being extraordinarily speedy just yesterday (for example, a 66 MHz word processor or an ISDN Internet connection) now seems extraordinarily slow. The shot lengths in movies, advertisements, and even documentaries have increased by a factor of at least fifty,[1] and the speed with which speeches are delivered in parliament has risen by 50 percent since 1945.[2] Athletes break speed records with frightening regularity. Although the velocities of trains, planes, and cars no longer appear to be increasing by much, traffic planners continue to promise abbreviated travel times. The time that elapses between an earthquake, a new disease, or a novel fashion in New Zealand and my being informed about it is getting shorter every year. Speed dating and drive-through funerals[3] remind us that even basic life activities appear to be speeding up: fast food, fast learning, fast love. Neighbors, fashions and lifestyles, jobs and lovers, political convictions, and even religious commitments appear to change at constantly heightened rates. Perhaps most significant, the time we're allowed to concentrate exclusively

---

1. Peter Wollen, "Speed and Cinema," *New Left Review*, no. 16 (2002): 105–14.

2. Thomas Hylland Eriksen, *Tyranny of the Moment: Fast and Slow Time in the Information Age* (London: Pluto Press, 2001), 71. Eriksen is referring to a study of the Norwegian parliament.

3. Both have recently made their appearance in the United States, and one can imagine that they are already being imitated elsewhere. Even the old English pastime of cricket is subject to the forces of acceleration. See Sarah Lyall, "Cricket for Our Time: It's Highly Condensed," *New York Times*, June 27, 2003, A4.

on one thing is progressively diminishing: we are constantly interrupted by a stream of incoming messages, phone calls, television and radio announcements, or merely by sudden breaks in our flow of consciousness that disrupt whatever activity we happen to be pursuing.

In what way, if any, are these phenomena interrelated? Do they signify an acceleration *of* society per se, or are they instead illustrations of separate processes of acceleration *within* society? Do they add up to a qualitative shift in the fabric of contemporary society? Have we crossed a critical threshold or speed barrier, or are recent experiences of speed only one-sided representations of an eternal interplay between the forces of movement and those of constancy and stability? These are among the most important questions that this book seeks to answer.

In debates about contemporary society, it is now something of a commonplace that core social and economic processes are undergoing a dramatic acceleration, while general rates of social change are intensifying no less significantly. Popular as well as scholarly literature includes innumerable assertions that society, history, culture, and even time itself evince substantial evidence of speeding up. In short, *acceleration* figures as a striking feature of prominent diagnoses of contemporary social development.[4] The observation of a change in (spatio-)temporal structures also underlies present debates about globalization, as does the postmodern fascination with experiences of simultaneity and instantaneousness and fragmentation of identity.[5] *Pace* Paul Virilio's innovative recent attempt to initiate a new science of speed or "dromology,"[6] however, the concept of acceleration generally remains elusive and poorly defined. Even in otherwise serious and analytically impressive intellectual work, too often the simplistic claim is made that in modern societies more or less everything is speeding up. While other structural features of Western capitalist modernity (for example,

4. From the popular literature see, for example, James Gleick, *Faster: The Acceleration of Just About Everything* (New York: Pantheon Books, 1999); Jeremy Rifkin, *Time Wars: The Primary Conflict in Human History* (New York: Henry Holt, 1987). The *New York Times*'s editorial writers recently joined the chorus by commenting that "speed and expediency have become the tyrants governing everyday life—walk (or drive) and talk on the phone, fast forward, multitask." "Read This Slowly," *New York Times*, September 28, 2002, A16.

5. On globalization and speed, see David Harvey, *The Condition of Postmodernity: An Enquiry into the Origins of Cultural Change* (Cambridge, Mass.: Blackwell, 1989), as well as Zygmunt Bauman, *Globalization: The Human Consequences* (Cambridge: Polity Press, 1998), and Manuel Castells, *The Rise of the Network Society* (Oxford: Blackwell, 1996). On speed and postmodernism, see Hartmut Rosa in this volume.

6. See Paul Virilio's and Stefan Breuer's contributions to this volume. More generally for Virilio's views, see *The Virilio Reader*, ed. James Der Derian (Oxford: Blackwell, 1998).

differentiation, rationalization, or individualization)[7] have long been the subject of extensive theoretical debate, its key temporal dimension, acceleration, has been largely ignored by social and political analysis. Despite a recent body of social theory that convincingly underscores the need to take social temporality seriously, this oversight probably derives from a dominant atemporal conceptual framework that continues to plague mainstream social science.[8] One aim of the present volume is to help fill that conceptual lacuna.

By clearing the path toward a better understanding of recent temporal trends, we hope to demonstrate that the concept of social acceleration is an indispensable tool for contemporary social and political analysis. Notwithstanding the intellectual and political distances separating the contributors to this volume, their insights help provide the necessary conceptual instruments if we are to distinguish better between serious social analysis and the superficial technobabble and imbalanced ideology ubiquitous in contemporary discourse about speed. The editors of this volume also hope to make a contribution, however modest, to a critical theory of society. In our view, the concept of acceleration holds out the promise of shedding fresh light on a host of political and social pathologies plaguing contemporary society. Although the diverse theoretical perspectives represented here offer no easy answers concerning the best way to overcome those pathologies, and although some of the authors included here endorse politically quiescent and even reactionary answers to the challenges of speed, we believe that paying closer attention to the high-speed contours of contemporary society ultimately places its core attributes in a critical light. If the unfulfilled quest for a decent society is to remain viable in the twenty-first century, a serious-minded analysis of the temporal driving forces underlying contemporary society will have to make up a crucial element of a renewed critical theory of society. We hope that the essays collected here, some by internationally renowned scholars and available for the first time to an English-speaking audience, can help generate a useful debate about social acceleration, as well as its causes and consequences.

Motivated by these theoretical and political concerns, this volume aims to provide a comprehensive survey of historical and contemporary perspectives on the following set of pressing temporal questions:

---

7. See Rosa in this volume.

8. For a survey, see Barbara Adam, *Time and Social Theory* (Cambridge: Polity Press, 1990). Among empirical-minded social scientists, the work of John P. Robinson and Geoffrey Godbey is noteworthy. See *Time for Life: The Surprising Ways Americans Use Their Time* (University Park: Pennsylvania State University Press, 1997).

1. First, how should we *conceptualize* acceleration? What forms of acceleration are empirically observable in modern society? Which social arenas, spheres, institutions, or structures in fact change at higher rates than in the past? Is social acceleration a linear process, or does it instead constitute a discontinuous process subject to countertendencies, obstacles, and sudden leaps? In what sense—if any—is it justifiable to speak of the acceleration *of* society, rather than of various forms of acceleration *within* society?

2. Which structures, processes, and institutions seem *immune* to change? How do processes of acceleration relate to evidence of social, historical, and cultural *deceleration*?

3. How can we best describe the *causes* of acceleration? What drives acceleration, and how exactly do the driving forces behind acceleration relate to other developmental trends in modern society?

4. What are the *consequences* of social acceleration on the individual and on the texture of social life? How does acceleration impact on politics and law?

5. Are there individual, social, and ecological limits to acceleration? Is there a logical end point toward which changes in temporal structure converge?

6. What critical potential might an analysis of the temporal structures of society yield?

As the diverse contemporary and historical discussions of social acceleration collected here will quickly reveal, a wide variety of answers to each of these questions is possible. Let us screen them one by one:

(1) One of the most difficult dilemmas in formulating a theory of acceleration is the fact that a mere collection of symptoms or instances of acceleration will not suffice. As a brief glance at the examples mentioned above shows, we can easily find evidence for a wide variety of manifestations of acceleration. In their sheer totality, they are sometimes interpreted as indications for the speedup of contemporary culture,[9] history,[10] or even time itself.[11] Before we embrace comprehensive diagnoses of this type, however, additional clarification seems necessary. First, it is essential that we pay attention to those realms of social life that do *not* accelerate and sometimes

9. See Hermann Lübbe below; see also Peter Conrad, *Modern Times, Modern Places* (New York: Norton, 1999).
10. For discussions of this idea, see Henry Adams and Reinhart Koselleck in this volume.
11. Georges Gurvitch, *The Spectrum of Social Time* (Dordrecht: D. Reidel, 1963).

even appear subject to deceleration. Otherwise, our temporal diagnosis will necessarily be one-sided and thus potentially misleading. Second, it seems obligatory that we investigate how different examples of social acceleration may turn out to be interconnected. The readings collected in this volume should help shed light on both tasks.

On closer examination, we find that theorists of social acceleration generally concentrate on one or more of the following types of phenomena. First, the sense of an enormous speedup is clearly fueled by the profound effects of the acceleration in transportation and communication that took place over the course of the nineteenth and twentieth centuries.[12] The revolution in transportation and communication has indisputably changed the way we perceive space and time. Not surprisingly, our perceptions of innumerable facets of social life have changed as well. In contrast, other authors barely mention this form of speedup. Instead, they tend to concentrate on the speedup of everyday life, that is, on the increasing scarcity of time and, consequently, the acceleration in our pace of life. As the contributions to this volume show, this form of acceleration is exceedingly difficult, though by no means impossible, to define and measure.[13] Yet another form of acceleration refers to increases in productivity and efficiency: we produce more goods in vastly reduced periods of time, and we also appear to consume them at a higher pace.[14] Finally, some have identified a speedup of a very different sort, namely increased social and cultural rates of change. The number of technical, social, and cultural innovations, so the argument goes, is increasing dramatically. As a result, the lifeworld is constantly dismantled at an ever-faster velocity: fashions, lifestyles, product cycles, jobs, relations to spouses and sexual partners, political and religious beliefs, forms of practice and association, as well particular orientations toward social action become increasingly contingent and unstable during the course of modernity. This perception fuels the case for an acceleration of culture.[15] To be sure, it might well turn out that this in fact is nothing more than an extension of a much older evolutionary principle of acceleration. Recall the familiar clock model of natural history often used to depict the history of

12. This form of acceleration is at the heart of the notion of "time-space compression," the term coined by David Harvey; it is crucial as well for the reflections of authors as diverse as the Italian Futurist F. T. Marinetti and the leading left-wing contemporary French analyst of speed, Virilio (see their contributions to this volume below).

13. For attempts to do so, see the contributions by Simmel and Rosa below.

14. Staffan Burenstam Linder, *The Harried Leisure Class* (New York: Columbia University Press, 1970).

15. For example, see Lübbe below.

life on earth in terms of the passing of one hour of time. During the course of most of the hour, nothing significant appears to happen; the clock's hands barely move. Yet minutes and seconds before the hour is up, events visibly speed up at an exponential rate, and the rate of change steadily grows higher as *Homo sapiens* appears on the scene; the clock's hands now spring forward.[16]

Not surprising, how these different realms of acceleration are interrelated is a matter of heated debate. The answers provided to this question depend significantly on one's view of the causes of acceleration (see Point 3 below).

(2) What aspects of social life are *not* speeding up? Aside from a whole range of more or less "natural" obstacles to speed and intentional slowdowns,[17] two phenomena deserve special attention. First, many of the processes of acceleration identified above do not affect (adversely or otherwise) a substantial portion of the world's population. In other words, there are many places where life pretty much goes on as it did in the past. In some regions subject to desperate poverty and crippling political disorder, core social processes understandably appear to have come to a standstill. Significant segments of the population of the developed world also appear to be excluded from key features of social acceleration: for the unemployed, the sick, the homeless, and many retirees, life sometimes seems subject to a slowdown rather than a speedup. To the extent that those who fall under these social categories now appear to be increasing in number as well, the experience of deceleration accordingly tends to appear relatively widespread. There are plausible reasons for postulating that this experience of deceleration primarily constitutes evidence of cultural and structural social exclusion. It does not necessarily undermine the claim that contemporary society is subject to a structural or cultural acceleration per se. Nevertheless, the fact that a significant portion of humanity experiences slowness at least as intensely as it does speed should caution us about the dangers of any overly general diagnosis concerning social acceleration.

Paradoxically, the widespread contemporary experience of sweeping social acceleration is also accompanied by an equally strong impression of a deeply rooted, complementary trend toward structural and cultural sclerosis and inertia. From this latter perspective, history is not speeding up at all; on the contrary, it has come to an end. Beneath all the frantic movement of events

16. See Henry Adams and Reinhart Koselleck in this volume.
17. For a discussion of how acceleration generates deceleration or "slowdowns," see Rosa below.

and appearance, we find what Nietzsche might have described as the eternal repetition of the ever-same: a terminal sclerosis of culture and ideas, or what Virilio has dubbed the "polar inertia" toward which we inevitably gravitate, notwithstanding widespread evidence of social acceleration.[18]

Another key question that needs to be tackled concerns the fundamental nature of the process (or processes) of acceleration. How exactly does acceleration proceed? How can it be it observed? As some of the volume's contributions suggest, there tend to be waves of acceleration that are subsequently followed by increases in the discourse on acceleration (along with futile calls for deceleration), as well as phases of relative stability. Since most authors agree that a significant period of acceleration took place between 1880 and 1920, it should come as no surprise that many of the most astute analyses of acceleration were written either during this period or slightly posterior to it.[19] With the fall of communist regimes and the takeoff of the digital revolution in the late eighties and nineties, another impressive round of acceleration probably occurred. This second round similarly generated a wide-ranging debate on the causes and effects of social acceleration, as much of the recent debate on globalization can be interpreted as an attempt to make sense of the ramifications of social speed.[20]

(3) Every diagnosis of acceleration remains conceptually fuzzy unless the question of its fundamental causes is tackled head-on. So what drives social acceleration? We can identify two main competing approaches to this question. One group of authors assumes that social acceleration is the consequence of a transhistorical anthropological or even biological principle. For them, speed is a successful strategy of survival, a basic biological imperative of effort reduction: to be fast is to save energy, demonstrate adaptability, and outrace competitors in the struggle for scarce resources.[21] In human history, this principle, as Virilio reminds us, seems to be transformed into a principle of power and dominance, and hence of war and politics: "Speed has always been the advantage and the privilege of the hunter and the warrior. Racing and pursuit are the heart of all combat. There is thus a hierarchy of speeds to be found in the history of societies, for to possess the earth, to hold terrain, is also to possess the best means to scan it in order to protect and defend it."[22] Human history can be interpreted as a ferocious temporal

---

18. See Paul Virilio, *Polar Inertia* (London: SAGE, 1999).
19. For example, Simmel, Adams, Marinetti, and John Dewey below.
20. See Bob Jessop and John Urry in this volume.
21. Peter Kafka, *Gegen den Untergang: Schöpfungsprinzip und globale Beschleuningungskrise* (Munich: C. Hanser, 1999).
22. Virilio, "Military Space," in *The Virilio Reader*, 24.

Darwinian struggle culminating in the "survival of the fastest." Other authors favor an alternative theoretical framework that similarly takes speed to be a transhistorical imperative, which we might describe as "catastrophism." They hold that major changes in social temporality are caused by forces external to the societies affected, such as natural disasters and war.[23] Whether or not a transhistorical principle of acceleration exists, however, there can be little doubt that the real takeoff of social acceleration starts with the advent of modernity. Just as it remains unclear exactly when modernity began, so too is it difficult to provide a precise date and place for the commencement of modern acceleration. Thus, we find a heated debate about whether the regime of modern time discipline, framed by the conceptions of abstract, linear time and dominated by clock time, originates most fundamentally in the cloisters, the capitalist markets, or the prisons and barracks essential to modern state development.[24]

Existing research suggests that the origins of modern acceleration are probably multiple. But what are its most important driving forces? Here as well, many potential causes have been identified. One popular argument tries to connect the acceleration of the pace of life and social and cultural change to advances in technology, where we find especially spectacular and easily measurable forms of acceleration. Yet the cultural sense of an increasing scarcity of time cannot be explained by technological acceleration alone: as we have known at least since Karl Marx, technological development potentially functions to save time and thus should augment free time and leisure. When properly employed, high-speed technology might very well function to slow down the pace of everyday existence. Therefore, technological acceleration is perhaps an effect rather than a cause of social acceleration as a general phenomenon: note that many sustained attempts at accelerating transportation and communication took place before any of the great technological breakthroughs of modernity occurred.[25] In part because of such considerations, another commonly held view attributes social acceleration more or less exclusively to the immanent dynamics of capitalism. Following Marx's famous account of the temporality of modern capitalism,

---

23. See, for example, Anatol Rapoport, *General System Theory* (Cambridge, Mass: Abacus Press, 1986).

24. Nigel Thrift, "Vivos Voco: Ringing the Changes in the Historical Geography of Time Consciousness," in *The Rhythms of Society,* ed. Michael Young and Tom Schuller (London: Routledge, 1988), 53–94; Gerhard Dohrn van Rossum, "Zeit der Kirche, Zeit der Händler, Zeit der Städte," in *Zerstörung und Wiederaneignung von Zeit,* ed. Rainer Zoll (Frankfurt am Main: Suhrkamp, 1988), 72–88; Jacques LeGoff, *Medieval Civilization, 400–1500* (Oxford: Blackwell, 1990).

25. See Koselleck's contribution in this volume.

the simple equation of time and money in the market is responsible for the speedup of production, and hence of circulation and consumption, too. The necessity of speed in economic competition certainly could explain the well-nigh permanent revolution in production, transportation, and communication technologies; for example, David Harvey argues that capitalism generates a compression of time and space that, operating in accordance with a classical base-superstructure explanatory model, produces far-reaching consequences for the cultural and political realms as well.[26] In contrast, other analysts suggest that capitalism is itself an effect rather than a cause of a culture of chronic time famine. For those who endorse this position, acceleration is a result of secularization, since the cultural experience of a loss of "eternal time" creates an unbridgeable gap between the time of the world and the individual lifespan. This is an idea suggested, for example, by the philosopher Hans Blumenberg. From a Christian perspective, the end of one's individual life and the end of the world imminent with Christ's return converge: both gravitate toward the same end point, after which another, more important form of time begins. From a secular perspective, however, the time and the offers of the world are virtually eternal and endless, whereas the end of the individual lifespan, meaning death, approaches quickly. Thus, living faster serves as a strategy to diminish the distance between the time of the world and the time of one's life. If we live twice as fast, we can realize twice as many worldly options within a single lifespan; that is, we can live two lives in one. Eventually, acceleration can thus serve as a functional equivalent to eternity.[27] Other possible candidates for the prime

26. Harvey, *The Condition of Postmodernity*. For those inspired directly by Marx, see Jessop in this volume. Simmel advances a slightly different perspective by seeing money rather than capitalist accumulation as a central driving force behind acceleration. For Linder, it is not so much capitalism as the success of our productive technologies that causes the veritable time famine plaguing contemporary society. In his view, potentially scarce goods such as time and money tend toward a rational allocation: people try to spend time as efficiently as possible. How much they work, rest, consume goods, care for their own bodies and belongings, or engage in philosophical or cultural activities depends on what they can expect in return. Thus, as productivity rises, they get more and more out of work and consumption, and this, in turn, leads to an increased scarcity of time and a corresponding shift in people's time budgets. Wealth in goods and wealth in time are inversely related: poor societies experience an abundance of time (to engage in work has no net effects, as there is little to consume), whereas rich societies are starved for time. In this way, Linder may actually fall into a cultural rather than economic school of explanation, but he can also be read as an attempt to bridge the gap between the two (see *The Harried Leisure Class*).

27. Hans Blumenberg, *Lebenszeit und Weltzeit* (Frankfurt am Main: Suhrkamp, 1986). See also Rosa in this volume. Max Weber provides an early version of this cultural approach by arguing that the temporal contours of the Protestant ethic, which later on became thoroughly secularized, triggered the rise of capitalism.

mover of social acceleration in modernity are the competitive dynamics of the modern state system and military rivalry, both of which incessantly generate high-speed forms of social action; or perhaps, as suggested by some practitioners of systems theory, the principle of functional differentiation.[28]

There is no need here to decide the matter of the fundamental driving forces, though there are good reasons to expect that modern social acceleration can only be explained as the joint result of a complex interlocking set of causes.

(4) We also need to examine the social consequences of the multiple processes of acceleration identified above. Since both collective and individual life experiences are necessarily temporal in character, changes in temporal structures tend to lead to far-reaching effects on them. Shifts in social temporality affect workplace experience, our love lives, and countless other facets of human existence. As the essays collected here demonstrate, acceleration has manifold cultural, ethical, psychological, political, and even ecological consequences: it changes the core of our fundamental being in time and space. For one thing, our capacity to transverse vast distances at rising speeds alters our perception of time and space. As early as the emergence of the railways, insightful social commentators noted that acceleration compresses and even annihilates distance. In the age of the Internet, spatial location sometimes comes to seem altogether irrelevant. As a result of acceleration, the anthropological preponderance of space over time is inverted and ultimately replaced by the dominance of time.[29] In addition, the phenomenological horizons of past, present, and future—and hence of the self and its relation to the social world—cannot remain unaffected by the speedup of social change: there are significant differences between relatively static cultures and those in which high rates of innovation in many spheres of activity incessantly revolutionize the lifeworld.[30] For example, processes of cultural reproduction are different in dynamic high-speed societies than in static ones,[31] because our perceptions of the relationship of the self to world, to tradition, and to history are similarly altered when the horizons of expectation—

---

28. See Virilio and Rosa in this volume.
29. See Breuer in this volume.
30. See Lübbe in this volume.
31. For example, some studies suggest that in the context of high-speed mass media, even language, the basic cultural tool per se, is incessantly transformed: lengthy and time-consuming linguistic constructions tend to be erased. For example, "sound bites" allow for nothing more than short expressions of opinion. Similarly, information has to be transmitted in ways that allow for short attention spans. This corresponds to familiar tendencies in aesthetic experience toward the dissolution of linear narration in favor of the simultaneity of fragmentary images.

that is, what we predict for the future with some degree of confidence—diverge significantly from our images of the past.[32] In cultures that systematically favor the short term over the long term, the idea of stable individual (or, for that matter, stable collective) identity risks becoming anachronistic. It tends to be replaced by more open, experimental, and fragmentary images of the self.[33] While some writers see this trend as threatening, those of a more postmodern bent typically celebrate its liberating and even redemptory power, suggesting that it bears the promise of liberation from the "terror of identity," of being the ever-same. From their perspective, it holds out the promise of an almost infinite plurality of forms of life within a single life course: acceleration thereby comes to serve as a functional equivalent to traditional ideas of an "eternal life." As the high speed of social change alters the relationship between generations, old age no longer is treated with reverence and as evidence of wisdom, but rather as a handicap and an anachronistic exemplar. Instead of having the advantage of years of accumulated wisdom, seniors suffer the disadvantage of no longer being at home in a lifeworld where past experience so often seems utterly irrelevant given the fast pace of social and cultural change. Psychologically as well as ethically, high-speed society clearly privileges the capacity to adapt at a rapid-fire pace to ever-changing circumstances. It demands flexibility on the part of the individual in the context of changing opportunity structures and high rates of contingency. The rhythm, sequence, and duration of a significant range of experiences shift as well: times allotted to work, relaxation, and shopping decreasingly follow a rigid predetermined schedule, and over the life course, key events (for example, marriage, childbirth and childrearing, work life, education) seem to lose the binding temporal order, sequence, and rhythm they once possessed.

Social acceleration also has a huge impact on many facets of collective experience. In particular, it raises difficult political questions. Whereas some emphasize the democratic potential of new high-speed communications technologies, or celebrate a speedup that frees people from the inertia of tradition and custom, others remind us that self-government inevitably takes time and may even require the existence of relatively stable publics. In other words, some writers embrace the political repercussions of speed,

---

32. This is Koselleck's argument (see in this volume).

33. For an anxious discussion of this trend, see Richard Sennett, *The Corrosion of Character: The Personal Consequences of Work in the New Capitalism* (New York: Norton, 1998); see also Kenneth Gergen, *The Saturated Self: Dilemmas of Identity in Contemporary Life* (New York: Basic Books, 2000).

whereas others believe that it poses a fundamental threat to democracy.[34] How, for example, can the democratic state hope successfully to regulate high-speed capitalism? Finally, acceleration plays a significant but typically unacknowledged role in the ecological crisis: contemporary society uses up natural resources like gas and oil at rates much higher than necessary for their reproduction, and produces and dumps large amounts of toxic waste at faster speeds than the ecosystem is able to dispose of them. In other words, familiar forms of pollution and climatic change can also be understood, at least in part, as resulting from the temporal gap separating contemporary society's use of natural resources and nature's capacity for regeneration.

(5) This takes us to the crucial question of the limits of speed. How much speed can and should we achieve? How much can we tolerate? Ever since our historical predecessors first grappled with the experience of social acceleration, worries about things going too fast have abounded. We only need to remind ourselves about the now seemingly quaint anxieties that greeted the appearance of the first steam engine or automobile: physicians and psychiatrists quickly diagnosed serious injuries and dangers likely to be caused by the unhealthy speed of ten or fifteen miles per hour, and since it took some time until people developed the capacity to adapt their senses to higher speeds, the fact that so many people were in fact sickened by their first train or automobile ride seemed to prove the skeptics right. These examples remind us of the dangers of underestimating individual and collective resources for temporal adaptation. The same holds true for so-called natural speed barriers of all kinds. Modern science has found ways to speed up many processes formerly thought to be fundamentally unchangeable (for example, cures for diseases previously thought incurable). Instead, we should conceive of limits to speed as primarily cultural and political: even though the precise nature of these limits calls for more thorough investigation, beyond a certain tempo of transformation, cultural reproduction might inevitably become strained and perhaps even impossible.[35] The erosion of institutions—which, by definition, necessarily embody elements of permanence and stability—might inadvertently unravel the fabric of high-speed society, since many processes of acceleration necessarily depend on stable institutional frameworks. This is perhaps most evident in the realm of law: modern democratic legislation possesses the double advantage of being, on the one hand, dynamic (as opposed to relatively static forms of

34. See Marinetti, Dewey, Schmitt, William E. Connolly, and William E. Scheuerman in this volume.
35. See Lübbe in this volume.

customary law) and, on the other hand, able to provide a stable framework for social action. The process of lawmaking cannot be sped up infinitely, however.[36] Legitimate democratic decision making and interest mediation are necessarily deliberate and thus time-consuming. Indeed, they tend to be even more slow-going in dynamic, constantly changing societies since political commitments there tend also to become short-lived. As a result, the identification, formulation, and representation of collective interests become increasingly arduous and thus time-consuming as well.[37]

There appear to be two possible limits to speed in terms of both individual and collective experience: acceleration might outpace our capacities for the successful integration of temporal experience as well as our ability to synchronize disparate temporal logics. For example, how much change and flexibility can we integrate into our lives without losing some minimal indispensable sense of coherence, history, and shared narrative? To be sure, individuals are forced to adapt to the temporal structures that confront them in different spheres of social activity (for example, in the economy or state). But even if we are capable of gradually increasing our tolerance for speed, there still seems to be no guarantee that we will do so in accordance with the temporal requirements of specific spheres of social life. This underscores the difficulties of synchronization: even if most spheres of social life are now speeding up, it seems unlikely that they are all doing so at the same pace. Hence, we are confronted with the distinct possibility that different institutional spheres (for example, the capitalist economy and democratic state) might grow progressively out of step with one another. In fact, many economic and technological changes already seem on the verge of becoming politically uncontrollable. Possibilities for temporal disintegration and desynchronization seem ubiquitous in contemporary society. For example, many political economists now point out that the immensely increased transaction speeds characteristic of the financial markets have completely uncoupled them from the "real" material economic realm; this may have potentially troublesome results. Similarly, experiences of the "non-simultaneity of the simultaneous" clearly seem to be on the rise between as well as within specific societies: social groups or individuals following very different temporal rhythms frequently coexist in any given territory, and dramatic

---

36. See Schmitt in this volume.

37. For example, the welfare state provided a stable institutional background and a safety net for many processes of economic and cultural speedup, yet it now faces severe pressures: what once appeared as a paragon of speed and temporal efficiency (e.g., modern bureaucracy) increasingly is a symbol of sluggishness and sclerosis.

temporal disjunctures might contribute to explosive social conflict. For example, one consequence of globalization is that we now find privileged social groups well acclimated to the worlds of high-speed global economic and cultural flows but structurally and culturally out of touch with a growing mass of socially excluded groups.[38]

This poses the question of whether there is something like a necessary end point to social acceleration, a temporal state of affairs toward which modernity inevitably gravitates. Here as well, two scenarios seem possible. First, even if we are correct to see temporal desynchronization and disintegration as growing problems in contemporary society, it remains conceivable that novel social, political, and legal institutions might bring about a new temporal equilibrium, where the forces of change and stability would be more or less successfully balanced at a higher and more complex level than at the present time. Such a development might mirror the emergence of the relatively stable institutional framework of modern society following a period of high insecurity and instability generated by capitalist industrialization, which, as Virilio and others have noted, can also be interpreted as a speed or "dromocratic revolution." It is the function of such an institutional framework to direct and steer the processes of acceleration along stable pathways. In due course, individual, cultural, and political life might adapt to new levels of social speed by developing corresponding forms of control, perhaps, but not necessarily, with the help of computer technology and other recent high-speed innovations.[39] In other words, one might still conceive of the possibility that our high-speed society might develop a sufficiently stable institutional and cultural substructure capable of providing a necessary minimum of constancy in social life. Yet it is no less conceivable that social speed has outgrown every possibility of successful reintegration and temporal balance: by setting everything in motion along the lines of a "total mobilization," modernity would thereby have lost its capacity to find a healthy balance between change and stability.[40] Of course, it is also possible that any of a host of imaginable catastrophes generated by our inability to harness speed effectively (for example, nuclear war, climatic disaster, new

38. Castells, *The Rise of the Network Society*. Of course, this argument has been made by others as well.

39. Think, for example, of novel possibilities for accelerating democratic decision making via computer technology. For a survey of the debate, see Ian Budge, *The New Challenge of Direct Democracy* (Cambridge: Polity Press, 1996).

40. Eventually, "hyperacceleration" might generate an uncontrolled process according to which total inertia, or the recurrence of the ever-same, results. See Jean Baudrillard, *The Illusion of the End* (Stanford: Stanford University Press, 2000), 217–25; Fredric Jameson, *The Cultural Turn* (New York: Verso, 1998), 50–72.

forms of disease, or a political breakdown followed by horrible forms of violence) might put an end to the process of social acceleration along with the project of modernity that spawned it. Conceivably, disastrous conflicts pitting those excluded from the ambivalent achievements of high-speed society against those benefiting from it might erupt.

(6) Such perils underscore the pressing need for a critical analysis of social acceleration. Our ultimate motive for putting together this volume is the intuition that a systematic analysis of social acceleration opens up new pathways for social and political criticism in the aftermath of the dissolution of the normative bases once provided by the philosophy of history and philosophical anthropology.[41] Ten years ago, an analogous idea was advanced by the controversial German philosopher Peter Sloterdijk, who attempted to develop a new critical theory of "political kinetics," conceived as a third version of critical theory after Marx and the Frankfurt School. In Sloterdijk's view, both earlier versions of critical theory ultimately failed because they misunderstood and uncritically supported the kinetic forces of modernity, which set everything in motion until they ultimately achieve a state of "total mobilization" ("totale Mobilmachung"), a warlike state where everything is determined by the logic of speed.[42] Unfortunately, Sloterdijk's own approach was overly speculative, unsystematic, and oblivious to the importance of empirical findings. Nonetheless, we believe that something useful can be retrieved from his otherwise highly problematic reformulation of critical theory. In our view, temporal structures provide a special point of access to the necessary connection between systemic macro- and individual micro- level perspectives on social experience. There is no question that structural social transformations (for example, the emergence of industrial capital- ism) yield corresponding changes in individual self-understandings and orientations towards action. Structural change and alterations in the domi- nant forms of culture and identity go hand in hand. But in highly individ- ualized and ethically pluralistic societies, it becomes notoriously difficult to disclose how systemic or functional needs (for example, the imperatives of growth and acceleration in capitalist economies) are translated into cul- tural perspectives as well as individual orientations toward action. The cen- tral nodal point for this mutual assimilation is the experience of time. As

---

41. On this situation, see Axel Honneth, "Pathologien des Sozialen: Tradition und Aktu- alität der Sozialphilosophie," in *Pathologien des Sozialen: Die Aufgaben der Sozialphilosophie* (Frankfurt am Main: Fischer Taschenbuch, 1994), 9–69.

42. Peter Sloterdijk, *Eurotaoismus: Zur Kritik der politischen Kinetik* (Frankfurt am Main: Suhrkamp, 1989), 12–14, 26–29, 52–54.

sociologists have long emphasized, the basic temporal horizons of action, and even the measurement and perception of time, vary in accordance with the basic structure of society.[43] Nevertheless, the experience of time takes the form of solid and seemingly "objective" facticity at the individual level: products of socialization, temporal structures and horizons are deeply rooted in our *habitus* and take on the form of a "second nature."[44] Consequently, time is both profoundly private—*how do I want to spend my time?* is perhaps the most fundamental ethical question we face—and simultaneously indisputably social: the core structures, patterns, and velocities of temporal experience are nonetheless beyond the immediate reach of any given individual. The normative character of such temporal structures manifests itself in many ways: social rhythms, sequences, and velocities are regularly sanctioned by various penalties, and in modern societies, ignoring the predominant temporal norms can lead to social exclusion.[45] It is precisely because of the dual character of temporal experience that temporal structures can be seen as a primary locus for the integration and coordination of individual perspectives and identities, on the one hand, and structural or functional imperatives, on the other. Since temporal structures are socially interpreted as factually given, as something objective and seemingly natural in character, they can achieve a maximum of social coordination and regulation, while simultaneously requiring only a minimum of externally imposed ethical or authoritative paternalism. If this interpretation is plausible, however, it becomes evident that the question about how we want to spend our time is not simply a private one, but political in the strongest possible sense. Thus, the drive toward social acceleration can be taken as an ethically and politically unregulated feature of collective social existence carrying substantial normative significance and a looming potential for the creation of social pathologies in the form of time pathologies.

As many contributions collected in this volume demonstrate, social acceleration changes our relationship toward space and time, the natural and material structures surrounding us (the objective world), toward our fellow

43. Norbert Elias, *Time: An Essay* (Oxford: Blackwell, 1992); Émile Durkheim, *The Elementary Forms of Religious Life* (New York: Free Press, 1995); Pitrin A. Sorokin and Robert Merton, "Social Time: A Methodological and Functional Analysis," *American Journal of Sociology* 42 (1937): 615–29; Niklas Luhmann, "The Future Cannot Begin," in *The Differentiation of Society* (New York: Columbia University Press, 1982), 271–88.

44. Elias, *Time: An Essay.*

45. Simonetta Tabboni, "The Idea of Social Time in Norbert Elias," *Time and Society* 10 (2001): 5–27, esp. 18 (taking temporal norms to be collective norms par excellence). See also Robert Lauer, *Temporal Man: The Meaning and Uses of Social Time* (New York: Praeger, 1981), 72.

human beings (the social world), and finally, toward ourselves (the subjective world). We have already discussed the phenomena of temporal disintegration and desynchronization that plague contemporary society. Yet the most striking problem with a hyperaccelerated society is that it undermines individual and collective autonomy. The promise of individual as well as collective autonomy, however, defines the modern project.[46] If it can be systematically demonstrated that the forces of acceleration have reached a point where they are destroying our fundamental capacity to exercise ethical and political autonomy, we might then have a sturdy basis for social criticism.[47] Many of the essays collected here provide strong indications of the potential merit of this approach. As we will see, there is substantial empirical evidence that the specter of desynchronization, for example, threatens political autonomy: social, economic, and technological change, it seems, have become so rapid-fire in character that they no longer are effectively steered by existing democratic institutions. And whether forms of self-government might counter this trend still remains a matter of controversy.

The analysis of social acceleration also potentially opens the door to a revitalized critique of ideology. From our perspective, postmodern approaches that deride any attempt at systematic critical theory as just another doomed "metanarrative," as nothing more than a stepping-stone toward totalitarianism, in favor of an uncritical celebration of a fragmentary, experimental, incoherent life course, represent forms of capitulation to the structural imperatives of high-speed society. By no means can we naïvely accept the postmodernist self-understanding that it represents a contribution to emancipation. The multiple or fragmentary selves endorsed by postmodernism, it turns out, may be dictated by the necessities of acceleration rather than the result of an autonomous ethical choice.

A close analysis of the effects of acceleration on fundamental temporal structures might finally lead to novel insights about individual pathologies widespread in contemporary society. Social actors are presented with the challenge of constantly negotiating and integrating at least three temporal perspectives. Typically, we focus on the temporal structures of everyday life

---

46. In this respect, we are in strong agreement with the critical theory tradition, as represented by the early Frankfurt School and Habermas, as well as its more recent practitioners.

47. Our starting point might provide a basis for social critique that is even stronger than the moral principles formulated by discourse ethics, since it would not be confronted with the motivational gap plaguing the latter: speed would not only threaten the abstract principles of justice, but also undermine the possibility of pursuing a good life that is our own creation.

and its routines and repetitive conundrums, but periodically (during crises or transitions in status) we compare how we are doing against the (linear) temporal perspectives of the life course as a whole, of our life plans and projects. Finally, we have to balance both against the perceived images and needs of the epoch in which we find ourselves, against the structurally based speeds, rhythms, and durations of collective historical time. Social acceleration impacts on our resources to negotiate and reconcile these perspectives. It risks undermining the capacity of social actors to integrate distinct temporal perspectives and thereby develop a coherent sense of self as well as those time-resistant priorities necessary for the exercise of autonomy. Widespread perceptions of growing fatalism,[48] along with an alarming rise in various forms of depression (both in the clinical and the metaphorical sense), arguably are related to temporal disorders.[49] Although further empirical research is obviously required, they might be taken as representing pathological forms of reaction to the pressures of acceleration. Formulated in more philosophical (and abstract) terms: social acceleration condenses episodes of action and experience; as such, it counteracts our capacity to relate episodes of experience to a sense of identity, history, and the communities we constitute. Episodes of experience thus would remain just that: episodes that pass without a trace without being transformed into lived experience, in the sense once described by Walter Benjamin.[50] In this way, critical analysis of speed might also serve as a starting point for reformulating the critique of alienation: the high-speed tempo of change potentially leads to manifold forms of alienation from space and time, the objective world, social world, and the self since the appropriation of novel experiences and subsequent familiarization with them requires time no longer readily available to individuals in a high-speed society.

A fundamental question is whether the pathologies of social acceleration can be overcome without attacking its central driving forces (for example, capitalism). Might it "merely" take a series of institutional reforms oriented toward gaining sufficient control over high-speed society, or, alternatively, is the only answer a dramatic pull of the emergency brake of high-speed

48. Sloterdijk, *Eurotaoismus*, 111. See also Manfred Garhammer, *Wie Europäer ihre Zeit nutzen: Zeitstrukturen and Zeitkulturen im Zeichen der Globalisierung* (Berlin: Edition Sigma, 2001).

49. Lothar Baier, *Keine Zeit! 18 Versuche über die Beschleunigung* (Munich: A. Kunstmann, 2000), 147; Alain Ehrenberg, *La fatigue d'être soi: dépression et société* (Paris: O. Jacob, 1998).

50. On this, see the instructive essay by Amir Ahmadi, "On the Indispensability of Youth for Experience: Time and Experience in Paul Valery and Walter Benjamin," *Time and Society* 10 (2001): 191–212.

society as an escape from the course of history altogether, along the lines Walter Benjamin argued in his famous critique of progress?[51]

Of course, the reader does not need to endorse such speculative arguments in order to acknowledge the rich potential for social analysis entailed by a critical-minded examination of social acceleration.

From Classical to Contemporary Perspectives

The present volume undertakes to tackle these questions in three parts. Part 1 consists of a selection of the most astute early to mid-twentieth-century statements about the phenomenon of social acceleration in modern thought. Part 2 includes more recent attempts to develop ambitious und undeniably impressive theoretical analyses of social speed or acceleration. Part 3 interrogates the political consequences of social acceleration.

The social experience of time in modern society has been widely analyzed by literary figures, political critics, social theorists, and philosophers. Yet our discussions here of social acceleration are more focused and, we believe, politically more pertinent. Among the innumerable nineteenth- and twentieth-century writers who thematized the social experience of time, a relatively elite group zeroed in on the specific dynamics of social acceleration or social speed. Because their prescient reflections on the temporal dynamics of modernity offer a necessary basis for formulating a coherent understanding of the dynamics of social acceleration, some of their most important contributions are considered in Part 1. Other authors than those represented here might legitimately have been included, but in our view Henry Adams, Georg Simmel, and Filippo Tommaso Marinetti grasped the centrality of social acceleration to recent social experience to a degree unmatched by their contemporaries. Although John Dewey and Carl Schmitt are not generally described as theorists of temporality, we believe that they also formulated, from radically antagonistic positions, unfairly neglected early analyses of the potential dangers of social acceleration for democratic political life, a chief preoccupation of Part 3 of this volume. The classical reflections on social speed brought together for the first time here are illuminating historical documents that record the profound temporal transformations experienced by Western modernity, especially since the Industrial Revolution.

---

51. Walter Benjamin, "Theses on the Philosophy of History," in *Illuminations*, ed. Hannah Arendt (New York: Harcourt, Brace and World, 1968), 253–64.

Typically neglected by contemporary social and political theorists, the historian and literary figure Henry Adams nonetheless perhaps came closest among early analysts of social temporality to grasping the general significance of speed for the dynamics of social development, and his idiosyncratic yet highly suggestive stab at formulating a "law of acceleration" as a way of making sense of human history is thus reprinted here (chapter 1). Even though many readers may justifiably find Adams' account of acceleration unduly unsystematic, and despite the fact that there exist sound reasons why we should be skeptical of his naïve claim that the entire course of human history can be neatly described by means of an invariable law or regularity, his 1904 essay remains original and uncannily prophetic. Indeed, the present volume might plausibly be taken as an attempt to confirm Adams's core intuition that the experience of acceleration provides fundamental and hitherto unappreciated insights about social life. The strength of Adams's analysis lies not only in his multifaceted description of how the general phenomenon of acceleration manifests itself in social and economic affairs, knowledge and scientific innovation, as well as military and political life, but also in his provocative assertion that the general pace of activity in most domains of social life has increased over the course of human history. In this view, acceleration is a permanent attribute of human existence, yet "behind the year 1400, the process [of acceleration] certainly went on, but the progress became so slight as to be hardly measurable." In contrast, in recent centuries, and especially since the Industrial Revolution, the tempo of scientific and technological innovation, many facets of economic life, and even the rate of innovation in military technology have taken on ever more dramatic proportions. Adams was also among the first writers to pose clearly the difficult question of what significance tradition and past history might come to possess in a high-speed society. As Adams predicts, to an increasing extent, "few lessons in the past . . . would be useful in the future" given the rapid pace of social change. Thus, "the attempt of the American of 1800 to educate the American of 1900 had not often been surpassed for folly; and since 1800 the forces and their complications had increased a thousand times or more." Adams thereby anticipates a major concern of recent theoretical work on social acceleration: in a social context subject to permanent change, the experiences of past generations risk appearing irrelevant and even alien.

In order to understand experiences of social acceleration in the nineteenth century, Adams points to the significance of modern capitalism. Indeed, a core theme of many of the readings included in this volume is the centrality of modern capitalism to social acceleration. Decreasing the turn-over time necessary to turn a profit, reducing the time necessary to produce a specific commodity, accelerating the rate of technological innovation, speeding up production in order to maximize the use of labor power, rap-idly moving goods to distant markets—countless familiar features of capi-talist production contribute directly to the acceleration of fundamental social and economic activities. Georg Simmel, whose fascinating analysis of the temporal consequences of modern economic life, from his landmark *Phi-losophy of Money*, is included here as chapter 2, represents a paradigmatic example of this genre. Simmel provides an engrossing phenomenology of the impact of the "money economy" on the pace of life, according to which the mere increase in the supply of money contributes in far-reaching ways to an acceleration of everyday life. It leads, for example, to the "temptation to spend money, and in so doing promotes a greater turnover in commodities, an increase, acceleration and multiplication" in possible forms of economic experience, as well as what he describes as additional "economic-psychic" consequences for the tempo of everyday life. The easy flow of cash charac-teristic of modern economies tends to promote a corresponding flow of potential economic offerings and thereby novel experiences, as well as "a constant sense of disorder and psychic shocks" resulting in part from an awareness of the gap between preexisting economic opportunities and new ones provided by the multiplication as well as heightened turnover of com-modities. Simmel's most original intuition concerning the marriage of money and speed is probably found in his discussion of their concentra-tion in the heart of modern big cities, which typically harbor financial cen-ters like London's City or New York's Wall Street: "It is a peculiar feature of monetary transactions that they tend to concentrate in a relatively few places." A striking aspect of the modern money economy is the growth of large centers for financial transactions. The urban areas that emerge in the shadows of concentrated capitalist finance offer a dramatically increased variety of possibilities for human experience, a crucial presupposition of the heightened pace of modern life. The metropolis is Simmel's core metaphor for modernity, as well as for speed and money, and its defining feature is the restless and transitory nature of all social activity. The money economy's central artery, the stock exchange, places its high-speed dynamics in the clearest possible light: "Its sanguine-choleric oscillations between optimism and pessimism, its nervous reaction to ponderable and imponderable mat-ters, the swiftness with which every factor affecting the situation is grasped and forgotten again—all this represents an extreme acceleration in the pace of life, a feverish commotion and compression of its fluctuations, in which the specific influence of money upon the course of psychological life becomes most clearly discernible." A central concern of recent theorists of globalization, namely 24/7 financial markets where major transactions are made electronically at the blink of an eye, arguably confirms Simmel's ideas about the pivotal role of speed "wherever money becomes the general center of interest."

The selections in Part I also demonstrate that early analysts of the high-speed texture of modern society were quick to grasp its potentially deleterious consequences for democratic politics. At the start of the twentieth century, Marinetti's *Futurist Manifesto* proclaimed an aesthetic or "religion-morality of speed," which Marinetti associated not only with beauty, but also with courage, aggression, war, and a desire for the new and unexpected. Marinetti's view illustrates how positive eudaimonistic expectations came to be connected to social acceleration: in his account, speed offers hitherto untapped possibilities for exhilarating forms of novel human experience; by no means should speed be interpreted as a negative or unpleasant necessity of capitalist production. Hostility to speed implies an antimodern endorsement of the "criminal slowness of Sunday crowds" and "decadent slow-moving Venetian lagoons" ("The New Religion-Morality of Speed," reprinted here as chapter 3). Marinetti soon transplanted the *Futurist Manifesto*'s simplistic temporal binary oppositions (we create a new good, speed, and a new evil, slowness) to the sphere of political institutions: liberal democracy, with its preference for slow-going deliberative legislatures and peaceful but time-consuming negotiations and compromise, offers a political counterpart to the Sunday strolls and Venetian lagoons despised by Marinetti, whereas an executive-dominated dictatorship, prepared to wage aggressive war against its foes at a moment's notice, constitutes an appropriate institutional embodiment of the religion-morality of speed.

In a discussion from *The Public and Its Problems* (excerpted here as chapter 4) of what he dubbed the "mania for motion and speed," John Dewey similarly describes the increasingly high-speed texture of social life at the outset of the twentieth century as posing fundamental challenges to the freewheeling deliberative publics on which a vibrant democracy necessarily depends. In stark contrast to Futurists like Marinetti, however, Dewey formulates the temporal dilemmas at hand as a series of constructive questions that he thought democrats must tackle successfully if they were to revitalize existing liberal society's unrealized radical democratic potential: "How can a public be organized, we may ask, when literally it does not stay in place?" To the extent that democratic citizenship minimally requires the possibility of effective action in concert with others, how might citizenship be sustained in a social world subject to ever more astonishing opportunities for movement and mobility? Speed attributes a shifting and unstable character to social life, as demonstrated by increased rates of change and turnover in many arenas of activity. If citizenship requires some modicum of constancy and stability in social life, however, might not shifts in the temporal conditions of human activity bode poorly for political participation? How might citizens come together and act in concert when contemporary society's "mania for motion and speed" makes it difficult for them to get acquainted with one another and form stable civic associations where collective interests gain expression, let alone identify objects of common concern? Although implicitly agreeing with the Futurists about the threats posed to democracy by new high-speed technologies, Dewey nonetheless implies the possibility of ultimately refurbishing democratic politics so as to make it better attuned to the temporal exigencies of our era.

The German right-wing authoritarian theorist Carl Schmitt eerily corroborates the Futurist expectation that speed is likely to undermine liberal democracy. In a 1950 essay excerpted here as chapter 5, Schmitt describes a "motorization" or acceleration of lawmaking that increasingly plagues liberal democratic legislatures, according to which an ever-decreasing amount of time is devoted to parliamentary deliberation. Statutory rulemaking is rushed and the resulting laws are poorly crafted, and temporally overwhelmed parliaments increasingly hand over substantial decision-making authority to the executive and administration. In Schmitt's disturbing account, the proliferation of emergency and exceptional powers, plaguing even the most well-established liberal democracies, needs to be interpreted as an institutional adaptation to the temporal pressures of acceleration.

More recent scholarship builds on the legacy of classical analysts of social speed, whose groundbreaking contributions too often remained incomplete and even aphoristic. Fortunately, a veritable renaissance has taken place in temporally oriented social and cultural theory in recent years, as a rich variety of writers have struggled to make sense of the unprecedented possibilities for instantaneousness and simultaneity made available by contemporary society.

In chapter 6, Hartmut Rosa offers a discussion of the concept of social acceleration in contemporary social theory. The essay not only provides a detailed survey of the main positions in the ongoing debate on social speed, but it also defends a number of central theses. Rosa seeks to clarify the notion of social acceleration by distinguishing between "technological acceleration," meaning that technical processes (in communication or production, for example) operate at a faster tempo than during earlier epochs; the "acceleration of social change or transformation," which refers to the heightened pace of change in key forms of social activity (the family or workplace, for example); and the "acceleration of everyday life," which he sees in the form of a speedup occurring in many arenas of activity (for example, shorter mealtimes). Rosa argues that the three forms of social acceleration interact to generate a relatively autonomous feedback cycle: new high-speed technologies (for example, the computer) often lead to increased rates of social transformation, which cause an acceleration of everyday life; this in turn is likely to lead social actors to pursue novel, purportedly time-saving technological devices in order to tackle the imperatives of an increasingly hectic everyday life. The paradox, however, is that new forms of high-speed technology are thereby likely to be created, and resulting technological innovations then generate subsequent forms of acceleration in the basic patterns of social life as well new temporal pressures in everyday life. Rosa insists, however, that this feedback cycle is ultimately driven by fundamental structural forces, and he follows most of the authors represented in this volume by underscoring the centrality of modern capitalism to speed. In partial contrast, he also argues that social acceleration rests on independent cultural and sociostructural factors neglected by competing accounts of the origins of social speed. Finally, Rosa considers a phenomenon that, with the possible exception of John Urry (chapter 10), has been widely neglected by theorists of speed: many examples of contemporary social deceleration can be inextricably linked to fundamental processes of acceleration; the relationship between social speed and slowness turns out to be dialectical in character.

In chapter 7, Reinhart Koselleck adds much-needed clarity to the concept of social acceleration while simultaneously documenting its far-reaching impact on Western modernity, especially since the end of the eighteenth century. In an exquisite excavation of historical sources, Koselleck traces social acceleration to trends predating the Industrial Revolution (for example, the construction of modern roads in absolutist Europe and the increasing temporal efficiency of horse-drawn carriages), but he concedes that "only since the French and the Industrial revolutions has the principle of acceleration begun to become a general experiential principle." Previously, Koselleck holds, acceleration served as an expectational rather than an experiential social category. While arguing in favor of the notion that acceleration constitutes a core feature of modern experience, Koselleck also persuasively delineates empirically verifiable claims about acceleration *in* history from the dubious notion of an acceleration *of* history: the latter plagues many modern philosophies of history, yet it ultimately represent a problematic secularization of premodern theological ideas having potentially disastrous political implications. For Koselleck, the concept of acceleration can aid our understanding of the dynamics of modern society, yet only if it is clearly distinguished from the residues of a theologically tinged philosophy of history that continued to haunt political movements well into the twentieth century.

Neo-Marxist scholars have played a key role in initiating the temporal turn in recent social theory. In chapter 8, Bob Jessop not only offers a survey of this recent shift in radical and neo-Marxist social analysis, but he also persuasively argues that we should interpret globalization as plagued by a series of spatiotemporal tensions derived in part from the high-speed dynamics of contemporary capitalism. Globalizing capitalism's obsession with fast profits and quick turnover times conflicts with the necessities of long-term system reproduction, including its own natural and ecological presuppositions; fast capitalism meshes poorly with the fundamental rhythms of human existence, thereby engendering intense stress and unease in everyday life; post-Fordism increasingly presupposes temporally long-term extraeconomic factors (for example, the heightened reflexivity and collective mastery of complex techniques) that are essential to successful economic competition but nonetheless clash with the temporality of core economic processes; a temporal tension also exists between the push to accelerate the circulation of capital via a shortening of production cycles and long-term infrastructural necessities that alone allow for a shortened product cycle; finally, high-speed capitalism compresses space by extending markets, yet it also continues to rely on fixed infrastructures. According to Jessop's account, a satisfactory theory of globalization will need to move beyond simplistic theses about a one-sided demise of state sovereignty, and most existing accounts of globalization fail adequately to capture the complex and multifaceted ways in which the nation-state plays a constitutive role in navigating the conflicting temporalities of the globalizing political economy.

Part 2 is rounded out by contributions from Hermann Lübbe and John Urry. In chapter 9, Lübbe sees the accelerated pace of innovation in research and development, production, and social organization as the chief driving force behind a "contraction of the present" which "entails a process whereby the space of time for which we can calculate our living conditions with a degree of constancy is shortened." Machiavelli famously thought it possible to rely on the history of ancient Rome to gain fungible novelty about military strategy for Renaissance Florence; in countless traditional societies, young people were taught to imitate the achievements of past generations. In contrast, the ever-increasing quantity of innovations per unit of time in the present era means that not only the lived experiences of our distant historical predecessors, but even those of our immediate forefathers (and mothers), seem as if from a veritable foreign country, distant and even alien, and unable to provide meaningful guidance for present action. But not only are the connections between the present and past increasingly tenuous. The present itself contracts or shrinks in the sense that its relevance for future experience declines as well: Lübbe refers to "experiences of a loss of rationality, which threaten us as the limits of planning become evident through the decreasing predictability of the premises of future action." As Henry Adams similarly observed a century ago, "The attempt of the American of 1900 to educate the American of 2000" must necessarily be even less successful than the attempt of someone from 1800 to provide useful guidance to one of Adams's own contemporaries in 1900. According to Lübbe, high-speed society's fundamental temporal tendencies pose difficult normative and institutional challenges, since even a dynamic, fast-paced society presupposes some measures of cultural, social, and political constancy and stability. Yet our accelerating society seems bent on blindly tearing down its own temporal supporting banisters.

In chapter 10, Urry offer a cautiously more hopeful diagnosis of contemporary temporal trends. Like many of the other authors in this volume, Urry is fascinated by the emergence of a mode of what he describes as "instantaneous time," according to which changes in information and communication technologies "allow information and ideas to be instantaneously transmitted and simultaneously accessed across the globe." He also shares their anxieties about the implications of high-speed or instantaneous temporality for the possibility of a decent human existence. Declining possibilities for effectively planning for the future, as Lübbe similarly finds, result from instantaneous time, as does a corresponding decline in trust about the future: "It no longer functions as something in which people appear to trust. Qualitative research suggests that almost all groups of British citizens are pessimistic about what is happening in the future and feel that the pace of life and the development of new life cycles are increasing stress, pressure, and short-termism." Yet Urry also points to evidence suggesting the possibility and even simultaneity of an alternative mode of social temporality, "glacial time," where heightened importance is attributed to changes that occur "over generations and indeed can only be observed intergenerationally."

Urry's analysis of glacial time tends to fuse normative and descriptive perspectives. Although he does provide empirical evidence for it (for example, the appearance of the British organization Common Ground, which advocates a "slowing down" of social life, or contemporary advocates of "slow food"), much of his argument relies on the hope that social experiences incongruent with instantaneous temporality ultimately will encourage social actors to challenge the hegemony of speed.

How might social acceleration impact our most fundamental political ideals? Central among these ideals, of course, is the unfinished struggle for self-determination and democracy. In the shadows of Marinetti, Dewey, and Schmitt, recent authors have undertaken to outline the significance of speed for democracy. They find themselves confronting precisely that question which preoccupied early twentieth-century analysts of the political repercussions of speed: must speed inevitable undermine democracy, as Marinetti and Schmitt argued, or might it instead be possible, in the spirit of Dewey's reflections from *The Public and Its Problems,* to transform speed into a democratic ally?

Albeit from an opposing normative and political perspective, Paul Virilio, in chapter 11, tends to support the view of reactionaries like Marinetti and Schmitt that speed inexorably decimates liberal democracy. From the radical Left, but in surprising diagnostic agreement with Schmitt's ideas about the motorization of law, Virilio posits that the "state of emergency" now represents a normal state of affairs in most political systems, as the pivotal role played by speed in war making and interstate competition systematically undermines traditional attempts to delineate the domestic and foreign realms. To an increasing degree, foreign threats now "collapse inwards" onto the domestic arena, and lawmaking devices (for example, executive prerogative) long considered suitable for the foreign realm now flourish in the domestic arena as well. High-speed war making undermines the privileged place of elected legislatures and democratic publics, augmenting the power position of the executive and thereby centralizing political power in the hands of narrow, unrepresentative cliques best able to exploit high-speed weapons of mass destruction. When the constant progress of rapidity within weapons technology "threatens from one day to the next to reduce the warning time for nuclear war *to less than one fatal minute,*" Virilio asks, what room is left for human reflection and deliberation, let alone public debate and exchange?

In chapter 12, however, Stefan Breuer takes Virilio to task for offering an oversimplified analysis of the origins of social acceleration. Virilio posits a perceptive description of the temporal dynamics of present-day society, Breuer concedes, yet his fascination with technological innovation (in particular, military technology) leads him to misdiagnose its structural origins. Breuer correctly picks up on a problematic tendency in Virilio's argumentation, namely the latter's tendency to waver uneasily between a vaguely Marxisant interpretation of military conflict and an alternative line of inquiry in which technology, and especially the technology of modern warfare, is accorded primary causal status. In short, Virilio's analysis ultimately suffers from an overemphasis on the noneconomic sources of speed.

In chapter 13, Herfried Münkler challenges the assumption endorsed by Virilio, as well as Marinetti and Schmitt before him, that speed and war making are necessarily two sides of the same coin. While conceding that war making has often contributed to social acceleration, Münkler calls for a more nuanced account of the temporalities of war. Although technologically and economically privileged states typically benefit from high-speed warfare, those political entities less well equipped with such resources have successfully decelerated military conflict in order to ward off economically and technologically superior foes—think, for example, of the numerous guerrilla wars successfully waged against rich Western powers. Slowness, no less than speed, sometimes proves a powerful military instrument. No less complicated are the temporal consequences of war making on the rhythm of economic and political development: we should avoid endorsing simplistic claims that war necessarily accelerates all facets of social life. Finally, even though substantial evidence suggests that the pace of events during war has been subject to dramatic acceleration, it would be incorrect to conclude that military superiority can be necessarily ensured via a monopoly on high-speed technology and military organization. According to the author, such a view badly underestimates the creative capacities of (technologically inferior) opponents, as history is filled with examples of "slow" political entities identifying the Achilles' heel of speedier military opponents. Münkler is not directly concerned with the impact of acceleration on democracy, yet to the extent that his argument challenges a central tenet of those who see democracy as threatened by speed—after all, they often argue that high-speed warfare undermines democracy—it may also open the door to a more complex view of the relationship between democracy and speed.

In this spirit, William E. Connolly and William E. Scheuerman, in chapters 14 and 15, both offer a somewhat less pessimistic gloss than Virilio's on the political implications of speed. Both concede that speed poses profound dangers, but interpret it "as an ambiguous medium that contains positive implications." Connolly explains why it is necessary to conceptualize speed as an ambivalent phenomenon in order to offer a defensible vision of cosmopolitanism able to appeal to "a variety of Christians, Jews, secularists, neo-Aristotelians, Islamists, Kantians, deep ecologists, Buddhists, and atheists." Scheuerman similarly acknowledges that social acceleration contributes directly to the dynamic character of modern society, generating historically unprecedented possibilities for individual self-realization and experimentation. Yet he also acknowledges many threats posed by social speed to meaningful democratic citizenship. In a high-speed society, the basic activities of democratic citizenship too often seem temporally sluggish and even wasteful, and their logic conflicts with contemporary society's preference for speed and temporal efficiency.

Whether analysts are justified in suggesting that social speed nonetheless might revitalize democracy remains an open question. However, their contributions undoubtedly offer a reminder of the political stakes at hand in the seemingly abstract theoretical debate about social acceleration. At the very least, the editors hope that the present volume can help explain why a critical-minded analysis of social acceleration can not only help clarify the nature of those political stakes, but also potentially prepare the way for a more decent political and social future.

PART 1

CLASSICAL PERSPECTIVES ON SOCIAL ACCELERATION

ONE

A LAW OF ACCELERATION

Henry Adams

Images are not arguments, rarely even lead to proof, but the mind craves them, and, of late more than ever, the keenest experimenters find twenty images better than one, especially if contradictory; since the human mind has already learned to deal in contradictions.

The image needed here is that of a new centre, or preponderating mass, artificially introduced on earth in the midst of a system of attractive forces that previously made their own equilibrium, and constantly induced to accelerate its motion till it shall establish a new equilibrium. A dynamic theory would begin by assuming that all history, terrestrial or cosmic, mechanical or intellectual, would be reducible to this formula if we knew the facts.

For convenience, the most familiar image should come first; and this is probably that of the comet, or meteoric streams, like the Leonids and Perseids; a complex of minute mechanical agencies, reacting within and without, and guided by the sum of forces attracting or deflecting it. Nothing forbids one to assume that the man-meteorite might grow, as an acorn does, absorbing light, heat, electricity—or thought; for, in recent times, such transference of energy has become a familiar idea; but the simplest figure, at first, is that of a perfect comet—say that of 1843—which drops from space, in a straight line, at the regular acceleration of speed, directly into the sun, and after wheeling sharply about it, in heat that ought to dissipate any known substance, turns back unharmed, in defiance of law, by the path on which it came. The mind, by analogy, may figure as such a comet, the better because it also defies law.

Motion is the ultimate object of science, and measures of motion are many; but with thought as with matter, the true measure is mass in its astronomic sense—the sum or difference of attractive forces. Science has quite enough trouble in measuring its material motions without volunteering help to the historian, but the historian needs not much help to measure some kinds of social movement; and especially in the nineteenth century, society by common accord agreed in measuring its progress by the coal-output. The ratio of increase in the volume of coal-power may serve as dynamometer.

The coal-output of the world, speaking roughly, doubled every ten years between 1840 and 1900, in the form of utilized power, for the ton of coal yielded three or four times as much power in 1900 as in 1840. Rapid as this rate of acceleration in volume seems, it may be tested in a thousand ways without greatly reducing it. Perhaps the ocean steamer is nearest unity and easiest to measure, for any one might hire, in 1905, for a small sum of money, the use of 30,000 steam-horse-power to cross the ocean, and by halving this figure every ten years, he got back to 234 horse-power for 1835, which was accuracy enough for his purposes. In truth, his chief trouble came not from the ratio in volume of heat, but from the intensity, since he could get no basis for a ratio there. All ages of history have known high intensities, like the iron-furnace, the burning-glass, the blow-pipe; but no society has ever used high intensities on any large scale till now, nor can a mere by-stander decide what range of temperature is now in common use. Loosely guessing that science controls habitually the whole range from absolute zero to 3000° Centigrade, one might assume, for convenience, that the ten-year ratio for volume could be used temporarily for intensity; and still there remained a ratio to be guessed for other forces than heat. Since 1800 scores of new forces had been discovered; old forces had been raised to higher powers, as could be measured in the navy-gun; great regions of chemistry had been opened up, and connected with other regions of physics. Within ten years a new universe of force had been revealed in radiation. Complexity had extended itself on immense horizons, and arithmetical ratios were useless for any attempt at accuracy. The force evolved seemed more like explosion than gravitation, and followed closely the curve of steam; but, at all events, the ten-year ratio seemed carefully conservative. Unless the calculator was prepared to be instantly overwhelmed by physical force and mental complexity, he must stop there.

Thus, taking the year 1900 as the starting point for carrying back the series, nothing was easier than to assume a ten-year period of retardation as far back as 1820, but beyond that point the statistician failed, and only the mathematician could help. Laplace would have found it child's-play to fix a ratio of progression in mathematical science between Descartes, Leibnitz, Newton, and himself. Watt could have given in pounds the increase of power between Newcomen's engines and his own. Volta and Benjamin Franklin would have stated their progress as absolute creation of power. Dalton could have measured minutely his advance on Boerhaave. Napoleon I must have had a distinct notion of his own numerical relation to Louis XIV. No one in 1789 doubted the progress of force, least of all those who were to lose their heads by it.

Pending agreement between these authorities, theory may assume what it likes—say a fifty, or even a five-and-twenty-year period of reduplication for the eighteenth century, for the period matters little until the acceleration itself is admitted. The subject is even more amusing in the seventeenth than in the eighteenth century, because Galileo and Kepler, Descartes, Huygens, and Isaac Newton took vast pains to fix the laws of acceleration for moving bodies, while Lord Bacon and William Harvey were content with showing experimentally the fact of acceleration in knowledge; but from their combined results a historian might be tempted to maintain a similar rate of movement back to 1600, subject to correction from the historians of mathematics.

The mathematicians might carry their calculations back as far as the fourteenth century when algebra seems to have become for the first time the standard measure of mechanical progress in western Europe; for not only Copernicus and Tycho Brahe, but even artists like Leonardo, Michael Angelo, and Albert Dürer worked by mathematical processes, and their testimony would probably give results more exact than that of Montaigne or Shakespeare; but, to save trouble, one might tentatively carry back the same ratio of acceleration, or retardation, to the year 1400, with the help of Columbus and Gutenberg, so taking a uniform rate during the whole four centuries (1400–1800), and leaving to statisticians the task of correcting it.

Or better, one might, for convenience, use the formula of squares to serve for a law of mind. Any other formula would do as well, either of chemical explosion, or electrolysis, or vegetable growth, or of expansion or contraction in innumerable forms; but this happens to be simple and convenient. Its force increases in the direct ratio of its squares. As the human meteoroid approached the sun or centre of attractive force, the attraction of one century squared itself to give the measure of attraction in the next.

Behind the year 1400, the process certainly went on, but the progress became so slight as to be hardly measurable. What was gained in the east or elsewhere, cannot be known; but forces, called loosely Greek fire and gunpowder, came into use in the west in the thirteenth century, as well as instruments like the compass, the blow-pipe, clocks and spectacles, and materials like paper; Arabic notation and algebra were introduced, while metaphysics and theology acted as violent stimulants to mind. An architect might detect a sequence between the Church of St. Peter's at Rome, the Amiens Cathedral, the Duomo at Pisa, San Marco at Venice, Sancta Sofia at Constantinople and the churches at Ravenna. All the historian dares affirm is that a sequence is manifestly there, and he has a right to carry back his ratio, to represent the fact, without assuming its numerical correctness. On the human mind as a moving body, the break in acceleration in the Middle Ages is only apparent; the attraction worked through shifting forms of force, as the sun works by light or heat, electricity, gravitation, or what not, on different organs with different sensibilities, but with invariable law.

The science of prehistoric man has no value except to prove that the law went back into indefinite antiquity. A stone arrow-head is as convincing as a steam-engine. The values were as clear a hundred thousand years ago as now, and extended equally over the whole world. The motion at last became infinitely slight, but cannot be proved to have stopped. The motion of Newton's comet at aphelion may be equally slight. To evolutionists may be left the processes of evolution; to historians the single interest is the law of reaction between force and force—between mind and nature—the law of progress.

The great division of history into phases by Turgot and Comte first affirmed this law in its outlines by asserting the unity of progress, for a mere phase interrupts no growth, and nature shows innumerable such phases. The development of coal-power in the nineteenth century furnished the first means of assigning closer values to the elements; and the appearance of supersensual forces towards 1900 made this calculation a pressing necessity; since the next step became infinitely serious.

A law of acceleration, definite and constant as any law of mechanics, cannot be supposed to relax its energy to suit the convenience of man. No one is likely to suggest a theory that man's convenience had been consulted by Nature at any time, or that Nature has consulted the convenience of any of her creations, except perhaps the *Terebratula*. In every age man has bitterly and justly complained that Nature hurried and hustled him, for inertia almost invariably has ended in tragedy. Resistance is its law, and resistance to superior mass is futile and fatal.

Fifty years ago, science took for granted that the rate of acceleration could not last. The world forgets quickly, but even today the habit remains of founding statistics on the faith that consumption will continue nearly stationary. Two generations, with John Stuart Mill, talked of this stationary period, which was to follow the explosion of new power. All the men who were elderly in

the forties died in this faith, and other men grew old nursing the same conviction, and happy in it; while science, for fifty years, permitted, or encouraged, society to think that force would prove to be limited in supply. This
mental inertia of science lasted through the eighties before showing signs
of breaking up; and nothing short of radium fairly wakened men to the
fact, long since evident, that force was inexhaustible. Even then the scientific authorities vehemently resisted.

Nothing so revolutionary had happened since the year 300. Thought had
more than once been upset, but never caught and whirled about in the vor-
tex of infinite forces. Power leaped from every atom, and enough of it to
supply the stellar universe showed itself running to waste at every pore of
matter. Man could no longer hold it off. Forces grasped his wrists and flung
him about as though he had hold of a live wire or a runaway automobile;
which was very nearly the exact truth for the purposes of an elderly and timid
single gentleman in Paris, who never drove down the Champs Élysées without expecting an accident, and commonly witnessing one; or found himself in the neighborhood of an official without calculating the chances of a
bomb. So long as the rates of progress held good, these bombs would double in force and number every ten years.

Impossibilities no longer stood in the way. One's life had fattened on
impossibilities. Before the boy was six years old, he had seen four impossibilities made actual—the ocean-steamer, the railway, the electric telegraph,
and the Daguerreotype; nor could he ever learn which of the four had most
hurried others to come. He had seen the coal-output of the United States
grow from nothing to three hundred million tons or more. What was far
more serious, he had seen the number of minds, engaged in pursuing
force—the truest measure of its attraction—increase from a few scores or
hundreds, in 1838, to many thousands in 1905, trained to sharpness never
before reached, and armed with instruments amounting to new senses of
indefinite power and accuracy, while they chased force into hiding-places
where Nature herself had never known it to be, making analyses that con-
tradicted being, and syntheses that endangered the elements. No one could
say that the social mind now failed to respond to new force, even when the
new force annoyed it horribly. Every day Nature violently revolted, causing
so-called accidents with enormous destruction of property and life, while
plainly laughing at man, who helplessly groaned and shrieked and shud-
dered, but never for a single instant could stop. The railways alone approached
the carnage of war; automobiles and fire-arms ravaged society, until an earthquake became almost a nervous relaxation. An immense volume of force

had detached itself from the unknown universe of energy, while still vaster reservoirs, supposed to be infinite, steadily revealed themselves, attracting mankind with more compulsive course than all the Pontic Seas or Gods or Gold that ever existed, and feeling still less of retiring ebb.

In 1850, science would have smiled at such a romance as this, but, in 1900, as far as history could learn, few men of science thought it a laughing matter. If a perplexed but laborious follower could venture to guess their drift, it seemed in their minds a toss-up between anarchy and order. Unless they should be more honest with themselves in the future than ever they were in the past, they would be more astonished than their followers when they reached the end. If Karl Pearson's notions of the universe were sound, men like Galileo, Descartes, Leibnitz, and Newton should have stopped the progress of science before 1700, supposing them to have been honest in the religious convictions they expressed. In 1900 they were plainly forced back on faith in a unity unproved and an order they had themselves disproved. They had reduced their universe to a series of relations to themselves. They had reduced themselves to motion in a universe of motions, with an acceleration, in their own case, of vertiginous violence. With the correctness of their science, history had no right to meddle, since their science now lay in a plane where scarcely one or two hundred minds in the world could follow its mathematical processes; but bombs educate vigorously, and even wireless telegraphy or airships might require the reconstruction of society. If any analogy whatever existed between the human mind, on one side, and the laws of motion, on the other, the mind had already entered a field of attraction so violent that it must immediately pass beyond, into new equilibrium, like the Comet of Newton, to suffer dissipation altogether, like meteoroids in the earth's atmosphere. If it behaved like an explosive, it must rapidly recover equilibrium; if it behaved like a vegetable, it must reach its limits of growth; and even if it acted like the earlier creations of energy—the saurians and sharks—it must have nearly reached the limits of its expansion. If science were to go on doubling or quadrupling its complexities every ten years, even mathematics would soon succumb. An average mind had succumbed already in 1850; it could no longer understand the problem in 1900.

Fortunately, a student of history had no responsibility for the problem; he took it as science gave it, and waited only to be taught. With science or with society, he had no quarrel and claimed no share of authority. He had never been able to acquire knowledge, still less to impart it; and if he had, at times, felt serious differences with the American of the nineteenth century, he felt none with the American of the twentieth. For this new creation, born since 1900, a historian asked no longer to be teacher or even friend; he asked only to be a pupil, and promised to be docile, for once, even though trodden under foot; for he could see that the new American—the child of incalculable coal-power, chemical power, electric power, and radiating energy, as well as of new forces yet undetermined—must be a sort of God compared with any former creation of nature. At the rate of progress since 1800, every American who lived into the year 2000 would know how to control unlimited power. He would think in complexities unimaginable to an earlier mind. He would deal with problems altogether beyond the range of earlier society. To him the nineteenth century would stand on the same plane with the fourth—equally childlike—and he would only wonder how both of them, knowing so little, and so weak in force, should have done so much. Perhaps even he might go back, in 1964, to sit with Gibbon on the steps of Ara Coeli.

Meanwhile he was getting education. With that, a teacher who had failed to educate even the generation of 1870, dared not interfere. The new forces would educate. History saw few lessons in the past that would be useful in the future; but one, at least, it did see. The attempt of the American of 1800 to educate the American of 1900 had not often been surpassed for folly; and since 1800 the forces and their complications had increased a thousand times or more. The attempt of the American of 1900 to educate the American of 2000, must be even blinder than that of the Congressman of 1800, except so far as he had learned his ignorance. During a million or two of years, every generation in turn had toiled with endless agony to attain and apply power, all the while betraying the deepest alarm and horror at the power they created. The teacher of 1900, if foolhardy, might stimulate; if foolish, might resist; if intelligent, might balance, as wise and foolish have often tried to do from the beginning; but the forces would continue to educate, and the mind would continue to react. All the teacher could hope was to teach it reaction.

Even there his difficulty was extreme. The most elementary books of science betrayed the inadequacy of old implements of thought. Chapter after chapter closed with phrases such as one never met in older literature: "The cause of this phenomenon is not understood"; "science no longer ventures to explain causes"; "the first step towards a causal explanation still remains to be taken"; "opinions are very much divided"; "in spite of the contradictions involved"; "science gets on only by adopting different theories, sometimes contradictory." Evidently the new American would need to think in contradictions, and instead of Kant's famous four antinomies, the new universe would know no law that could not be proved by its anti-law.

To educate—one's self to begin with—had been the effort of one's life for sixty years; and the difficulties of education had gone on doubling with the coal-output, until the prospect of waiting another ten years, in order to face a seventh doubling of complexities, allured one's imagination but slightly. The law of acceleration was definite, and did not require ten years more study except to show whether it held good. No scheme could be suggested to the new American, and no fault needed to be found, or complaint made; but the next great influx of new forces seemed near at hand, and its style of education promised to be violently coercive. The movement from unity into multiplicity, between 1200 and 1900, was unbroken in sequence, and rapid in acceleration. Prolonged one generation longer, it would require a new social mind. As though thought were common salt in indefinite solution it must enter a new phase subject to new laws. Thus far, since five or ten thousand years, the mind had successfully reacted, and nothing yet proved that it would fail to react—but it would need to jump.

TWO

THE PACE OF LIFE AND THE MONEY ECONOMY

Georg Simmel

The Pace of Life, Its Alterations, and Those of the Money Supply

Finally, there is a third influence by which money contributes to determining the form and order of the contents of life. It deals with the *pace* of their development, which is different for various historical epochs, for different areas of the world at any one time and for individuals of the same group. Our inner world extends, as it were, over two dimensions, the size of which determines the pace of life. The greater the differences between the contents of our imagination at any one time—even with an equal number of conceptions—the more intensive are the experiences of life, and the greater is the span of life through which we have passed. What we experience as the pace of life is the product of the sum total and the depth of its changes. The significance of money in determining the pace of life in a given period is first of all illustrated by the fact that a *change* in monetary circumstances brings about a *change* in the pace of life.

It has been asserted that an increase in the quantity of money—whether through the import of metals or the debasement of currency, through a positive balance of trade or through the issue of paper money—would leave the internal situation of a country completely unchanged. For aside from the few people whose income is fixed and not multipliable, every commodity or piece of work would increase in money value if the supply of money increased; but since everyone is a producer as well as a consumer, then the individual would earn only that much more as he had to spend, and the situation would remain unchanged. Even if such a proportionate increase in prices were the objective effect of an increase in money supply, quite basic psychological changes would occur. No one readily decides to pay a higher price for a commodity than he did hitherto even if his income has increased in the meantime; on the other hand, everyone is easily tempted by an increased income to spend more, without considering that the increased income is balanced by price increases in daily needs. The mere increase in the supply of money that one has in one's hand intensifies—quite regardless of any awareness of its mere relativity—the temptation to spend money, and in so doing promotes a greater turnover in commodities, an increase, acceleration and multiplication in economic conceptions. The basic human trait of interpreting what is relative as an absolute conceals the transitory character of the relationship between an object and a specific amount of money and makes it appear as an objective and permanent relationship. This brings about disturbance and disorientation as soon as one link of the relationship changes. The alteration in what is active and passive is in no way immediately balanced by its psychological effects. When such changes occur the awareness of the economic processes in their previous stability is interrupted from every side and the difference between present and previous circumstances makes itself felt on every side. As long as the new adjustment does not occur, the increase in the quantity of money will cause a constant sense of disorder and psychic shocks, and will thus deepen the differences and the comparative disparity between current conceptions and thereby accelerate the pace of life. It would therefore be to invite misinterpretation were one to infer a "consolidation of society" from the continuous increase in income. It is precisely because of the increase in money income that the lower strata become agitated, a condition that—depending upon one's political viewpoint—is interpreted either as rapacity and mania for innovation, or as healthy development and energy, but which in any case is avoided where a greater stability of income and prices exists. The latter implies at the same time the stability of social distances.

The accelerating effects of an increase in the supply of money on the development of the economic–psychic process are most conspicuously displayed by the after-effects of debased paper money, in the same way as some aspects of normal physiology are most clearly illustrated by pathological and abnormal cases. The unnatural and unfounded influx of money brings about, first of all, a shaky and illogical increase in all prices. The first plethora of money only suffices to satisfy the demand for certain categories of goods. Therefore one issue of unreliable paper money is followed by another, and the second issue by yet another. "Any pretext"—it was stated of Rhode Island at the beginning of the eighteenth century—"served for the additional multiplication of notes. And if paper money had driven all coins out of the country, *the scarcity of silver* would have been an additional reason for further paper money issues." The tragic consequence of such operations is that a second paper money issue is unavoidable in order to satisfy the demands that are the result of the first issue. This will make itself felt all the more where money itself is the immediate centre of the movements: price revolutions that are the result of the inundation of paper money lead to speculation, which in turn requires constantly growing supplies of money. One might say that the acceleration in the pace of social life that is brought about through an increase in the supply of money is most clearly discernible when the purely functional importance of money, without reference to its substantial value, is in question. The acceleration in the whole economic tempo is here raised to a still higher pitch, because, as it were, its origin is purely immanent; that is, it first manifests itself in the acceleration in the printing of money. This interrelationship is demonstrated by the fact that, in countries with a rapid pace of economic development, paper money is particularly apt to increase in quantity. A monetary expert states with reference to North America: "One cannot expect people who are so impatient with small gains, so convinced that wealth can be produced out of nothing or at least out of very little, to be willing to impose upon themselves the self-restrictions which in England or Germany reduce the dangers of paper money issues to a minimum." In particular, however, the acceleration in the pace of life that is brought about through an increase in the supply of paper money results from the upheaval in ownership. This is clearly discernible in the North American paper money economy prior to the War of Independence. The abundantly printed money which had originally circulated at a high value suffered tremendous losses in value. Whoever was wealthy yesterday could be poor today; and conversely, whoever had secured fixed values for borrowed money paid his debts back in devalued money and thus became rich. Not only did it become everyone's urgent interest to transact his economic operations as quickly as possible, to avoid long-term transactions and to learn to take up opportunities immediately; but also, these fluctuations in ownership brought about a sense of continuous change, sudden rifts and convulsions within the economic scene that spread to many other areas of life and were thus experienced as the growing intensity in the trend of economic life or as a quickening of its pace. Compared with stable money, debased money has even been considered to be of specific utility: it has been claimed that it is desirable to have debts repaid in debased money, because debtors are generally active economic producers, whereas creditors are mostly passive consumers who contribute much less positively to economic transactions. The fiduciary note-issue was not yet legal currency at the beginning of the eighteenth century in Connecticut and at the beginning of the nineteenth century in England, yet every creditor was obliged to accept it in payment of debts. The specific significance of money for the pace of economic life is further substantiated by the fact that the crisis that occurs after the excessive issue of paper money retards and paralyses economic life to a corresponding degree. Here too the role of money in the objective development of the economy corresponds to its functions as a mediator in the subjective aspect of that development: for it has been rightly pointed out that exchange is slowed down by the multiplication of the means of exchange beyond what is actually required, just as the increase in the number of brokers eases transactions up to a certain point beyond which, however, it operates as a barrier to transactions. Generally speaking, the more mobile money is, the less secure is its value because everyone tries to get rid of it as quickly as possible. The obvious objection, that trade requires two people and that the ease with which base money is given away is paralysed by the hesitancy to accept it, is not quite valid, because base money is still better than no money at all (and the same cannot always be claimed for poor merchandise). The interest in money as such has to be discounted against the distaste for base money on the part of the seller of merchandise. Hence the interest of the buyer and the reluctance of the seller to exchange commodities for base money do not exactly balance since the latter is weaker and cannot adequately limit the acceleration of circulation through the former. On the other hand, the owner of base money, or money that is valuable only under specific circumstances, has a lively interest in the preservation of the circumstances that give value to his possessions. When in the middle of the sixteenth century the princes' debts had grown to such an extent that there were widespread national bankruptcies, and when in France the sale of annuities was practised to an excessive extent, then it was stated in their defence—since they were very insecure— that in so doing the loyalty of the citizen as an owner of annuities to the king and his interest in saving him would thereby be greatly strengthened. It is significant that the term "partisan" originally referred to a money-lender who was party to a loan to the Crown, while later, owing to the solidarity of interests between such bankers and the minister of finance under Mazarin and Fouquet, the term acquired the meaning of an "unconditional supporter" and it has preserved this meaning ever since. This occurred during the period of greatest unreliability in the French finances, whereas during their improvement under Sully the partisans (money-lenders) moved into the background. And later Mirabeau, when introducing the *assignat* (paper currency), emphasized that wherever the currency existed the desire for its reliability ought to exist: "You consider a defender necessary for the measures taken and a creditor interested in your success." Thus, such money creates a specific grouping of interests and, on the basis of a new tendency towards inertia, a new animation of contrasts.

However, this assumption that these consequences of an increasing amount of money in circulation make themselves felt to a greater extent in so far as cheaper money affects producers and consumers to the same extent is far too simple. In reality such phenomena are much more complicated and volatile. This may be seen, first of all, in objective terms. The increase in the supply of money at first brings about an increase in the prices of only some commodities and leaves others as they were. It has been assumed that because of the influence of American precious metals the prices of European goods since the sixteenth century have risen in a definite and slow order of succession. The increase in the supply of money within a country always at first affects only a specific group that takes care of the flood of money. First and foremost, a rise in the prices of those goods will occur for which members of this group compete, whereas other commodities, the price of which is determined by mass consumption, will remain cheap. The gradual influx of larger supplies of money leads to attempts to balance them out, the previous price relationship of commodities is disrupted, and the budget of each household becomes accustomed to disturbances and shifts. In short, the fact that any increase in the supply of money affects the prices of goods *unevenly* necessarily has a disturbing effect upon the process of interpretation of the situation on the part of economically active persons. It leads to widespread experiences of differentiation, to the breakdown of existing parities and to demands for attempts to balance them out. It is certainly true that this influence—partly accelerating, partly retarding—is a result not only of the unevenness of prices but also of the unevenness within money values themselves. That is, it is the result not only of the devaluation of money but, perhaps even more so, of the continuous fluctuation in the value of money. It has been said of the period prior to the great English coinage reform of 1570 that "if all shillings had been reduced to the value of groats, transactions would have adjusted themselves relatively easily. But the fact that one shilling equalled 6 pence, another 10, and a third one 8, 6 or even 4 pence made every exchange a controversy!"

The unevenness in the prices of commodities results in a situation in which certain persons and occupations profit by a change in money values in a quite specific manner while certain others suffer considerably. In former times this was especially true of the peasantry. Towards the end of the seventeenth century, the English peasant, ignorant and helpless as he was, actually became squeezed between those people who owed him money and paid him its face value, and those to whom he owed money and insisted on payment by weight. Later the same was true in India at every new devaluation of money: if the farmer sold his harvest, he never knew whether the money received would suffice to pay the rent for his mortgage. It has long been known that wages are the last to be adjusted to a general increase in prices. The weaker a social group is, the slower and more sparingly does the increase in the amount of money trickle through to it. Frequently, an increase in income is attained only after an increase in the prices of that strata's consumer goods has long been in force. Out of this process, shocks and agitations of all kinds emerge. The growing differences between the strata require constant alertness because, in view of the new circumstances, conservative and defensive attitudes are no longer sufficient. Instead, positive struggle and conquest are required in order to preserve the *status quo ante* with regard to the relationship between the strata as well as the standard of living of individual strata. This is one of the basic reasons why every increase in the quantity of money has such a disturbing effect upon the pace of social life, since it produces new differences on top of the existing ones and divisions, even in the budget of the individual family, that must constantly accelerate and deepen the level of awareness. It is quite obvious that a considerable decline in the amount of money will bring about similar effects except that they will be in reverse. The close relationship between money and the pace of life is illustrated by the fact that an increase as well as a decrease in the amount of money, as a consequence of its uneven diffusion, brings about those manifestations of differentiation that are mirrored psychologically in break-downs, irritations and the compression of mental processes. This implication of *changes* in the quantity of money is only a phenomenon or an accumulation of the significance of money for the relationship of objects, that is for their psychic equivalents. Money has brought about new equations between objects. We compare them, one with another, according to their utility value, their aesthetic, ethical, eudaemonistic and labour value, with reference to hundreds of relationships of quantity and quality, so that their identity in one of these relationships may coincide with total lack of identity in another. Thus, their money value creates an equation and comparison between them that is in no way a constant function of other values, yet is always the expression of some notions of value that are the origin and combination of others. Every value standpoint that orders and ranks things differently and cuts across the usual mode of ordering things provides, at the same time, a new vitality for their relationship, a suggestion of as-yet unknown combinations and syntheses, of the discovery of their affinities and differences. This is because our minds are constantly endeavouring to counterbalance what is irregular and to force differentiation upon the uniform. In so far as money confers upon things within a given sphere a sameness and differentiation to a greater extent than any other value standpoint, it thereby stimulates innumerable endeavours to combine these with the ranking derived from the other values in the sense of these two tendencies.

The Concentration of Monetary Activity

In addition to the results of changes in the supply of money, which suggest that the pace of life is, as it were, a function of those changes, the compression of the contents of life is evident in another consequence of monetary transactions. It is a peculiar feature of monetary transactions that they tend to concentrate in a relatively few places. As far as local diffusion is concerned, it is possible to establish a scale of economic objects. Here I shall indicate only some of the characteristic levels. The scale commences with agriculture, which by its very nature resists every attempt to concentrate its different areas; agriculture is inevitably bound up with the original dispersal of space. Industrial production can be compressed to some extent: the factory is a spatial condensation compared with artisan production and domestic industry while the modern industrial centre is a manufacturing microcosm, in which every kind of raw material in the world is transformed into objective forms, whose origins are dispersed throughout the world. The most remote link in this scale is money transactions. Owing to the abstractness of its form, money has no definite relationship to space: it can exercise its effects upon the most remote areas. It is even, as it were, at any moment the central point of a circle of potential effects. On the other hand, it also enables the largest amounts of value to be condensed into the most minute form—such as the $10 million cheque that was once signed by Jay Gould. To the possibility of condensing values by means of money and of condensing money by means of its increasingly abstract forms, there corresponds the possibility of condensing monetary transactions. In so far as the economy of a country is increasingly based upon money, financial activities become concentrated in large centres of money transactions. In contrast to the country, the city has always been the seat of money transactions and this relationship also holds for comparisons between small towns and cities. An English historian has stated that in its whole history London, though it never functioned as the heart of England but sometimes as its brain, always operated as its purse. Similarly, it was said that already at the end of the Roman Republic every penny that was spent in Gaul entered the books of financiers in Rome. This centrifugal force that finance possesses supports the interest of both parties: that of the borrowers because they can obtain cheaper money because of the competition of inflowing capital (the interest rate in Rome was 50 per cent lower than the average in ancient times), and that of the creditors because, although money does not have such a high value as in outlying areas, they are sure of chances for investment at any time, which is more important than lending the money at a higher rate in isolated areas. As a result, it has also been pointed out that contractions in the central money market can be more easily overcome than at the various outlying points on the periphery. Through the process of centralization that is inherent in money, the preliminary stage of accumulation in the hands of scattered individuals has been surmounted. The centralization of monetary transactions on the stock exchanges counteracted the superior power that individuals could wield by monetary means. For instance, even though the stock exchanges of Lyons and Antwerp brought enormous gains to individual money magnates during the fifteenth century, they objectified the power of money in a central institution that was superior to the power and rules of even the most powerful individuals, and they prevented the situation from arising in which a single financial house could determine the trend of world history to the extent that the Fuggers had once done.

The more basic reason for the evolution of financial centres is obviously to be found in the relativity of money. This is because, on the one hand, money expresses only value relationships between commodities, while on the other the value of every definite quantity of money cannot be as directly ascertained as can that of any other commodity; it has significance only in comparison with the total amount that is offered. Therefore, the maximum concentration of money at one point, the continuous competition of huge amounts, the balancing of a major part of supply and demand as such, will lead to the more accurate determination of its value and to its greater utilization. A bushel of grain has a particular importance at any one place, no matter how isolated and regardless of its money value. A certain quantity of money, however, is important only in relation to other values. Hence, in order to attain a stable and just valuation, money has to be confronted with as many other values as possible. This is the reason why not only "everything presses for gold"—men as well as things—but also why money itself presses for "everything." It seeks to come together with other money, with all possible kinds of values and their owners. The same interrelationship operates in the opposite direction: the convergence of large numbers of people brings about a particularly strong need for money. In Germany, one of the main demands for money arose out of annual fairs organized by local lords in order to profit from the exchange of currency and the tax on goods. Through this enforced concentration of commercial transactions at a single point in a larger territory, the inclination to buy and sell was greatly increased and the need for money thereby first became a general necessity. Wherever increasingly large numbers of people come together, money becomes relatively that much more in demand. Because of its indifferent nature, money is the most suitable bridge and means of communication between many and diverse people. The more people there are, the fewer are the spheres within which they can base their transactions except through monetary interests.

The Mobilization of Values

All this illustrates to what great extent money symbolizes acceleration in the pace of life and how it measures itself against the number and diversity of inflowing and alternating impressions and stimuli. The tendency of money to converge and to accumulate, if not in the hands of individuals then in fixed local centres; to bring together the interests of and thereby individuals themselves; to establish contact between them on a common ground and thus, as determined by the form of value that money represents, to concentrate the most diverse elements in the smallest possible space—in short, this tendency and capacity of money has the psychological effect of enhancing the variety and richness of life, that is of increasing the pace of life. It has already been emphasized elsewhere that the modern concept of time—as a value determined by its usefulness and scarcity—first became accepted with the growth of capitalism in Germany when, during the fifteenth century, world trade and financial centres developed together with the quick turnover of cheap money. It was in this period that the church clocks began to strike at every quarter of an hour; and Sebastian Franck, who was the first to recognize the revolutionary significance of money even though in a most pessimistic manner, first called time an expensive commodity. The most characteristic symbol of all these correlations is the stock exchange. Economic values and interests are here completely reduced to their monetary expression. The stock exchange and its representatives have achieved the closest possible local assembly in order to carry out the clearance, distribution and balancing of money in the quickest manner possible. This twofold condensation of values into the money form and of monetary transactions into the form of the stock exchange makes it possible for values to be rushed through the greatest number of hands in the shortest possible time. The New York Stock Exchange, for instance, has a turnover every year that is five times the amount of the cotton harvest through speculation in cotton, and even in 1887 fifty times the total yearly production of oil was sold there. The frequency of the turnover increases with fluctuations in the quoted price of a particular value. Indeed, the fluctuations in the rate of exchange was the reason why regular stock exchange dealings in royal promissory notes [Königsbriefen] developed at all in the sixteenth century. For these notes, which reflected the changing credit status of, for instance, the French Crown, provided a completely different inducement to buying and selling than had previously existed with stable values. Changes in valuation are greatly increased and even often brought about by the flexible quality of money to express them directly. And this is the cause as well as the effect of the fact that the stock exchange is the centre of monetary transactions. It is, as it were, the geometrical focal point of all these changes in valuation, and at the same time the place of greatest excitement in economic life. Its sanguine-choleric oscillations between optimism and pessimism, its nervous reaction to ponderable and imponderable matters, the swiftness with which every factor affecting the situation is grasped and forgotten again—all this represents an extreme acceleration in the pace of life, a feverish commotion and compression of its fluctuations, in which the specific influence of money upon the course of psychological life becomes most clearly discernible.

Finally, the relative speed of circulation of money in relation to all other objects must immediately increase the general pace of life wherever money becomes the general centre of interest. The roundness of coins which makes them "roll" symbolizes the rhythm of the movement that money imparts to transactions. Even where coins originally possessed corners, their constant use must have smoothed the corners and rounded them off; physical necessity has thus provided the most useful form of instrument for the intensity of transactions. For centuries in the countries bordering on the Nile there even existed globular money composed of glass, wood or agate—the differences in the material used suggests that its form was the reason for its popularity. It is no coincidence that the principle of "rounding off" is applied with reference to large sums of money, since this principle corresponds to the expanding money economy. "Rounding off" is a relatively modern term. The most primitive form of cheques payable to the English Treasury were tallies for any irregular amount and they frequently circulated as money. Only in the eighteenth century were they replaced by endorsable paper bills which represented rounded-off amounts from £5 upwards. It is surprising how little attention was formerly paid to rounding off, even for large amounts of money. That the Fuggers in 1530 agreed to pay 275,333 florins and 20 crowns to the Emperor Ferdinand, and that Emperor Maximilian II in 1577 owed them 220,674 florins, are not isolated cases. The development of the institution of shares followed a similar course. The joint stock of the East India Company in the Netherlands in the seventeenth century could be split up into any proportions that might be desired. Only the acceleration of transactions finally brought about the situation in which a fixed unit of 500 Flemish pounds became the only possible unit of ownership or "share" in its trade. Even today in the retail trade, monetary transactions are calculated in rounded off amounts in places with a considerable volume of money transactions, whereas prices in more remote regions would appear to be rarely rounded off.

The above-mentioned development from inconveniently large to smaller coins and money orders clearly has the same significance for the acceleration of the speed of transactions as the rounding off process, which itself suggests a physical analogy. The need to have money in small amounts increases with the speed of transactions. In this context, it is significant that in 1844 an English bank note circulated on average for fifty-seven days before being redeemed, whereas in 1871 it circulated for only thirty-seven days! If one compares the velocity of circulation of landed property with that of money, then this immediately illustrates the difference in the pace of life between periods when the one or the other was the focal point of economic activity. One thinks, for example, of the character of tax payments with reference to external and internal fluctuations depending on the object on which they were levied. In Anglo-Saxon and Norman England taxes were imposed exclusively upon land ownership: during the twelfth century levies were imposed on the possession of cattle; shortly afterwards, certain portions of mobile property (the fourth, seventh and thirteenth parts) became taxable. The objects of taxation became more and more diverse until finally money income was made the proper basis of taxation. In so doing, taxation attains a hitherto-unknown degree of flexibility and adjustability, and the result is a much greater variability and yearly fluctuation in the contribution of individuals, combined with a greater stability of the total revenue produced. The direct significance of and emphasis upon landed property or money for the pace of life may explain the great value that very conservative peoples place upon agriculture. The Chinese are convinced that only agriculture secures the peace and perpetuation of states, and perhaps for this reason they have imposed a huge tax upon the sale of land, so that most sales of land are carried out privately and without official registration. But where the acceleration of economic life that is instigated by money has asserted itself, it seeks to impose its rhythm upon the resistant form of landed property. During the eighteenth century the state of Pennsylvania provided mortgages for private land purchase and permitted the bills to be circulated as paper money. Benjamin Franklin stated that these bills were, in reality, *coined land*. Similarly, in Germany it has been asserted by conservatives that the legislation of recent decades concerning mortgages will bring about a liquidation of landed property and will transform it into some kind of paper money that could be given away in bills of any desired amount so that, as Waldeck also puts it, landed property would seem to exist only in order to be sold by auction. Not surprisingly, modern life too mobilizes its contents in the most superficial sense and in several less well known respects. In medieval times and also during the Renaissance, what we today term "movables" or furnishings in the strict sense were little in demand. Wardrobes, sideboards and benches were built into the panelling; tables and chairs were so heavy that they were often immovable, and small movable fixtures were almost non-existent. Subsequently, furniture, like capital, has become mobile.

Finally, I wish to illustrate by means of a legal regulation the power of the trend in the money economy to subject other contents of life to its own pace. It is an old legal precept that an object that has been taken away from its legal owner has to be returned to him in all circumstances, even if the present owner has acquired it legitimately. Only with reference to money is this precept invalid: according to Roman as well as modern law, money that has been stolen cannot be taken away from a third person who has acquired it in good faith and returned to the original owner. This exception is obviously necessitated by the practice of business transactions which would otherwise be considerably handicapped, disturbed and disrupted. But recently, however, this restitutory dispensation has been extended to cover all other objects that come under rule of the commercial code. This implies that the acceleration in commercial transactions makes every commodity similar to money. It allows them to function only as money value and subjects them to the same regulations that money itself requires for the purpose of facilitating its transactions!

Constancy and Flux as Categories for Comprehending the World

The following consideration may serve to characterize the contribution that money makes to the determination of the pace of life by its specific nature and in addition to its technical consequences that have already been mentioned above. The more precise analysis of the concepts of constancy and change reveals a dual opposition in the form in which they are realized. If we consider the substance of the world, then we easily end up in the idea of an ἐύχαίπᾶν, of an unchangeable being, that suggests, through the exclusion of any increase or decrease in things, the character of absolute constancy. If, on the other hand, we concentrate upon the formation of this substance, then constancy is completely transcended; one form is incessantly transformed into another and the world takes on the aspect of a *perpetuum mobile*. This is the cosmologically, and often metaphysically interpreted, dual aspect of being. However, if a thorough-going empirical method is applied, this contrast between constancy and flux takes on a different aspect. If we observe the image of the world as it immediately presents itself to us, then there are certain forms that do persist through time, whereas the real elements of which they are composed are in continuous motion. Thus, for example, the rainbow persists despite the constantly changing position of the water particles; the organic form persists despite the constant exchange of material of which it is composed. Indeed, in every inorganic object only the relationship and the interaction of the smallest parts persist, whereas the parts themselves, hidden to our eyes, are in constant molecular flux. Thus, reality itself is in a restless flux, and though we are unable to observe this because, as it were, we lack the sharpness of sight, the forms and constellations of movements solidify in the appearance of the enduring object.

As well as these two contrasts in the application of the concepts of constancy and flux to the world as it is perceived, there exists a third. Constancy may have a meaning that goes beyond any extended period of time. The simplest, but in this context a sufficient, instance of this is the law of nature. The validity of the law of nature rests on the fact that a certain constellation of elements necessarily results in a definite effect. This necessity is totally independent of *when* the preconditions present themselves in reality. Whether it be once or a million times, at this moment or in a hundred thousand years hence, the validity of the law is eternal in the sense of timelessness. Its essence and very notion exclude any change or motion. It does not matter, at this point, that we cannot ascribe unconditional validity with unconditional certainty to any single law of nature. This is not only because our comprehension, which cannot distinguish between the recurrent but fortuitous combination of phenomena and actual causal relationships, is necessarily subject to correctibility, but rather, and above all, because each law of nature is valid only for a definite state of mind, whereas for another one the truth would lie in a different formulation of the same factual state of affairs. However, since the human mind is liable to develop no matter how slowly and indiscernibly, there can be no law that is valid at a given moment that is not subject to change in the course of time. Yet this change refers only to the perceptible content of the law of nature and to its meaning and concept. The notion of a law—which exists regardless of any instance of its imperfect realization but which none the less justifies the idea and gives it meaning—rests upon that absence of all motion, upon that validity that is independent of all given conditions because they are changeable. There must be a corresponding phenomenon in the form of motion to this distinctive absolute form of persistence. Just as constancy may extend over any extent of time, no matter how long, until any relationship to a specific moment of time is simply dissolved by the eternal validity of the law of nature or the mathematical formula, so too change and motion may be conceived of as absolutes, as if a specific measurement of time for them did not exist. If all motion proceeds between a "here" and a "there," then through this absolute motion—the *species aeternitatis* in reverse—the "here" completely disappears. Whereas timeless objects are valid in the form of permanency, their opposites are valid in the form of transition, of non-permanency. I am in no doubt that this pair of opposites is comprehensive enough to develop a view of the world out of them. If, on the one hand, one knew all the laws that control reality, then reality would actually be reduced to its absolute contents, to its eternal timeless significance. This would be true even though reality could not yet be constructed on this basis since the law as such, according to its ideal content, is completely indifferent towards any individual instance of its realization. But it is precisely because the content of reality is completely absorbed in these laws, which constantly produce effects out of causes and simultaneously allow these effects to operate as causes, that it is possible, on the other hand, to perceive reality, the concrete, historical, experiential appearance of the world in that absolute flux that is indicated by Heraclitus' symbolic formulation. If one reduces the view of the world to this opposition, then everything of duration, everything that points beyond the immediate moment, is extracted from reality and assembled in the ideal realm of mere laws. In reality itself things do not last for any length of time; through the restlessness with which they offer themselves at any moment to the application of a law, every form becomes immediately dissolved in the very moment when it emerges; it lives, as it were, only by being destroyed; every consolidation of form to lasting objects—no matter how short they last—is an incomplete interpretation that is unable to follow the motion of reality at its own pace. The unity of the whole of being is completely comprehended in the unity of what simply persists and what simply does not persist.

Money as the Historical Symbol of the Relative Character of Existence

There is no more striking symbol of the completely dynamic character of the world than that of money. The meaning of money lies in the fact that it will be given away. When money stands still, it is no longer money according to its specific value and significance. The effect that it occasionally exerts in a state of repose arises out of an anticipation of its further motion. Money is nothing but the vehicle for a movement in which everything else that is not in motion is completely extinguished. It is, as it were, an *actus purus*; it lives in continuous self-alienation from any given point and thus forms the counterpart and direct negation of all being in itself.

But perhaps it represents, no less as a symbol, the opposite form, that of defining reality. The individual amount of money is, in fact, by its very nature in constant motion. But this is only because its value relates to the individual objects of value, just as the general law relates to the concrete conditions in which it realizes itself. If the law, which itself stands above all motions, none the less represents the form and basis of all motions, then the abstract value of wealth that is not subdivided into individual values and that is represented by money is, as it were, the soul and purpose of economic activities. As a tangible item money is the most ephemeral thing in the external-practical world; yet in its content it is the most stable, since it stands as the point of indifference and balance between all other phenomena in the world. The ideal purpose of money, as well as of the law, is to be a measure of things without being measured itself, a purpose that can be realized fully only by an endless development. Money expresses the relationship that exists between economic goods. Money itself remains stable with reference to the changes in relationships, as does a numerical proportion which reflects the relationship between many and changing objects, and as does the formula of the law of gravity with reference to material masses and their infinitely varying motion. Just as the general concept in its logical validity is independent of the number and modification of its realizations, indicating, as it were, their lawfulness, so too money—that is, the inner rationale by which the single piece of metal or paper becomes money—is the general concept of objects in so far as they are economic. They do not need to be economic; but if they wish to be, they can do so only by adjusting to the law of valuation that is embodied in money.

The observation that this one institution participates equally in the two basic forms of reality may explain the relationship of these two forms. Their significance is actually a relative one; that is, each finds its logical and psychological possibility for interpreting the world in the other. Only because reality is in constant motion is there any sense in asserting its opposite: the ideal system of eternally valid lawfulness. Conversely, it is only because such lawfulness exists that we are able to comprehend and grasp that stream of existence that would otherwise disintegrate into total chaos. The general relativity of the world, at first glance familiar to only one side of this opposition, in reality also engulfs the other side and proves to be its mistress where it only appeared to be a party. In the same way, money transcends its significance as a single economic value in order to represent abstract economic value in general and to entwine both functions in an indissoluble correlation in which neither is first.

Money, as an institution of the historical world, symbolizes the behaviour of objects and establishes a special relationship between itself and them. The more the life of society becomes dominated by monetary relationships, the more the relativistic character of existence finds its expression in conscious life, since money is nothing other than a special form of the embodied relativity of economic goods that signifies their value. Just as the absolutist view of the world represents a definite stage of intellectual development in correlation with the corresponding practical, economic and emotional conditions of human affairs, so the relativistic view of the world seems to express the momentary relationship of adjustment on the part of our intellect. More accurate, it is confirmed by the opposing images of social and subjective life, in which money has found its real effective embodiment and the reflected symbol of its forms and movements.

THREE

THE NEW RELIGION-MORALITY OF SPEED

Filippo Tommaso Marinetti

In my First Manifesto (February 20, 1909) I declared: the magnificence of the world has been enriched by a new beauty, *the beauty of speed*. Following dynamic art, the new religion-morality of speed is born this Futurist year from our great liberating war. Christian morality served to develop man's inner life. Today it has lost its reason for existing, because it has been emptied of all divinity.

Christian morality defended the physiological structure of man from the excesses of sensuality. It moderated his instincts and balanced them. The *Futurist morality* will defend man from the decay caused by slowness, by memory, by analysis, by repose and habit. Human energy centupled by speed will master Time and Space.

Man began by despising the isochronal, cadenced rhythm, identical with the rhythm of his own stride, of the great rivers. Man envied the rhythm of torrents, like that of a horse's gallop. Man mastered horse, elephant, and camel to display his divine authority through an increase in speed. He made friends with the most docile animals, captured the rebellious animals, and fed himself with the eatable animals. From space man stole electricity and then the liquid fuels, to make new allies for himself in the motors. Man shaped the metals he had conquered and made flexible with fire, to ally himself with his fuels and electricity. He thereby assembled an army of slaves, dangerous and hostile but sufficiently domesticated to carry him swiftly over the curves of the earth.

Tortuous paths, roads that follow the indolence of streams and wind along the spines and uneven bellies of mountains, these are the laws of the earth. Never straight lines; always arabesques and zigzags. Speed finally gives to human life one of the characteristics of divinity: *the straight line*.

The opaque Danube under its muddy tunic, its attention turned on its inner life full of fat libidinous fecund fish, runs murmuring between the high implacable banks of its mountains as if within the immense central corridor of the earth, a convent split open by the swift wheels of the constellations. How long will this shuffling stream allow an automobile, barking like a crazy fox terrier, to pass it at top speed? I hope to see the day when the Danube will run in a straight line at 300 kilometers an hour.

One must persecute, lash, torture all those who sin against speed.

Grave guilt of the passéist cities where the sun settles in, slows down, and never moves again. Who can believe that the sun will go away tonight? Nonsense! Impossible! It has been domiciled here. Squares, lakes of stagnant fire. Streets, rivers of lazy fire. No one can pass, for the moment. You can't escape! An inundation of sun. You would need a refrigerated boat or a diving suit of ice to cross that fire. Dig in. A despotism, a police raid of light, about to arrest the rebels in their blazons of coolness and speed. A solar state of siege. Woe to the body that leaves home. A sledgehammer blow on the head. Finished. Solar guillotine over every door. Woe to the thought that leaves its skull. Two, three, four leaden notes will fall on it from the ruined bell tower. In the house, sultrily, a madness of nostalgic flies. A stir of thighs and sweaty memories.

Criminal slowness of Sunday crowds and the Venetian lagoons.

Speed, having as its essence the intuitive synthesis of every force in movement, is naturally *pure.* Slowness, having as its essence the rational analysis of every exhaustion in repose, is naturally *unclean.* After the destruction of the antique good and the antique evil, we create a new good, speed, and a new evil, slowness.

Speed = synthesis of every courage in action. Aggressive and warlike.

Slowness = analysis of every stagnant prudence. Passive and pacifistic.

Speed = scorn of obstacles, desire for the new and unexplored. Modernity, hygiene.

Slowness = arrest, ecstasy, immobile adoration of obstacles, nostalgia for the already seen, idealization of exhaustion and rest, pessimism about the unexplored. Rancid romanticism of the wild, wandering poet and long-haired, bespectacled dirty philosopher.

If prayer means communication with the divinity, running at high speed is a prayer. Holiness of wheels and rails. One must kneel on the tracks to pray to the divine velocity. One must kneel before the whirling speed of a gyroscope compass: 20,000 revolutions per minute, the highest mechanical speed reached by man. One must snatch from the stars the secret of their stupefying, incomprehensible speed. Then let us join the great celestial battles, vie with the star 1830 Groombridge that flies at 241 km. a second, with Arthur that flies at 413 km. a second. Invisible mathematical artillery. Wars in which the stars, being both missiles and artillery, match their speeds to escape from a greater star or to strike a smaller one. Our male saints are the numberless corpuscles that penetrate our atmosphere at an average velocity of 42,000 meters a second. Our female saints are the light and electromagnetic waves at 3×10^{10} meters a second.

The intoxication of great speeds in cars is nothing but the joy of feeling oneself fused with the only *divinity*. Sportsmen are the first catechumens of this religion. Forthcoming destruction of houses and cities, to make way for great meeting places for cars and planes.

FOUR

THE MANIA FOR MOTION AND SPEED

John Dewey

The increase in the number, variety and cheapness of amusements represents a powerful diversion from political concern. The members of an inchoate public have too many ways of enjoyment, as well as of work, to give much thought to organization into an effective public. Man is a consuming and sportive animal as well as a political one. What is significant is that access to means of amusement has been rendered easy and cheap beyond anything known in the past. The present era of "prosperity" may not be enduring. But the movie, radio, cheap reading matter and motor car with all they stand for have come to stay. That they did not originate in deliberate desire to divert attention from political interests does not lessen their effectiveness in that direction. The political elements in the constitution of the human being, those having to do with citizenship, are crowded to one side. In most circles it is hard work to sustain conversation on a political theme; and once initiated, it is quickly dismissed with a yawn. Let there be introduced the topic of the mechanism and accomplishment of various makes of motor cars or the respective merits of actresses, and the dialogue goes on at a lively pace. The thing to be remembered is that this cheapened and multiplied access to amusement is the product of the machine age, intensified by the business tradition which causes provision of means for an enjoyable passing of time to be one of the most profitable of occupations.

One phase of the workings of a technological age, with its unprecedented command of natural energies, while it is implied in what has been said, needs explicit attention. The older publics, in being local communities, largely homogeneous with one another, were also, as the phrase goes, static. They changed, of course, but barring war, catastrophe and great migrations, the modifications were gradual. They proceeded slowly and were largely unperceived by those undergoing them. The newer forces have created mobile and fluctuating associational forms. The common complaints of the disintegration of family life may be placed in evidence. The movement from rural to urban assemblies is also the result and proof of this mobility. Nothing stays long put, not even the associations by which business and industry are carried on. The mania for motion and speed is a symptom of the restless instability of social life, and it operates to intensify the causes from which it springs. Steel replaces wood and masonry for buildings; ferro-concrete modifies steel, and some invention may work a further revolution. Muscle Shoals was acquired to produce nitrogen, and new methods have already made antiquated the supposed need of great accumulation of water power. Any selected illustration suffers because of the heterogeneous mass of cases to select from. How can a public be organized, we may ask, when literally it does not stay in place? Only deep issues or those which can be made to appear such can find a common denominator among all the shifting and unstable relationships. Attachment is a very different function of life from affection. Affections will continue as long as the heart beats. But attachment requires something more than organic causes. The very things which stimulate and intensify affections may undermine attachments. For these are bred in tranquil stability; they are nourished in constant relationships. Acceleration of mobility disturbs them at their root. And without abiding attachments associations are too shifting and shaken to permit a public readily to locate and identify itself.

The new era of human relationships in which we live is one marked by mass production for remote markets, by cable and telephone, by cheap printing, by railway and steam navigation. Only geographically did Columbus discover a new world. The actual new world has been generated in the last hundred years. Steam and electricity have done more to alter the conditions under which men associate together than all the agencies which affected human relationships before our time. There are those who lay the blame for all the evils of our lives on steam, electricity and machinery. It is always convenient to have a devil as well as a savior to bear the responsibilities of humanity. In reality, the trouble springs rather from the ideas and absence of ideas in connection with which technological factors operate. Mental and moral beliefs and ideals change more slowly than outward conditions. If the ideals associated with the higher life of our cultural past have been impaired, the fault is primarily with them. Ideals and standards formed without regard to the means by which they are to be achieved and incarnated in flesh are bound to be thin and wavering. Since the aims, desires and purposes created by a machine age do not connect with tradition, there are two sets of rival ideals, and those which have actual instrumentalities at their disposal have the advantage. Because the two are rivals and because the older ones retain their glamor and sentimental prestige in literature and religion, the newer ones are perforce harsh and narrow. For the older symbols of ideal life still engage thought and command loyalty. Conditions have changed, but every aspect of life, from religion and education to property and trade, shows that nothing approaching a transformation has taken place in ideas and ideals. Symbols control sentiment and thought, and the new age has no symbols consonant with its activities. Intellectual instrumentalities for the formation of an organized public are more inadequate than its overt means. The ties which hold men together in action are numerous, tough and subtle. But they are invisible and intangible. We have the physical tools of communication as never before. The thoughts and aspirations congruous with them are not communicated, and hence are not common. Without such communication the public will remain shadowy and formless, seeking spasmodically for itself, but seizing and holding its shadow rather than its substance. Till the Great Society is converted into a Great Community, the Public will remain in eclipse. Communication can alone create a great community. Our Babel is not one of tongues but of the signs and symbols without which shared experience is impossible.

FIVE

THE MOTORIZED LEGISLATOR

Carl Schmitt

The Crisis of Positive Statutory Legality: The Twentieth Century

The situation of the nineteenth century, which was in many respects favorable to legal studies and jurisprudence, has changed since the First World War. Since 1914 all major historical events and developments in every European country have contributed to making the process of legislation ever faster and more summary, the path to realizing legal regulation ever shorter, and the role of legal science ever smaller. The war and the postwar period, mobilization and demobilization, revolution and dictatorship, inflation and deflation—each of them, despite their differences, led to the same result throughout Europe: the process of legislation became increasingly simplified and accelerated. Ever new and more expansive authorizations were pronounced by which legislative bodies delegated power to issue decrees and orders having the force of law. "Decree" and "orders" supplanted the statute. Constitutional considerations always spoke against the practice of delegation, and such concerns were appropriate. For in the end legislative bodies are called upon by the constitution to make laws themselves, not to empower other agencies to legislate; as Locke, the legal-philosophical founder of modern constitutional law, had said, they should "make laws, but not legislators." At the 1921 Congress of German Jurists, the Berlin legal theorist Heinrich Triepel noted that the "misfortune" of the displacement of law by decree began in Germany right at the start of the First World War with the Enabling Act of 4 August 1914.[1] This was indeed a significant date for those interested in the transformation of the nature of law. Triepel also

1. [Editor's note: Triepel (1868–1946) was a prominent conservative jurist.]

read aloud the following report from a letter written to him by his great teacher, Karl Binding, shortly before the latter's death: "The next great task is the struggle against the decree in its presumption against the law."[2]

Many jurists who worked in quieter branches of the law believed that they were safe and reassured themselves with sayings like "public law passes away, private law endures," failing to note that the core of their positivism up until then, the concept of the legal norm itself, was being called into question. In contrast, Binding, a genuine jurist not only of criminal but also of constitutional law, scented with sure instinct both the structural transformation of law and the mortal danger to the whole existing normativism. In fact, everywhere the trend quickly overran all constraints—indeed, directly into the areas of economic, financial, and tax law, the native soil of the formal, constitutional conception of law.[3] In Germany the first Emergency Tax Law of 7 December 1923, enacted immediately after the end of the period of inflation, was not even issued under the Enabling Act, but instead under Article 48 of the Weimar Constitution, i.e., as a presidential emergency measure, since the Enabling Act was not promulgated in time. At the end of 1923, this only seemed to be a small disruption destined soon to blow over. For the next two Emergency Tax Laws, enacted after currency stabilization, could refer to a formal Enabling Act (of 8 December 1923). At the 1924 Congress of German Legal Theorists in Jena, the overwhelming majority remained completely blind to the structural transformation of the legislative process that was already underway. The 1925 finance reforms, the work of Secretary of State Johannes Popitz, were even passed via normal legislative channels. But just a few years later the Enabling Law too had been hopelessly overtaken, and after July 1930 financial and economic legal arrangements in general came to be enacted on the basis of Article 48 of the Weimar Constitution, i.e., as presidential emergency measures.[4]

2. [Editor's note: Schmitt offers no citation for the quote. Binding (1841–1920) was a famous German criminal lawyer.]

3. [Editor's note: An excellent survey of the interwar legal trends summarized by Schmitt here is provided by Clinton Rossiter, *Constitutional Dictatorship: Crisis Government in the Modern Democracies* (New Brunswick, N.J.: Transaction, 2002). Like Schmitt, Rossiter describes a proliferation of "emergency" methods of government, most of which pose difficult challenges for traditional liberal models of lawmaking.]

4. See my "L'évolution récente de problème des délégations legislatives," in *Introduction à l'étude du droit comparé: recueil d'études en l'honneur d'Édouard Lambert* (Paris: Société anonyme du recueil Sirey, 1938). Johannes Popitz himself took a position on the constitutional side of the question with the following statement: "The sharpest legal examination has must lead one to realize that the extent to which one can use Article 48 depends on the extent of the danger, and when the emergency is so great that something absolutely has to happen in order to present the financial collapse of the state, one cannot shy away from using Article 48 itself to

Compared to Germany, the victorious French Third Republic at the time seemed to be a surer bulwark of constitutionality. But here too legislative delegation won out. In the classic country of the legist tradition, the home of great constitutional jurists like Paul Esmein, Maurice Hauriou, and Leon Duguit, constitutional anxieties were naturally especially keen. But here too, as in other countries, ingenious distinctions between streamlined legislation and permissible delegation emerged, appeasing the constitutionalist conscience and inserting at least some constraints and delimitations. All to no avail. In France as in other countries—warring and neutral, victorious and defeated, parliamentary states as well as so-called dictatorships—the pressure to adapt legal provision to rapidly changing circumstances was irresistible. The warning of the Lord Chief Justice of England, Lord Gordon Hewart, against the "new despotism" (1928) changed nothing about the issue.[5] Even in mid-May 1944 the unsettling question of "executive powers" was debated in English Parliament without a single new idea being added to the arguments and perspectives of earlier discussions of this question in Germany, France, or other European countries. Julius von Kirchmann's prediction from nearly a century before that scholarship could never overtake positive law proved true—indeed, beyond all expectations. The legislative machine increased its tempo to a hitherto unimaginable extent, and positivist jurisprudential commentary and interpretation could hardly keep up. Long before the full torrent of decrees was unleashed, scholarly and systematic commentaries written by professors of law had already been replaced by the growing volume of practical commentaries composed by practitioners or ministerial experts, who, in many cases, by doing so in no way disowned their outstanding legal training.[6]

It has been said of decree that it is "motorized law." Should legal scholarship now run after and likewise try to "motorize" itself? Any researcher who thinks scientifically will perceive the inherent impossibility of keeping up. But with the motorization of law through mere decree the pinnacle of simplification and acceleration has not yet been reached. New accelerations have resulted from market regulation and state direction of the economy, with its numerous delegations to authorities and subauthorities making up

---

impose taxes. But at the same time it follows from this that of course the greatest caution is exercised and that this kind of procedure is only justifiable in such difficult time as hopefully lie forever behind us." "Die staatsrechtlichen Grundlagen des öffentlichen Finanzwesens," in *Recht und Staat im Neuen Deutschland,* ed. Bernhard Harms (Berlin: Hobbing, 1929).

5. [Editor's note: The reference is to Hewart's widely read *The New Despotism* (New York: Cosmopolitan, 1929).]

6. [Editor's note: Kirchmann (1802–84) was a vocal critic of positive legislation.]

different kinds of regulatory offices, interest groups, and commissioners. It is thus precisely in this field that in Germany the concept of the "order" [*Verordnung*] follows in the path of the "decree" [*Anordnung*]. The order is "the most elastic form of legislation" and surpasses the decree with regard to the speed of its realization and the simplicity of its promulgation. If the decree is "motorized law," the order could be called "motorized decree."[7] Here the space for an independent, purely positivistic theory of the legal norm comes to an end. Law is transformed into an instrument of planning,[8] the administrative act into an act of steering. With an order issued by one of the responsible authorities, not publicly announced but often shared only with those immediately affected, without possibility of further amendment and entirely adapted to the rapidly changing circumstances, it is no longer possible to insert an independent third authority between the order and the person who issues it, the measure and the person to whom it applies, the act of regulation and the regulatory office, as was still possible in the nineteenth century between the enactment and he who enacts it [*Setzung und Setzer*], the law and the legislator. It can make sense to say that the law is smarter than the legislator; but it is something completely different to claim that a regulatory measure, issued according to the circumstances, is smarter than the directing authority best informed about the situation.

Legal Scholarship as the Last Refuge of Legal Consciousness

Seen from the broad historical perspective of many centuries, the situation of European legal scholarship has always been determined by two oppositions: to theology, metaphysics, and philosophy on the one side, and to a merely technical demand for norms on the other. European legal scholarship developed as an independent science beginning in the twelfth century in struggle against theology and by disentangling itself from faculties of theology. Friedrich Carl von Savigny defended legal science on this flank

7. So reports ministerial counselor Rieger in an extremely important essay, "Rückblick und Ausblick auf die Form der wirtschaftlichen Gesetzgebung," Ministerialblatt of the RWM [Reports of the Reichswirtschaftsministerium], January 28, 1941; see Werner Weber in *Zeitschrift für die gesamte Staatswissenschaft* 102 (1946): 116–17; Kurt Emig in *Deutsche Rechtswissenschaft.* 7 (1942): 220–21; and W. Gäthgens, "Die rechtlichen Grundlagen der Waren-Bewirtschaftung," in *Probleme der gelenkten Wirtschaft,* ed. Friedrich Dorn (Berlin: De Gruyter, 1942), 52, where the notion of an order as the most elastic form of legislation is discussed.

8. Law as an instrument of planning is discussed in the 1938 Berlin *Habilitationsschrift* of Georg Daskalakis (Athens).

by recognizing the secularized theology of the seventeenth- and eighteenth-century philosophy of natural law, as well as Hegel's system of philosophy, as a threat to its internal autonomy.[9] But at the same time he fought on the other flank against the positivism of the mere enactment of enactments [*Setzung von Setzungen*], the mere ought-rule [*Sollensregel*], as hostile to science, and recognized the danger of the legal positivism of the Napoleonic codification. In both cases, he objected to the "positivism of historical sources" in order to save legal scholarship from becoming either mere philosophy or a "mere craft." By giving itself over to theology and philosophy, legal science would cease being, in a specific way, its own autonomous science; it would dissolve itself into other faculties and give up the results of half a millennium. It would then no longer be "positive" in the historical sense given to this ambiguous word, which Savigny also liked to use, by the specificity of legal science. By being subjected to the mere legality of an enacted "ought," it would completely lose its dignity as a science and be reduced to a not particularly useful instrument of a subsidiary technical field, treating the world as a tabula rasa for territory-less, lawless planning. Legal science would then not only no longer be a faculty, it would have lost its academic character altogether. It would no longer belong to the university—assuming that this institution retains the meaning that historically befits it as a concrete order of European intellectual life.

European legal scholarship is the first-born child of the modern European mind, of modern "occidental rationalism." The modern natural sciences followed only later. The first trailblazers of this rationalism were the legists, great revolutionaries who shared the fate of true revolutionaries. In the twelfth- and thirteenth-century rebirth of Roman law in the cities of north and central Italy, "commentaries" gave rise to the *corpus juris*. These chaotic times in no way corresponded to the nineteenth-century ideal of security, but precisely such circumstances made people aware of the indispensability of legal scholarship that drew on scientific sources. Legal science asserted itself as a faculty through fierce struggle with the Church and theology in the thirteenth and fourteenth centuries, and maintained itself through the tumultuous dissolution of feudalism. The sixteenth century, which saw the flowering of humanistic legal scholarship, was also a time of bloody sectarian civil wars. Great jurists of this period fell victim to intolerant fanaticism, so that each side had its legal martyrs, like John Story on the side of

9. [Editor's note: Savigny (1802–84) was an important figure in Schmitt's critique of positive legislation. For a discussion, see William E. Scheuerman, *Liberal Democracy and the Social Acceleration of Time* (Baltimore: Johns Hopkins University Press, 2004), 127–43.]

the old faith, and Donelus and Albericus Gentilis on the side of the new one. A typical jurist of this time, Jean Bodin, creater of modern public law and the concept of sovereignty, only escaped death at the hands of murderers on Saint Bartholomew's night in 1572 by a miracle. No one can say that legal scholarship was lacking in intellectual courage, which belongs to all the sciences, during this horrific time of sectarian war.

Since the nineteenth century, the situation of European legal scholarship has been characterized by a splitting up of law into legality and legitimacy. The threat to the European legal-theoretical mind today no longer comes from theology, and only occasionally from philosophical metaphysics, but rather from an unrestrained technicism, which serves statutory law as a tool. Now legal science has another flank on which to defend itself. The scientific jurist is not a theologian or a philosopher, but neither is he merely a function in some kind of enacted "ought" and its enactment of enactments [*Setzung von Setzungen*]. We thus have to defend ourselves against subaltern instrumentalization, as in other times we defended ourselves against dependence on theology. In relations with both sides we practitioners of both remain science and jurisprudence: this is the reality of our intellectual existence, which we do not allow to be eroded from outside by methodological, psychological, or general philosophical categories. For we fulfill a task that no other form of human activity can take away from us. We cannot select changing power holders and regimes according to our taste, but in the changing situation we perceive the basis of a rational essence of power that the principles of law cannot do without. Among these principles is the recognition of the person, based on reciprocal respect, which does not disappear even in struggle; the sense for the logic and consistency of concepts and institutions; a sense of reciprocity and for the minimum of an orderly process, the *due process of law* [English in original—trans.] without which there is no law.[10] Here, in the fact that we preserve this indestructible kernel of all law against all the measures that corrupt it, lies the

10. The formula "due process of law," which has a central significance in the practice of courts in the United States of America, is of European origin. Hermann von Mangoldt, *Rechtsstaatsgedanke und Regierungsform in den Vereinigten Staaten von Amerika: Die geistigen Grundlagen des amerikanischen Verfassungsrechts* (Essen: Essener Verlagsanstalt, 1938), 13. It is, to put it in our terms, an "institutional guarantee," not a status quo guarantee; for since the *Hurtado* case (1884) it has remained constant in the practice of the Supreme Court that "due process of law" means a minimum of form and process, not simply and traditionally the ancient process of the common law. See John Rogers Commons, *The Legal Foundations of Capitalism* (New York: Macmillan, 1924), 33; Rodney L. Mott, *Due Process of Law* (Indianapolis: Bobbs-Merrill, 1926), 246.

dignity that is entrusted to us, in Europe today more than at any other time and in any other part of the world.

English-style traditionalism, borne by legal practitioners, is no longer intellectually up to significant new problems. The legalization of the law in the French style, and its transformation into state legality and a functional mode of the public administration and the judiciary, carries with it the danger of paralysis—or, for Germany as the strongest industrialized country, of mechanization, technicization, and corruption [*Termitisierung*]; its fate is catching up with it in the growing motorization of the legislative machinery. The idea of deadly legality, "légalité qui tue," pronounces the dangers of this corruption of law in the network of ever-newer "enacted" normative prescriptions. So all that really remains for us is the call to legal scholarship as the last guardian of the unintended rise and development of law.

When Savigny raised his voice in protest in 1814, the jurists of Europe were still entirely spellbound by the model of Napoleonic codification, and above all by the *Code Civil*. In the brilliance of this glory, most were not even aware of the situation of French legal scholarship at the time, and especially of its sad role as teachers and professors of law.[11] The hypnosis that resulted from the Napoleonic codification was even stronger than the military and political success of the new Caesar, and outlasted his military and political breakthrough. France was the land of the legists and the most modern legal codification. The alleged or real statement of the French legal teacher Begnet was typical of France; two generations before our German positivists, he offered his audience the cheap wisdom that for him there was no civil law, only the civil lawbook.[12] For the dominant opinion of the time, French legal development, with its positivistic transformation of law into state legality, stood at the pinnacle of the progress of civilization and humanity. It was also in France that one first became aware of the splitting up of law into legality and legitimacy.[13] Very few people, among them Tocqueville, recognized at the time that in reality this acclaimed progress of civilization was nothing other than progressive centralization, and that the apparent advance of law signified nothing other than the rising scaffolding of ever-newer legal prostheses in service to centralization, which in essence

---

11. See Julien Bonnecase's presentation of *L'École de l'exégèse en droit civil*, 2nd ed. (Paris: E. de Boccard, 1924).

12. Ibid., footnotes at 29 and 128.

13. The significance of this was already expressed by Felicité de Lamennais with the greatest clarity and fullest awareness in 1829. [Editor's note: Lamennais was a French Catholic political thinker.]

only worked to make the revolution permanent and accepted only revolution as a legitimate power overlaid with legality. A French jurist of European stature, Hauriou, bore witness to this connection in 1916, during the First World War.[14] This makes it easier to see Savigny's farsightedness and his extraordinary significance for European legal science. The terrifying shock of 1848, at least for a moment, opened many eyes. It is no accident that the bad news of the deadly legalization of law, of "légalité qui tue," the idea of deadly legality on which governments and people die, emerged in France, the land of the legists, shortly before the outbreak of 1848.

Of course, after the revelatory shock of 1848 a positivistic reaction and resignation set in, and nineteenth-century development slid further along the rails of progress toward the prevailing legality of the prevailing status quo of prevailing measures. This was not only the case in France, where the split between legality and legitimacy first appeared. In every European country, even in England—where I will only mention the names Jeremiah [sic] Bentham and John Austin—one finds many examples and parallels to the statement of the French teacher of civil law, who turned away from law and fled to the *sécurité* of the civil lawbook and positivistic normativism. In Germany we have a crude example of the most naïve legal positivism in Karl Bergbohm's 1892 book *Jurisprudenz und Rechtsphilosophie*. But it is also precisely in Germany that there are still the strongest intellectual reserves, through whose power the name Savigny could become a symbol. We should not forget the origin of this symbol, and we shall never give up its future actuality.

More than one hundred years ago, when Savigny wrote and published his treatise, the danger of an empty, legalistic technicism was not nearly as great as it is today, in the age of motorized law and motorized decrees. So much greater and more admirable is the intellectual power that was required to recognize the danger at that time and take up resistance against it at the beginning of the era that started with the splitting of law into legality and legitimacy, and ended with the total transformation of historical legitimacy

14. In Hauriou's words: "Thus, the Revolution of 1789 is nothing other than the absolute advent of written law and the systematic destruction of customary institutions. It has resulted in a state of perpetual revolution, since the mobility of the written law is no longer balanced by the stability of certain customary institutions, the forces of change are more powerful than the forces of stability. In France, social and political life, absolutely emptied of institutions, can only provisionally sustain themselves, with many somersaults, thanks to the high level of general morality." Maurice Hauriou, *Principes de droit publique* (Paris: Recueil Sirey, 1916), XI. If, against this, the great French jurist then, in 1916, hoped to find a remedy in the distinction between simple and constitutional law, European constitutional experience since 1919 has sadly disappointed him.

into revolutionary legitimacy.[15] Only within this larger picture does the arcanum of the 1814 warning become visible. Whoever understands it will understand and not misinterpret our invocation of the names Savigny and Johann Jakob Bachofen.[16] At a time when legality has become a poisoned weapon with which one party stabs another in the back, legal scholarship becomes the last refuge of legal consciousness. In a time of tests and trials, legal scholarship is also thereby protected against the threat of historicization, which must collapse in a century of security. Even in the fact of the terror of the means of annihilation, which modern natural science places at the disposal of every power holder, a legal science thrown back on its own resources will be able to find the secret crypt in which the buds of its spirit are protected from every persecutor. This trust, and not, for example, a program for unearthing and publishing, is what we make of Savigny's warning, which for us has become a document of the first resistance. European legal scholarship does not have to die along with the myths of the law and the legislator. If we keep in mind our sad history, our strength is rooted in our grief. Thus, genius will not leave us, and it will show that even the confusion of language can be better than a Babylonian unity.

[Translated by James Ingram]

15. "Revolutionaries who do not know to connect illegal forms of struggle with *all* legal ones are bad revolutionaries" (emphasis in original). Thus Lenin in *Der "Radikalismus," die Kinderkrankheit des Kommunismus* (Leipzig: Francke, 1920), 74. See also the philosophical explanation by Georg Lukács in 1920 on legality and illegality, reprinted in *Geschichte und Klassenbewusstsein: Studien über marxistische Dialektik* (Berlin: Malik, 1923), 261–75, an essay that is more important and current than the great bulk of writings on legal philosophy and natural law that have appeared since 1920, since it rightly posed the question under the concepts "legality and legitimacy."

16. [Editor's note: The latter was a Swiss jurist (1815–87).]

PART 2

HIGH-SPEED SOCIETY
THEORETICAL FOUNDATIONS

SIX

SOCIAL ACCELERATION:
ETHICAL AND POLITICAL CONSEQUENCES
OF A DESYNCHRONIZED HIGH-SPEED SOCIETY

Hartmut Rosa

I. Social Acceleration in the Process of Modernization

In 1999, James Gleick, exploring everyday life in contemporary American society, noted the "acceleration of just about everything": love, life, speech, politics, work, TV, leisure, etc.[1] In this observation he certainly is not alone. In popular as well as scientific discourse about the current evolution of Western societies, acceleration figures as the single most striking and important feature.[2] But despite the noticeable increase in the discourse about acceleration and the shortage of time in recent years, the feeling that history, culture, society, or even "time itself" in some strange way accelerates is not new at all; it seems to be a constitutive trait of modernity as such. As historians such as Reinhart Koselleck have persuasively argued, the general sense of a speedup has accompanied modern society since at least the middle of the eighteenth century.[3] And indeed, as many have observed and

1. James Gleick, *Faster: The Acceleration of Just About Everything* (New York: Pantheon Books, 1999).

2. William E. Scheuerman, "Liberal Democracy and the Empire of Speed," *Polity* 34, no. 1 (2001): 41: "Any attempt to make sense of the human condition at the start of the new century must begin with an analysis of time and space compression." "Time-and-space compression" is David Harvey's term for acceleration; see *The Condition of Postmodernity: An Enquiry into the Origins of Cultural Change* (Cambridge, Mass.: Blackwell, 1989).

3. Cf. Reinhart Koselleck, *Futures Past: On the Semantics of Historical Time* (Cambridge, Mass.: MIT Press, 1985). Koselleck demonstrates that complaints about the overwhelming speed of modern history start well before the French Revolution and long before there is a noticeable development of *technological* speed. The discourse on acceleration then periodically peaks again and again during the following centuries. For example, in 1877 W. G. Greg observed

empirical evidence clearly suggests, the history of modernity seems to be characterized by a wide-ranging speedup of all kinds of technological, economic, social, and cultural processes and by a picking up of the general pace of life. In terms of its structural and cultural impact on modern society, this change in the temporal structures and patterns of modernity appears to be just as pervasive as comparable processes of individualization or rationalization. Like them, it seems, social acceleration is not a steady process but evolves in waves (most often brought about by new technologies or forms of socioeconomic organization), with each new wave meeting considerable resistance as well as partial reversals. Most often, a wave of acceleration is followed by a rise in the "discourse of acceleration," in which cries for deceleration in the name of human needs and values are voiced but eventually die down.[4]

However, contrary to the other constitutive features of the modernization process, which have all been the object of extensive analysis—individualization, rationalization, differentiation (both functional and structural), and the instrumental domestication of nature—the concept of acceleration still lacks a clear and workable definition and a systematic sociological analysis. Within systematic theories of modernity or modernization, acceleration is virtually absent, with the notable exception of Paul Virilio's "dromological" approach to history, which, alas, hardly amounts to a theory. This surprising absence in the face of the empirical and discursive omnipresence of processes of acceleration is arguably a reflection of the neglect of the temporal dimension and processual nature of society in twentieth-century sociological theory—a neglect noted by many authors, most famously perhaps by Anthony Giddens and Niklas Luhmann.[5] In the history of sociology, modernization has mainly been analyzed from four different perspectives,

---

that the most significant feature of his age was its high speed and the pressure it put on life, and he voiced severe doubts whether this gain in speed was a good that was worth its price. In 1907, Henry Adams formulated his famous "law of acceleration" (of history; reprinted in this volume); cf. Robert Levine, *A Geography of Time* (New York: Basic Books, 1997) for further historical observations of social acceleration. The subtitle of Douglas Coupland's celebrated novel *Generation X* fits perfectly with this long tradition. *Generation X: Tales for an Accelerated Culture* (New York: St. Martin's Press, 1991).

4. Thus, the protests and anxieties relating to the introduction of the steam engine, the railway, the telephone, or the personal computer mirror in many respects the various "communitarian" anxieties and protests against manifestations of individualization, or traditionalist opposition against ensuing waves of rationalization—with rationalization generally being victorious in the process of modernization.

5. See Barbara Adam, *Time and Social Theory* (Cambridge: Polity Press, 1990), for an attempt to systematically and comprehensively introduce the temporal dimension into social theory.

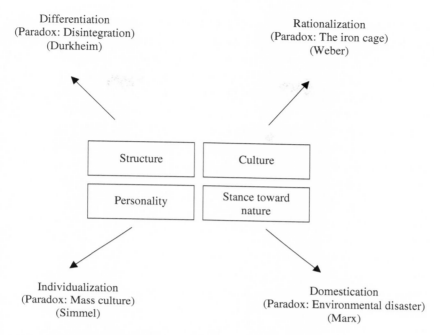

Figure 1. The process of modernization I

prevalent, for example, in the works of Weber, Durkheim, Simmel, and Marx, respectively: culture, social structure, personality type, and relation to nature.[6] From these perspectives, or material dimensions, the process of modernization is identifiable as a process of rationalization, differentiation, individualization, or instrumental domestication, respectively (fig. 1).

My claim here is that we cannot adequately understand the nature and character of modernity and the logic of its structural and cultural development unless we add the temporal perspective to our analysis. Of course, the temporal dimension runs across the four material dimensions of society and cannot neatly be separated from them in phenomenological terms; there is no "social time" independent of these dimensions. The dominant changes in them are closely linked to the cardinal change in temporal patterns (acceleration), which alternatingly appears as their cause or their effect. In fact, it can be argued that many instances are actually driven by the logic of acceleration. As I will briefly try to demonstrate in the closing section of

6. This conceptualization of sociological attempts to grapple with processes of modernization is suggested by Hans van der Loo and Willem van Reijen in *Modernisierung. Projekt und Paradox*, 2nd ed. (Munich: Deutscher Taschenbuch, 1997), loosely adhering to Talcott Parsons's (notoriously static) outline of a "general system of action."

this chapter, the drive toward social acceleration in modern societies might in fact be so overriding that we might actually find phenomena of de-differentiation and deindividualization in cases where differentiation and individualization have become hindrances to social acceleration.

Interestingly, Van der Loo and Van Reijen state that for each of the four central processes of modernization there is a paradoxical flipside that has also frequently been the focus of social analysis. For example, individualization goes hand in hand with the evolution of "mass culture," the result of rationalization could be imprisonment in a thoroughly irrational "iron cage" (doomed to economic growth even when the only scarcity is the scarcity of scarcity), and the instrumental control and domination of nature could lead to a backlash in which manmade natural disasters wipe out our entire civilization. And sure enough, such a flipside is evident for social acceleration as well. Hence, no analysis of social acceleration will be complete unless it takes into account those strange corresponding phenomena of social deceleration and slowdown that have become particularly visible toward the turn of the twenty-first century, with the rise of theories of "hyperacceleration," "turbo-capitalism," and the "digital speed revolution" on the one hand, and conceptions of "polar inertia," the "end of history," the "closing of the future," and the sclerotic inescapability of the "iron cage" on the other.[7] From the latter perspective, all the apparent speed and transformation of society appear to be only changes on the "user surface,"[8] beneath which processes of paralysis and sclerosis predominate.

But what is social acceleration? Does it refer to an acceleration of society itself, or does it only capture accelerating processes within (a static) society? In what sense can we talk of social acceleration in the singular, when all we see is a host of possibly unrelated processes of acceleration, such as in sports, fashion, video editing, transport, and job succession, as well as some phenomena of social deceleration? In the following I present an analytic framework that will allow, at least in principle, a theoretically thorough

7. Paul Virilio, "Polar Inertia," in *The Virilio Reader*, ed. James Der Derian (Oxford: Blackwell, 1998), 117–33; Francis Fukuyama, *The End of History and the Last Man* (New York: Free Press, 1992); Jean Baudrillard, *The Illusion of the End* (Cambridge: Polity Press, 1994); Charles Taylor, "Marx statt Tocqueville: Über Identität, Entfremdung und die Konsequenzen des 11. September: An Interview with Hartmut Rosa and Arto Laitinen," *Deutsche Zeitschrift für Philosophie* 50, no. 1 (2002): 9.

8. Lothar Baier, *Keine Zeit! 18 Versuche über die Beschleunigung* (Munich: A. Kunstmann, 2000). This sense is strongly expressed in the novels of Douglas Coupland too. I have explored this at length in "Am Ende der Geschichte: Die Generation 'X' zwischen Globalisierung und Desintegration," in *Neustart des Weltlaufs? Fiktion und Faszination der Zeitenwende*, ed. Karsten Fischer (Frankfurt am Main: Suhrkamp, 1999).

and empirically justifiable (or at least contestable) definition of what it could mean for a society to accelerate and of the ways in which Western societies can be understood as acceleration societies.

II. What Is Social Acceleration?

It is obvious that contrary to Gleick's observation of the "acceleration of just about everything," there is no single, universal pattern of acceleration that speeds up *everything*. To the contrary, many things slow down, like traffic in a traffic jam, while others stubbornly resist all attempts to make them go faster, like the common cold. Nevertheless, there are certainly a great many social phenomena to which the concept of acceleration can properly be applied. Athletes seem to be running and swimming faster and faster, computers compute at ever-higher speeds, transport and communication need only a fraction of the time they took a century ago, people appear to sleep less and less (some scientists have found that the average sleeping time has decreased by two hours since the nineteenth century and by thirty minutes since the 1970s[9]), and even our neighbors seem to move in and out of their apartments more frequently.

But even if we can prove these changes are not accidental but follow a systematic pattern, is there anything these very different processes have in common so that they can be brought under the one concept of social acceleration? Not directly, I want to claim. Rather, when we look more closely at this range of phenomena, it becomes apparent that we can separate them into three analytically as well as empirically distinct categories, which I will present in the rest of this section. In the next section, I will explore the connection between the different spheres of acceleration and the mechanisms or motors that lie behind them. In the fourth section, I will discuss some problems for the sociological analysis of "acceleration societies" that arise from the fact that we have to account for a range of social phenomena that remain constant or even decelerate. I will then discuss some of the most pressing and transformative political and ethical consequences of social acceleration before returning in the conclusion to the problem of the proper conceptualization of the process of modernization.

---

9. Manfred Garhammer, *Wie Europäer ihre Zeit nutzen: Zeitstrukturen und Zeitkulturen im Zeichen der Globalisierung* (Berlin: Edition Sigma, 1999), 378.

1. Technological Acceleration

The first, most obvious, and most measurable form of acceleration is the speeding up of intentional, goal-directed processes of transport, communication, and production that can be defined as "technological acceleration." Although it is not always easy to measure the average speed of these processes, the general tendency in this realm is undeniable. Thus, the speed of communication is said to have increased by 10^7, the speed of personal transport by 10^2, and the speed of data processing by 10^6.[10]

It is predominantly this aspect of acceleration that is at the center of Paul Virilio's "dromology," a narrative of historical acceleration that proceeds from the revolution in transport to that in transmission and finally to the "transplantation" revolution dawning in the emergent possibilities of biotechnology.[11] The effects of technological acceleration on social reality are certainly tremendous. For example, the "natural" (that is, anthropological) priority of space over time in human perception (rooted in our sense organs and the effects of gravity, which allow for an immediate distinction of "above" and "below," "in front of" and "behind," but not "sooner" and "later") seems to have been inverted: in the age of globalization of the Internet, time is increasingly conceived as compressing or even annihilating space.[12] Space, it seems, virtually "contracts" and loses its significance for orientation in the late modern world. Processes and developments are no longer located, and locations become "non-lieux," without history, identity, or relation.[13]

2. Acceleration of Social Change

Whereas phenomena of the first category can be described as acceleration processes *within* society, the phenomena of this second category can be classified as accelerations *of* society itself. When novelists, scientists, and journalists since the eighteenth century have observed the dynamization of Western culture, society, or history—and sometimes of time itself[14]—they

10. Karlheinz Geißler, *Vom Tempo der Welt: Am Ende der Uhrzeit* (Freiburg: Herder, 1999), 89.

11. Paul Virilio, *Open Sky* (London: Verso, 1997), 9–15.

12. See Harvey, *The Condition of Postmodernity*, 201–10.

13. Marc Augé, *Non-lieux: introduction à une anthropologie de la surmodernité* (Paris: Seuil, 1992). Harvey, however, referring to an inverse spatialization of time, cautions us to not dismiss space too quickly (*The Condition of Postmodernity*, 272).

14. See, e.g., Georges Gurvitch, "Social Structure and the Multiplicity of Time," in *Sociological Theory, Values, and Sociocultural Change*, ed. E. A. Tiryakian (London: Free Press of Glencoe, 1963); or Gerhard Schmied, *Soziale Zeit: Umfang, "Geschwindigkeit" und Evolution* (Berlin: Duncker and Humblot, 1985), 86–90.

have been concerned not so much with the spectacular technological advancements as with the (often simultaneous) accelerated processes of social change that rendered social constellations and structures as well as patterns of action and orientation unstable and ephemeral. The underlying idea is that rates of change themselves are changing. Thus, attitudes and values as well as fashions and lifestyles, social relations and obligations as well as groups, classes, or milieus, social languages as well as forms of practice and habits, are said to change at ever-increasing rates. This has led Arjun Appadurai to replace the symbolization of the social world as consisting of stable social aggregates that can be localized on maps with the idea of fluid, flickering screens representing cultural flows that only occasionally crystallize into "ethno-, techno-, finan-, media- and ideoscapes."[15]

However, empirically measuring rates of social change remains an unresolved challenge. There is little agreement in sociology as to what the relevant indicators of change are and when alterations or variations actually constitute a genuine or "basic" social change.[16] Here sociology might avail itself of approaches developed in social philosophy. The German philosopher Hermann Lübbe claims that Western societies experience what he calls the "contraction of the present" (*Gegenwartsschrumpfung*) as a consequence of the accelerating rates of cultural and social innovation.[17] His measure is as simple as it is instructive: for Lübbe, the past is defined as that which no longer holds/is no longer valid, while the future denotes that which does not yet hold/is not yet valid. The present, then, is the time span for which (to use an idea developed by Reinhart Koselleck) the horizons of experience and expectation coincide. Only within these time spans of relative stability can we draw on past experiences to orient our actions and infer conclusions from the past with regard to the future. Only within these time spans is there some certainty of orientation, evaluation, and expectation. In other words, social acceleration is defined by an increase in the decay rates of the reliability of experiences and expectations and by the contraction of

15. Arjun Appadurai, "Disjuncture and Difference in the Global Cultural Economy," in *Global Culture: Nationalism, Globalization, and Modernity,* ed. Mike Featherstone (London: Sage, 1990), 295–310.

16. Cf. Pjotr Sztompka, *The Sociology of Social Change* (Oxford: Blackwell, 1993), or Hans-Peter Müller and Michael Schmid, eds., *Sozialer Wandel: Modellbildung und theoretische Ansätze* (Frankfurt am Main: Suhrkamp, 1995). In "Social Structural Time: An Attempt at Classifying Types of Social Change by Their Characteristic Paces," *The Rhythms of Society,* ed. Michael Young and Tom Schuller (London: Routledge, 1988), 17–36, Peter Laslett distinguishes nineteen (!) different rates of internal social change (economic, political, cultural, etc.).

17. See chapter 9 of this volume.

the time spans definable as the "present." Now, according to Lübbe, we can apply this measure of stability and change to social and cultural institutions and practices of all kinds: the present contracts in the political as well as the occupational, the technological as well as the aesthetic, the normative as well as the scientific or cognitive dimensions—that is, in cultural as well as in structural respects.

But how could we verify this empirically? There seems to be fairly general agreement in the social sciences that the basic structures of society are those that organize the processes of production and reproduction. For Western societies since the early modern period, these have essentially included the family and the occupational system. And in fact, most studies of social change focus on exactly these domains, along with political institutions and technology. I will later turn to the question of how technological and social change, and hence technological acceleration and the acceleration of social change, are interrelated. For the moment I want to suggest that change in these two realms—family and work—has accelerated from an *intergenerational* pace in early modern society to a *generational* pace in "classical" modernity to an *intragenerational* pace in late modernity. Thus, the ideal-typical family structure in agrarian society tended to remain stable over the centuries, with generational turnover leaving the basic structure intact. In classical modernity, this structure was built to last for just a generation: it was organized around a couple and tended to disperse with the death of the couple. In late modernity, there is a growing tendency for family life cycles to last less than an individual lifespan: increasing rates of divorce and remarriage are the most obvious evidence for this.[18] Similarly, in the world of work, in premodern societies the father's occupation was inherited by the son—again, potentially over many generations. In classical modernity, occupational structures tended to change with generations: sons (and daughters) were free to choose their own profession, but they generally chose only once, that is, for a lifetime. In late modernity, occupations no longer extend over the whole of a work life; jobs change at a higher rate than generations.[19]

If we try to formulate the argument more generally, the stability of social institutions and practices could serve as a yardstick for the acceleration (or deceleration) of social change. In the work of authors like Peter Wagner and Beck, Giddens, and Lash, theoretical as well as empirical support can

18. Laslett, "Social Structural Time," 33.
19. For some empirical evidence on this, cf. Garhammer, *Wie Europäer ihre Zeit nutzen,* and Richard Sennett, *The Corrosion of Character: The Personal Consequences of Work in the New Capitalism* (New York: Norton, 1998).

be found for the thesis that institutional stability is generally on the decline in late modern societies.[20] In a sense, the whole discourse about postmodernity and contingency hinges on this idea, although for now it is only meant to serve as a starting point for future empirical research.

3. Acceleration of the Pace of Life

Interestingly, there is a third type of acceleration in Western societies that is neither logically nor causally entailed by the first two, but rather seems, at least at first glance, paradoxical with respect to technological acceleration. The "acceleration of the pace of (social) life, which has been postulated again and again in the process of modernity (e.g., by Simmel or, more recently, by Robert Levine),[21] is the central focus of much of the discussion about cultural acceleration and the alleged need for deceleration. Now, if we assume that the "pace of life"—an admittedly fuzzy concept—refers to the speed and compression of actions and experiences in everyday life, it is hard to see how it relates to technological acceleration. Since the latter describes the decrease of the time needed to carry out everyday processes and actions of production and reproduction, communication and transport, it should entail an increase in free time, which in turn would slow down the pace of life. If less time is needed, time should become abundant. But if, quite to the contrary, time becomes more and more scarce, this is a paradoxical effect that calls for a sociological explanation[22]

But first we must be able to measure the pace of life.[23] In my view, attempts to do so could follow a subjective or an objective approach, with

20. Peter Wagner, *A Sociology of Modernity: Liberty and Discipline* (London: Routledge, 1994); Ulrich Beck, Anthony Giddens, and Scott Lash, *Reflexive Modernization: Politics, Tradition and Aesthetics in the Modern Social Order* (Cambridge: Polity Press, 1994).

21. Georg Simmel, "The Metropolis and Mental Life," in *On Individuality and Social Forms,* ed. Donald N. Levine (Chicago: University of Chicago Press, 1971); and chapter 2 of this volume. See also Levine, *A Geography of Time.*

22. For a very interesting economic explanation, see Staffan B. Linder, *The Harried Leisure Class* (New York: Columbia University Press, 1970). I take up some of his arguments in the following.

23. American sociologist Robert Levine and his team recently conducted a cross-cultural comparative empirical study in which three indicators for the speed of life were used: the speed of walking in inner cities; the time it takes to buy a stamp in a post office; and the exactness of public clocks. For a number of reasons I have discussed at length elsewhere, this approach can at best serve as a very rough preliminary attempt. See "Temporalstrukturen in der Spätmoderne: Vom Wunsch nach Beschleunigung und der Sehnsucht nach Langsamkeit: Ein Literaturüberblick in gesellschaftstheooretischer Absicht," *Handlung, Kultur, Interpretation* 10, no. 2 (2001): 335–81. It certainly remains very unsatisfactory as an instrument in a thorough sociological analysis of the temporal structures of late modernity.

the most promising route probably being a combination of the two. On the subjective side, an acceleration of the speed of life (as against the speed of life itself) is likely to have effects on individuals' experience of time: it will cause people to consider time as scarce, to feel hurried and under time pressure and stress. Typically, people will feel that time goes by faster than before and they will complain that "everything" goes too fast; they will worry that they might not be able to keep up with the pace of social life. Hence, the fact that this complaint has accompanied modernity ever since the eighteenth century does not prove that the speed of life was high all the time—in fact it does not help to determine the speed of life at all—but it does hint at its continuous acceleration. As we might expect, recent studies indicate that in fact people in Western societies do feel under heavy time pressure and they do complain about the scarcity of time. These feelings seem to have increased over recent decades,[24] making plausible the argument that the "digital revolution" and the processes of globalization amount to yet another wave of social acceleration.[25]

On the objective side, an acceleration of the speed of life can be measured in two ways. First, it should lead to a measurable contraction of the time spent on definable episodes or "units" of action like eating, sleeping, going for a walk, playing, talking to one's family, etc., since acceleration implies that we do more things in less time. This is a domain where time-use studies are of the highest importance. And in fact, some studies have found plenty of evidence for this: thus, for example, there appears to be a clear tendency to eat faster, sleep less, and communicate less with our families than our ancestors did.[26] Nevertheless, one needs to be very careful with such results—first, because the data for longitudinal time-use studies are extremely limited; second, because we always find counterinstances (such as that the time fathers spend with their children in at least some sections of Western societies is clearly increasing) without being able to adequately determine the significance of these findings; and third, because it is frequently unclear what drives the measured accelerations (for example, that people on average sleep less today than previous generations might simply

24. Geißler, *Vom Tempo der Welt*, 92; Garhammer, *Wie Europäer ihre Zeit nutzen*, 448–55; Levine, *A Geography of Time*, 196.

25. It thus remains rather doubtful that John P. Robinson and Geoffrey Godbey's diagnosis of the beginning of "The Great American Slowdown" can be confirmed by further investigation. See *American Demographics* 18, no. 6 (1996): 42–48. In January 2002, Robinson confirmed to the author by personal communication that he didn't yet have conclusive evidence in either direction.

26. Cf. Garhammer, *Wie Europäer ihre Zeit nutzen*.

be attributable to the fact that they reach an older age and don't work as hard physically). The second way to objectively explore the acceleration of the pace of life consists in measuring the social tendency to "compress" actions and experiences, that is, to do and experience more within a given period of time by reducing the pauses and intervals or by doing more things simultaneously, like cooking, watching TV, and making a phone call.[27]

III. What Drives Social Acceleration?

When we look for the social forces that drive the wheels of acceleration, it becomes necessary to rethink the connection between the three spheres of acceleration discussed so far. The major problem here lies in the paradox of the simultaneity of technological acceleration (1) and the increasing scarcity of time (3). If free time decreases in spite of technological acceleration, the only possible explanation is that the quantum of work itself has changed, or, more precisely, has risen faster than the corresponding technological rate of acceleration. Thus, free time is produced when the technological acceleration rate is above the rate of growth, where "growth" refers to all kinds of time-consuming actions and processes. Conversely, time becomes scarce when growth rates are higher than the acceleration rates. For example, when between two points in time (t_1, t_2) the speed of transport increases by the factor 4, and the average distance crossed in a given period of time rises by the factor 2, half of the time used for transport at t_1 is available as "free time" at t_2. However, if the speed rate only doubles between t_1 and t_2 whereas the distance crossed rises by the factor 4, twice as much time is needed for transport; hence, at t_2 twice as many time resources are needed: time gets scarce. The same holds for processes of production, communication, and so on. It is important to note that growth and acceleration are neither logically nor causally interconnected, since only the acceleration of constant processes logically entails a corresponding augmentation, whereas processes of transport, communication, or production are not necessarily constant. Hence, we should apply the term "acceleration society" to a society if and only if technological acceleration and the growing scarcity of time (that is, an acceleration of the pace of life) occur simultaneously, that is, if growth rates outgrow acceleration rates.

27. See also Friederike Benthaus-Apel, *Zwischen Zeitbindung und Zeitautonomie: Eine empirische Analyse der Zeitverwendung und Zeitstruktur der Werktags- und Wochenendfreizeit* (Wiesbaden: Deutscher Universitätsverlag, 1995).

Now this, interestingly, is one way in which the acceleration of the pace of life and technological acceleration are interconnected: technological acceleration can be seen as a social answer to the problem of scarce time, that is, to the acceleration of the pace of life. Examining the causal relations between the three spheres of social acceleration reveals a surprising feedback loop: technological acceleration, which is frequently connected to the introduction of new technologies (like the steam engine, the railway, the automobile, the telegraph, the computer, the Internet), almost inevitably brings about a whole range of changes in social practices, communication structures, and corresponding forms of life. For example, the Internet has not only increased the speed of communicative exchange and the virtualization of economic and productive processes; it has also established new occupational, economic, and communicative structures, opening up new patterns of social interaction and even new forms of social identity.[28] Hence, it is easy to see how and why technological acceleration is prone to go hand in hand with the acceleration of change in the form of changing social structures and patterns, orientations, and evaluations of action. Furthermore, if the acceleration of social change entails a contraction of the present in the sense discussed above, this naturally leads to an acceleration in the pace of life. The explanation for this is to be found in the "slippery-slope" phenomenon, well known in the realm of capitalist production: the capitalist cannot pause and rest, stop the race, and secure his position, since he either goes up or goes down; there is no point of equilibrium because standing still is equivalent to falling behind, as Marx and Weber pointed out. Similarly, in a society with accelerated rates of social change in all spheres of life, individuals always feel that they stand on a slippery slope: taking a prolonged break means becoming old-fashioned, outdated, anachronistic in one's experience and knowledge, one's equipment and clothing, one's orientations, and even one's language.[29] Thus, people feel pressed to keep up with the speed of change they experience in their social and technological world in order to avoid the loss of potentially valuable options and connections (*Anschlußmöglichkeiten*). This problem is aggravated by the fact that in a world of incessant change it gets increasingly difficult to tell which options will eventually turn out to be valuable. Hence, accelerated social change will in turn lead to an acceleration of the pace of life. And finally, as we saw

28. Sherry Turkle, *Life on the Screen: Identity in the Age of the Internet* (New York: Simon and Schuster, 1995).

29. Thus, elderly people in Western society are frequently unable to understand the "technobabble" the young use when talking about their Game Boys, e-mails, DVDs, etc.

at the outset, new forms of technological acceleration will be called for to speed up the processes of productive and everyday life. Thus, the acceleration cycle is a closed, self-propelling process (fig. 2).

Yet the acceleration cycle by itself is not sufficient to explain the inherent dynamics of Western societies, or to understand its origins and the specific ways in which the logic and dynamic of speed and growth are interwoven. When looking for the driving forces of acceleration beyond the feedback cycle itself, one finds that there are three (analytically independent) primary factors that can be identified as the external key accelerators behind the three dimensions of social acceleration. In each of them, the logics of growth and speed are connected in a particular way characteristic of one of the dimensions of social acceleration.

1. The Economic Motor

The most obvious source of social acceleration in Western societies is, of course, capitalism. Within a capitalist economy, labor time figures as a crucial factor of production, such that saving time is equivalent to making (relative) profit, as expressed in Benjamin Franklin's famous equation of time and money. Also, time leads over competitors in the introduction of new technologies or products are a key element of market competition because they allow for crucial extra profits before competitors catch up. Finally, the accelerated reproduction of invested capital is crucial with respect to what Marx called the "moral consumption" of technology and to the credit system. As a consequence, the circle of production, distribution, and consumption constantly accelerates. This certainly explains the restless competition for technological acceleration in capitalist societies. In short, the functioning of the capitalist system rests on the accelerating circulation of goods and capital in a growth-oriented society. Thus, the logic of capitalism connects growth with acceleration in the need to increase production (growth) as well as productivity (which can be defined in terms of time as output per unit time).

It is therefore not surprising that many authors concerned with the problem of social acceleration have attributed not only technological but all forms of acceleration to capitalism.[30] However, this assumption of enforced

---

30. Sennett, *The Corrosion of Character;* Fritz Reheis, *Die Kreativität der Langsamkeit: Neuer Wohlstand durch Entschleunigung,* 2nd ed. (Darmstadt: Primus, 1998); Harvey, *The Condition of Postmodernity;* also Scheuerman, "Liberal Democracy and the Empire of Speed," 43–49. See Moishe Postone, *Time, Labor, and Social Domination: A Reinterpretation of Marx's Critical Theory* (Cambridge: Cambridge University Press, 1996), for a contemporary Marxist reinterpretation of the roles of growth and time in capitalist societies.

capitalist acceleration by itself seems insufficient to explain a whole range of acceleration phenomena in dimensions two and three (see fig. 2), some of which reveal that processes of acceleration are by no means always or even usually enforced by competition, but are frequently associated with eudaimonistic or even eschatological undertones.[31] This is where the cultural motor of acceleration comes in, a motor that seems indispensable for explaining the very success of capitalist forms of production.

2. The Cultural Motor

The acceleration of social change in Western societies is indissolubly linked to the dominant cultural ideals of modernity. These have gradually shifted the balance between tradition and innovation toward the priority of change, such that "real life," as Friedrich Ancillon observed in 1828, is to be sought in "change for the sake of change."[32] Now, without denying that the evolution of industrial and capitalist forms of production and the accompanying social practices played a key role in the institutionalization of this idea, it is important to see that its roots reach further back. The ideal formulated by Ancillon is the consequence of a conception of life in which the good life is the fulfilled life, a life that is rich in experiences and developed capacities. This dominant modern cultural ideal evolved in the secularization of time and of conceptions of human happiness, analyzed at length by Hans Blumenberg and more recently by Marianne Gronemeyer and Gerhard Schulze.[33] The idea of the fulfilled life no longer supposes a "higher life" waiting for us after death, but rather consists in realizing as many options

31. The clearest expression of the "eudaimonism of speed" is probably Marinetti's *Futurist Manifesto*, where speed is celebrated as a glorious new, omnipresent, and immortal goddess. See chapter 2 of this volume.

32. "Everything has begun to move, or has been set in motion, and with the intention or under the pretense of fulfilling and completing everything, everything is placed in question, doubted, and approaches a general transformation. The love of movement in itself, without purpose and without specific end, has emerged and developed out of the movement of the time. In it, and in it alone, one seeks and sets real life" (quoted in Koselleck, *Futures Past*, 251). It is remarkable how closely these observations resemble Marx and Engels' famous passage from the *Communist Manifesto*, where "all that is solid melts into air." However, whereas in the *Manifesto* this transformation appears to be simply an unintended by-product of economic relations, Ancillon (and Koselleck) point out that it is also driven by cultural currents. The question of the "prime mover" can safely be set aside at this point.

33. Hans Blumenberg, *Lebenszeit und Weltzeit* (Frankfurt am Main: Suhrkamp, 1986); Marianne Gronemeyer, *Das Leben als letzte Gelegenheit: Sicherheitsbedürfnisse und Zeitknappheit*, 2nd ed. (Darmstadt: Primus, 1996); Gerhard Schulze, "Das Projekt des schönen Lebens: Zur soziologischen Diagnose der modernen Gesellschaften," in *Lebensqualität: Ein Konzept für Praxis und Forschung*, ed. A. Bellebaum and K. Barheier (Opladen: Westdeutscher, 1994). On the secularization of time, cf. Charles Taylor, *Modern Social Imaginaries* (Durham: Duke University Press, 2004).

as possible from the vast possibilities the world has to offer. To taste life in all its heights and depths and in its full complexity becomes a central aspiration of modern man.[34] But, as it turns out, the world always seems to have more to offer than can be experienced in a single lifetime. The options offered always outgrow those realizable in an individual's life; or, in Blumenberg's terms, the perceived time of the world (*Weltzeit*) and the time of an individual life (*Lebenszeit*) dramatically diverge for individuals in the modern world. Acceleration of the pace of life appears to be a natural solution to this problem: if we live twice as fast, if we take only half the time to realize an action, goal, or experience, we can double what we can do within our lifetime. Our "efficacy," the proportion of realized options to potentially realizable options, doubles. It follows that in this cultural logic, too, the dynamics of growth and acceleration are intricately interwoven.

Now, by this cultural logic, if we kept increasing the speed of life, we could eventually live a multiplicity of lives within a single lifetime by taking up all the options that would define them. Acceleration serves as a strategy to erase the difference between the time of the world and the time of our life. The eudaimonistic promise of modern acceleration thus appears to be a functional equivalent to religious ideas of eternity or eternal life, and the acceleration of the pace of life represents the modern answer to the problem of finitude and death.

However, due to the self-propelling dynamic of the acceleration cycle, the promise of acceleration never is fulfilled, for the very same techniques, methods, and inventions that allow for an accelerated realization of options simultaneously increase the number of options (of "world time" or "world resources," so to speak) at an exponential rate. For example, the Internet not only speeds up information and communication, it also opens up wholly new domains of exchange, service, communication, and entertainment. Hence, whenever we surf the Net, we could potentially surf hundreds and thousands of other sites that might even better serve our purposes. The same holds true for cable TV: whereas thirty years ago we missed only two or three other programs by watching one channel, we now miss hundreds.[35] This, of course, has created the cultural phenomenon of "zapping." As a

---

34. Famous literary illustrations of this idea can be found in the work of Goethe, such as in *Faust* or *Wilhelm Meister*.

35. Of course, this multiplication of options is only a cultural problem if the options are considered to be (at least potentially) valuable. An increase in uninteresting options would not affect the pace of life. However, as we will see in Section 4 of this chapter, one problem of "acceleration societies" is that the (future) relevance of present options becomes increasingly unpredictable. We don't know what we will need, like, own and use tomorrow.

consequence, our share of the world, the proportion of realized world options from potentially realizable ones, decreases (contrary to the original promise of acceleration) no matter how much we increase the pace of life. And this is the cultural explanation for the paradoxical phenomenon of simultaneous technological acceleration and increasing time scarcity.

3. The Structural Motor

Apart from the economic and the cultural explanations for the dynamics of modern Western acceleration, some sociologists have identified a third external engine in the social structure of modern society. According to this view, which is advocated predominantly in the context of Niklas Luhmann's systems theory, social change is accelerated by modern society's basic structural principle of functional differentiation. In a society that is not primarily segregated into hierarchical classes but rather structured along the lines of functional systems, such as politics, science, art, the economy, and law, complexity increases immensely. As a result, the future opens up to almost unlimited contingency and society experiences time in the form of perpetual change and acceleration.[36] Now, increasing complexity and contingency create an abundance of options and possibilities. Since these cannot be handled simultaneously, Luhmann argues that complexity in modern societies is "temporalized" in order to enable the sequential processing of a higher number of options and relations than could be processed simultaneously. The ensuing needs for synchronization and selection of increasing (future) options can in turn only be satisfied if the processing itself is accelerated. Thus, we find a surprising structural duplication or "reflection" of the cultural dilemma outlined in the preceding paragraph (or vice versa). Here, too, we find a variant of the internal dialectics of growth and acceleration that is characteristic of modern societies, here as a driving motor for (structural) social change (fig. 2).

IV. The Form and Relevance of Social Deceleration

Even if we find convincing evidence for acceleration in all three spheres defined above, it is crucial not to be drawn into a logic of subsumption

36. Otthein Rammstedt, "Alltagsbewußtsein von Zeit," *Kölner Zeitschrift für Soziologie und Sozialpsychologie* 27 (1975): 50; Niklas Luhmann, *The Differentiation of Society,* trans. Stephen Holmes and Charles Larmore (New York: Columbia University Press, 1982); Armin Nassehi, *Die Zeit der Gesellschaft: Auf dem Weg zu einer soziologischen Theorie der Zeit* (Opladen: Westdeutscher, 1993).

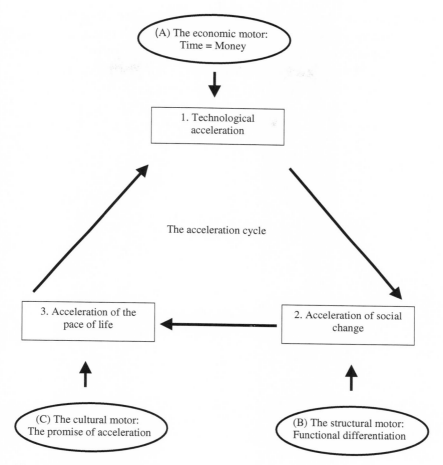

Figure 2. Motors of acceleration

where every social process or phenomenon is seen as determined by the dynamics of acceleration. Hence, before we can adequately determine the sense in which we can speak *of the acceleration of Western societies,* we need to understand the status, function, and structure of those phenomena that escape dynamization or even represent forms of slowdown and deceleration. Analytically, we can distinguish five different forms of deceleration and inertia, which cut across the spheres of acceleration identified so far.

1. Natural and anthropological speed limits. Some things cannot be accelerated in principle. Among these are most physical processes, like the speed of perception and processing in our brains and bodies or the time it takes for most natural resources to reproduce.

2. Territorial as well as social and cultural niches that have not yet been touched by the dynamics of modernization and acceleration. They have simply been (totally or partially) exempted from acceleration processes, although they are accessible to them in principle. In such contexts, time seems to be "standing still," as the saying goes: forgotten islands in the sea, socially excluded groups or religious sects such as the Amish, or traditional forms of social practice (like producing whiskey in the famous Jack Daniels commercial). Arguably, these "oases of deceleration" come under increasing pressure in late modernity unless they are deliberately protected against acceleration, and thus they fall under category 4.

3. Slowdown as an unintended consequence of acceleration and dynamization. This frequently entails dysfunctional and pathological forms of deceleration. The best-known version of the former is the traffic jam, whereas recent scientific findings identify the latter in some forms of psychopathological depression that are understood as individual (deceleratory) reactions to overstretched pressures of acceleration.[37] This category could also include the structural exclusion of workers from the sphere of production, which is often a consequence of their inability to keep up with the flexibility and speed required in modern Western economies. The excluded thus suffer extreme deceleration in the form of long-term unemployment.[38] Economic recessions—called economic slowdowns—could also be interpreted along these lines.

4. Intentional forms of (social) deceleration, contrary to the unintentional forms of slowdown. These include ideological movements against modern acceleration and its effects. Such movements have accompanied more or less every new step in the history of modern acceleration, and in particular of technological acceleration. Thus, the steam engine, the railway, the telephone, and the computer were met with suspicion and even hostility; in all cases, the oppositional movements eventually failed.[39] Hence, within this fourth category, we need to distinguish between two forms of deliberate deceleration:

37. Cf. Levine, *A Geography of Time;* several articles in *Psychologie Heute* 26, no. 3 (1999); or Baier, *Keine Zeit!* 147–62.

38. Sennett, *The Corrosion of Character,* chap. 7; Marie Jahoda, "Time: A Social Psychological Perspective," in *The Rhythms of Society,* ed. Michael Young and Tom Schuller (London: Routledge, 1988), 154–72.

39. Cf. Levine, *A Geography of Time;* Wolfgang Schivelbusch, *Geschichte der Eisenbahnreise: Zur Industrialisierung von Raum und Zeit im 19. Jahrhundert,* new ed. (Frankfurt am Main: Fischer Taschenbuch, 2000).

(a) Limited or temporary forms of deceleration that aim at preserving the capacity to function and further accelerate within acceleratory systems. On the individual level, we find such accelerating forms of deceleration as people taking time out in monasteries or taking yoga courses, which promise a rest from the race; these have the purpose of allowing a more successful participation in acceleratory social systems afterwards. Similarly, there is a huge self-help literature suggesting a deliberate slowdown in work or learning in order to increase the volume of overall work or learning in a given period of time, or recommending pauses in order to increase energy and creativity.[40] On the social and political level, too, moratoria are sometimes suggested to solve technological, political, legal, environmental, or social obstacles that stand in the way of modernization.[41]

(b) Diverse, often fundamentalist, antimodernist social movements for (radical) deceleration. This is hardly surprising given that acceleration appears to be one of the fundamental principles of modernity. Among these we find radical religious as well as "deep ecological" or politically ultraconservative or anarchist movements. Thus, for German politician and scholar Peter Glotz, deceleration has become the new ideological focus of the victims of modernization.[42] However, to straightforwardly dismiss the cry for deceleration as ideological is dangerously simplistic, for the more important arguments for intentional deceleration are those that follow the lines of thought of the first form, 4(a). The central insight here is that the enormous processes of acceleration that have shaped modern society were firmly grounded and enabled by the stability of *some* central modern institutions like law, democracy, the industrial work regime, and the standardized or institutionalized biographies or life trajectories of modernity.[43] Only within

---

40. For such accelerating forms of deceleration, see Lothar J. Seiwert, *Wenn Du es eilig hast, gehe langsam: Das neue Zeitmanagement in einer beschleunigten Welt*, 5th ed. (Frankfurt am Main: Campus, 2000).

41. Cf. Matthias Eberling, *Beschleunigung und Politik* (Frankfurt am Main: P. Lang, 1996).

42. Peter Glotz, "Kritik der Entschleunigung," in *Die Beschleunigungsfalle oder der Triumph der Schildkröte*, 3rd ed., ed. Klaus Backhaus and Holger Bonus (Stuttgart: Schäffer-Pöschel, 1998), 75–89; Levine, *A Geography of Time*.

43. See Rosa, "Temporalstrukturen in der Spätmoderne"; Martin Kohli, "Lebenslauf und Lebensalter als gesellschaftliche Konstruktionen: Elemente zu einem interkulturellen Vergleich," in *Im Lauf der Zeit: Ethnographische Studien zur gesellschaftlichen Konstruktion von Lebensaltern*, ed. G. Elwert, M. Kohli, and H. K. Müller (Breitenbach: Saarbrücken, 1990), 11–32; Holger Bonus, "Die Langsamkeit der Spielregeln," in Backhaus and Bonus, *Die Beschleunigungsfalle*, 41–56.

a stable framework formed by such institutions can we find the necessary preconditions for long-term planning and investment and thus for long-term acceleration. Furthermore, as Lübbe argues, the preconditions of cultural reproduction in an accelerating society are such that flexibility is only possible on the basis of some stable and unchanging cultural orientations and institutions. Institutionally as well as individually—or structurally as well as culturally—there seem to be certain limits to flexibilization and dynamization that may be in danger of erosion in late modernity.[44] Hence, it is quite possible that, much more than the antimodernist radicals, it is the very success and ubiquity of acceleration that undercuts and erodes the preconditions for future acceleration. In this sense, deceleration in some respects could be a functional necessity of acceleration society rather than an ideological reaction to it.

5. Finally, we find the perception that in late modern society, despite widespread acceleration and flexibilization (which create the appearance of total contingency, hyperoptionality, and unlimited openness), real change is in fact no longer possible: the system of modern society is closing in and history is coming to an end in a "hyperaccelerated standstill" or "polar inertia." Advocates of this diagnosis include Paul Virilio, Jean Baudrillard, and Francis Fukuyama. They claim that there are no new visions and energies available to modern society, and hence the enormous speed of events and alterations is a superficial phenomenon barely covering up deep-rooted cultural and structural inertia.[45] For a sociological theory of acceleration society, it is vital to account for this possibility of (extreme) paralyzation in its very conceptual scheme.

The fundamental question that arises at this point is the relationship between processes of social acceleration and deceleration in modern society. Two general possibilities are conceivable. First, the processes of acceleration and deceleration are by and large in balance such that we find both types of changes in the temporal patterns of society without a clear and sustained dominance of one or the other. Second, the balance in fact shifts toward the powers of acceleration such that the categories of deceleration

---

44. See chapter 9 of this volume. See also above, section II.2 and below, section IV.2.

45. Fukuyama, in fact, takes part in the discourse on "post-histoire" that follows a long tradition going back to Kojève and Hegel. For Lothar Baier (*Keine Zeit!*), acceleration and change only happen on the "user interface" of modern societies while their deep structures remain unchanged.

have to be interpreted either as *residual* or as *reactions* to acceleration. I would suggest that the second is in fact correct, though this is rather difficult to prove empirically. My claim rests on the supposition that none of these forms of deceleration amounts to a genuine and structurally equal countertrend to modern acceleration. The phenomena listed under categories 1 and 2 merely denote the (retreating) limits of social acceleration; they are not counterpowers at all. The decelerations of category 3 are effects of acceleration and as such derivative of and secondary to it. Category 4(a) identifies phenomena that, on closer examination, turn out to be either elements of acceleration processes or *enabling conditions* of (further) acceleration. The intentional resistance to the speedup of life and the ideology of deceleration 4(b) clearly are reactions to pressures of and for acceleration; as pointed out above, all of the main tendencies of modernity have met considerable resistance, but so far all forms of resistance have turned out to be rather short-lived and unsuccessful. Thus, the only form of deceleration that seems not to be derivative or residual is category 5. This dimension seems to be an inherent, complementary feature of modern acceleration itself; it is the paradoxical flipside characteristic of all the defining forces of modernity (individualization, differentiation, rationalization, domestication, and acceleration).

V. Ethical and Political Implications

For the analysis of the temporal structures of society, it is of central importance to realize that the speedup of processes frequently amounts to more than a mere quantitative change that leaves the nature of those processes untouched. To the contrary, just as speeding up a sequence of images can bring them to life in the transition from photography to film, or the acceleration of molecules can transform ice into water into steam, changes in the temporal structures of modern societies transform the very essence of our culture, social structure, and personal identity (and, of course, our experience of nature, too). Thus, the much-discussed but little-agreed-upon distinction between modernity and post- or late modernity may in fact be best captured with reference to the temporal dimension: we can say that late modernity is nothing other than modern society accelerated (and desynchronized) beyond the point of possible reintegration. I would like to show this by exploring two major and related transformations: the transition in personal identities and the decline of politics in late modernity.

1. Situational Identity and the Detemporalization of Life

Of the three dimensions of social acceleration, the acceleration of the pace of life is most directly linked to personality. Since the notion of "personality" has become rather obscure in the social sciences and humanities (probably owing to its essentialist ring), the relevant changes are instead most often discussed in terms of shifting patterns of identity.[46]

From the model developed above, the acceleration of the pace of life could be explained by two different factors. On the one hand, individuals could feel pressed to speed up in response to the social change around them, because of what I have called the "slippery-slope" phenomenon. Acceleration in this sense would be enforced by the fear of losing out in light of the speed and flexibility demands of the social and economic world. On the other hand, speeding up the pace of life could be a (voluntary) response to "the promise of acceleration," that is, a consequence of people's conception of the good life. Of course, fear and promise might well both be driving factors of acceleration (as they are, following Max Weber's famous Protestant ethic thesis, the driving factors of capitalism).[47] Common parlance might serve as a guide for testing the slippery-slope hypothesis: even a casual look at how people explain or justify their use of time is puzzling in light of the dominant ideology of individual freedom. In a strange opposition to the idea that individuals in Western societies are free to do whatever they please, the rhetoric of obligation abounds: "I have to read the newspaper, exercise, call and visit my friends regularly, learn a second language, scrutinize the market for job opportunities, have hobbies, travel abroad, keep up with contemporary computer technologies, etc."[48] However, we have to be careful to scrutinize the source of this kind of "must"—it might well stem from an underlying cultural ideal as well as from social and economic pressures. Interestingly, we find an analogous semantic slip in contemporary politics: whereas in early and classical modernity processes and technologies of acceleration were legitimized in the rhetoric of "progress," which mirrored the promise of acceleration, in late modernity political language has adopted

---

46. See my *Identität und kulturelle Praxis: Politische Philosophie nach Charles Taylor* (Frankfurt am Main: Campus, 1998).

47. Cf. Hartmut Rosa, "Wachstum und Beschleunigung—Angst und Verheißung der kapitalistischen Gesellschaft," *Erwägen, Wissen, Ethik* 13, no. 3 (2002): 330–33, review of Elmar Altvater, "Kapitalismus: Zur Bestimmung, Abgrenzung und Dynamik einer geschichtlichen Formation," *Erwägen, Wissen, Ethik* 13, no. 3 (2002): 281–92.

48. For an impressive list of such "musts," see Horst W. Opaschowski, *Freizeitökonomie: Marketing von Erlebniswelten*, 2nd ed. (Opladen: Leske and Budrich, 1995), 85–86.

the terminology of "inherent necessity" and "unavoidable adjustment" (to a fiercely competitive world)—a clear indication of the felt pressures of the slippery slope.

However, common parlance might serve as an indicator of the nature of subtle connections between the different spheres of social acceleration in yet another sense. The acceleration of rates of social change to an intra- rather than intergenerational pace is mirrored in language that avoids identity predicates and uses temporary markers instead. People speak of working (for the time being) as a baker rather than being a baker, living with Mary rather than being Mary's husband, going to the Methodist Church rather than being a Methodist, voting Republican rather than being a Republican, and so on. This use of language indicates that the awareness of contingency has increased even where the actual rates of change have not yet done so: things (jobs, spouses, religious, political commitments) could be otherwise, they could change at any time because of either my own or other people's decisions. Although increased contingency is not equivalent to acceleration, it surely contributes to the perception of slippery slopes and time pressure. The introduction of temporary markers in identity statements (I *was* a Methodist, I *am* married to Mary, I *will be* a consultant *after* my next degree) reflects a temporal contraction of identity reflecting the contraction of the present identified above. It is measurable, to some degree, by indicators for the deinstitutionalization of biographies and life trajectories.

Accordingly, a number of recent studies suggest a significant change in the time perspectives by which people organize their lives. As Martin Kohli has convincingly argued, modernity was characterized by a "temporalization of life": people were no longer absorbed with handling their life on a day-to-day basis but started to conceive their lives along the lines of a three-tiered temporal pattern (the modern standard biography of education, work life, retirement or childhood, adult life, old age) that defined an institutionalized, reliable structure and orienting perspective around which individuals could plan their lives.[49] Classical modern identities were consequently long-term projects supposed to evolve like a bildungsroman. In late modernity, however, this pattern no longer holds: neither work nor family life can be foreseen or planned for a lifetime. Instead, people develop a new perspective that has been oddly termed the "temporalization of time": time spans and the duration of activities or commitments are no longer planned ahead

49. Kohli, "Lebenslauf und Lebensalter"; above, Section II.2.

but left to evolve.[50] Such a temporalization of time, however, is equivalent to the detemporalization of life: life is no longer planned along a line that stretches from the past into the future; instead, decisions are taken from time to time according to situational and contextual needs and desires. As Richard Sennett argues, stability of character and adherence to a time-resistant life plan are incompatible with the demands of the late modern world.[51] Thus, a conception of the good life based on long-term commitments, duration, and stability is thwarted by the fast pace of social change.[52]

But even when this new perspective is depicted in neutral or even positive terms, it is evident that a new form of situationalism is replacing the temporally extended identity characteristic of classical modernity.[53] This new situationalism in a way resembles premodern forms of existence in which people had to cope with unforeseeable contingencies on a day-to-day basis without being able to plan for the future; however, whereas the dangers, events, and contingencies that threatened the earlier forms of life (natural disasters, wars, diseases, etc.) were exogenous to society, the new situationalism is an endogenous product of social structures themselves. However we evaluate this phenomenon, the incompatibility of situational identities with the modern ideal of individual ethical autonomy is apparent. The ideal of the autonomous and reflective leading of a life requires adopting long-term commitments that bestow a sense of direction, priority, and "narratability" to life.[54]

---

50. Cf. Mike Sandbothe, *Die Verzeitlichung der Zeit: Grundtendenzen der modernen Zeitdebatte in Philosophie und Wissenschaft* (Darmstadt: Wissenschaftliche Buchgesellschaft, 1998); and Karl H. Hörning, Daniela Ahrens, and Anette Gerhard, *Zeitpraktiken: Experimentierfelder der Spätmoderne* (Frankfurt am Main: Suhrkamp, 1997).

51. See, e.g., Hörning, Ahrens, and Gerhard's characterization of the late modern figure they term "the gambler"; this character resembles the "drifter" described by Richard Sennett, although Sennett is much more critical with respect to the desirability of such a time perspective. For a philosophical critique of such a "reduced" sense of time that exclusively focuses on the present, see Dieter Sturma, "Die erweiterte Gegenwart: Kontingenz, Zeit und praktische Selbstverhältnisse im Leben von Personen," in *Die Wiederentdeckung der Zeit: Reflexionen, Analysen, Konzepte,* ed. A. Gimmler, M. Sandbothe, and W. C. Zimmerli (Darmstadt: Primus, 1997), 63–78. For a further discussion of the causes and consequences of the "temporalization of time," see Rosa, "Temporalstrukturen in der Spätmoderne."

52. For this, see my "On Defining the Good Life: Liberal Freedom and Capitalist Necessity," *Constellations* 5, no. 2 (1998): 201–14.

53. Hörning, Ahrens, and Gerhard, *Zeitpraktiken.*

54. Interestingly, the findings of some authors suggest that there is a tendency toward a "new fatalism" that assumes that we cannot control or plan the conditions of our lives (e.g., Garhammer, *Wie Europäer ihre Zeit nutzen*). This, too, could be read as evidence for the increasingly "situational" instead of "temporal" perspective. Hörning, Ahrens, and Gerhard also point out that the incapacity to develop a persistent sense of relevance, direction, and priority is a serious problem for the late modern "gambler" personality type. See *Zeitpraktiken;*

The incapacity to engage in long-term commitments and to develop a frame of time-resistant priorities and long-term goals frequently seems to lead to a paradoxical backlash in which the experience of frantic change and temporalized time gives way to the perception of "frozen time" without (a meaningful) past and future and consequently of depressing inertia. German philosopher Klaus-Michael Kodalle has tried to explain this phenomenon philosophically, while Douglas Coupland's *Generation X* illustrates it metaphorically in the stories of "Texlahoma," a place in which time is eternally frozen in the year 1974—making for a nice contrast with the book's subtitle: "Tales for an Accelerated Culture." Finally, Peter Conrad observes that historically, the problem of *l'ennui* (boredom) became vexing precisely at the moment when the Industrial Revolution "increased velocity in all areas of human experience" and created a climate of "hectic, propulsive dynamism" in which history itself was imagined as a fast-running railway.[55]

In sum, the individual's reaction to social acceleration in late modernity seems to result in a new, situational form of identity, in which the dynamism of classical modernity, characterized by a strong sense of direction (perceived as progress), is replaced by a sense of directionless, frantic motion that is in fact a form of inertia.

2. The "End of Politics" and the Detemporalization of History

Interestingly, an exactly analogous phenomenon can be observed in late modern politics. Here we have the same constellation of a political temporalization of time that results in a detemporalization of politics. Politics in classical modernity had a temporal index in the very labels "progressive" versus "conservative" (or left versus right), while history was perceived of as (directed) progress: progressive politics sought to accelerate progress, whereas conservative politics was "reactionary" in opposing the forces of change and acceleration. Today, ironically, if the distinction between left and right has retained any discriminatory power at all, "progressives" tend to sympathize with the advocates of deceleration (stressing locality, political

---

and "Do Technologies Have Time? New Practices of Time and the Transformation of Communication Technologies," *Time and Society* 8 (1999): 293–308.

55. Peter Conrad, *Modern Times, Modern Places* (New York: Knopf, 1999), 16–17; Klaus-Michael Kodalle, ed., *Zeit-Verschwendung: Ein Symposon* (Würzburg: Königshausen and Neumann, 1999), 12; cf. Garhammer, *Wie Europäer ihre Zeit nutzen*, 482; Sennett, *The Corrosion of Character*, 121; at length in Rosa, "Am Ende der Geschichte."

control of the economy, democratic negotiation, environmental protection, etc.), whereas "conservatives" have become strong defenders of the need for further acceleration (embracing new technologies, rapid markets, and fast administrative decision making). This is yet another example of how the forces of acceleration have outgrown the very agents and institutions that set them in motion: bureaucracy, the nation-state, the strict time regime of the factory, democratic politics, stable personal identities—all of these institutions historically played a key role in enabling social acceleration by providing stable and calculable background conditions, but are now in danger of being eroded by the very forces of acceleration they set in motion.[56] In late modernity, they have become obstacles to further acceleration. The very idea of an "institution," whose Latin root indicates its static, durable character, is incompatible with the idea of total acceleration (table 1).

As a result, politics, too, has become situationalist: it confines itself to reacting to pressures instead of developing progressive visions of its own. Very often, political decisions no longer aspire to actively steer (acceleratory) social developments, but are defensive and deceleratory. It seems that just as it has become virtually impossible to individually plan one's life in the sense of a life project, it has become politically impossible to plan and shape society over time; the time of political projects, it seems, is also over. Individually as well as politically, the sense of a directed movement of history has given way to a sense of directionless, frantic change. For Armin Nassehi, a German author in the systems-theoretic tradition, this loss of political autonomy (corresponding to the loss of individual autonomy discussed above) is an inevitable consequence of the temporal structures of modern society:

> The present . . . loses its capacity for planning and shaping. As the present of action it is always oriented toward the future, but it cannot shape this future because of the dynamics, risks, and vast amount of simultaneity within the present, which it cannot control at all. Early modernity promised the capacity to shape and control world and time and to initiate and historically legitimate future progress. But in late modernity, time itself has come to destroy the

---

56. Thus, the neoliberal cry for deregulation is clearly a reaction to the perceived slowness of a bureaucracy that was once hailed by Max Weber as the fastest and most efficient institution conceivable. Similarly, the power of the nation-state seems to be on the decline because its reactions are too slow in a world of high-speed global transactions. The slowness of the state was arguably a key factor in the fall of the Soviet Empire.

Table 1.   The dialectics of acceleration and institutional stability: Modern accelerators as late modern decelerators

Societal core institutions	As accelerators in classical modernity	As decelerators in late modernity
Bureaucracy	Acceleration of administrative processes	Deceleration of social and economic processes
Nation-state	Acceleration via standardization (time, language, law)	Deceleration of supranational circulatory processes
Representative democracy	Accelerated adaptation to sociopolitical needs	Deceleration of vital decision making
Political regulation	Acceleration through progressive politics	Deceleration through the claim to regulation
Spatial and temporal separation of work and life/leisure	Uninhibited acceleration of productive economic processes	Inhibited acceleration of the lifeworld
Stable personal identities	Acceleration through individualization	Deceleration/inhibited change through inflexibility
Individual life plans	Acceleration through the temporalization of life	Decelerated adaptation to social change

potential for any form of social or substantial control, influence, or steering."[57]

The structural problem at the heart of this disappearance of politics is the political system's fundamental inability to accelerate. Here we touch on a central structural feature of late modern societies: the desynchronization of social and functional spheres, which takes two forms. First, there is a desynchronization of different groups and segments of society. Not all social groups accelerate equally: some, like the sick, the unemployed, the poor, or, in some respects, the elderly, are forced to decelerate, while others, like the Amish, refuse to adopt the temporal structures and horizons of modernity. This desynchronization entails an increasing "simultaneity of the non-simultaneous": high-tech and stone-age methods of warfare, transport, or communication persist side by side, not only between different countries, but even within the same society, and fast and slow paces of life can be

57. Nassehi, *Die Zeit der Gesellschaft,* 375. Similarly, Baudrillard holds that history has lost its sense of (linear) progression: it is no longer moving toward an imaginary end point (which is why Baudrillard argued the "symbolic year 2000" would never be reached), but rather "is disintegrating into its simple elements in a catastrophic process of recurrence and turbulence" (*The Illusion of the End,* 11). Cf. Baier, *Keine Zeit!* 17–18.

observed on one and the same street.[58] The result of this "multitemporality" is likely to be a progressive disintegration of society. At first, the desynchronization of various segments might aggravate the problem of ghettoization, transforming society into a mosaic of temporal ghettos. Some of these ghettos may resist the forces of acceleration, but wherever these forces are in operation, they will eventually enforce the dissolution of the boundaries between groups and segments, since these boundaries are effective speed limits (the increasing irrelevance of state borders is just the most striking example of this tendency). The resulting postmodern dedifferentiation, however, may lead not to reintegration, but to a fast-paced, atomized, kaleidoscopic social amalgam in which highly volatile associations and lifestyle milieus replace the mosaic of ghettos.

This, in turn, may aggravate the political problem of desynchronization in its second form. Contrary to a widespread opinion, modernity has not just established a single, unitary form of abstract, linear time that synchronizes its various subsystems. Rather, the process of functional differentiation has resulted in a series of almost autopoietic subsystems like the economy, science, law, politics, the arts, and so on, all of which follow their own temporal rhythms, patterns, and horizons. Just as there is no unifying social or substantial center governing the subsystemic operations, there is also no integrating temporal authority, and this, in turn, results in increasing temporal desynchronization.

For the political system, this entails truly paradoxical temporal horizons. On the one hand, the time needed for democratic political decision making is not just hard to accelerate, since processes of deliberation and aggregation in a pluralistic democratic society inevitably take time;[59] it is actually increasing for a number of reasons. First, the less consensus there is within society, the less conventionalist the legitimating principles of society are, the longer it takes to reach consensus—and disintegrated modern acceleration societies tend to become both more pluralistic and less conventionalist,

58. Of course, the acceleration thesis presented in this chapter can only be upheld if it can be shown that the predominance of processes of deceleration and time abundance (if they can be found at all) is a phenomenon characteristic of socially excluded or underprivileged groups like the old, the unemployed, and the poor or sick rather than the trend-setting elites. Deceleration, then, is a sign of deprivation and exclusion and thus plays a dysfunctional rather than a functional role in modern societies, which can partially be explained as an unintended effect in the sense of category three above.

59. See Scheuerman, "Liberal Democracy and the Empire of Speed," 56–63. Scheuerman points out that there is a long-standing trend in politics toward shifting political powers from the legislative to the executive branches of government in order to accelerate decision-making processes and retain political control in the "empire of speed."

making it hard to know in advance even which social groups or associations are going to be relevant for negotiations. Hence, in a volatile political world, the time needed for the effective organization of collective interests increases.[60] Second, the less certainty there is about future conditions, the longer it takes to plan for the future and to make decisions.[61] Due to the acceleration of social change and the contraction of the present, background conditions become increasingly contingent; instead of providing yardsticks for decision-making process, they become complicating factors. Third, the *effects* of political decisions tend to extend further and further into the future—most visibly in the area of nuclear power or genetic engineering, where decisions seem to be irreversible. The longer the temporal range of a particular decision, the more time it takes to make it rationally. Here, perhaps, the paradoxical nature of policy making today is most visible: the effects of crucial decisions extend in time just as the time available for making them shrinks.

On the other hand, contrary to this need for more time for political decision making, the acceleration of the surrounding systems—especially economic circulation and technological-scientific innovation—decreases the time given to politics to decide an issue. If politics aspires to steer and control the basic conditions of technological and economic development, it must either keep up with their accelerating pace or seriously infringe on their autonomy, virtually ending functional differentiation. At present, policy makers are always in danger of making completely anachronistic decisions: when, after years of deliberation and negotiation, they finally pass a law regulating the use of, say, some forms of stem-cell research or cloning, technological progress may already have made it obsolete.[62] Second, because of the contraction of the present and the increase in contingency, not just the rate, but also the number and range of social issues in need of political regulation rise, leaving less time for each decision.

60. "How can a public be organized, we may ask, when literally it does not stay in place? . . . Without abiding attachments associations are too shifting and shaken to permit a public readily to locate and identify itself," John Dewey noted in 1927 in *The Public and Its Problems* (Chicago: Swallow Press, 1954), 140–41; cf. Scheuerman, "Liberal Democracy and the Empire of Speed," 60–62.

61. Thus, it might be difficult to develop a good pension plan even in the face of stable demographics when the proportion of old-age pensioners to working people is known. But this task is almost impossible when it is uncertain (a) how long future generations will live, (b) how long they will work, (c) what percentage of the population will work at what time, (d) whether the insurance system will be privatized anyway, (e) whether the nation-state will lose its power to decide over pension schemes altogether, etc.

62. This was the argument of the supporters of a Swiss proposition called the *Beschleunigungsinitiative* (acceleration initiative), which sought to reduce democratic processes in order to speed up lawmaking. It was rejected in a March 2000 referendum.

Third, since, as we have seen, background conditions change quickly and the temporal horizon for which political effects can be rationally planned and controlled continuously contracts, fewer and fewer things can be durably and effectively regulated. Instead, politics shifts to "muddling through" (described by Luhmann as the primacy of the short term) with increasingly temporary and provisional solutions, which ensure that issues keep reappearing on the agenda. The result of these contradictory and incompatible time pressures seems to be consistent with our finding above: politics not only becomes situationalist and loses its sense of direction; it also tends to shift the decision-making process toward other, faster arenas: the legal system (juridification), or the economy and individual responsibility (privatization and deregulation). Thus, precisely at a point in history where the human power to steer and control its own fate seems to reach an unprecedented technological zenith (foremost, of course, in the shape of genetic engineering), society's political capacity to do so reaches its nadir. The deliberate and democratic political shaping of our society and form of life, the political project and promise of enlightened modernity, may be becoming obsolete in the late modern "acceleration society" (fig. 3).[63]

As a result, the inability to control social change has brought about an overwhelming sense of directionless change in an "iron cage" that itself has become fundamentally inert. Within its structures, parallel to the individual experience of time and life delineated above, the frantic pace of political events covered in the news can barely cover up the virtual standstill of the history of ideas—or of history itself. As Baudrillard puts it:

> This is the most significant event within [our] societies: the emergence, in the very course of their mobilization and revolutionary process (they are all revolutionary by the standards of past centuries), of an immense indifference and the silent potency of that indifference. This inert matter of the social is not produced by a lack of exchanges, information or communication, but by the multiplication and saturation of exchanges. . . . It is the cold star of the social and, around that mass, history is also cooling. Events follow one upon another, canceling each other out in a state of indifference. The masses, neutralized, mithridatized by information, in turn

63. Scheuerman, "Liberal Democracy and the Empire of Speed," 67. Scheuerman, however, is still somewhat optimistic about the possibility of resynchronizing socioeconomic and political processes by way of institutional reform; cf. Scheuerman, "Reflexive Law and the Challenges of Globalization," *Journal of Political Philosophy* 9, no. 1 (2001): 81–102.

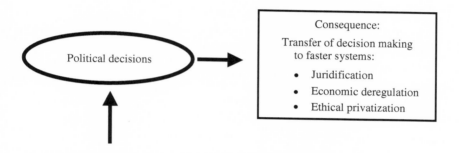

Contraction of the temporal horizon/
Increasing scarcity of time resources

- Time span for decisions decreases (speed of technological and social innovation increases)
- Number of necessary decision increases, reducing the available time per decision
- Horizon of calculability decreases (contraction of the present)

Political decisions

Consequence:

Transfer of decision making to faster systems:

- Juridification
- Economic deregulation
- Ethical privatization

Expansion of the temporal horizon/
Increasing demand for time resources

- Increasing temporal range of effects of decisions
- Increasing demand for political regulation in consequence of growing contingencies
- Erosion of cultural and sociostructural common ground for decision making (disintegration) results in increasing demand on time resources per decision
- Increasing demand for information and planning in consequence of the increase in variability of background conditions increases demand on time resources per decision

Figure 3. Paradoxes of political time

neutralize history and act as an *écran d'absorption*. . . . Political events already lack sufficient energy of their own to move us. . . . History comes to an end here, not for want of actors, nor for want of violence . . . , nor for want of events . . . , but by deceleration, indifference and stupefaction. . . . It is being buried beneath its own immediate effect, worn out in special effects, imploding into current events. Deep down, one cannot even speak of the end of history here, since history will not have time to catch up with its own end. Its effects are accelerating, but its meaning is slowing inexorably.

It will eventually come to a stop and be extinguished like light and time in the vicinity of an infinitely dense mass.[64]

VI. Conclusion

At the outset of this chapter, I tried to pinpoint the relevance of the logic of acceleration for the overall process of modernization. I noted that in the sociological tradition, modernization has been analyzed from four different perspectives, relating to society's structure, culture, personality type, and relation to nature. Now, when we try to reconceptualize the acceleration process along the lines of these four dimensions, it appears that change in the temporal structures is relevant to each of them (fig. 4). While all segments of the world's population are certainly not equally affected by social acceleration—to the contrary, in some parts of the world and some segments of Western societies many processes in fact appear to decelerate—the logic of social acceleration is decisive for the structural and cultural evolution of contemporary society. Thus, it is evident that technological acceleration is a crucial feature of modern society's relation to nature, while the acceleration of the pace of life is of overriding importance for the late modern personality. Furthermore, the overall acceleration of social change is intimately related to both cultural and structural transformation.

With respect to social structure, two distinct but related aspects of acceleration were identified. On the one hand, if we take functional differentiation to be the main structural feature of modern societies, there clearly is a speedup of (sub)systemic processing: financial transactions, economic production and distribution, scientific discoveries, technological inventions, artistic productions, and even lawmaking[65] have unmistakably sped up following their own logics without much outside interference. This has led to desynchronization, since not all subsystems are equally capable of acceleration.[66] On the other hand, if we take the basic structure of society to be the

64. Baudrillard, *The Illusion of the End*, 3–4.
65. See chapter 5 of this volume; see also Scheuerman "The Economic State of Emergency," *Cardozo Law Review* 21 (2000): 1891.
66. It remains an open question whether at some point in the future the drive for further acceleration will cause an eventual dedifferentiation, as some advocates of postmodernity argue, since strict systemic boundaries might eventually become obstacles to "total" acceleration. If this should happen, functional differentiation could be a further feature in the dialectics of acceleration and stability (fig. 3): it accelerated social processes in "classical" modernity but comes to function as a decelerator in late modernity. Some authors suggest that postmodernity

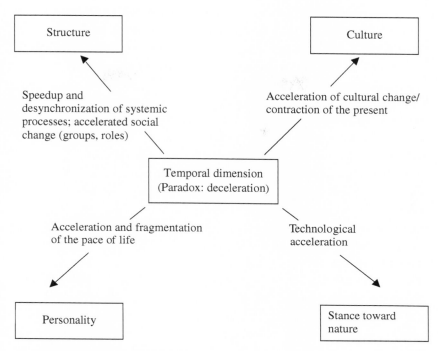

Figure 4. The process of modernization II

structure of its associations, groups, and collectivities and the corresponding role structures—as suggested, for example, by Parsons[67]—then processes of social acceleration have clearly increased the speed of social change; family and occupational structures as well as associations and milieus have become highly volatile, shifting, and contingent, making it difficult to identify politically and socially relevant and stable associational structures at all. This, as we have seen, further aggravates the problem of social integration for late modern societies.

With respect to the cultural dimension, the contraction of the present— that is, the shortening of the time spans within which action orientations and social practices remain stable—is the most important effect of social

has to be understood as a process of dedifferentiation in which the borders between science and religion, art and technology, economy and politics, etc. are crumbling; see Harvey, *The Condition of Postmodernity*, 291; Fredric Jameson, *The Cultural Turn: Selected Writings on the Postmodern, 1983–1998* (London: Verso, 1998).

67. Talcott Parsons, *The System of Modern Societies* (Englewood Cliffs, N.J.: Prentice-Hall, 1971), 4.

acceleration. Lifestyles, fashions, practices, occupational, familial, territorial, political, and religious commitments all change at a faster pace and become increasingly contingent and revisable. Late modern culture thus clearly appears to be highly dynamic.

However, as pointed out throughout this chapter, in at least three of the four dimensions (structure, culture, and personality) we also find complementary signs of deceleration or inertia—the paradoxical flipside of social acceleration. Thus, individuals at times, despite the frantic pace of events, experience their loss of direction, priorities, and narratable "progress" as "frozen time" or virtual inertia, just as the entrenched logics of subsystemic operations appear to be so reified that notions of the "end of history," the "exhaustion of utopian energies," and the "iron cage" abound amidst the discourse of permanent and total social change.[68] Similarly, with respect to culture, what from one perspective appears to be a vast contingency of value orientations and lifestyles in which "anything goes" can be interpreted from another perspective as an entrenchment of the basic value orientations of modernity, that is, as strict adherence to the values of activity, universality, rationality, and individuality.[69] From the deceleratory perspective, Western societies' apparently fast pace of change is only a surface phenomenon beneath which we find inertia. Only with respect to nature does there seem to be no complementary deceleration. Here, only the looming possibility of environmental disaster figures as a potential for (exogenous) deceleration.

A final question concerns whether acceleration really is an independent feature of modernity or just a perspective from which its core processes (individualization, domestication, rationalization, differentiation) can be reinterpreted. After all, all four processes traditionally associated with modernization are intricately connected with increases in speed: thus, individualization can be a cause as well as an effect of acceleration, since individuals are more mobile and adaptive to change and faster in making decisions than collectivities. Similarly, one of the main reasons for, as well as a consequence of, organizational differentiation is the speeding up of systemic processes, and the same holds true for rationalization as the improvement of

---

68. Even if there is eventually a postmodern dedifferentiation of social subsystems, this will, in my view, not alter the perception of inertia and powerlessness, since the resulting "kaleidoscopic chaos" will be even less controllable. The operative blundering of systemic borders will not reverse the uncontrollable, nonintentional functioning of systemic processing.

69. For this argument, see Gerd Günter Voß, "Wertewandel: Eine Modernisierung der protestantischen Ethik," *Zeitschrift für Personalforschung* 3 (1990): 263–75; and Schulze, "Steigerunglogik und Erlebnisgesellschaft," *Politische Bildung* 30, no. 2 (1997): 79.

means-ends relationships and domestication as an improvement of instrumental control. Nevertheless, I would suggest that we regard modernization
as a process of social acceleration for at least three reasons. First, individual
as well as collective human existence is in its very essence temporal and
processual; changes in temporal structures are changes in individual and
social existence.[70] Hence, it is only with respect to the significant changes
in its temporality that the nature and impact of modernization become
fully visible. Second, social acceleration reveals the unitary logic underlying
all four dimensions of modernization. And third, it is only from a temporal perspective that we can fully understand the fundamental transformations in contemporary society, which are the result of social acceleration
within the unaltered framework of modernity but beyond the limits of individual and social integration and autonomy. As such, they amount to a silent
but sweeping qualitative social revolution by a mere quantitative change in
the realm of speed.

70. "The self is process; the temporal dimension is fundamental. To neglect the temporal
dimension is to neglect the essence. We shall never understand the human by simply analyzing the individual as a stable configuration of traits, qualities, or attitudes," argues, Robert
Lauer, reminiscent of Heidegger, in *Temporal Man: The Meaning and Uses of Social Time* (New
York: Praeger, 1981), 56. He convincingly adds that exactly the same is true for social inter-
actions and society as well (86–88).

SEVEN

IS THERE AN ACCELERATION OF HISTORY?

Reinhart Koselleck

Make haste, my smith, to fit the steed!
Day passes away as you tarry o'er the deed.—
"How your great horse steams in its might!
Where do you rush to, my worthy knight?"[1]

With these rather hackneyed verses in the familiar, half-uncanny style of late Romantic balladry begins the first German railroad poem. Its title is "The Steam Horse." It dates from 1830—thus five years before the first German railroad rolled from Nuremberg to Fürth—and its author is Adelbert von Chamisso.

As the title indicates, the change from horse to locomotive is thematized in the immense horse, or, to put it nonmetaphorically, acceleration. First of all, our locomotive gains a day by driving around the globe from east to west. This remains within the compass of calendrical experience. But then it picks up speed:

> My steamhorse, model of all that is fast,
> Leaves the course of time itself in the past.
> Now racing off into the setting sun,
> It appears from the east 'fore the day has begun.[2]

Chamisso's locomotive as it were throws off the shadow that the future casts on the past. It overcomes not only natural but also historical time; it

---

1. "Schnell! Schnell, mein Schmied! Mit des Rosses Beschlag! / Dieweil De zauderst, versteicht der Tag.— / 'Wie damfet Dein ungeheures Pferd! / Wo eilst De so him, mein Ritter wert?'" Adelbert von Chamisso, "Das Dampfroß" [The Steamhorse], in *Chamissos Werke*, vol. 1, pt. 1, *Gedichte*, ed. Max Sydow (Berlin: Bong, 1907), 66.

2. "Mein Dampfroß, Muster der Schnelligkeit, / läßt hinter sich die laufende Zeit / Und nimmt's zur Stunde nach Westen den Lauf, / Kommt's gestern von Osten schon wieder herauf." Ibid.

circumnavigates the earth so quickly that it overtakes its breakneck rotation, and hence the past. "I have robbed time of its secret, / It spiraled back from yesterday to yesterday."[3] So the knight of the locomotive becomes the witness of his own birth; he disturbs his grandfather by flirting with his betrothed at his wedding, from which he is rudely ejected; now he wants to deliver posterity's greetings to Napoleon on St. Helena, then to seek him out in 1804 and warn him before he crowns himself emperor—"Oh, had he heeded the warning!" Chamisso the critical Bonapartist adds.

The smith, however, who received a fee of nineteen hundred gold pieces for his services—the nineteenth century was compensated in gold—wants to know something else, namely the future: whether the market will rise or fall, and, "just between you and me," whether it is wise to trust in the House of Rothschild. But by then the rider, pushing a spring, had already disappeared with his steamhorse.

Chamisso's poem is not only the first in Germany, but also the most astonishing of the lyrics of railroad technology to arise at that time. In the poetry of steam, which soon became a fashion, all kinds of attitudes that could be taken as social or political were represented: from hymns to progress—"with every rail that we lay, a new life is brought into the world" (Louise Otto-Peters)[4]—to terror in the face of energies that, once unleashed, threaten to destroy culture and spirit. The rise of speed unleashed a true shock as well as many challenges. What had previously been accomplished by horses, wind, or water was now done by machines. The transition from a time of movement bound to nature to a time manageable through technology was certainly hard to describe. So at first metaphors from nature offered themselves: exotic animals or mythical figures that the locomotive was intended to be. Rhinoceros, dragon, elephant, colossus, giant—these were attempts to indicate what the locomotive could do even more than a horse: namely, (twenty-four kilometers in an hour, conveying a whole wagon train, including people, luggage, freight, and even horses, from one place to another.

Now, Chamisso was the only one who outdid the metaphorics of the technological generation of power and thematized acceleration itself. This called forth something unexpected. In a fable-like inversion, he saw acceleration

---

3. "Ich habe der Zeit ihr Geheimnis geraubt, / Von gestern zu gestern zurück sie geschraubt." Ibid.

4. "Mit jeder Schine, die wir legen, wird neues Leben in die Welt gebracht." From *Lieder eines deutschen Mädchens,* cited in "Vom Biedermeier zum Maschinenzeitalter," by Manfred Riedel, *Archiv für Kulturgeschichte* 43, no. 1 (1961): 109. Riedel finds extensive evidence in different literary genres of the rapid change in experience brought about by the steamship and the railroad.

itself increasingly rising, so that it caught up with the past but not the future. The more the one opened up, the more the other escaped. After reading Chamisso's poem, one is almost led to say that historicism is the true shape of progress, for what the past was becomes increasingly known, while what the future will bring is ever less so.

Chamisso is ultimately not alone in this fantastic interpretation. It belongs to the pre-1848 generation's experience of acceleration. "A new phase of world history is beginning," as Heine reported from Paris upon the opening of the Rouen-Orléans line, "and our generation may boast of having been there." The witnesses to that event experience both more and less than those who heard the roar of the cannons at Valmy: "We merely note that our whole existence is taking off on a new track, is being hurled forth, that new conditions, joys, and hardships await us and the unknown exercises a terrible charm, alluring and at the same time disquieting."[5]

Because of this new unforeseeability of the future, another contemporary, Eduard Beurmann, wrote of governments that they are "suspicious of these enterprises whose end they cannot calculate themselves, but time lets nothing stand in its way."[6] And even a monarch who himself promoted railroads, Ludwig I of Bavaria, took up his quill and addressed himself to the future: the Earth will go up in smoke, so it is written. "Everywhere and nowhere at home, the human race roams erratically over the earth, just like steam. / Only now has the racing cart begun its revolving course / Its goal is obscured to the eye" (1847).[7]

Even today's generation, witnesses of trips to the moon and Sputniks, of live television coverage, of rockets and jet airplanes, has not undergone a revolution of experience like that of the pre-1848 generation. It is as if the plane's takeoff from the ground were the actual experience—not the flight itself and its acceleration. Apparently, accelerating processes can also become a habit. Prophylactically, Brockhaus wrote in 1838 that even air travel, should it ever happen, would not be equal to the revolution achieved by the railway in regard to the technological mastery of time. In order to answer the

5. Heinrich Heine, *Lutetia* LVII, May 5, 1843, in *Sämtliche Schriften*, vol. 9, ed. Klaus Briegleb (Munich: Hanser, 1976), 448–49.

6. Cited in Riedel, "Vom Biedermeier zum Maschinenzeitalter," 102.

7. "Überall und nirgends daheim, streift über die Erde unstät, so wie der Dampf, unstät das Menschengeschlecht. / Seinen Lauf den umwälzenden, hat der Rennwagen begonnen / Jetzo erst, das Ziel lieget dem Blacke verhüllt." "Die Dampfwagen," in *Gedichte des Königs Ludwigs von Bayern*, pt. 4 (1847), 275—with thanks to to Erich Maschke for this reference. For an analysis of the context and meaning, see Wolfgang Frühwald, "Der König als Dichter: Zu Absicht und Wirkung der Gedichte Ludwig des Ersten, Königs von Bayern," *Deutsche Vierteljahresschrift für Literaturwissenschaft und Geistesgeschichte* 50 (1976): 146.

question of acceleration in history, or simply the acceleration *of* history, in the following, I will divide it into two subquestions:

First, I will treat the singularity of the experience of acceleration in its empirical relation to the rise of the Industrial Revolution. My thesis will be that acceleration corresponds to a denaturalization of the hitherto traditional experience of time. It is indicative of a specifically modern history.

Second, I will use a history-of-ideas approach to investigate the theoretical or mythological metaphors that were utilized before the Industrial Revolution for something resembling historical acceleration. I hope to show that acceleration as a category of historical expectation has a long history, and that new formulations of expectations had accrued since the sixteenth century, but could only become a fully fleshed-out experiential concept with the Industrial Revolution. In other words, the foreshortening of time, previously formulated in apocalyptic terms, became a metaphor for acceleration that employed concepts that were not on the horizon of Christian eschatology in the sixteenth century.

I. The Denaturalization of Temporal Experience Through Factors of Technological Acceleration

I am aware that with the expression "denaturalization of time" I am using an unguarded figure of speech. Time always has to do with nature, with the stars and the course of human biological processes, no matter how these processes are used, reworked, or transformed by human society. One need only recall the famous Soviet joke "Sleep faster, comrade!" to indicate a border that no planning can go beyond. My aim here is to show that the factors that establish man as a historical being in his temporal experience result in a relatively greater independence from a nature on which man always continues to rely, and that the acceleration that man brings about himself is unmistakable evidence of this process.

The introduction of the mechanical clock in the fourteenth century had already effected a denaturalization of temporal experience. It led to the quantification of the day into twenty-four equal hours. Le Goff speaks of mercantile time, the time of businesspeople, which competed with religious-liturgical time and, under the influence of the developing science of physics, represented an enormous achievement of abstraction.[8] The whole history

8. Jacques Le Goff, "Zeit der Kirche und Zeit des Händlers im Mittelalter" (1960), in *Schrift und Materie der Geschichte*, ed. Claudia Honegger (Frankfurt am Main: Suhrkamp,

of the measurement of time can also be described with regard to its social function as a story of increasing abstraction.

Ethnologists tell us how deeply the early measures of time remained embedded in the context of human action.[9] In Madagascar, for example, there is a unit of time "for the time it takes to cook rice" or for the split second required "to roast a grasshopper." Measures of time and the course of action thus entirely converge. Such expressions are much more concrete than something like the German *Augenblick* ("moment"—literally, blink of an eye), which itself represents a unit of time, or the "present," which originally meant "in the presence of" and only around 1800 mutated into a determination of time.

The elementary time measurements of advanced cultures, which indicate the passage of time by the dwindling of their material—sand or water—were also geared to the completion of concrete actions: they measured the length of a sermon, determined the hour of Mass, or, like Cicero's water clock, marked the duration of a pleading in court. To these elementary measures of time was added the sundial, which indicated different times depending on the season and geographical position, since it showed the time according to the natural trajectory of the sun.

Mechanical clocks could adjust as well. In the nineteenth century the Japanese still used clocks that made the passage of time variable, so that daytime hours were in reverse relation to nighttime hours, and depending on the season lasted longer in the summer or shorter in the winter. The seasonal difference between daytime and nighttime hours passed unmediated in these clocks into the rhythm of work, from which they received their purpose. Such clocks correspond as much as the early measures of time to the daily routines of agriculture or handcrafts rather than to the mechanized workplace, whose temporal rhythms, derived from the machine and all equal, are prescribed for man.

Introduced in the fourteenth century, the mechanical clock descended from the castle or church tower to the town hall, then to the living room,

---

1977), 393–414, as well as in the meantime (the opposition of religious and commercial time brought down that the mechanical clock ringing of the prince above all, and of course in working together with the Church, if it was also introduced for the benefit of businesspeople) the fundamental investigations of Gerhard Dohrn-van Rossum, *Die Geschichte der Stunde: Uhren und moderne Zeitordnung* (Munich: Hanser, 1992). Laying the groundwork and bringing together numerous investigations is Arno Borst, *Computus: Zeit und Zahl in der Geschichte Europas* (Berlin: Wagenbach, 1990; rev. ed., Munich: Deutscher Taschenbuch, 1999).

9. For this and the following dates and reflections, see E. P. Thompson, "Time, Work-Discipline, and Industrial Capitalism," *Past and Present* 38 (1967): 56–97.

and finally found its way into the vest pocket. These clocks, which could indicate minutes by the sixteenth century and seconds by the seventeenth, were, to be sure, an indicator as much as a stimulator of discipline, the rationalizing of the human work world and the latitude for action within it. In the first half of the nineteenth century, many industrial workers in England already carried their own watches, not least to verify those of their overseers. Standardized time was finally introduced with the emergence of the railroad network and its standardized timetables—in Prussia, before the 1848 revolution—which differed completely from the various local times and the position of the sun. Henry Ford began his career as an entrepreneur by having watches made with two hands so that they could simultaneously show standard time and local time. This was final evidence of the development of technologically determined units of time, which detached themselves from traditional temporal rhythms connected to nature. Day and night seemed to be assimilated as soon as railroad times made it possible, thanks to trains running on tracks, to solve the problem of night travel. This process corresponded with the rise in the great nineteenth-century factories of nightshifts, which had already existed in the dark mines of the sixteenth century and were now increasingly being introduced to increase production.

All of these processes have often been described, if insufficiently investigated. We can distinguish roughly between three phases of increasing abstraction:

1. The measurement of time was first embedded in the context of human action.
2. The sundial succeeded in, so to speak, objectivizing natural time.
3. The mechanical clock and later the pendulum clock began a transformation of the everyday through quantified units of time that helped secure and promote an all-encompassing organization of society, a process that extended from the fourteenth to the eighteenth centuries. The Sun King, Louis XIV, was celebrated as the *maître du temps*[10] because he ruled the present by his wisdom, the past by his memory, and the future by his foresight—symbolized by the clocks that were dedicated to him and those he had displayed.

For our way of posing the question, it is important to see that the regularly running clocks that intruded into everyday life were the origin and the

10. Klaus Maurice, *Die Französische Pendule des 18. Jahrhunderts: Ein Beitrag zu ihrer Ikonologie* (Berlin: De Gruyter, 1967), 102.

indicators of a lasting order, but not of acceleration,[11] however much they allowed it to be measured in the physical domain. The dwindling hourglass and its flowing time became the allegory of transitoriness, vanity; the mechanical clock, to the contrary, became the allegory of constancy, of cleverness and utility. Only toward the end of the eighteenth century, when the clock had become thoroughly commonplace, could it also iconographically represent vanity.

Machine metaphors, especially clockwork, that were applied to the cosmos, society, and people in the seventeenth century were still preprogressive metaphors: they evoked regularity, the household of God, which had been set up and then ran steadily; they could apply to nature or man, but not their acceleration.[12] The clock could measure acceleration, but it could not symbolize it. It was the railroad and its metaphorics that made it possible to symbolize acceleration: Marx spoke of revolution as the "locomotive of history," not the clock of history. This new metaphor indicates the threshold at which acceleration could first coalesce into the dominant experiential principle of a new generation.[13]

It now belongs to the character of our epochal threshold that even before the invention of the steam engine, the mechanical loom, and the telegraph, which respectively accelerated traffic, industrial production (led by textiles), and the transmission of news, an increase in speed in life as a whole had already been registered. The period that began after this threshold had been crossed inevitably led to a new dimension in temporal experience. "One also began to live more quickly and intensively," thought Niebuhr, looking back at the eighteenth century, "but this was first taking shape at the time of the Revolution and has essentially developed since."[14]

The premechanical increase in speed had been apparent in many ways since the seventeenth century. The construction of networks of roads and canals increased the volume of freight and the distance it could be carried.

11. Compare Comenius (1592–1670): "In omni Republica sit una suprema potestas, cui caeterae subordinentur: in uno judico unus judex, quem admodum un una civitae unum commune Horologium esse expedit, ad quod omnia publica negotia disponantur." *De rerum humanarum emendatione consultatio catholica*, 2 vols. (Prague: Academia Scientiarum Bohemoslovaca, 1966), 2:511.

12. "The world is a clock which is wound once and then continues as long as God decides to let it run," J. H. S. Formey, "Conversation," in *Encyclopédie ou dictionnaire raisonné des sciences, des arts et des métiers*, 4 vols. (Paris: Briasson, 1754), 4:38.

13. Karl Marx, *Die Klassenkämpfe in Frankreich, 1848 bis 1850* (1850) (Berlin: Vorwärts, 1895), 90, quoted in Karl Griewank, *Der neuzeitliche Revolutionsbegriff: Entstehung und Entwicklung* (Weimar, 1955; 2nd ed., Frankfurt am Main: Europäische Verlagsanst, 1969), 218.

14. Barthold Georg Niebuhr, *Geschichte des Zeitalters der Revolution* (1829), 2 vols. (Hamburg: Agentur des Rauhen Hauses, 1845), 1:55.

The motivation could be mercantile or political. In England, for example, which always enjoyed the advantage of cheap and fast waterways throughout the island, a network of roads was first constructed after Bonnie Prince Charlie of Scotland had driven so deep into England in 1745 that no troops could quickly be mustered against him. But we are concerned here not with causation, but with phenomena.

The average speed of private carriages on French roads more than doubled from 1814 to 1848, from 4.5 to 9.5 kilometers per hour. In Prussia during the same period the time of the mail coach journey from Berlin to Cologne shrank from 130 to 78 hours. Government investments in road building made governments hesitate for a long time to create cheaper competition for themselves by subsidizing railways—as is well known, one of the indirect causes of the 1848 revolutions.

We find another precursor of increasing speed in the seas.[15] In the first decade of the nineteenth century, North Americans developed the clipper ship, a narrow sailing ship with tall masts, which cut the time to travel from New York around Cape Horn to San Francisco (19,000 km) from 150–190 to 90 days. The record for a day was more than 750 km, an average speed of around 15 nautical miles per hour, which steam would only beat much later.

Something similar can be observed in communications. Before the electrical telegraph prevailed—Sömmering had invented one in 1810, but it proved unusable—optical telegraph networks, whose tradition stretched back to antiquity, were developed to their final perfection.[16] The speed of signaling was increased enormously, whether through the necessary shortening of baroque administrative texts or the construction of a system of signals, which were transmitted from tower to tower. This reporting system, which was at the same time a control system, was systematically developed during the French Revolution. For example, in 1794 the capture of Condé-sur-L'Escaut was reported from Lille to Paris by optical telegraph many hours before the arrival of the mounted courier. Napoleon's successes were also made possible by the acceleration of the means of communication. The

15. On this, see Wolfgang Zorn, "Verdichtung und Beschleunigung des Verkehrs als Beitrag zur Entwicklung der 'modernen Welt,'" in *Studien zum Beginn der modernen Welt*, ed. R. Koselleck (Stuttgart: Klett-Cotta, 1977), 115–34. Cf. Philip S. Bagwell, *The Transport Revolution* (London: Routledge, 1988); and Brian Austen, *British Mail-Coach Services, 1784–1850* (New York: Garland, 1986).

16. These are described vividly and with many examples in Hermann Kellenbenz and Hans Pieper, *Die Telegraphenstation Köln-Flittard: Eine Kleine Geschichte der Nachrichtentechnik* (Cologne: Rheinland-Westphalia Wirtschaftsarchiv der Köln, 1973).

order to kill Andreas Hofer was transmitted by the same medium, although the majority of judges had voted against it. Political and military interests claimed a preeminence that would only later be taken over by mercantile society. As Professor Büsch of Hamburg explained toward the end of the eighteenth century, "It would be possible to think of cases in which news, had it only arrived a few hours earlier, could have been worth greater sums than the annual cost of the telegraph lines, including the entire cost of set-ting them up"[17]—a guiding principle of the world of trade and finance in the coming centuries. Saving time increases costs, but it increases profits even more.

Now, what is the common testimony of these dates? Modern state and civil society had already achieved an astonishing acceleration in the means of transportation before the invention of technological instruments of accel-eration. To be sure, these achievements were up against an absolute limit set by nature. Roads could be improved, carriages refined, but horses them-selves remained the same. Sailing ships could be perfected, but their speed finally depended on the wind. Optical telegraphy could be rationalized, but transmissions were thwarted by nightfall, and in the day by rain and clouds, not infrequently for days or weeks. Sometimes a report would lie unsent or incomplete for days; thus, victory was reported from Spain without anyone in Paris learning whether Wellington or Napoleon was the victor.

Once acceleration was unleashed in interpersonal transport, it could be driven further only once technological inventions allowed it to overstep these barriers. It was after the French and the Industrial revolutions that accel-eration began to become a general experiential principle.

Some of the criteria of this principle formulated at the time are as follows.

The most familiar emerging yardstick for acceleration was the disappear-ance of space. In an eloquent 1838 article, the *Brockhaus der Gegenwart* de-fined the nature of the railroad thus: "It overcomes spatial separations by bringing things closer in time. . . . Thus, all spaces are only distances for us by virtue of the time we need to pass through them; as we accelerate these times, the influence of space itself on life and transport is foreshortened." With touching naïveté, the article makes individual calculations for the work world and politics, while studiously overlooking the coming significance of the train for the military. By taking the train, the traveling apprentice would be able to gain four and a half days of working time per week. Adjacent

---

17. Johann Georg Büsch, *Abhandlung von dem Geldumlauf in anhaltender Rücksicht auf die Staatswirtschaft und Handlung*, pt. 2 (Hamburg: C. E. Bohn, 1800), 43.

cities would grow together into an "artificially concentrated space." The division between the city and the countryside in general would be overcome by a common economic space. "Land and sea trade places"; "Railroads reduce Europe to approximately the area of Germany."[18]

It is unnecessary to cite further examples. Without any mitigating political or social factors, the data of acceleration are projected in a linear fashion into the future. And this is not without political purpose. The democratizing effect of the railroad, which conveyed all the existing estates in four classes at the same speed, was seen and feared by its enemies. The railroad as initiator of the age of equality is part of topology. It is almost superfluous to mention that the advancing unification of legal spaces at the cost of traditional regional titles belongs to the same stock of experience.

But acceleration was registered in other areas as well. In 1793 the analyses of Adam Smith found their way into the current German encyclopedia. The division of labor induced "not only a proportionate growth of productive power, but also a saving in the expenditure of time, whereby the time that was lost by the passage of work from one to another is gained. This gain in time further multiplies the quantity of work markedly." Finally, the gain in time saves wages, and all of this together is owed to machines. The working time thus liberated is in turn used for the satisfaction of new needs, which emerge because existing needs have already been satisfied by the machines.[19]

Analyses of the structure of needs, which since the 1790s had returned to a temporal perspective, belong to this context. Luxury lost its stigma of being a prerogative of the upper classes. Rather, the need for increasing needs was driven by the accelerating change of fashion noted by Garve. Instead of satisfying the minimal demands of natural necessity, growing

18. Karl August Espe, ed., *Conversations-Lexikon der Gegenwart*, 4 vols. (Leipzig: F. A. Brockhaus, 1838), 1–2:1115–36, section 41; from the same author, cf. "Die Eisenbahnen, eine europäische Notwendigkeit," in *Scherz und Ernst* (Leipzig, 1836). The overcoming of spatial separation by bringing things nearer in time was ironized by Heine (*Lutetia* VII, 449): "Even the basic concepts of space and time have become unstable. Space will be killed by the railroad, and only time will remain to us. If only we had enough money to also properly kill the latter!"

19. Under the title "Dampfüberschuss und Zeitüberschuss," *Der bayerische Gewerbefreund*, no. 13 (1848): 55, asked itself what should be done with the millions of hours that were saved by use of the railroad and steamship. It feared that the "immense accumulation of freed time" would not be employed by the rising proletariat for education and morality. Cited in *Aufbruch ins Industriezeitalter*, vol. 3, *Quellen zur Wirtschafts- und Sozialgeschichte Bayerns*, ed. Konrad von Zwehl (Munich: Oldenbourg, 1985), 140–41. The challenge of noneconomically useful free time is a direct consequence of the increase, and to that extent also the acceleration, of productivity.

needs now pressured the order of the estates. Everywhere developments made it clear that what was experienced as acceleration was no longer reversible. Thus, the static metaphor of the machine was also burst apart from the economic side: in 1800 Büsch, in analyzing the circulation of money, described the classes as different driving wheels according to their occupation. But then he continued: "We must not force this comparison too far. For these driving wheels do not work only alone and all as a whole, namely for the welfare of the state, but also back on one another, and each promotes and accelerates the others' motion—an arrangement for which I can venture no mechanical example that is in complete agreement."[20]

Everywhere it was acceleration that distinguished the temporal experience of this time from all the times that came before. But metaphors for a self-inducing and thus accelerating system were sought in vain. Acceleration seemed to take hold of one domain after another, not only the technical world of industry, the empirically verifiable heart of all acceleration, but everyday life, politics, the economy, and population growth.[21]

The world of the bourgeois unfolded under its sign. Thus, ever more pianos—status symbols of every bourgeois salon—were produced in ever-shorter periods of time. In 1750, a piano maker produced perhaps twenty instruments per year. Thanks to the mechanical production of metal frames, Broadwood of London was manufacturing four hundred pianos annually in 1802 and fifteen hundred in 1825. "Prices sank, pitch rose," achieving a brilliant frequency of 435. Mozart and Beethoven were angry that their pieces were played faster than they had intended. Reading, too, was accelerated, so to speak, in bourgeois households. To repeated readings of the Bible and the classics came the consumption of constantly encroaching new products, above all the novel. Starting in 1814, the rotary press promoted turnover, to which Brockhaus, one of our chief witnesses, adapted himself. While his first encyclopedia was brought up to date with supplementary volumes, between 1830 and 1840 the publisher moved to offering a *Brockhaus der Gegenwart,* an encyclopedia of the present, which presented a cross-section of modernity. Soon afterwards came the current journal *Die Gegenwart,* which delivered the events of a bustling time to the kitchen table month by month.

Let us pause in my enumeration of empirical findings and their contemporary meaning and ask what provides the experiential principle of acceleration.

20. Büsch, *Abhandlung von dem Geldumlauf,* 2:17.
21. Cf. Rolf Peter Sieferle, *Bevölkerungswachstum und Naturhaushalt: Studien zur Naturtheorie der klassischen Ökonomie* (Frankfurt am Main: Suhrkamp, 1990).

The increasing use of that principle since the turn of the nineteenth century bears witness first of all to a change in the sensation and consciousness of time, without of course the everyday use of language being able to have theoretical or systematic stringency. It apparently gives the impression of registering an experience that had never before existed: here, of course, lies precisely the point of acceleration. It is in the first place the moment of surprise that is articulated here. Allow me to try briefly to elucidate this.

The question of acceleration is embedded in the general question of what historical time is. If one may designate progress as the first genuine historical category of time—despite its historico-theological implications—then acceleration is a specific variety of this progress. From a theoretical perspective, there can also be progress when it takes a regular path, so that the mere speed of change or improvement provides no additional indication that anything is changing at all in a progressive way. The rise of production can, for example, always remain the same within the same interval of time. Only if productivity is increased does it become an acceleration of production. (There is a well-known research problem in economic history here that has not yet been adequately solved. The transition from manual to mechanical spinning and weaving is only a symptom of many others that can be differently weighted.)

Only when rates, which are measured in the same intervals of natural chronology, increase geometrically and no longer arithmetically can something accordingly be registered as acceleration. Thus, around 1900 Henry Adams considered the whole of modern history from the perspective of the law of acceleration.[22] This model is useful as a heuristic determination for the technological-industrial conditions of modern history, although it cannot be applied in an unmediated way to general history. In any case, it is quite clear to us that acceleration is more than simply change and more than mere progress. It qualifies the "progress of history," an expression that became sayable only after 1800.

Change, *mutatio rerum,* can be reported in all histories. What is modern, however, is change that calls forth a new temporal experience: namely, that everything changes faster than could have been expected or had earlier been

22. Henry Adams, *The Education of Henry Adams* (see chapter 1 of this volume): "A dynamic theory would begin by assuming that all history, terrestrial or cosmic, mechanical or intellectual, would be reducible to this formula if we knew the facts." Adams brings examples from all spheres of life to support his contention that spirit could now only react, although he later understood this; in the future it will have to learn to jump in order to adapt.

experienced. Through the shorter spaces of time, a component of unfa-
miliarity enters the everyday of those affected that cannot be derived from
any previous experience: this distinguishes the experience of acceleration.
As Goethe has Eduard say in *Elective Affinities:* "It is bad enough that now
one can no longer learn for one's whole life. Our forefathers held to the
teaching that they received in their youth; but we have to learn everything
anew every five years if we do not want to be completely out of date."[23]

In other words, temporal rhythms and developments are articulated that
can no longer be derived from any natural time or sequence of generations.
The formerly constant reproducibility of learning and the lasting application of what has been mastered are interrupted for the mastery of what is
now new. Measured against the preceding experience of learning, the temporal rhythm of learning anew becomes shorter and shorter, which induces
the experience of accelerating change. This kind of acceleration refers to a
history conceived of as time constantly outstripping itself, as it were, even
as the modern period with its emphasis on the new.

Here, of course, a second explanation is due that should warn us against
establishing the concept of the modern period thus attained absolutely in
its singularity. Acceleration is also always a perspectival concept whose evidence is acquired from the comparison of contemporaneous generations
that share a common if also perspectively refracted space of experience.
Perthes formulated this in a letter to Jacobi when he sought to interpret the
"unbelievable speed" with which his time rearranged all thought and desire.[24]
Earlier changes of experience came over centuries; today they are crowding
one upon the other and accordingly expanding the struggle. "Our time . . .
has united what cannot be united in the three generations now living. The
immense contrasts of 1750, 1789, and 1815 dispense with any transitions
and appear not one after another but one next to the other in the people

23. Goethe, *Die Wahlverwandtschaften* 1:4, in *Sämtliche Werke: Briefe, Tagebücher und Ges-
präche*, vol. 8, *Romane*, ed. Waltraud Wiethölter (Frankfurt am Main: Deutscher Klassiker,
1994), 300.

24. Undated letter (ca. 1815), in *Friedrich Perthes' Leben: Nach dessen schriftlichen und münd-
lichen Mittheilungen aufgezeichnet*, 6th ed., by Clemens Theodor Perthes, 3 vols. (Gotha: F. A.
Perthes, 1872), 2:146. Cf. also the analogous but dualistically high-styled polemic against the
"advice of the five hundred": "Outside France presented the spectacle of two enemy nations";
the morals, language, and opinions of each stood in strict opposition. One nation followed the
empire of philosophy ("the reign of philosophy"), the other its prejudices; the one freedom,
the other servitude; the Republic stood against the monarchy: "in a word, the space of two
centuries between the inhabitants of the same fatherland." Félix Bonnaire, Corps législatif,
Conseil des Cinq-Cents: Rapport fait par Bonnaire sur le calendrier républicain, séance du 4
thermidor an 6 (1798) (Paris: Imprimerie nationale, 1798). Thanks to Michael Meinzer for
this reference.

now living, according to whether they are grandfathers, fathers, or grand-children." It is the chronological contemporaneity of those who are not polit-ically or socially contemporaneous that calls forth conflicts, where attempts to resolve the point at issue as measured by earlier times are experienced as acceleration.

Our category of acceleration can thus also refer to an instrument of knowl-edge that aims at a theory of political crisis, without having to thereby deduce further acceleration for the future. The French Revolution and its progress were conventionally conceived in this sense. Thus, for instance, Georg Friedrich Rebmann gave a funeral oration for the revolutionary cal-endar, revoked in 1805. He gives a typological summary of the previous revolution that had established its own calendar. Then he continues: "Briefly, it [the calendar] saw everything that had come to pass in twenty centuries before it in the space of a few years and finally died of a stroke, while the doctors prophesied its consumption, just as child prodigies rarely grow old. Alas, but had it also learned that people become cleverer and better, that their experiences would become useful for them and their descen-dents! *Requiescat in pace!*"[25]

The topos of the compressed and therefore accelerated time of revolu-tionary events ends here in semiresignation, since progress has not mate-rialized to the degree hoped for.

Görres reacted similarly after the Restoration in the conventional sense seemed to have been reinstated: he thought then that one could learn little from earlier history: "But if you want to learn from it [history], take the Rev-olution as your instructor; in it the lazy course of centuries has accelerated into a carousel."[26]

Here, then, we become acquainted with an interpretive concept of accel-eration that out of the dimension of the surprise at an unknown future returns to the structural possibilities of a history that can be analogously repeated. A revolution is, so to speak, only the accelerated concentration of all possible histories. Thus, even the accelerated history, as it were, still remains a history that is not only modern.

Of course, the last two witnesses come from political experience, not indus-trialization. In the horizon of the technologizing society of the nineteenth

25. Georg Friedrich Rebmann, *Der revolutionäre Kalender* (n.d.), in *Insel-Almanach auf das Jahr 1966* (Frankfurt am Main: Isel, 1966), 80–85.

26. Joseph Görres, *Teutschland und die Revolution* (1819), in *Gesammelte Schriften*, vol. 13, *Poli-tische Schriften*, ed. Günther Wohlers (Cologne: Gilde, 1929), 81; R. Koselleck, "Geschichte, His-torie," in *Geschichtliche Grundbegriffe*, vol. 2, ed. Otto Brunner (Stuttgart: Klett-Cotta, 1975), 677.

century, this political variety of acceleration was always called upon as revolutionary impetuses happened, but on the whole they did not determine the meaning of everything that happened. We must therefore theoretically distinguish between two types of acceleration:

1. Acceleration that is registered in times of crisis in constitutional-political life. There have been examples of this since Thucydides that apply to today's experience as well, as "Geschwindigkeit" (speed) in early modern usage also referred to unrest and civil war. What characterizes interpretations of the French Revolution is the oft-repeated thesis that Polybius's exemplary constitutional cycles of nine generations were now compressing into a single generation, or even shorter, in the rush of events. This type of acceleration draws on something long familiar, merely seeing it as happening in a shorter time.

2. Acceleration that results from technological-industrial progress and—in contrast to the past—can be registered as the experience of a new time. Of course, these types of acceleration, which can be strictly distinguished by temporal theory, blend together and reinforce one another in everyday speech and can thereby contribute to supplying arguments for a comprehensive historical crisis theory of modernity, like that masterfully brought together by Jakob Burckhardt.[27]

As a first preliminary finding, then, let us note that there are surely accelerations, not *of* history, but rather only *in* history, according to the stratum of experience, whether they are primarily politically or technologically and economically determined. "History itself" or "history in and for itself" can hardly be thought of as an appropriate subject of action that could act in an accelerated way. For this history in and for itself contains within itself all standards of comparison by which one would have to measure whether it was accelerating or slowing down. The concept of a history that is theoretically abstracted from empirical histories, and that constitutes at once its own subject and object, that is, a history that carries within itself the condition of all possible histories: this concept, first developed in the eighteenth century, does not allow a measure to be set up outside itself that could indicate an acceleration of history, let alone measure it. Hegel, who tried to deduce the stages of world history from the work of the world

---

27. See Reinhart Koselleck, "Krise," in *Geschichtliche Grundbegriffe*, vol. 3, ed. Otto Brunner (Stuttgart: Klett-Cotta, 1982), 639–40.

spirit, clearly recognized this, though he conceded that the writing of history had accelerated: "In modern times the relations are entirely altered. Our culture is essentially comprehensive and immediately changes all events into historical representations."[28] But the world spirit, which works its way through nations and individuals at their cost, progresses only through detours and mediations: "It not only has enough time," it does not even take time into account. And "as for the slowness of the world spirit, it should be considered like this: it doesn't have to hurry; it has time enough—millennia are before you like a day; it has time enough because it is outside of time, because it is eternal." Moreover, this slowness "is increased by each seemingly backward step, by times of barbarity."[29]

It was no accident that Hegel, who sought to develop and comprehend the One History simply out of the spirit of a formerly Christian god, quoted that verse of the Psalm 90, to demonstrate that each situation could equally call for slowing down and for acceleration: "For a thousand years in thy sight are but as yesterday when it is past, and as a watch in the night." This ambiguous comparison leads us back to the apocalyptic presuppositions of modern axioms of acceleration.

II. The Category of Temporal Foreshortening Between Apocalypse and Progress

So far we have become acquainted with acceleration as an experiential concept of modernity and in thereby discovered two kinds: we can conceive of acceleration either as the possibility of repeating history or as a result of technological-industrial innovation. Now we will look at the criteria of acceleration that were in use before the threshold of our period in order, as it were, to gain a new insight from the past.

The foreshortening of time plays a repeatedly activated role in the apocalyptic texts of the Judeo-Christian tradition. This foreshortening of time could be defined as a category of religious experience, but it takes its meaning from Christian expectation, by which temporal foreshortening is a favor bestowed by the grace of God: he will not suffer us to wait so long for the end of the world (Mark 13:20, Matthew 24:22). The end is to occur sooner

28. G. W. F. Hegel, *Die Vernunft in der Geschichte*, ed. J. Hoffmeister (Hamburg: F. Meiner, 1955), 9.
29. G. W. F. Hegel, *Einleitung in die Geschichte der Philosophie*, ed. J. Hoffmeister (Hamburg: F. Meiner, 1959), 62, 64.

than it would in any case. The measure of this foreshortening is the prophesied overcoming of time itself.[30]

The longer the second coming of Christ fails to materialize, the more another kind of expectation leads to the question, how much longer? The basis of this expectation is the stubborn wish of the faithful to shorten time in order to be able to participate in salvation as soon as possible. In 2 Peter 3:8 the answer (from Psalm 90) is offered that a day is like a thousand years before the Lord, and a thousand years like a day. This phrase, too, should offer comfort in the face of all too empirical hopes—namely to refer to God's grace that his message will first reach all the Earth's inhabitants in order to complete the number of the elect. The delay of the end is thus as much an indication of God's grace as the prophesied foreshortening of time. There is no contradiction here, provided that the Pauline transposition of both varieties of expectation could be transcribed into the conviction of believers. For our question, what is decisive is only that the foreshortening or delay has its guiding point outside of time altogether. Both expressions secure evidence only of the eternality of God, whose renewed entrance into this world would bring a new world into being. We are faced with two relational temporal determinations in the vicinity of the apocalypse, which would, to be sure, allow historical events to be interpreted, but whose interpretive grid could not primarily be read from the temporal structure of these events themselves. It is consequently not a matter of a historical foreshortening of lapses of time, but rather of a foreshortening of the time of history, an anticipated end of the world.

Finally, a third variety represents the chiliastic interpretation of the intermediate condition between expectation and arrival of the end. This too could be vouchsafed by Peter's epistles and above all John's Apocalypse. If a thousand years are only a day before God, they are introduced as a time of blessed expectation of the final return of Christ to Earth. This teaching of an intermediate condition, in which the foreshortening and the delay of the expiry date are so to speak neutralized, also draws on an extrahistorically determined telos. If apocalyptic images are nevertheless employed again and again for empirical events, institutional problems immediately present themselves concerning who decides the correct exegesis. Heresy lurks behind each empirical verification of apocalyptic interpretation, however much these interpretations also influenced and advanced the history of Christianity.

---

30. Cf. Reinhart Koselleck, "Zeitverkürzung und Beschleunigung: Eine Studie zur Säkularisation," in *Zeitschichten: Studien zur Historik* (Frankfurt am Main: Suhrkamp, 2000), 177–202.

While the teaching of the thousand-year empire was made taboo by the Church Fathers, and especially by Augustine, the determinations of both temporal foreshortening and delay remained an inherent moment of Christian expectation. Luther, who in contrast to his theological writings always formulated down-to-earth apocalyptic expectations in his table talks, provides good testimony for this both by asking for a delay and by prophesying and desiring the imminence of the Day of Judgment. Thus, the two arguments concerning delay sometimes blend together—that a thousand years are only a day before God and that empirical history is being foreshortened.

One criterion of the extrahistorical character of apocalyptic prophecy is its reversibility. An unfulfilled prophecy or apocalyptic expectation can continually be repeated; indeed, the probability that the prophesied and expected will still come to pass rises with each disappointed expectation. That is, evidence of its prospective fulfillment lies precisely in the error concerning the timing, and becomes all the more certain. In this way, the temporal framework of the form of foreshortening is metahistorically determined. The empirical data for confirming the fact that accelerating events are also omens of the end of time could be exchanged from time to time. This obtains as long as recourse is made to these texts, that is, up to Luther and well into the seventeenth century, only to be reduced in the further course of the modern period to an ever smaller circle of people who no longer had access to the sphere of political decisions.

From this exemplarily foreshortened position, we gain new access to the proliferation of statements in the sixteenth century that time was being foreshortened that did not call upon the apocalypse. The expression of self-foreshortening temporal frameworks indeed remained harnessed to a horizon of expectation (namely, that in the future ever-faster progress would appear), but the expression was also enriched by other, new stocks of experience that were not construed in a Christian sense. The hard kernel of experience from which they above all were derived was the discoveries and inventions of the rising natural sciences. A general tendency can be noted for the period from the sixteenth to the nineteenth centuries: the hopes and expectations, initially stimulated by Christianity, enriched by utopianism, and connected to the history of inventions and discoveries, were increasingly taken over by the experiential principles of the natural sciences.

From the temporal foreshortening that had previously fixed an earlier end to history from outside, an acceleration of determinable sectors of experience was now registered within history itself. What is new here is that the end was no longer approaching more quickly; rather, measured against the slow progress of the previous centuries, contemporary progress was setting in ever more quickly. The telos of mastering nature and justly organizing society became a sliding goal, and each intention of advancement could be interpreted as long-delayed progress.

It is therefore a matter of something more and other than merely secularization. However much apocalyptic expectations in the guise of millennial hopes sought to enter into the new concept of acceleration, the experiential kernel to which the new expectations referred was no longer deducible from the apocalypse.

However, the mutual imbrication with the apocalyptic tradition goes further. It always reemerges, mediated in many ways, where it is a matter of determining the goal of history, which it is humanity's task to reach ever more quickly. This becomes clear in the eighteenth century, when the category of acceleration was widened from increasing mastery of nature to include society, the development of morality, and history as a whole. One can even say that the whole of history itself was first revealed as a particular human way of being when it was interpreted as progressive and accelerating.

Toward the end of the eighteenth century, above all during the French Revolution, voices proliferated that came to see the whole of history from the perspective of increasing acceleration. The question of whether the succession of foreshortening periods was objectively ascertainable or whether it was only a matter of subjective perception was taken up, implicitly or explicitly, by many authors. Still keeping his distance from the enlightened chiliasts, Lessing attested that he wanted to accelerate the production of the future itself. With this he announced the actual course of history and human hopes, plans, and actions that Kant would seek to ground in a way that was as subtle as it was engaged. Kant believed he could empirically realize the moral duty to attempt and promote progress in the events of the French Revolution and especially in people's reaction to these events, generating hope that a just republic and a peaceful order of peoples could be brought about in ever-shorter intervals of time.

He never went as far as Condorcet, who was convinced that one could foresee, guide, and accelerate the progress of the human race "as soon as one found the right leading thread in the history of all previous progress."[31]

---

31. Jean-Antoine-Nicolas de Caritat, marquis de Condorcet, *Esquisse d'un tableau historique des progrès de l'esprit humain* (1793), trans. Wilhelm Alff as *Entwurf einer historischen Darstellung der Fortschritte des menschlichen Geistes* (Frankfurt am Main: Europäische Verlagsanstalt, 1963), 27, 43, 371, 385; and R. Koselleck, *Futures Past: On the Semantics of Historical Time*, trans. Keith Tribe (Cambridge, Mass.: MIT Press, 1985), 52.

But in both theorems the duty, wishfulness, or establishment of accelerated progress was tied back to human action itself, however much historical-philosophical reinsurance was taken out in a plan of nature (Kant) or a universal law (Condorcet).

The experience of a series of natural scientific successes and the beginning of technologization were the godparents of Condorcet's self-assurance. In any case, for the philosophy of history-laden eighteenth-century concept of acceleration, this meant that it could only be meaningfully used if there was an aim to attain in an accelerated manner. Here lies the formal analogy to the extratemporally determined aim that had long been familiar from apocalyptic texts.

Thus, at the Festival of the Constitution in 1793, Robespierre conjured up happiness and freedom as the destiny of humankind, which had now in the Revolution become the duty of all citizens to attain in an accelerated way. And in the same year, Condorcet formulated the "loi révolutionaire," whose goal was to maintain, guide, and accelerate the Revolution.[32]

What Joseph Görres speculatively deduced a quarter-century later—that the "great world train of history . . . steadily accelerates," that the "foreshortening of periods, as they approach the present," was undeniable[33]—this transposition of apocalyptic expectation into the interpretation of history also impregnated the French positivist school. What was expected in the apocalypse from God's secret counsel was now to be achieved by men. With recourse to Condorcet, Saint-Simon too demanded that the preceding centuries be arranged as the successive steps forward of human spirit so that "you will see clearly the means to be used to accelerate its perfection."[34] All the interlocking social, economic, and political analyses of world history by Saint-Simon and his student Comte remain within the framework of factually observed increases in speed as well as under the guiding principle of continuing to accelerate them. Here the Last Judgment is included—as by Schiller—in history itself. "La grande crise finale" would be the French

---

32. [Editor's note: for further discussion see Reinhart Koselleck, "Zeitverkürzung und Beschleunigung: Eine Studie zur Säkularisation," in *Zeitschichten: Studien zur Historik* (Frankfurt am Main: Suhrkamp, 2000), 192.] On the different scales of pronouncements of acceleration, see Horst Günther, ed., *Die Französische Revolution: Berichte und Deutungen deutscher Schriftsteller und Historiker* (Frankfurt am Main: Deutscher Klassiker, 1985), 552, 831, 837 (Wieland), 652 (Forster), 1054, 1070 (Wilhelm Schulz).

33. Görres, *Europa und die Revolution*, 188–89.

34. Henri, comte de Saint-Simon, "Esquisse d'une nouvelle encyclopédie," in *Oeuvres de Saint-Simon et d'Enfantin* (Paris: E. Dentu, 1865–78), 15:89, cited in Rolf Peter Fehlbaum, *Saint-Simon und die Saint-Simonisten: Vom Laissez-Faire zur Wirtschaftsplanung* (Basel: Kyklos, 1970), 12.

Revolution, which would lead to the peaceful reordering of society. Its precondition would of course be sociological theory, for only it provides "the total reorganization which alone can end the great crisis of modernity"[35] by converting knowledge of the past into long-range planning for the future. Even if the word of the last judgment is maintained, the apocalyptic metaphor fades.

Now, what is common to these testimonies? Clearly, this acceleration, which here is claimed and confirmed for the whole of world history, is much less a controlling experiential concept than a utopian concept of expectation.

A quasireligious promise had colored spaces of time that were to be laid aside in an accelerated manner. But the determination of the goal remained inner-worldly and received new support in the nineteenth century from technological progress. Thus, in an 1838 essay on the railroad, Brockhaus defined the organization of world peace by a self-determining humanity as a morally necessary postulate. And he continued: "Indeed, history has been directed toward this truly holy aim all along, but it will reach it centuries sooner on the furiously forward-rolling wheels of the railroad."[36]

One can certainly assert that there is the formal temporal structure of an apocalyptic expectation here. But no more than that, for the authority of experience remains a technical instrument, which, as very quickly became apparent, was unable to redeem the demand of such a sacred history. Anyone who wanted to continue to cling to inner-worldly goal determination had to be on the lookout for other accelerators.

By recourse to the apocalyptic tradition and its transformation since the early modern period, we have thus found another answer. Historical acceleration can be registered in two possible cases:

First, it can be traced back to the foreshortening of time arising from the expectation of a goal: then processes of acceleration are always possible as a postulate and can constantly be conjured up anew, irrespective of whether they can be fulfilled. In this case it is a matter of a concept of expectation that can be repeated at any time. Purely subjective, it can be deduced from temporal slowdowns, foreshortenings, or delays—categories of things wished for or of disappointed hopes.

Second, acceleration can be deduced from the comparison with previous conjunctures of events: thus it remains empirically verifiable and can deliver data for further planning. Then it is a matter of a purely experiential concept.

35. Auguste Comte, *Cours de philosophie positive*, ed. Charles Le Verrier, 2 vols. (Paris: Garnier, 1949), 2:114, 157–58.
36. See note 18.

Finally, and here I come to the conclusion, there is a combination of both possibilities that perhaps appears most frequently today: it consists in the idea that the technological-industrial condition that the developed countries achieved in the past is to be made up by the less developed countries in the future. It necessarily follows from this that the need to catch up can only be satisfied by acceleration. Here too it is a matter of a determination of the contemporaneity of the noncontemporaneous, which carries a great potential for conflict. Further, there is here a shrinking of experience and expectation; the difference between them demands to be quickly bridged. One's experience is the other's expectation. Condorcet, Comte, and Friedrich List investigated and promoted the acceleration of historical events with this third possibility above all in view. In our time, it does not belong only to the everyday business of political planning (I am reminded of a Khrushchev or a Mao Zedong); without it, politics and economics in an international context would be unthinkable. Of course, we do not know how long this will hold.

Let us listen once more to Chamisso, with whose help we boarded the earlier train of acceleration: "In autumn 1837 I visited Leipzig with the intention of traveling on the railroad, harnessing the zeitgeist—I could not have died in peace had I not looked from the high seat of this triumphal car into the unrolling future."[37] A year later, Chamisso was dead.

[Translated by James Ingram]

37. Adelbert von Chamisso, in *Chamissos Werke*, 136.

EIGHT

THE SPATIOTEMPORAL DYNAMICS OF GLOBALIZING CAPITAL AND THEIR IMPACT ON STATE POWER AND DEMOCRACY

Bob Jessop

This chapter argues, only partly in a willfully contrarian spirit, that the spatial turn associated with the study of what is conventionally called (economic) globalization has been overdone and that a temporal (re)turn is now overdue.[1] For, if we choose to separate time and space, then temporality is at least as important as, if not more important than, spatiality in the unfolding logic (and illogic) of the growing integration of the world market and its various conditions of existence. Thus, one of my aims below is to highlight the temporality of capital accumulation on a world scale. Time and space are so closely related in this unfolding, however, that we should talk instead of the uneven spatiotemporal dynamics of the world market. Accordingly, I also explore their conjoint (if often uneven) impact in contemporary political economy and the spatiotemporal manifestations of the various contradictions and dilemmas of accumulation. Next I consider the implications of these dynamics for states (especially national states) as they seek to deal with the integration of the world market and to meet its challenges to their temporal as well as territorial sovereignty. The chapter ends with comments on the problems posed by time-space compression for economic and political democracy.

This chapter has benefited from discussions with Ulrich Beck, Neil Brenner, Christina Colclough, Gene Desfor, Edgar Grande, Joachim Hirsch, Martin Jones, John Jørgensen, Gordon MacLeod, Jamie Peck, Andrew Sayer, Kirsten Simonsen, Ngai-Ling Sum, and John Urry. The usual disclaimers apply.

1. Some portions of this chapter appeared under the title "Time and Space in the Globalization of Capital and Their Implications for State Power," *Rethinking Marxism* 14, no. 1 (2002): 97–117. I am grateful for the journal editors for allowing me to use them here as well.

Globalization Defined

"Globalization" is a deeply problematic notion that tends to obscure more than it reveals about recent economic, political, social, and cultural changes. Here I use it to denote a multicentric, multiscalar, multitemporal, multiform, and multicausal process that includes, but is not exhausted by, the formation of the world market and the reorganization of the interstate system. It is multicentric because it emerges from activities in many places rather than from a single center. It is multiscalar because it emerges from actions on many scales—which are no longer seen as nested in a neat hierarchy but seem to coexist and interpenetrate in a tangled and confused manner—and because it develops and deepens the scalar as well as the spatial division of labor and thereby requires more complex forms of interscalar articulation. Thus, what could be described from one perspective as globalization might appear quite differently (and perhaps more accurately) from other scalar viewpoints: for example, as internationalization, triadization, regional bloc formation, global city network building, cross-border cooperation, international localization, glocalization, glurbanization, or transnationalization.[2] It follows that the dynamics of the world market derive from diversely scaled processes and their interaction: they are not confined to processes that operate purely on a global scale, even if these could be isolated from those occurring elsewhere. Globalization is also multitemporal because it involves the ever more complex restructuring and rearticulation of temporalities and time horizons. This aspect is captured in the notions of time-space distantiation and time-space compression. The former process involves the stretching of social relations over time and space so that relations can be controlled or coordinated over longer periods of time (including into the ever more distant future) and longer distances, greater areas, or more scales of activity. Time-space compression involves the intensification of "discrete" events in real time and/or the increased velocity of material

2. On glocalization, see Neil Brenner, "Global Cities, Global States: Global City Formation and State Territorial Restructuring in Contemporary Europe," *Review of International Political Economy* 5, no. 1 (1997): 1–37; Neil Brenner, "Beyond State-Centrism? Space, Territoriality, and Geographical Scale in Globalization Studies," *Theory and Society* 28, no. 1 (1999): 39–78; and Erik A. Swyngedouw, "Neither Global nor Local: 'Glocalization' and the Politics of Scale," in *Spaces of Globalization: Reasserting the Power of the Local*, ed. Kevin R. Cox (New York: Guilford Press, 1997), 137–66. On glurbanization, see Bob Jessop and Ngai-Ling Sum, "An Entrepreneurial City in Action: Hong Kong's Emerging Strategies in and for (Inter-)Urban Competition," *Urban Studies* 37, no. 12 (2000): 2287–2313. And, on transnationalization, see Michael P. Smith, *Transnational Urbanism: Locating Globalization* (Oxford: Blackwell, 2001).

and immaterial flows over a given distance.[3] Globalization is clearly multi-causal because it results from the complex, contingent interaction of many different causal processes. It is also multiform. It assumes different forms in different contexts and can be realized through different strategies—neo-liberal globalization is only one and, indeed, requires complementary and flanking strategies even where it does take root.[4] Overall, these features mean that, far from globalization being a unitary causal mechanism, it should be understood as the complex, emergent product of many different forces operating on many scales. Hence, nothing can be explained in terms of the causal powers of globalization—let alone causal powers that are inevitable and irreversible and get actualized on some intangible stage behind our backs or on some intangible plane above our heads. Instead, it is global-izations (in the plural) that need explaining in all their manifold spatiotem-poral complexity. Moreover, once we understand how globalizing processes are generated and how they operate, we can better intervene in their pro-duction and better resist some of their effects.

Thus seen, globalization has both structural and strategic moments. Struc-turally, it involves the objective processes whereby increasing global inter-dependence is created among actions, organizations, and institutions within (but not necessarily across) different functional systems (economy, law, pol-itics, education, science, sport, etc.) and the lifeworld that lies beyond them. These processes occur on various spatial scales, operate differently in each functional subsystem, involve complex and tangled causal hierarchies rather than a simple, unilinear, bottom-up or top-down movement, and often dis-play an eccentric "nesting" of the different scales of social organization. They also develop unevenly in space-time. Nonetheless, globalization can be said to increase insofar as the covariation of actions, events, and institutional orders involves more (and more important) relevant activities, is spatially more extensive, and occurs more rapidly. Strategically, globalization refers to conscious attempts to promote global coordination of activities in (but not necessarily across) different functional subsystems and/or in the life-world. This does not require that the actors involved are physically present at all points in the planet but only requires them to monitor relevant activ-ities, communicate about these, and try to coordinate their activities with others to produce global effects. Coordination efforts range from generalized

---

3. I use time-space compression here to describe actual processes rather than a sense of dis-orientation produced by the complex spatiotemporal changes associated with globalization.
4. Winifried Ruigrok and Rob van Tulder, *The Logic of International Restructuring* (Lon-don: Routledge, 1995).

metasteering (based on constitutional or institutional design) intended to produce a more or less comprehensive global order through creation of international regimes to particularistic pursuit of specific economic-corporate interests within such (meta-)frameworks. Not all actors are (or could hope to be) major global players but many more must monitor the global as a horizon of action, the implications of changing scalar divisions, and the impact of time-space distantiation and compression on their identities, interests, and strategies. The overall course of globalization is the unintended, relatively chaotic outcome of interaction among various strategies to shape or resist globalization in a complex, path-dependent world society.

Globalization is part of a proliferation of scales and temporalities as narrated, institutionalized objects of action, regularization, and governance. The number of scales and temporalities of action that can be distinguished is immense,[5] but far fewer ever get explicitly institutionalized. How far this happens depends on the prevailing technologies of power—material, social, and spatiotemporal—that enable the identification and institutionalization of specific scales of action and temporalities. It is the development of new logistical means (of distantiation, compression, communication), organizational technologies, institutions with new spatiotemporal horizons of action, broader institutional architectures, new global standards (including world time), and modes of governance that helps to explain this growing proliferation of economically and politically significant institutionalized scales and temporalities. Moreover, as new scales and temporalities emerge and/or existing ones gain in institutional thickness, social forces also tend to develop new mechanisms to link or coordinate them. This in turn often prompts efforts to coordinate these new coordination mechanisms. Thus, as the triad regions have begun to acquire institutional form and identity, new forums have developed to coordinate their bi- and trilateral relations. Analogous processes occur on other scales. The overall result is growing scalar complexity, greater scope for deliberate interscalar articulation, and more problems in making such interscalar articulation work. Similar issues are occurring around time and its governance. This can be seen in the rise both of nanotemporalities and long-term action oriented to environmental sustainability and more general problems of intertemporal governance.

5. Alfred North Whitehead argues that "there are an indefinite number of discordant time-series and an indefinite number of distinct spaces." Hence it is important to examine how "multiple processes flow together to construct a single consistent, coherent, though multifaceted, time-space system." *The Principle of Relativity with Applications to Physical Science* (Cambridge: Cambridge University Press, 1922), cited by David Harvey, *Justice, Nature, and the Geography of Difference* (Oxford: Blackwell, 1996), 259.

Globalization and the Spatial Turn

Social theorists often suggest that globalization is a key factor behind the "spatial turn." For example, noting a major paradigm shift in the social sciences from concern with modernization to interest in globalization, Arif Dirlik links this reorientation "to the spatial turn or, more accurately, the ascendancy of the spatial over the temporal."[6] More generally, insofar as globalization is inherently spatial, many social scientists seem to agree on the need to address issues of space, place, and scale. But what is involved in making a spatial turn? First, a thematic spatial turn would take spatial issues as its immediate object of analysis; and second, a methodological spatial turn would investigate more complex issues by taking their spatial moments as its entry point but would then move beyond them in its final account. Whether thematic, methodological, or both, this might involve little more than an innocent, belated, and welcome recognition that space does matter. But it could also imply, as David Harvey suggests, that an earlier interest in time and temporal issues was mistaken, overdone, or misleading. Thus, he presents the spatial turn as an important reaction against the privileging, in conventional dialectics, of time over space.[7] Theoretically this involves an "escape from the teleologies of Hegel and Marx [that] can . . . most readily be achieved by appeal to the particularities of spatiality (network, levels, connections)."[8] In addition, practically, it favors "militant particularism" based *in the first instance* on "local mobilization."[9]

Such arguments can engender a paradox. Authors often link globalization to the spatial turn and condemn the overly temporal and teleological nature of the dialectic at the same time as they cite Marx, himself a major dialectical thinker, as a far-sighted analyst of globalization. It is often claimed that *The Communist Manifesto* anticipated many aspects of contemporary globalization.[10] However, although its authors identified important spatial moments of capitalism in the *Manifesto* and, indeed, presented the world market as the ultimate horizon of capital accumulation, it does not follow that their own analysis was essentially spatial. Indeed, as Neil Smith notes, commenting on Marx's work as a whole, "the lively spatial implications of

6. Arif Dirlik, "Globalization as the End and the Beginning of History: The Contradictory Implications of a New Paradigm," *Rethinking Marxism* 12, no. 4 (2000): 6.

7. David Harvey, "Globalization in Question," *Rethinking Marxism* 8, no. 4 (1996): 4.

8. Harvey, *Justice*, 109.

9. David Harvey, *Spaces of Capital: Towards a Critical Geography* (Edinburgh: Edinburgh University Press, 2002).

10. For example, Dirlik, "Globalization," 11–12; Harvey, "Globalization," 2.

Marx's analyses were rarely developed."[11] This is especially clear in the *Manifesto* itself. For, if it has a grand narrative, this is essentially temporal. It describes a history of class struggles that must end in the victory of the proletariat as the universal class. When dealing specifically with capitalism, of course, it also presents a spatial narrative. The *Manifesto* argues that capitalism is inherently global in its scope and dynamic, involving cosmopolitan production, the world market, the rise of world literature, etc. But this spatialization is still subordinate to a revolutionary telos: it serves to universalize the capital relation and so prepare the conditions for a worldwide revolution. Likewise, as capitalism develops, workers are concentrated in factories and cities and power is centralized in the hands of a few large capitalists. This also stimulates revolutionary consciousness and politically isolates the exploiting class before, finally, the workers of the world unite to overthrow it.

A similar subordination of space to time, albeit one that regards capitalism as having a broad direction rather than a specific telos, occurs in *Capital*.[12] This great work covers many general spatial issues, also discussed by the founders of historical materialism elsewhere, that concern production and innovation in various modes of production: supplies of raw materials or semifinished products, the spatial division of labor, forms of cooperation, relative population density, the role of transportation, and the nature of barter and trade. There are also many incidental comments on space and place, town and country, changes in means of transportation and communication, the spatiotemporality of circulation, and so on. More importantly, it offers a spatialized account of merchant capital, primitive accumulation, colonialism, the Industrial Revolution (including the transition from "putting out" to the factory system),[13] England's prefigurative role in industrial capitalism (*de te fabula narratur*), integration of the home market, the expansion of the world market, and many other topics.[14]

When Marx unfolds the basic logic of the fully constituted capitalist mode of production, however, he systematically privileges time over space.[15] Thus,

---

11. Neil Smith, *Uneven Development: Nature, Capital, and the Production of Space* (Oxford: Blackwell, 1984), 81.

12. Moishe Postone, *Time, Labor, and Social Domination: A Reinterpretation of Marx's Critical Theory* (Cambridge: Cambridge University Press, 1993).

13. This involves, inter alia, the transition from "putting out" to machinofacture in factories.

14. Often, when Marx alludes to spatial themes in *Capital*, he adds that it is necessary to pass over them for the present, it is not the place to detail them, etc., indicating that, while important, they are secondary to the initial emphasis on the economy of time.

15. Booth suggests that, for Marx, "(a) all economic formations can be grasped as ways in which persons produce and distribute free time (or surplus time—the difference will be

place and space appear both as the material support[16] and material effect of the logic of capitalism considered as an economy of time.[17] The *inner* determinations of capital accumulation are primarily temporal, and this is reflected in Marx's order of presentation in his various analyses. "Starting from simplified notions of accumulation, Marx gradually explicates the complex dynamics of an interconnected triple accelerator of: increasing accumulation of capital, increasing productive forces of labour, and an increasing composition of capital."[18] He explains capital's self-expansion in terms of the complex articulation between multiple concrete temporalities and the singular abstract time of exchange value[19]—especially as integrated through the widening and deepening of the world market. He was the pioneer here, and, given the absence of relevant concepts in classical political economy, Marx had to develop a suitable language for addressing the dialectic among the concrete and abstract moments of the time factor. Among his key concepts were labor time, absolute surplus value, socially necessary labor time, relative surplus value, machine time, circulation time, turnover time, turnover cycle, socially necessary turnover time, interest-bearing capital, and expanded reproduction.[20]

The key point here is that the spatial *dynamic* of consolidated capitalism (as opposed to its spatial conditions of existence) derives initially from the primacy of production within the capitalist mode of production. This entails competition among capitalists to gain a competitive advantage by reducing labor time below what is currently socially necessary and/or the total time

---

discussed further on); (b) the distinctions between these formations can be expressed as differences in the use and distribution of time; and (c) the idea of time as the realm of freedom and as the scope or space for human development leads to the embedding of the economic conception of time (and so, indirectly, the idea of the economic sphere itself) in an overarching normative inquiry." William J. Booth, "Economies of Time: On the Idea of Time in Marx's Political Economy," *Political Theory* 19, no. 1 (1991): 9.

16. Phil Graham, "Space and Cyberspace: On the Enclosure of Consciousness" (2001).

17. Indeed, Marx notes that the organization of production in all periods can be reduced to an economy of time—e.g., *Grundrisse: Foundations of the Critique of Political Economy*, trans. Martin Nicolaus (Harmondsworth: Penguin, 1973).

18. Geert Reuten, "The Inner Mechanism of the Accumulation of Capital: The Acceleration Triple," in *The Constitution of Capital: Essays on Volume I of Marx's "Capital,"* ed. Riccardo Bellofiore and Nicola Taylor (Basingstoke: Palgrave, 2004), 274.

19. Postone, *Time, Labour*, 292–93 and *passim*.

20. This point was emphasized by Henryk Grossman, *Das Akkumulations- und Zusammenbruchgesetz des kapitalistischen Systems* (Leipzig: C. L. Hirschfield, 1929), as cited by Daniel Bensaïd, *Marx for Our Times: Adventures and Misadventures of a Critique*, trans. Gregory Elliott (London: Verso, 2002), 74. I have extended the list of temporal categories to reinforce its significance and link it to more recent scholarship on the centrality and originality of Marx's work on time.

involved in the production and circulation of their commodities below the prevailing socially necessary turnover time.[21] This dynamic is propelled by the interaction of socially necessary labor and turnover times as mediated through class struggle and capitalist competition. Thus, Marx's analysis "seeks to justify the temporal determination of both production and the dynamic of the whole, and not—as it might seem at first—simply as one of the regulation of exchange."[22] This is most clear when Marx explores the roles of machinofacture and relative surplus value as the most adequate technological form and social form respectively of the capital relation.[23]

Critically, the more integrated the world market, the greater the acceleration of this competition and its pressures on capital accumulation, with the result that they become the decisive features of capital accumulation in the long run. Indeed, as Marx and Engels noted about the early stages of capitalist development: "The movement of capital, although considerably accelerated, still remained, however, relatively slow. The splitting up of the world market into separate parts, each of which was exploited by a particular nation, the exclusion of competition among themselves on the part of the nations, the clumsiness of production itself and the fact that finance was only evolving from its early stages, greatly impeded circulation."[24] As these frictions are overcome through the increasing integration of the world market, the speed of the capitalist treadmill accelerates.[25] This also reinforces the dominance of the logic of capital such that the formation of the world market is not only the result of capitalist dynamics but, once consolidated, a crucial precondition for its realization. Indeed, as Marx argued,

> it is only foreign trade, the development of the market to a world market, which causes money to develop into world money and *abstract labour* into social labour. Abstract wealth, value, money, hence *abstract labour*, develop in the measure that concrete labour

21. David Harvey, *The Limits to Capital* (Oxford: Blackwell, 1982); Postone, *Time, Labour*; Bensaïd, *Marx*.

22. Postone, *Time, Labour*, 190, cf. 269.

23. Rob Beamish, *Marx, Method, and the Division of Labor* (Urbana: University of Illinois Press, 1992); Postone, *Time, Labour*, 284.

24. Karl Marx and Friedrich Engels, *The German Ideology*, in *Collected Works*, vol. 5 (London: Lawrence and Wishart, 1976), 56n.

25. Cf. Heinz D. Kittsteiner, "Reflections on the Construction of Historical Time in Karl Marx," *History and Memory* 3, no. 2 (1991): 59. On the importance of the logic of acceleration in capitalism, see Helmut Rosa, chapter 6 of this volume, as well as "The Speed of Global Flows and the Pace of Democratic Politics," *New Political Science* 27, no. 4 (2005): 444–59, esp. 448–49.

becomes a totality of different modes of labour embracing the world market. Capitalist production rests on the *value* or the transformation of the labour embodied in the product into social labour. But this is only [possible] on the basis of foreign trade and of the world market. This is at once the pre-condition and the result of capitalist production.[26]

In addition to the historically specific, capitalistically generic pressures to reduce socially necessary labor and turnover times, capitalists also face pressure to innovate in other ways that affect the spatial and scalar divisions of labor. In this sense, although place and space are certainly regarded as a basic presupposition of all social activities and *Capital* provides many ad hoc comments on these issues, they enter Marx's analysis as major variables much later in his order of presentation. Thus, disregarding general comments on the importance of the division of labor for any and all production arrangements, they are first seriously introduced in terms of particular capitals rather than capital in general; in terms of relative surplus value as opposed to absolute surplus value; in terms of turnover time rather than production time; and in the context of use value (e.g., transportation) rather than that of value or exchange value.[27] In general, as Marx moves from the analysis of capital in general through the analysis of the different circuits of capital towards his (never completed) analysis of the overall movement of capital within the framework of the world market, he pays increasing attention to the complex articulation of concrete time and place with the more fundamental dynamic of socially necessary labor time in the form of both absolute and relative surplus value (for a brief summary of some basic dimensions of this in the three published books of *Capital*, see table 2).

Turning to ontological aspects of the capital relation, the time of abstract (or general) labor central to exchange value exists only in and through concrete, particular labors performed in specific times and places. In other words, value as a measure of abstract time is indissolubly linked to activities that occur in concrete times and places and, indeed, actually depends on current rather than historical levels of productivity—a criterion that is often linked to uneven development and the displacement of the cutting-edge centers of innovation and productivity. This said, as Wilson also notes,

---

26. Karl Marx, *Theories of Surplus Value*, vol. 3 (London: Lawrence and Wishart, 1971), 253.
27. Yves de la Haye, *Marx and Engels on the Means of Communication (the Movement of Commodities, People, Information, and Capital)* (New York: International General, 1988). On the division of labor, see Marx and Engels, *German Ideology*.

Table 2. Marx's *Capital*, time, and space

Vol.	Successive concepts of capital	How time enters the analysis	How space enters the analysis	Premature closure of analysis of this concept of capital
1	Class relations involved in the appropriation of surplus value.	Linear production time: class struggle over necessary and surplus labor time, including absolute and relative surplus value.	Extension of so-called primitive accumulation to noncapitalist social formations. First remarks on unequal exchange.	Based on a quasi-embodied labor theory of value, not on an abstract social labor theory of value. Thus, the worker becomes exploited object, not an active subject.
2	Value in motion (unity of circuits of productive, commodity, and money capital).	Syllogisms of time: metamorphoses and circulation of capital.	International mobility of money and commodities.	Continuity of circuit of capital is emphasized at the expense of possible ruptures.
3	Transformation of values into prices: value as the price of production. Nature of profit and its division and distribution among fractions of capital.	Expanded reproduction as a whole. Living time of conflicts and crises is rooted in capitalist competition and in transformation of surplus value into profit.	Internationalized prices of production. World market audits economic practices through global competition.	Eruptions in circuit of capital are introduced in an ad hoc manner, as digressions, so that no unified theory of crisis is presented.

Sources:

Column 2: Daniel Bensaïd, *Marx for Our Times: Adventures and Misadventures of a Critique*, trans. Gregory Elliott (London: Verso, 2002).

Column 3: Dick Bryan, "The Internationalisation of Capital and Marxian Value Theory," *Cambridge Journal of Economics* 19, no. 3 (1995): 421–42.

Column 4: Felton C. Shortall, *The Incomplete Marx* (Aldershot: Avebury, 1994).

"exchange values tend to prioritize time over space while use-values tend to prioritize space over time."[28] Interestingly, even this contrast is transcended through the money form itself because the circulation of commodities overcomes the temporal, spatial, and personal barriers that are associated with direct exchange of products.[29] This is reflected in the contrast between the mobility of abstract money capital in a space of flows and the consumption of specific use values in specific times and places. Yet even this prioritization is only ever tendential and relative, for "in every instance when we accentuate space or time, the other aspect is still present, although hidden."[30] Harvey echoes this point in citing Rescher's view that "space and time are 'mutually coordinate in such a way that neither is more fundamental than the other.'"[31] There are also "contradictory movements in which time is simultaneously compressed and expanded, depending on which part of the system one examines, so that the general progression is uneven and punctuated by more or less significant reverses."[32] This suggests the need to make a thematic and methodological *temporal* (re)turn to redress one-sided concern with space in globalization studies. Interestingly, just such a temporal (re)turn is found in a growing recognition of the need to bring time (back) into the analysis of globalization among those who had previously privileged the spatial.[33] This prompted Harvey, the leading postwar Anglophone theorist of capital's spatiality, to argue that "[u]nder capitalism . . . the meaning of space and the impulse to create new spatial configurations of human affairs can be understood only in relation to such temporal requirements."[34]

Some Spatiotemporal Contradictions of Globalizing Capitalism

I now explore five spatiotemporal contradictions in contemporary capitalism. These are not contradictions of globalization as such; my approach to

28. Wilson, "Time, Space, and Value: Recovering the Public Sphere," *Time and Society* 8, no. 1 (1999): 162.

29. Postone, *Time, Labour*, 264.

30. Barbara Czarniawska and Bernward Joerges, "Travels of Ideas," in *Translating Organizational Change*, ed. Barbara Czarniawska and Guje Sevón (New York: Walter de Gruyter, 1996), 21.

31. Harvey, *Justice*, 252.

32. Erica J. Schoenberger, *The Cultural Crisis of the Firm* (Oxford: Blackwell, 1997), 19.

33. For a discussion of three representative cases, see Jessop, "Time and Space in the Globalization of Capital and Their Implications for State Power," *Rethinking Modernism* 14, no. 1 (2002): 97–117.

34. David Harvey, *The Condition of Postmodernity* (Oxford: Blackwell, 1989), 37.

the latter rules this out. But they become more severe with the increasing complexity and flexibility in the circuits of capital associated with economic globalization. For its multicentric, multiscalar, multitemporal, multiform, and multicausal character enhances capital's capacity to defer and displace its internal contradictions, if not to resolve them, by increasing the scope of its operations on a global scale, reinforcing its capacities to disembed certain of its operations from local material, social, and spatiotemporal constraints, enabling it to deepen the spatial and scalar divisions of labor, creating more opportunities for moving up, down, and across scales, commodifying and securitizing the future, deferring past and present material problems into the future, promoting long-term technology forecasting, organizational learning, and trust building, and rearticulating time horizons.

These enhanced capacities reinforce tendencies to uneven development as the search continues for new spatiotemporal fixes and new ways of displacing and deferring contradictions and conflicts.[35] Above all, globalization helps to emancipate the exchange-value moment of capital from extraeconomic and spatiotemporal frictions and constraints, increases the emphasis on speed, acceleration, and turnover time, and enhances capital's capacity to escape the control of other systems insofar as these are still territorially differentiated and fragmented.[36] This is linked to its increased capacity for discounting events (so collapsing the future into the present), its increased capacity for time-space compression, its resort to complex derivative trading to manage risk, and its capacities to jump scale. In addition, economic globalization weakens the capacity of national states to guide capital's expansion within a framework of national security (as reflected in the "national security state"), national welfare (as reflected in social democratic welfare states), or some other national project with a corresponding spatiotemporal fix. Conversely, it increases pressures on national states to adjust to the time horizons and temporalities of mobile capital able to operate beyond their frontiers. Thus, just as the formation and consolidation of the world market enables the full realization of the logic (or illogic) of capital accumulation, it also concentrates and intensifies the expression of its contradictions. As Marx notes: "By Free Trade all economic laws, with their most astounding contradictions, will act upon a larger scale, upon a greater extent of

35. For a discussion of spatiotemporal fixes, see Bob Jessop, *The Future of the Capitalist State* (Cambridge: Polity, 2002).

36. Conversely, the growth of global legal and political systems and other international regimes means that mobile capital will remain subject to their constraints.

territory, upon the territory of the whole earth . . . uniting of all these contradictions into a single group."[37]

A globalizing capitalism typically intensifies the spatiotemporal contradictions and tensions inherent in the capital relation and/or in the articulation and coevolution of that relation with the more general spatialities and temporalities of the natural and social world. The increasing emphasis on speed and the growing acceleration of social life have many disruptive and disorienting effects on modern societies.[38] Here I want to note five tensions they introduce into the globalizing economy: the first is ecological, the second is existential, the third concerns the relation between the economic and extraeconomic moments of capital appropriate the local bounties of first and second nature without regard to their long-term reproduction and move on whenever it becomes expedient to do so. Indeed, the growing emphasis on artificial short-term profit means that, "as capital speeds up, it diminishes or degrades the conditions of the natural reproduction of natural things."[39]

Second, there is a tension among the many and varied substantive temporalities of human existence (biological, sentient, sociocultural, self-reflexive) and the abstract time inherent in the commodification of labor power and the dominance of formal market rationality.[40] This is reflected in the stresses of everyday life and in a growing sense of time-space compression.[41]

Third, contemporary capitalism involves a paradox that "the most advanced economies function more and more in terms of the extra-economic."[42] This rests on the increasing interdependence between the economic and extraeconomic factors making for structural competitiveness. This is linked to the growth of new technologies based on more complex transnational, national, and regional systems of innovation, to the paradigm shift from

---

37. Friedrich Engels, "The Free Trade Congress at Brussels," in *Karl Marx, Friedrich Engels: Collected Works*, vol. 6 (London: Lawrence and Wishart, 1976), 290.

38. See chapter 11 of this volume and, more generally, Paul Virilio, *Speed and Politics: An Essay on Dromology*, trans. Mark Polizzotti (New York: Semiotext(e), 1986); and Paul Virilio, *The Virilio Reader*, ed. James der Derian (Oxford: Blackwell, 1998). See also John Armitage and Phil Graham, "Dromoeconomics: Towards a Political Economy of Speed," *Parallax* 7, no. 1 (2001): 111–23.

39. Teresa Brennan, "Why the Time Is Out of Joint: Marx's Political Economy Without the Subject," *Strategies*, nos. 9–10 (1995): 31.

40. A. W. Stahel, "Time Contradictions of Capitalism," *Capitalism, Nature, Socialism* 10, no. 1 (1999): 108. See Karl Polanyi, *The Great Transformation: The Political and Economic Origins of Our Time* (New York: Farrar and Rinehart, 1944).

41. Thomas H. Eriksen, *Tyranny of the Moment: Fast and Slow Time in the Information Age* (London: Pluto Press, 2001).

42. Pierre Veltz, *Mondialisation, villes et territoires: L'économie d'archipel* (Paris Presses universitaires de France, 1996), 12.

Fordism with its emphasis on productivity growth rooted in economies of scale to post-Fordism with its emphasis on mobilizing social as well as economic sources of flexibility and entrepreneurialism, and to the more general attempts to penetrate microsocial relations in the interests of valorization. It is reflected in the emphasis now given to social capital, trust, and communities of learning as well as to the competitive role of entrepreneurial cities, enterprise culture, and enterprising subjects. This paradox generates major contradictions in both temporal and spatial terms. Thus, temporally, short-term economic calculation (especially in financial flows) comes into increasing conflict with the long-term dynamic of "real competition." For the latter is rooted in resources (skills, trust, heightened reflexivity, collective mastery of techniques, economies of agglomeration and size, cluster effects) that may take years to create, stabilize, and reproduce. Likewise, spatially, there is a basic contradiction between the economy seen as a deterritorialized, socially disembedded space of flows and as a territorially rooted, socially embedded system of extraeconomic as well as economic resources, competencies, and activities.[43] The latter moment is reflected in wide range of emerging concepts to describe the knowledge-based economy—national, regional, and local systems of innovation, innovative milieus, systemic or structural competitiveness, learning regions, social capital, trust, learning-by-doing, speed-based competition, and so on.

Fourth, temporally, there is a tension between the drive to accelerate the circulation of capital by shortening the production cycle between design and final consumption and the long-term infrastructural development on which this depends. Harvey is especially incisive here. He notes that "it takes a specific organization of space to try and annihilate space and it takes capital of long turnover time to facilitate the more rapid turnover of the rest. But the reduction of spatial barriers has an equally powerful opposite effect; small-scale and finely graded differences between the qualities of places (their labor supply, their infrastructures, and political receptivity, their resource mixes, their market niches, etc.) become even more important because multinational capital is better able to exploit them."[44] This set of contradictions is aggravated by the increasing capacity for temporal compression permitted by the latest developments in information and communication technologies. In general, the scope that time-space compression opens for disjunction between the short-term interests of hypermobile capital and the interests

---

43. Michael Storper, "Territories, Flows, and Hierarchies in the Global Economy," in Cox, *Spaces of Globalization*, 19–44.
44. Harvey, *Justice*, 246–47.

of other social agents often causes distress to other fractions of capital and also puts pressure on inherited state forms and less mobile social forces.

Fifth, spatially, there is a tension between extending the scope of markets through the annihilation of space by time and the need for fixed infrastructure to enable rapid movement through space (which must be destroyed in turn as the next round of accumulation develops).[45] This contradiction may be aggravated by the expansion of production through mechanization and scale economies. Because this requires larger markets, it extends the time of commodity circulation and may also extend the overall turnover time due to the higher proportion of fixed to total capital. It can also lead to a dialectic of spatial concentration (agglomeration economies) and dispersal (congestion, land prices, unionization, etc.).[46]

There are spiral processes at work in the last two contradictions that tend to increase the spatiotemporal complexities of regularizing and governing capital accumulation. "Every local decentralization presupposes a renewed form of centralization at a higher level. Every temporal flexibilization requires, with increasing complexity, new mechanisms in order to hold the seemingly loosening temporal connections together. Flexibility becomes possible against the background of a previously unattained degree of constant temporal availability, as the prerequisite and consequence of which it functions."[47] There are also oscillations in the relative importance of time and space. Thus, whereas mass production compressed time in production, it extended it in product life cycles to valorize dedicated fixed capital and allow for the unmanageability of time required for product development. Now the situation is reversed. The current emphasis is on speeding up product development times and order-to-delivery cycle. This also involves maximum flexibility in organization of production, economies of scope, and so on.[48]

The Implications of Globalization for (National) States

Much has been written on the competing claims that globalization undermines the national state and that the latter has a key role in sustaining globalization. Such writings have been plagued by false oppositions and

45. Harvey, "Globalization," 6.

46. Schoenberger, *Cultural Crisis,* 19–21.

47. Helga Nowotny, *Time: The Modern and Postmodern Experience,* trans. Neville Plaice (Cambridge: Polity Press, 1994), 99.

48. Schoenberger, *Cultural Crisis,* 45.

assumptions. One such opposition is that between the state as a "power container" that operates exclusively within defined territorial frontiers and the economy as a borderless exchange mechanism with no important territorial anchoring. This opposition illustrates four common errors. First, there is no reason to assume the fixity of its frontiers or temporal horizons, for states (and the social forces they represent) are actively involved in constituting and reconstituting the spatiotemporal matrices that organize politics, including its interstate and international moments.[49] Second, as form-determined condensations of a changing balance of social forces, state apparatuses and state power reflect the manifold processes involved in globalization. Thus, the state apparatus may interiorize the interests of foreign capital as well as project the interests of national capital abroad.[50] Third, the economy should not be reduced to a market-mediated space of flows operating in timeless time: markets also operate in accordance with other spatiotemporalities, and the economy more generally involves various non-market governance mechanisms with yet other spatiotemporal dynamics. Therefore, the regularization and governance of globalization is bound to involve many different scales and temporal horizons. And fourth, the specificity of many economic assets and their embedding in extraeconomic institutions mean that much economic activity remains place- and time-bound.[51] Combining these objections, one could conclude that the state operates as a *power connector,* that is, as a nodal or network state within a broader political system,[52] as well as a *power container;* and, likewise, that the economy has important territorial dimensions (reflected in concepts such as industrial districts, agglomeration economies, global cities, and regional or national capitalisms). Thus we should focus on the changing organization of politics and economics and their respective institutional embodiments and see frontiers and borders as actively reproduced and contingent rather than as pregiven and fixed.

Another false opposition involves treating the state as a political force and globalization as an economic process with the corollary that they have

49. David Gross, "Temporality and the Modern State," *Theory and Society* 14, no. 1 (1985): 53–81; Nicos Poulantzas, *State, Power, Socialism,* trans. Patrick Camiller (London: NLB, 1978).

50. Poulantzas, *Classes in Contemporary Capitalism,* trans. David Fernbach (London: NLB, 1975); Poulantzas, *State, Power, Socialism.*

51. Storper, "Territories, Flows"; Michael Storper and Allen J. Scott, "The Wealth of Regions: Market Forces and Policy Imperatives in Local and Global Context," *Futures* 27, no. 5 (1995): 505–26; Polanyi, *Great Transformation.*

52. Steven Brunn, "A Treaty of Silicon for the Treaty of Westphalia? New Territorial Dimensions of Modern Statehood," in *Boundaries, Territory, and Postmodernity,* ed. David Newman (London: Frank Cass, 1999), 114.

a zero-sum relationship. This ignores how states help to constitute the economy as an object of regulation and how far economic globalization continues to depend on politics, for the capital relation is constitutively incomplete and needs extraeconomic supplementation if the inherently improbable process of accumulation is to continue.[53] States are heavily involved in this supplementation both directly and through their modulation of other extraeconomic modes of regulation, and their equally improbable capacity to achieve this depends in part on revenues and resources derived from the accumulation process. In short, state-economy relations inevitably involve reciprocal interdependence, prompt attempts at strategic coordination, and produce structural coupling. They cannot be understood in zero-sum terms. Attempts to do so also ignore the complexities of globalization. Not only are many states actively involved in constituting the conditions for globalization, which is multiform and hence contested, but globalization is also linked to processes on other scales, such as regionalization, triadization, international localization, and cross-borderization, and states engage in promoting/resisting these processes too. Finally, zero-sum analyses ignore the extent to which the unfolding economic logic (and illogic) of globalization can constrain firms as well as political actors.[54]

This leads us to a third area of conceptual confusion: the claim that globalization puts pressure on the sovereign state. This is misleading for four reasons. First, sovereignty is only one aspect of the form of the modern state. As a specific juridicopolitical form, sovereignty certainly organizes key features of state power; but it is struggles over state power(s) that are ultimately primary, not the particular forms in which it is (they are) exercised. Forms of sovereignty have been reorganized in the past, and a postsovereign international system is imaginable. Second, it is not the state as such (sovereign or otherwise) that is pressured by globalization. The processes that generate globalization can only put pressure on particular forms of state with particular state capacities and liabilities, such as the Keynesian welfare national state in Atlantic Fordism or the Listian workfare national state in East Asian exportism.[55] In so doing, it also modifies the balance of forces

53. Jessop, *Future of the Capitalist State*.

54. Bob Jessop, "Reflections on the (Il)logics of Globalization," in *Globalisation and the Asia Pacific: Contested Territories*, ed. Kris Olds, Peter Dicken, Philip F. Kelly, Lily Kong, and Henry Wai-chung Yeung (London: Routledge, 1999), 19–38.

55. On Listian workfare national states and East Asian exportism, see ibid.; and Ngai-Ling Sum, "Theorizing the Development of East Asian Newly-Industrializing Countries: A Regulationist Perspective," in *Dynamic Asia*, ed. Ian Cook, Marcus A. Doel, Rex Y. F. Li, and Yongjiang Wang (Aldershot: Ashgate, 1998), 44–78.

within states, for any differential loss of capacities will favor some fractions, classes, and social forces over others; it also creates space for, and prompts, struggles to reorganize state forms and capacities. Important aspects of such pressures are the acceleration of economic decision making and temporal compression of significant economic events relative to the time required for considered political decision making. This weakens what one might call the "time sovereignty" of the state in its current form.[56] Third, since globalization is not a single causal mechanism with a universal, unitary logic but is multicentric, multiscalar, multitemporal, and multiform, it does not generate a single, uniform set of pressures. All states and state capacities will be pressured by globalization, but each will be affected in different ways. Indeed, while some states actively promote globalization, others can be seen as its victims. Thus, even if one agreed that globalization mainly means Americanization, the "Great Satan" would still experience pressures emanating from other centers and forms of globalization as well as from the internal impact of its own neoliberal form and the resistance it inevitably generates at home and abroad. Similar arguments hold for the differential impact of the multiscalar nature of globalization, with states being differentially involved in various scalar projects and processes; and about that of its multitemporal nature, with some states more actively involved in and/or more vulnerable to time-space distantiation and compression. And fourth, we should note that some aspects of globalization might actually enhance rather than diminish state capacities.

Having clarified possible misconceptions, we can now consider how (national) states are involved in, and affected by, globalization.[57] In broad terms, states are actively engaged in redrawing the spatiotemporal matrices within which capital operates. In doing so, they are trying to manage the tension between potentially mobile capital's interests in reducing its place dependency and/or liberating itself from temporal constraints, on the one hand, and, on the other hand, their own interest in fixing (allegedly beneficial)[58] capital within their own territories and rendering capital's temporal horizons and rhythms compatible with their statal and/or political routines, temporalities, and crisis tendencies. For, as globalization increases, national

56. See William E. Scheuerman, *Liberal Democracy and the Social Acceleration of Time* (Baltimore: Johns Hopkins University Press, 2004).

57. This is a complex topic, and I have discussed other aspects in other places: see Jessop, "Reflections"; and Jessop, *Future of the Capitalist State*.

58. Excluded here, for example, might be heavily polluting industries that may be encouraged to relocate—with their products being imported—rather than to undertake expensive environmental protection measures.

states in the advanced capitalist economies can no longer presume, as they did in the heyday of Atlantic Fordism, that their primary economic task is to govern a relatively closed national economy—instead they are increasingly involved in managing a range of transnational processes and creating the spatial and temporal fixes appropriate thereto. Particularly important here is the changing relationship between the economic and the extraeconomic factors bearing on competitiveness and state roles in redefining the boundaries between the economic and extraeconomic and/or reorganizing the latter and subordinating them to the perceived demands and pressures of globalization. Thus, to take a paradoxical example, even as neoliberal states seem to disengage from the market economy, they intervene more in the extraeconomic field and subordinate it to the demands of valorization.[59]

More generally, the activities of capitalist states, almost regardless of their specific form and projects, have been reshaping the spatiotemporal matrices of globalization. Their roles here reflect the balance of internal and external forces, with some states being more willing and active participants in these processes than others. Nonetheless, among many relevant activities, we can mention deregulating, liberalizing, and shaping the institutional architecture of finance, facilitating thereby its accelerating internationalization and its global acceleration;[60] modifying institutional frameworks for international trade and foreign direct investment; planning and subsidizing the spatial fixes that support the activities of financial, industrial, and commercial capital within and across borders; promoting uneven development through policies for interurban and interregional as well as international competition; cooperating in the rebordering and rescaling of state functions, including decentralization and cross-border region formation, regional bloc formation, and participation in forums for intertriad negotiation; destatizing current state functions by transferring them to private-public partnerships or place-bound market forces and thereby linking them to market-oriented temporalities;[61] deterritorializing some state functions by transferring them to private forms of functional authority (including international regimes) and/or to mobile market forces; attempting, conversely, to fit some nonterritorial problems into an areal structure (e.g., making national states responsible for enforcing international agreements on

59. See Jessop, *Future of the Capitalist State*.

60. Relevant measures range from creating and protecting its offshore bases to bailing out bad loans.

61. For an interesting example of the temporal implications of privatization on social security and pension funds, see Javier Santiso, "Political Sluggishness and Economic Speed: A Latin American Perspective," *Social Science Information* 39, no. 2 (2000): 233–53.

global warming); and, finally, addressing the multiformity of globalization processes by engaging in the struggle to define the rules for harmonizing or standardizing a wide range of technological, economic, juridicopolitical, sociocultural, and environmental issues.

More specifically, given the multicentric and multiform nature of globalization, some states are committed to promoting their own national or regional capitalisms and the appropriate conditions for the expanded reproduction of these forms of capitalism on a global scale. The neoliberal project has, of course, been the model most successfully promoted politically and ideologically in the past two decades (its material effects are another matter). But it has not gone uncontested; the European model in particular may be regaining ground, and the BRICS (Brazil, Russia, India, China, and South Africa) economies are reviving interest in different forms of developmental states. States are also establishing new scales of activity (and dismantling others) and thereby rescaling and rearticulating various state powers, institutional forms, and regulatory capacities and creating the possibility for themselves and other actors to "jump scales" in response to specific problems. They are promoting the space of flows by organizing conditions favorable to the international mobility of technologies, industrial and commercial capital, intellectual property, and at least some types of labor power. And, conversely, they are engaged in complementary forms of *Standortpolitik* and other forms of place-based competition in the attempt to fix mobile capital in their own economic spaces and to enhance the interurban, interregional, or international competitiveness of their own place-bound capitals.

The Temporal Sovereignty of the State

An important source of pressure on states comes from the growing complexity of the political economy of time and its implications for politics as the "art of the possible." States increasingly face temporal pressures in their policy making and implementation due to new forms of time-space distantiation, compression, and differentiation, for, as the temporalities of the economy accelerate relative to those of the state, the time to determine and coordinate political responses to economic events shrinks—especially in relation to superfast and/or hypermobile capital. This reinforces conflicts between the time(s) of the state and the time(s) of the market. One solution to the state's loss of time sovereignty is laissez-faire. This approach reinforces the temporality of deregulated exchange value, however, which becomes problematic when market forces provoke economic crises and states are expected to respond. Two other options are for states to try to compress their own decision-making cycles so that they can make more timely and appropriate interventions and to attempt to decelerate the activities of "fast capitalism" to match existing political routines.

A strategy of temporal compression increases pressures to make decisions on the basis of factors such as unreliable information, insufficient consultation, and lack of participation, even as state managers believe that policy is still taking too long to negotiate, formulate, enact, adjudicate, determine, and implement. The commitment to "fast policy" is reflected in the shortening of policy development cycles, fast-tracking of decision making, rapid program rollout, continuing policy experimentation, institutional and policy Darwinism, and relentless revision of guidelines and benchmarks. Scheuerman has summarized some of these trends in the general claim that there has been a shift to "economic states of emergency" characterized by executive dominance and constant legal change and dynamism.[62] This privileges those who can operate within compressed time scales, narrows the range of participants in the policy process, and limits the scope for deliberation, consultation, and negotiation. This can significantly affect the choice of policies, the initial targets of policy, the sites where policy is implemented, and the criteria adopted to demonstrate success. For example, as Wilson notes, an emphasis on rapid policy formulation and neglect of implementation serves the interests of efficiency criteria and productivity at the expense of concern with effectiveness and thereby reinforces instrumental rationality and exchange value over deliberation and use value.[63] An emphasis on speed also affects whether any lessons learned are relevant to other targets, sites, or criteria; and it discourages proper evaluation of a policy's impact over different spatiotemporal horizons, including delayed and/or unintended consequences and feedback effects. In such situations, "spin" trumps substance and modifies the nature of politics and policy making. It may also help to accelerate policy making and implementation cycles so that different approaches are tried in rapid succession as each is seen to fail. One symptom of this is the shortening half-life of legislation and other policies.[64] And it produces the dilemma that unchanged policies

62. William E. Scheuerman, "The Economic State of Emergency," *Cardozo Law Review* 21 (2000): 1890.
63. Wilson, "Time, Space, and Value," 175.
64. William E. Scheuerman, "Reflexive Law and the Challenges of Globalization," *Journal of Political Philosophy* 9, no. 1 (2001): 91–92.

become irrelevant or even counterproductive while constant changes in policies risk being seen as opportunistic or illegitimate.[65]

Even if fast policy appears irrational from a purely policy-making perspective, it may still be rational for some interests in politics- or polity-making terms. Fast policy is antagonistic to corporatism, stakeholding, the rule of law, formal bureaucracy, and, indeed, to the routines and cycles of democratic politics more generally. It privileges the executive over the legislature and the judiciary, finance over industrial capital, consumption over long-term investment. In general, resort to fast policy undermines the power of decision makers who have long decision-taking cycles, because in having to adapt to the speed of fast thinkers and fast policy makers they lose the capacity to make decisions in terms of their own routines and procedures. It also tends to destroy institutional memory, on the grounds that new circumstances require new approaches, and to block efforts to anticipate future difficulties and policy failures. Hence the present is extended at the expense of both past and future, and politics is lived in the mediatized world of spin and presentation, the quick fix, rapid churning of policies, and plebiscitarian democracy.[66]

An alternative strategy is not to compress absolute political time but to create relative political time by slowing the circuits of capital. Perhaps the most celebrated, if not yet implemented, example of this strategy is the Tobin tax, which would decelerate the flow of superfast and hypermobile financial capital and limit its distorting impact on the real economy.[67] Other examples include an energy tax on fossil fuels and nuclear power, consistent introduction of the polluter-pays principle on a global scale, resort to a worldwide prudential principle in the introduction of new technologies, inclusion of recycling and disposal costs in pricing goods, and the shift

65. On the case of law, for example, see Boaventura de Sousa Santos, "The Postmodern Transition: Law and Politics," in *The Fate of Law*, ed. Austin Sarat and Thomas R. Kearns (Ann Arbor: University of Michigan Press, 1991), 79–118.

66. Cf. Jean Chesneaux, "Speed and Democracy: An Uneasy Dialogue," *Social Science Information* 39, no. 3 (2000): 407–20; Andries Hoogerwerf, "Policy and Time: Consequences of Time Perspectives for the Contents, Processes, and Effects of Public Policies," *International Review of Administrative Sciences* 56, no. 4 (1990): 671–92; Javier Santiso and Andreas Schedler, "Democracy and Time: An Invitation," *International Political Science Review* 19, no. 1 (1998): 5–18. For a possible counterargument that simplistic, short-term, populist "spin" by a charismatic leader is a useful complement to—or front for—more complex, medium- to long-term, behind-the-scenes, lobbying, negotiation, and policy-making, see Edgar Grande, "Charisma und Komplexität: Verhandlungsdemokratie, Mediendemokratie und der Funktionswandel politischer Eliten," *Leviathan* 28, no. 1 (2000): 122–41.

67. Bruno Jetin and Suzanne de Brunhoff, "The Tobin Tax and the Regulation of Capital Movements," in *Global Finance: New Thinking on Regulating Speculative Capital Markets*, ed. Walden Bello, Nicola Bullard, and Kamal Malhotra (London: Zed Books, 2000), 195–214.

toward "slow food" and other forms of deceleration.[68] These could tilt the balance away from globalization in favor of regional and local economies, slow the rate of environmental destruction, and allow proper evaluation of the likely consequences of technological innovation. This could be supplemented by a fourth political time-management option, to establish the institutional framework for subsiditarian guided self-regulation on various scales as well as for continuous monitoring of how well such self-regulation is operating in the light of agreed criteria.[69] This strategy of reflexive metagovernance would enable the state to retain the capacity to coordinate activities across different time zones and temporalities without the risk of overload.[70]

More generally, on the temporal front, states are getting involved in promoting new temporal horizons of action and new forms of temporal flexibility, in coping with the increased salience of multiple time zones (in commerce, diplomacy, security, etc.), in recalibrating and managing the intersection of temporalities (e.g., regulating computer-programmed trading, promoting the twenty-four-hour city as center of consumption, managing environmental risk), and socializing long-term conditions of production as short-term calculation becomes more important for marketized economic activities. Of particular importance is the restructuring of welfare regimes to promote flexible economic and social adjustment and socialize its costs as economies become more vulnerable to the cyclical fluctuations and other vagaries of the world market.[71] Such a welfare orientation was always a feature of small open economies but is now becoming more general, for, "the more the welfare state is able to guarantee security and a 'future' beyond the market place, the more political space there is to relax closure vis-à-vis world markets."[72] More generally, in the spirit of Marx's analysis of time, wealth should be regarded as free time, not as the accumulation of the products of labor time. In this context a postcapitalist order would be oriented to maximizing free time and production would be subordinated to needs, among which unbound time would be central.[73]

68. Elmar Altvater and Birgit Mahnkopf, *Grenzen der Globalisierung: Ökonomie, Ökologie und Politik in der Weltgesellschaft*, 7th ed. (Münster: Westfälisches Dampfboot, 2007); Wendy Parkins, "Out of Time: Fast Subjects and Slow Living," *Time and Society* 13, nos. 2–3 (2004): 363–82; Carl Honoré, *In Praise of Slow: How a Worldwide Movement Is Challenging the Cult of Speed* (London: Orion, 2004).

69. Scheuerman, "Reflexive Law."

70. Hoogerwerf, "Policy and Time."

71. Jessop, *Future of the Capitalist State*.

72. Elmar Rieger and Stephan Leibfried, "Welfare State Limits to Globalization," *Politics and Society* 26, no. 3 (1998): 368.

73. Booth, "Economies of Time," 19.

Conclusions

The national territorial state has long played a key role in establishing and regulating the relation between the spatial and the temporal matrices of social
life.[74] This remains true in a period of globalization, but the forms of this
engagement have been changing. States are modifying the spatiotemporal
matrices of capitalism and the nation, and they have significant roles in managing uneven spatiotemporal development generated by the capital relation.
In key respects the processes that produce globalization have undermined the
effectiveness of national states as they developed during the postwar period.
In particular, some of the distinctive powers and capacities they developed as
Keynesian welfare national states have become less relevant to the new spatiotemporal matrices associated with globalization; wages are increasingly
regarded as a cost of production rather than a source of demand, and it is
harder to control the circulation of money as national money with the deregulation of international currency markets; and forms of competition and the
state have become much more critical sites of contradictions and dilemmas
in a globalizing, knowledge-based economy.[75] Nonetheless, a restructured
national state remains central to the effective management of the emerging
spatiotemporal matrices of capitalism and the emerging forms of post- or
transnational citizenship to be seen in multiethnic, multicultural, melting
pot, tribal, cosmopolitan, "playful" postmodern, and other identities. National
states have become even more important arbiters of the movement of state
powers upwards, downwards, and sideways; they have become even more
important metagovernors of the increasingly complex multicentric, multiscalar, multitemporal, and multiform world of governance; and they are
actively involved in shaping the forms of international policy regimes. They
are also responding to the crisis in traditional forms and bases of national citizenship. Their activities in these respects have far less to do with globalization in the strongest sense of this polyvalent, promiscuous, and controversial word (i.e., the emergence of a borderless planetary economy—an entity
widely and rightly regarded as mythical) than they do with the more general
spatiotemporal restructuring of contemporary capitalism. This is why I have
focused above on the complex spatiotemporal logics of globalization and their
implications for state power. In doing so I hope to have contributed in some
small measure to demystifying globalization and suggesting how its associated spatiotemporal transformations can be modified and controlled.

74. Poulantzas, *State, Power, Socialism*, 114.
75. Jessop, *Future of the Capitalist State*.

NINE

THE CONTRACTION OF THE PRESENT

Hermann Lübbe

The quantity of innovations per unit of time in some cultural domains, especially research and development, production, and organization, continues to increase constantly. This compression of innovation has a temporal consequence for contemporary culture that has long since become unmistakable: it makes the present contract.[1]

The contraction of the present—this distinguishing feature of the condition that I want to analyze here—is quite unusual and therefore requires explanation. What does it mean? It means that in a dynamic civilization, in proportion to increases in the number of innovations per unit of time, the number of years decreases over which we can look back without seeing a world alien to our trusted present-day lifeworld as well as outdated in significant experiental respects. The world we see instead represents a past that has become strange, even incomprehensible, to us.

Moreover, the innovation-dependent contraction of the present implies that in accordance with the shortening of the chronological distance to a past that has become alien, the number of future years for which we can infer the likely conditions of life decreases. Beyond these years, the future can no longer be compared in its essential respects to our present living conditions.

In short, the contraction of the present entails a process whereby the space of time for which we can calculate our living conditions with a degree of constancy is shortened. Reinhart Koselleck has described the consequence of this for the perception of historical time: the space of experience

---

1. The comprehensive cultural-theoretical context of this essay is set out in my *Im Zug der Zeit: Verkürzter Aufenthalt in der Gegenwart* (Berlin: Springer, 1992).

and the horizon of the future become incongruous.[2] With the transformation of our living conditions, our experiences and those of our fathers, which drew on the bases of prior life conditions, become progressively less qualified as a basis for the judgments that we, our children, or our children's children will have to make.

Let me try to elucidate the concept of a contraction of the present deriving from the compression of innovation by contrasting it with an experience of historical time having a much more expansive present. As late as the time of Machiavelli's interest in Roman history, as passed down to him by Livy, the predominant interest in past circumstances and events served as models for present judgments. They even seemed to offer a suitable basis for deriving abstract norms capable of guiding present action. Events in Roman military or political history functioned as examples for rules of action and strategy; their validity outside the period in question seemed to be indifferent to time. In temporal terms, this meant that the present—a space of time marked by a certain constancy of important elements of cultural life—extended over one and a half thousand years. The temporal space of experience stretched very far, and the horizon of the future corresponded to it in expanse and content.

In stark contrast, at least from the standpoint of strategic action dependent on the developmental dynamics of weapons technology, the present has contracted in chronological terms to an extreme degree. The applicability even of the most recent wars as models for strategic contingencies is sharply limited under present technological conditions. In correspondence with this shift, the teaching of military history no longer has as its primary purpose the presentation of still-valid models from the past. This raises a key question: what purpose, then, can the teaching of military history now have at all?

Whether Machiavelli's failure to acknowledge the existence of significant cultural evolution between the beginning of recorded time and his own present was because he was predominantly interested in learning from Roman history, or because he was simply not interested in that evolution, cannot be decided here. There have certainly been forms of cultural-historical evolution whose dynamics have been so negligible that it is absurd to posit that they could have been perceived as evolution. Of course, even the extended periods of primeval or early history were not lacking in innovation.

---

2. Reinhart Koselleck, *Futures Past: On the Semantics of Historical Time* (Cambridge, Mass.: MIT Press, 1985).

But the measures of time in these historical epochs had, as Karl J. Narr has impressively shown in a highly pertinent discussion,[3] a "subgeological" dimension. In the simplest terms, this means that the extraordinary progress of grinding techniques in producing sharper stone axes between the Neo-Paleolithic and the Neolithic periods could certainly not have been an object of significant attention for the subjects of this process.

It would be entirely speculative to conjecture how great the compression of innovation in cultural evolution must have become before it became obtrusive enough to compel its thematization. In any case, it must have reached a degree that sufficed to make the experience of being out of date or obsolete important enough to the life practices of three generations living at the same time and bound together by cultural unity in their immediate experiences. Experiences of the contraction of the present involve what only appears as a paradoxical effect of the temporal compression of innovation. The effect I have in mind here is that as the rate of innovation increases, so too does the pace of obsolescence. The cultural consequences of this progress-dependent increase in the speed of cultural obsolescence are considerable. In a dynamic civilization, the quantity of civilizational elements that are still contemporary, but already on the verge of being out of date or antiquated, increases. Put differently, the noncontemporaneity of the contemporary increases in a dynamic civilization. This noncontemporaneity of the contemporary was a subject of Friedrich Nietzsche's cultural-theoretical analyses more than a hundred years ago. But Friedrich Schlegel had already noticed and described it before Nietzsche.

Expressed in terms of evolutionary theory, this means that the evolutionary dynamic generates a corresponding increase in the quantity of relics. This is not a sufficient but is certainly a necessary condition for the likewise only apparently paradoxical trend that alongside the dynamic character of our culture, its degree of "museumification" also grows. Complementing its dynamism, the museumification of our civilization has progressively developed.

What, then, are museums?[4] Seen from this perspective, museums are nothing other than mortuaries for civilizational relics. Every curator knows that in our flourishing technical museums,[5] for example, the spans of time

---

3. See Karl J. Narr, *Zeitmaße in der Urgeschichte* (Opladen: Westdeutscher, 1978).
4. On the philosophy of museums, see Kenneth Hudson, *Museums for the 1980s: A Survey of World Trends* (Paris: UNESCO; London: Macmillan, 1977).
5. On their history, see Friedrich Klemm, *Geschichte der naturwissenschaftlichen und technischen Museen* (Munich: Oldenbourg, 1973).

in which new sections of the museum are due to open also shorten in accordance with the temporal compression of technological innovation.

Let me reiterate my view that the contraction of the present as outlined here, which complements the process of cultural museumification, represents a necessary but by no means sufficient condition for museumification. Indeed, this question borders on that of why we do not, analogously to the case of natural evolution, simply leave the accumulating relics of cultural evolution to natural processes of recycling. Why do we at least try to hold on to representative exemplars of what is directly characterized by its obsolescence, as well as by its distance from relevant current functional contexts?

Precisely this question, posed from the perspective of the by no means culturally marginal example of museumification, is that of the function of historical consciousness in dynamic civilizations. The answer to the question of the function of historical consciousness, and with it the achievements of the historical sciences in modern civilizations, will concern us here only in passing.[6] I restrict myself to a few remarks. What humanity is, we read in Wilhelm Dilthey, is told to us by our history. There is relatively little difficulty in realizing what we are by recounting the histories of our individual and collective provenance when these histories are realizations of pasts that we can still take as models of the present, and on the basis of whose life experiences we can judge. But difficulties arise with the realization of particular individual and above all collective pasts when, owing to the innovation dynamic sketched above, one's own past becomes alien ever more quickly. Then the more explicit achievements of a scientifically disciplined historical consciousness are needed in order to understand one's own alien past, and thereby to enable us to appropriate it, as well as to make sense of the past of our forebears.

In short: the achievements of historical consciousness are compensations for a temporally variable loss of confidence in one's cultural moorings. The necessity of these achievements increases with modernity. The preservation of historical monuments is an especially illuminating example of this connection between modernization and historicizing preservation. The faster the economically and technologically determined dynamics of building construction render our urban and rural architectural lifeworlds alien before our very eyes, the more intense becomes our concern with conservation, especially in regard to those objects suited to giving expression

---

6. The scientific and cultural theory of the historical sciences is worked out in my *Geschichtsbegriff und Geschichtsinteresse: Analytik und Pragmatik der Historie* (Basel: Schwabe, 1977).

to our ties to an experience that stays the same over time. For example, as the Frankfurt skyline comes to approximate that of Dallas or Denver, the more intolerable for us becomes the thought that the great monument of architectural historicism, the old Frankfurt Opera House, was sacrificed to this progress and, on the recommendation of Frankfurt's mayor, its ruins blown into smithereens.

Historical culture, then, is a specifically modern culture whose necessity increases with the dynamism of modern civilization, and this necessity is nothing other than that which holds that the expanding past can be connected to the present under the conditions of the contracting present sketched above. With recourse to the category of identity (which in this connection becomes unavoidable), the same thing can also be expressed in the following manner: the achievements of historical consciousness compensate for the dangers of the temporal diffusion of identity.

I would also add, in order to bring together the historical cultural sciences, on the one hand, and the natural sciences, on the other, that at the same time the historicity of culture is discovered, so too is the historicity of nature. In conventional bourgeois visions of education, too, cultural historiography and natural historiography have from the outset held equally weighty places. For good reason a fitting memorial to both Humboldt brothers—the cultural historian Wilhelm and the natural historian Alexander—was placed in front of the entry to the old Friedrich-Wilhelm (now Humboldt) University on Unter den Linden in Berlin. Analogously, the two museums on Vienna's Ringstraße, the Museum of Cultural History and the Museum of Natural History, are both distinguished by their prominent domed structures. In both cases, that of natural history as well as cultural history, historical consciousness furnishes an analogous achievement of order. This is an achievement in the production of a genetic connection between natural or cultural evolutionary relics: unconnected, they would make for chaos, but by producing a coherence based on interpreting their genetic dependence on one another, they are united into the structure of a single recountable history.[7]

Having understood this, one can also recognize that the cultural-historical sciences, on the one hand, and the natural sciences, on the other, are not distinguished by the former having to do with historical objects and the latter with ahistorical objects. Natural histories are histories like cultural

---

7. And thereby constitute a specifically modern concept of natural history. See also Wolf Lepenies, *Das Ende der Naturgeschichte: Wandel kultureller Selbstverständlichkeiten in den Wissenschaften des 18. und 19. Jahrhunderts* (Frankfurt am Main: Suhrkamp, 1978).

histories.[8] In this respect, the particularity of cultural history consists in nothing other than the linguistic-symbolic form of intergenerational transfers of cultural information, in contrast to the genetic form of intergenerational information transfers in biological evolution. The linguistic-symbolic mode of transferring cultural information between generations, as characteristic of cultural history, is at the same time the decisive condition for the extreme increase in cultural as compared to biological evolution.

However, the functions of historical consciousness should not occupy us further here. Historical consciousness is only one of the cultural consequences of modern civilization's experiences of acceleration. Another is the experience of increasing time pressure, under which one experimentally attempts, individually as well as institutionally, to culturally digest the temporally compressed assault of innovations. This condition is evinced by a cultural-historical process as significant as it was meaningful: the transformation in the so-called culture of reading, which, simultaneous with the rise of historical consciousness, took a dramatic turn in the eighteenth century. Two hundred years before today's well-known record-breaking numbers (outstripping themselves every year) at book fairs, we already encounter a century characterized by incessant complaints about the rising flood of publications, which surprises people over and over again at the annual Frankfurt Book Fair. What this means quantitatively can be found in David A. Kronick's useful *History of Scientific and Technical Periodicals*.[9] It is unnecessary to produce the striking columns of figures here.

Along with these complaints, however, the standard reaction of the reading public to the compression of cultural innovation was as obvious as it was rich in consequences: a culture of extensive reading developed, partially supplanting the art of intensive reading.[10] Put still more simply: in reaction to the compression of innovation in publishing, the capacity for reception was increased by raising the tempo of reading.

A prominent case exemplifies this: as he mentioned to Chancellor von Müller in 1830, Goethe read on the average one octavo volume per day. If

---

8. I have pointed out the structural identity of natural histories and cultural histories in my *Die Einheit von Naturgeschichte und Kulturgeschichte: Bemerkungen zum Geschichtsbegriff* (Mainz: Akademie der Wissenschaften und der Literatur zu Mainz, 1981).

9. David A. Kronick, *A History of Scientific and Technical Periodicals: The Origins and Development of the Scientific and Technological Press, 1665–1790* (New York: Scarecrow Press, 1962).

10. On the history of culture of reading, see esp. Rolf Engelsing, "Die Perioden der Lesergeschichte in der Neuzeit: Das statistische Ausmaß und die soziokulturelle Bedeutung der Lektüre," in *Börsenblatt für den den deutschen Buchhandel—Frankfurter Ausgabe*, no. 51 (27 July 1969): 1541–69.

one has an idea of the course of Goethe's days and years, it is clear that the reading technique required for such a reading load could not have involved hermeneutic meditation and careful exegesis, along the lines Faust demonstrates by his famous approach to the first sentence of the Gospel of John. Similarly extreme quantities were achieved in other prominent cases at the time. Schlosser, according to his own testimony, consumed more than four thousand books in three years as a *Gymnasium* student in Jever.

The compression of cultural innovation specific to this period increased time pressure in the form of an experience of a time shortage: the growing structural incongruity of the rising wealth of possible acquisitions on offer, on the one hand, and the relatively decreasing opportunities to make use of them, on the other, constrained as the latter were by the duration of a life course that remained fundamentally constant.

More culturally significant than the simple technique of increasing the speed of reception of published material is the dramatically increased pressure to select carefully from among a dramatically growing stock of offerings. One of the most important effects of this pressure of selection is obviously this: the relative quantity of what can be added to the canon of compulsory reading decreases, and with it the cultural homogeneity of the education of cultural contemporaries achieved by common reading. No longer canonical or set by the curriculum, incidental factors increase the differentiation of what is in fact appropriated by individuals, even among individuals in closely knit groups. Thus, the unequal distribution of the whole of culturally available knowledge rises. In other words, the age of emerging journalistic mass production unleashes not massification but, on the contrary, processes of individualization.

It is unnecessary to describe in greater detail the cultural consequences of the refraction of innovation compression through the narrow temporal boundaries of the individual life course. Against this background, one can recognize the significance of Ernst Robert Curtius's observation that the Enlightenment smashed the authority of the book.[11] The relative quantity of canonically bound cultural goods decreases in favor of the dramatically increasing quantity of information that is at once freely produced and freely received.

This description of cultural evolution as a process immediately poses the question of how it can continue and where it will end. "Surely it can't go

---

11. Ernst Robert Curtius, *Europäische Literatur und lateinisches Mittelalter,* 9th ed. (Bern: Francke, 1978), 352.

on like this forever!"—this response gives expression to the experience of the process of innovation compression sketched above. How the individual can hope to hold her ground under the pressure of this experience is given striking expression by two prominent figures, once again from the example of the developing culture of a reading public. Before he himself reached the public at large as a successful author, Schopenhauer put forth the view that one should not read "whatever the public at large concerns itself with at the moment."[12] The precondition and consequence of this comment is evidently the growing degree of arbitrariness in reference to what is topical at the moment, and thus a decreasing possibility of obliging a cultural community to keep up. This effect of growing cultural indifference, unleashed by innovation compression, will concern us later in another context. The relative quantity of what can be imposed on everyone as obligatory decreases with the total quantity of available cultural goods. While Schopenhauer drew from this the recommendation that one should no longer concern oneself with the latest thing, the question of course arises of what one should concern oneself with instead. Friedrich Schiller had already commented on this some decades earlier, when in a 1788 letter to Körner he wrote that "in the next two years" he would "no longer read any modern writers," but only old ones.[13] Precisely in contrast to the rising quantity of now only selectively receptive goods caused by innovation compression, which could no longer be reasonably obligatory for the common culture, the cultural phenomenon of the classics is constituted in the specifically modern sense: a classic is what is very old, what has demonstrated its power through its effective history as well as in the present, and what is in exactly this sense not obsolete, irrespective of its age.

Expressed in temporal categories, this means that in contrast to the rapidly rising quantity of quickly aging cultural resources, classics gain in interest as a resource promising heightened validity over time. In terms of evolutionary theory: the quantity of orientations, of literary and other norms, the quantity of everyday and also scientifically achieved knowledge through which the unity of a culture is expressed, does not change in toto at an analogous rate. Instead, as the cultural dynamic increases, out of the countless resources, those with more or less constant value are always singled out.

12. Arthur Schopenhauer, *Parerga und Paralipomena: Kleine philosophische Schriften*, vol. 2 (Leipzig: F. A. Brockhaus, 1891), 590.

13. Friedrich Schiller to Christian Gottfried Körner, August 20, 1788, in *Briefwechsel zwischen Schiller und Körner von 1784 bis zum Tode Schillers*, vol. 1, ed. Ludwig Geiger (Stuttgart: J. G. Cotta, 1892), 249.

Precisely this differentiation of cultural resources with apparently greater or lesser resistance to change now generates, as can easily be seen, previously unavailable possibilities to engage either with the changing or with the enduring. Progressive and conservative lines of cultural development can be perceived as isolated from each other, and finally also ideologized and even politicized.

I would now like to devote some attention to these ideological and political consequences of the experience of acceleration in cultural processes. A significant early appearance of this process is the futurization of utopia, impressively described by Reinhart Koselleck.[14] The perception and criticism of the world we in fact live in from the perspective of an imagined better world is not specifically new. On the contrary, it is a cultural constant that belongs to the classical tradition. Deep into the modern period, right up to the Renaissance, so-called utopias had primarily a spatial status, meaning that they showed us the image of a better world as one already realized in another distant place. With the conquest of space, which ultimately left no more objects of supposedly greater attractiveness on earth, the possibility of imagining a better counterworld to our own world elsewhere on earth disappeared. The temporalization of utopia, by transposing the perfection realized in literature from distant places to distant times, also presupposed that the social condition in which we now find ourselves is at the same time part of a directed process of transformation. This compels the moral-political validation of the future, whereby one must calculate things under conditions of what is experienced as a directed process of transformation, and the utopia of salvation represents in literary form a positive result by validating what one expects for the future. From this arise significant cultural and ultimately ideological and political consequences. First, in order to see the future as something better than the present, one is now compelled to attempt to extend originary histories into histories of the future. Second, in the interest of a concrete determination of aspirations for the present, one must attempt to articulate the path of history between the past and the future in epochal terms so as to discern the ephemeral quality of our present epoch in such a succession of epochs. Third, the insight into the greater moral and political validity of the future results in the duty to accelerate our movement into it.

The transformation of the classical philosophy of history into political

14. See Reinhart Koselleck, "Die Verzeitlichung der Utopie," in *Utopieforschung*, vol. 3 (Frankfurt am Main: Suhrkamp, 1982), 1–14.

ideology is thereby described as concisely as possible. A special ruse in this connection is the suitability of historicist ideology for politically self-privileging its subject. That is, the politically and ideologically transformed philosophy of history has the peculiarity that, owing to its special insight into the epochal course of history, it enables its carriers to say how it is that they, by virtue of their historical position, are the first and only ones capable of such insight into the whole course of history. From this comes their self-ascribed role of already representing the present vanguard position of future humanity as a party, and the right, even the duty, to make the corresponding aspirations politically binding. The resulting political program is, so to speak, every program of emancipation the educator carries out on her charges. Indeed, the educator already knows what the charges cannot, and just this circumstance of relational asymmetry, which determines the relation of the young and the old in the succession of generations, is transferred onto a singular development of the species, in a concept of the political education of the human race, as it were.

The consequences of such a historical-philosophical-ideological orientation of politics on a fundamentally assured course of history are considerable. First, potentials for revolutionary change are set loose, legitimated by the duty of acceleration indicated above. Second, politics becomes potentially capable of terror to a hitherto unknown extent owing to the consequences for political discrimination of the congruency now produced between old and new on the one side, and bad and good on the other. Third, wherever it prevails, a politics ideologically oriented in this way veers inevitably toward ultraconservatism and dogmatism. Indeed, nothing is more in need of conservation than a doctrine that claims to find itself in a temporal position privileged by world history.

As we all know, this philosophy of history-turned-ideology has made world history. Especially for Germans, it is touching, or at least unsettling, to glimpse on occasion the huge portraits of German lecturers, professors, and intellectuals who were educated in the school of so-called German Idealism—Karl Marx or Friedrich Engels and occasionally even their teacher, Hegel—in political processions in Moscow, Beijing, or Tirana.

Karl Popper called the purported insight into the law-governed character of historical events "historicism," and dedicated his book *The Poverty of Historicism* to the victims of the false belief in the existence of laws of history.[15] Expressed in the understated language of the philosophy of science, this error

---

15. See Karl Popper, *The Poverty of Historicism* (London: Routledge and Kegan Paul, 1969).

is that the unmistakable lawfulness of civilizational evolution is in fact directed toward no goal at all. The accelerating, order-producing or even order-dissolving innovations within this process have a contingent character, with the effect that evolution as such, irrespective of its lawfulness, is not open to prognoses. More simply put: the future of cultural evolution is open, yet a politics instead oriented toward an ideology that treats the future as fixed by a law-governed succession of epochs inevitably transforms an open society into a closed one.

It remains to point out that, from a historical-cultural perspective, this ideological-political reaction to the experience of history as a directed and at the same time accelerating process—the self-imposed task of additionally promoting the acceleration of history through one's own activities—is the secularization of an older, religiously formed experience of eschatological time pressure. Ernst Benz has described this brilliantly in his empirically rich essay on the acceleration of time as a problem in history and eschatology.[16] If the end of all things is approaching, the time for the necessary preparations becomes scarce. The practice of missionaries required acceleration, and in religiously inspired emigration one reacts not only to domestic material need. Instead, one at the same time loosens one's connections to the old world in order better to prepare for the new, heavenly one. One exists restlessly and hopes that precisely by doing so the approach of what is hoped can be accelerated.

However, quite apart from the imperatives of ideology or the philosophy of history, the pressure of cultural-evolutionary experiences of acceleration creates an objective compulsion to attempt to stay on top of the recognizable movement. This compulsion becomes especially virulent under the conditions of the disengagement of production and distribution systems from guild regulations and the system of estates. David S. Landes has described this with the lovely metaphor of "Prometheus unbound."[17] From a conceptual perspective, the most important elements of this description of industrial development from 1750 to the present are the following:

1. The preconditions of this process are the already familiar resources of a dramatic increase in the rate of innovation in the scientific and technological systems.

---

16. See Ernst Banz, *Akzeleration der Zeit als geschichtliches und heilsgeschichtliches Problem* (Mainz: Akademie der Wissenschaften und der Literatur, 1977).

17. See David S. Landes, *Der entfesselte Prometheus: Technologischer Wandel und industrielle Entwicklung in Westeuropa von 1750 bis zur Gegenwart* (Cologne: Kiepenheuer and Witsch, 1973).

2. The intervals between scientific-technological innovation and its economic use shorten.

3. Technological innovations, for their part, are intended for the most part to increase productivity, that is, the speed of production or the quantity of goods that can be produced per unit of time.

4. The economic advantages of reducing production costs thus made available through mechanisms of economic competition compel general participation in the pertinent modernization processes.

5. The regional and social reach of markets increases due to the quantity of products to be distributed and their dramatically rising specialization, which depends on modern modes of production.

6. With this rises the extension of transport, especially the mass transport of goods and people, which, as an extension in space, can only be made up for by raising the speed of transportation.

7. This last trend in itself compels a hitherto unprecedented standardization of time as the medium of action coordination. It suffices in this connection to recall that in many nation-states it was in fact the development of railway systems that compelled the development and institutionalization of standard time.

8. The increasingly obtrusive characteristic of time as a medium that must be taken into account in the coordination of action compels a transformation in modes of behavior. The virtue of punctuality becomes a necessity. Lack of punctuality results in exclusion from opportunities for social cooperation, and instruments for synchronizing actions and plans—from the pocket watch to the appointment calendar—become culturally indispensable. Time discipline is accordingly described by Norbert Elias as one of the subtlest consequences of the civilizing process.

Among philosophers and other theorists of time, we repeatedly find the inescapable reference to the Augustinian reflection that time is no problem for we who live in time, but that we always encounter difficulty when we reflexively ask what it is. From the last perspective treated above—the standardization of time compelled by social development—we can now readily formulate a pragmatic concept of time: time is the medium of action coordination, and the necessity of this coordination grows with the degree of differentiation and the transformational dynamics of modern societies. How it happened, then, that in the context of recent German ideologies of education the secondary virtue of punctuality was occasionally defamed as repressive is not to be examined here. Where one really believes this and teaches accordingly, the consequences must be described as follows: self-exclusion from the differentiated opportunities to cooperate that are open to us as participants in modern social life—with the consequence that one loses freedom in the sense of sovereignty over time and experiences oneself as an object, that is, as a victim of circumstances.

It is among the amusements of the present age to mock earlier generations' anxieties about tempo as expressed in popular cultural-historical observations. Especially in the railroad jubilees currently taking place in many countries, no opportunity is missed to quote from historical documents demonstrating such anxieties. These documents undoubtedly exist. But the dominant cultural-historical truth is that the dynamism of modern civilization has always been met predominantly with overwhelming agreement, and certainly not only in the ideological-political contexts treated above. This agreement is plausible in view of the evident advantages for life that modern civilization first was able to provide. Liberating humanity from the dull compulsion of hard physical labor, and thereby increasing the productivity of labor, as well as subsequently contributing to the general welfare, social security, and ultimately social peace—these evident advantages of life in modern society even today should by no means be lost in the fog. They remain unchanged, recognizable for everybody as commonplaces. The overwhelming acceptance of modern society, still a fact of life today, is explained by the evidence of such advantages for human life. Meanwhile, we have become so accustomed to the dynamic of civilization, as legitimated by these achievements, that irrespective of the resulting burdens that have yet to be dealt with here, considerable problems would assuredly arise from getting used to a less dynamic condition, or perhaps even to stagnation. I would like to suggest one of these problems by way of an example: income differentials, even when they increase, are relatively easy to deal with socio-psychologically and therefore politically if growth can be found to at all levels, especially the lowest. The pacifying effect of experiencing growth, it seems, is typically greater than the sensitivity produced by looking upon differences between levels. Precisely this changes, however, under conditions of stagnation—with the effect of sharpening struggles over distribution.

One way or another, from the perspective of cultural history, civilizational critique in the form of a critique provoked by the burdens of social dynamism is a relatively late phenomenon. In the early days of industrialization, we not only find calls for political movements, along the lines described above, desiring a political acceleration of history. We also find the celebration of gains from rationalization, which can after all be interpreted as a gain of usable time achieved by increases in the speed of production. There was even pleasure in speed as an aesthetically cultivated pleasure—the history of music from the late Baroque through Viennese Classicism to Romanticism, for example, is marked in part by a dramatization of changes in tempo. Tempo markings, which had not existed previously, now appeared in the technique of composition, the increase in tempo outdoing itself into the realm of the absurd. Robert Schumann's Piano Sonata in G minor, opus 22, is the most conspicuous example: "As fast as possible," it says right at the beginning, whereupon some bars later follows the command, "Even faster."

This account of the contents of modern temporal experience as the experience of acceleration could continue indefinitely. Those phenomena that provoke that experience and that I initially marked as instances of innovation compression have in part taken on the attributes of exponential growth. In the meantime, nearly every consumer of the mass media has come to rely on the upward-curving graphs that journalistically express the spread of events measuring such civilizational progress. This explains why the symbolization of this can be found today even in the art scene. At one recent Basel exhibition of modern art, which by no means coincidentally included civilization-critical themes today typically symbolized by the color green, a so-called exponential staircase was exhibited. It began comfortably enough, but rapidly ran into a steep wall, making a plunge likely. Of course, only in mathematics can an exponential series be extrapolated into infinity. In reality, the end of such a progression would be that symbolized in Basel by the plunge of the exponential staircase, unless more sustainable solutions can be found in response to the experience of such developments. I would like to outline some actually observable ways of responding to cultural developments. Of course, as a matter of life experience, whether or not the processes in question have been measured is not always significant. It is sufficient that contemporaries perceive them as having the alarming quality seeming that they cannot go on like this. Let me demonstrate this first of all in the case of art. Here, too, the phenomenon of innovation compression can be impressively established. From a calendar of conventional art history period concepts compiled by Hans Robert Jauss, the Romance Studies scholar at the University of Konstanz, we learn that in the half century between 1850 and 1900 seven large stylistic movements in visual art are conventionally distinguished, from Realism to the beginnings of Secessionism.[18] In contrast, more than twice this number of stylistic movements is distinguishable during the single decade between 1960 and 1970, in this case from Magic Realism to Environmentalism. This means a rise in the rate of artistic innovation by a factor of ten over 120 years.

Nothing has advanced this acceleration more strongly than the self-imposed artistic duty of avant-gardism,[19] which is understood here simply as putting a premium on innovation as innovation. It includes the gesture of storming museums in the wild years of Futurism, as well as the thematization of speed as a subject and the aestheticization of technology as the real medium of the speeding up of the course of civilization.

Meanwhile, the consequences of artistic production's self-imposed obligation to outdo itself by a type of permanent innovation are paradoxical— or, more precisely, apparently paradoxical. For the individual, first of all, the consequence is that whoever wants to be of tomorrow today only ensures that the day after tomorrow she will be yesterday's news. Accordingly, the number of artists steadily increases who in their later stages of life are no longer anything more than representatives of a great innovation for which they stood the day before yesterday. Here, too, the price of avant-gardism is an increase in the rate of obsolescence, and in the quantity of products that are already ready for the museum as soon as they are delivered.

Another moment follows from this: the absorption capacities of historical meaning are overtaxed. Concretely, this means that anyone who today wants to exhibit the development of contemporary art over the short space of a half century, from the beginning of the 1930s to the present, with effectively representative material in a limited space, requires objects in a quantity that conventional museums and art galleries can no longer accommodate. Accordingly, it was necessary, in the case of a representative exhibition of art in Cologne in 1983, to utilize huge exhibition halls in order to present fifty years of artistic developments. In any event, it is evident that only a specialist could discern a genetic order in the profusion of highly disparate objects connected to avant-gardism, the chaos of this host of relics. The nonspecialist art lover no longer perceives lines of development, but rather chaos, and the appropriate response to the perception of chaotic profusion is eclecticism. So she goes through the exhibition halls, hurried in groups,

18. Hans Robert Jauss, *Toward an Aesthetic of Reception* (Minneapolis: University of Minnesota Press, 1982).

19. See my "Historisierung und Ästhetisierung: Über Unverbindlichkeiten im Fortschritt," in *Oikeiosis: Festschrift für Robert Spaemann,* ed. Reinhart Löw (Weinheim: Acta Humaniora, 1987), 149–66.

pausing where, on the basis of a contingent whim, a work pleases her or emphatically does not. In short, the intellectual way of maintaining one's sovereignty in the face of the manifest chaos of this unmanageable quantity of relics is eclecticism. It is therefore no accident that eclecticism is the primary attitude and principle of perception in so-called postmodernism. Against the background of what is portrayed here, this is an understandable and even rational reaction to the descent of avant-gardist production into perceptual chaos. Postmodernism legitimizes preferences for the bygone, for anything old, whose special advantage is aging less rapidly than what is less old amidst highly dynamic developments, and thereby allowing some experience of continuity. A structural conservatism develops out of this, which, reduced to a formula, could be characterized as the restriction of innovative practice to strict necessity instead of possibility.

The reach of this formula extends far beyond the art scene into the general realm of morally regulated life. This may be demonstrated by another important case of specifically modern temporal experience. Under conditions of innovation compression, time does not only become a scarce good. With the rise of productivity, time, as a share of one's lifetime, is released as free time, meaning that for the majority of members of modern civilization, the span of the lifetime in which nothing happens if it is not self-determined extends ever further. It is precisely this that makes the capacity for productive self-determination—the ability to spend one's time productively and in ways that contribute to one's welfare—more important than ever before, and it is therefore no accident that the significance of "self-realization" for orienting one's life in the context of changing values becomes dominant, extending well into the lifestyle advice in the family and women's magazines.

In general, it can be attested of our present culture that in response to the experience of time shedding its necessity, the time freed up by progress in productivity turns out to be creative. One could place a portrayal of this under the fine heading of the "flowering of everyday culture"—from the unchanged blossoming of reading culture to the renaissance of domestic music, from the culture of horticulture to the productive use of professional capacities in "time-off" spaces in the context of the so-called shadow economy. Of course, there is also a flipside to the flourishing condition of everyday culture: the psychic and social consequences of an incapacity for self-determination, where the individual, instead of developing, himself becomes the greatest problem and experiences himself as a victim of circumstances. The decisive question is what the capacity for self-determination depends on. The factors that make one capable of self-determination are many and diverse. In each case a necessary if not sufficient factor is an education in classical virtues, even secondary ones that have maintained their constancy and validity over time through all kinds of cultural change. These include the so-called secondary virtues of orderliness, discipline, and punctuality, and the in no way secondary, but indeed primary, virtue of moderation. This means that a lifetime freed from necessity, which complements the scarcity of time, does not only make room for seemingly arbitrary variations in spheres of activity according to which individuals are differentiated according to their cultural level. Simultaneously complementing this trend, it also necessitates an orientation toward cultural resources distinguished precisely by the constancy of their validity notwithstanding cultural change.

Summed up as a general evolution-theoretical formula, this means that the quantity of elements in which culture's communicative unity consists cannot be changed as quickly as one would like. Highly dynamic cultural development presupposes a high constancy in the validity of some cultural elements. Dynamic cultures put themselves at risk from the rapid obsolescence of tradition that complements their dynamism, and in order to cope with this, declining traditional resources, whose validity demonstrates constancy, become all the more important.

In other words, there seem to be limits, from both an individual and an institutional perspective, to the capacity to process innovation. The intergenerational transfer of cultural information is potentially threatened if the cultural orientations of the two generations living together in the small modern family unit drift too far apart. Processes of growing up, just like processes of growing old, become precarious if the quantity of cultural resources that have consistent validity over the short duration of an average life dissolves with disorienting consequences.

The high level of dynamism is also culturally significant for the sciences. In the nineteenth century, the educated public still had a general cultural obligation to be familiar with scientific worldviews. The more the results from which today's scientific worldviews are produced descend from the regions of the very large, the very small, and the very complex—the greater the dynamism of the accumulation of such research-based knowledge— the less temporal consistency scientific worldviews necessarily have. Hence, chances dwindle that they can be consistently transferred through the educational curriculum into our general culture and become persistent cultural knowledge for at least one generation. This means that if the picture of the world we live in changes over a certain temporal limit, the obligation to stay up to date with regard to its orienting worldview becomes less and less feasible and ultimately dies out, and science suffers a potential loss of cultural validity.[20] Its legitimating principle, *curiositas*, loses validity, while the principle of relevance acquires cultural value to the same degree.

Limits to processing scientific progress may appear in some research fields even from a financial perspective. In the subfields concerned with research and development, the cost of research practices rises more rapidly than the desired gains in knowledge. This seems to be the case in the field of atomic physics, with the rising cost of the increasingly powerful particle accelerators required. Briefly, the research process seems to be characterized by a sinking threshold of utilization, which means that beyond a certain limit we must face the question whether, from the perspective of educational policy, the expected gains from research are as valuable to us as they are expensive.

There also seem to be limits to processing innovation in the economic field. We know from the industrial history of the nineteenth century that in many branches of production the productivity increase of the mechanical infrastructure moved within limits that made it economically possible to wait to install a new generation of machines until the older ones wore out. Meanwhile, in many sectors the write-off periods set by financial authorities sank far below the required working life of the machines in question. One recognizes that in the end there are also economic limits to processing innovation in the field of research and development.

Finally, there are limits to our capacity to process innovations; these can be characterized as limits on how much the future can be planned. On the one hand, the necessity of increasing the temporal reach of our action plans is extended ever further into the future along with the social and natural reach of our technological-instrumental actions. In our lifeworld we are familiar with this condition in the form of the appointment books we carry with us in filofaxes, which include ever-expanding stretches of planned time—now up to three years—to which we have to attend. In other words, under innovation compression, the future taken up by plans for action expands. Certainly, the attempt to calculate long periods into the future is an old element of our culture. Foresters always had to calculate between reforesting and harvesting over the course of many generations. Modern planning

20. See my *Die Wissenschaften und ihre kulturellen Folgen: Über die Zukunft des common sense* (Opladen: Westdeutscher, 1987).

times, however, have a completely different temporal structure. They compel planning as action coordination through the anticipatory synchronization of action, and do so under increasing uncertainty, due to innovation, regarding the conditions one will have to deal with in the future. Since cognitive innovations, at the very least, are not in principle foreseeable, along with the key factor causing the civilizational dynamic per se—namely, cognitive innovation arising from research—and the expansion of the periods of the future taken up by planning techniques, the chances decrease of successfully calculating the conditions one will have to reckon with in the future. The dynamic of modern civilization accordingly increases at once our reach into the future and the difficulty of finding reliable, future-oriented premises for conceptualizing future action.

I will dispense with further examples of experiences with the limits of our cultural capacity to process innovations. To conclude, I will list some of the possible reactions to the trends described above, in part by summarizing my key claims:

1. We react to the experience of the evolutionary character of our civilization by historicizing civilization. The aim of this historicizing is to maintain our own past, which becomes strange to us more and more quickly, as a past that can be appropriated as our own, and others' pasts as something that can be ascribed to them, and thus we continue to be able to say who we are.

2. We react to the increased rate of cultural obsolescence caused by innovation with structural conservatism, meaning that we turn for compensation to what has more constant validity as things change. We cultivate the classics and deal with traditions that promise some constant value akin to the manner by which we deal with scarce resources, that is, economically. This conservatism no longer has anything in common with the traditional political-ideological conservatisms that developed in the early nineteenth century. It does not have to do with a preference for the old by identifiable social groups whose privileged social position is attached to the conservation of old conditions. Instead, it is a matter of what I have called structural conservatism, which develops at precisely the moment when we experience being troubled less by the inconveniences than by the precarious secondary consequences of a form of progress that has long since prevailed. At the risk of repetition, I again propose the formula that in dynamic civilizations the very old, in the sense of a classic, acquires

the uncommonly important advantage of aging less rapidly than what is less old.

3. Complementing the growing esteem for classical resources, we react to the increasing pressures of innovation sketched above with eclecticism, with the cultivation of willful individual preferences, individualization, and specialization. This means that along with the growing importance of classical resources, we increase the quantity of things at one's disposal, thus decreasing the relative quantity of what can be demanded of all participants in the culture as obligatory. Modern constitutional development, for example, can be described in precisely this manner. Human and civil rights, as basic rights, can certainly be described as marking out precisely those domains of life that we would not want to place at the disposal of political decision-making bodies, especially not at the disposal of majorities, and that therefore, in precisely this sense, cannot be democratized. This means, in other words, that we let the quantity-of life-orientations increase in which we reciprocally concede to one another the right to be different.

4. Under innovation pressure we become cost-conscious—not only with the above-described effect of an increase in the rate of innovation through the compulsion of rationalization, but also by insisting on economic and, occasionally, user-competence-related limits on the replacement of the new by the newer in the field of investment.

5. The increase of innovation is limited by experiences of a loss of rationality, which threaten us as the limits of planning become evident through the decreasing predictability of the premises of future action.

6. The cultural position of the most important factor of cultural dynamism, science, changes as well. Not least because of the disproportional growth of its costs, the legitimating political and cultural scientific principle of relevance attains dominance against that of curiositas, while the cultural significance of scientific worldviews diminishes anyway because the common culture's capacity to receive it has long since been outpaced. This means that with the systematic scientization of science in our civilization, our cultural relation to the sciences becomes ever more pragmatic.

[Translated by James Ingram]

TEN

SPEEDING UP AND SLOWING DOWN

John Urry

The Problem of Time

A reconfigured social science has to place time at its very center. This is partly because time has come onto the academic agenda, crisscrossing disciplinary boundaries and offering opportunities for novel intellectual developments. Further novel technologies appear to be generating new kinds of speeded up time that dramatically transform the opportunities for, and constraints upon, the mobilities of peoples, information, and images. Also, new metaphors of time have become very influential—particularly the notion of "timeless" or "virtual" or "instantaneous" time.

But time and its various speeds are not a simple topic. First, unlike some aspects of space, time is invisible to the senses.[1] We always have to view time through indicators, such as the clock or the calendar. There is then a complexly mediated relationship between measuring devices and "time." Some writers propose that time is merely these methods of measurement; others that they are metaphors for time; and others again that it is a kind of category mistake to conflate lived or real time with its forms of measurement. There are of course many indicators of the passage of time that impose different temporal divisions upon human history. Such divisions often engender powerful emotional sentiments, as with the recent millennium.[2]

Some parts of this chapter are drawn from chapters 5 and 6 of John Urry, *Sociology Beyond Societies: Mobilities for the Twenty-First Century* (London: Routledge, 2000). It has been significantly further developed and benefited from collaborations with Scott Lash, Phil Macnaghten, and Bron Szerszynski.

1. Norbert Elias, *Time: An Essay* (Oxford: Blackwell, 1992), 1.
2. Stephen Jay Gould, *Questioning the Millennium: A Rationalist's Guide to a Completely Arbitrary Countdown* (London: Jonathan Cape, 1997).

Second, there is no single time but a variety of times. Hawking states: "There is no unique absolute time, but instead each individual has his own personal measure of time that depends on where he is and how he is moving."[3] Moreover, the meaning of time is relative to its system of measurement. According to Einstein, we can imagine as many clocks as we want to.[4] Much historical research also shows enormous variation in the meaning of time and in the degree to which words denoting time feature within the languages of different cultures.[5]

Third, there is a dispute as to whether time and its speeds are an absolute entity, possessing its own nature or particularity as Newton maintained; or whether time, as Leibniz argued, is "an *order* of successions"[6] (emphasis in original). So is time an absolute, separate from any objects in nature, or is the universe comprised of various objects that happen to exhibit temporal relationships between each other while time itself does nothing? A further dispute is whether time possesses directionality. Is there an arrow of time such that irreducible effects result from time's passage; or is time reversible and is there no distinction between what is past and what is future, as Newton and Einstein both presume?

Fourth, human activities with regard to these various times are extremely diverse. Some social organizations are structured around speeding up and hence the saving of time, since "time is money" or at least something like money, and hence minimizing time or maximizing activity (especially someone's else's activity) within a fixed period of time is sought. But with other social practices it is the slow speed of time that is enjoyable and desired. The pleasures of time are especially intertwined with the embodied (or sensed) nature of people's relationships with objects and environments.

Finally, most social scientists have operated with a conception of "social time" seen to be separate from, and opposed to, the sense of time employed by the natural sciences. Social scientists have held that natural and social times are substantially different from each other. However, what they have treated as the specifically "human" aspects of time are, it seems, characteristics of the physical world as well. "Past, present, and future, historical time, the qualitative experience of time, the structuring of 'undifferentiated

---

3. Steven W. Hawking, *A Brief History of Time* (New York: Bantam, 1988), 33. Such a personal sense of time is normally known as *Eigenzeit:* see Helga Nowotny, *Time: The Modern and Postmodern Experience* (Cambridge: Polity Press, 1994).

4. Nowotny, *Time,* 20.

5. See work in the anthropology of time: Alfred Gell, *The Anthropology of Time: Cultural Constructions of Temporal Maps and Images* (Oxford: Berg, 1992).

6. Quoted in Stephan Körner, *Kant* (Harmondsworth: Penguin, 1955), 33.

change' into episodes, all are established as integral time aspects of the subject matter of the natural sciences."[7] Social science has thus operated with an out-of-date conception of time within the natural sciences. Indeed, "clock time, the invariant measure, the closed circle, the perfect symmetry, and reversible time [are] our creations."[8] Thus, the one component of time that cannot be generalized throughout nature is in fact that of clock time, a human creation. But this is the very time taken by the social sciences as the defining feature of natural time, as natural time came to be separated from social time with the development of industrial capitalism.

Clock time is Newtonian, based on the notion that time is absolute, that from "its own nature, [it] flows equably without relation to anything eternal. . . . The flowing of absolute time is not liable to change."[9] Such absolute time is invariant, infinitely divisible into space-like units, measurable in length, expressible as a number and reversible. It is time seen essentially as space, as comprising invariant measurable lengths that can be moved along, both forwards *and* backwards. However, twentieth-century science transformed its understanding of the times of nature as no longer Newtonian. Hawking summarizes: "Space and time are now dynamic qualities: when a body moves, or a force acts, it affects the curvature of space and time—and in turn the structure of space-time affects the way in which bodies move and forces act."[10] Various scientific discoveries of the twentieth century transformed the understanding of the times of nature.[11]

First, Einstein showed that there is no fixed or absolute time independent of the system to which it refers. Time, or *Eigenzeit*, is thus a local, internal feature of any system of observation and measurement. Further, time and space are not separate from each other but are fused into a four-dimensional time-space curved under the influence of mass. Among other consequences is the possibility of the past catching up with the future, of traveling through time down a wormhole, and of the incredible warping of

7. Barbara Adam, *Time and Social Theory* (Cambridge: Polity Press, 1990), 150.
8. Ibid..
9. Newton quoted ibid. And see Peter Coveney and Roger Highfield, *The Arrow of Time* (London: W. H. Allen, 1990), 29–31.
10. Hawking, *A Brief History of Time*, 33.
11. See many sources including Fritjof Capra, *The Web of Life: A New Scientific Understanding of Living Systems* (London: HarperCollins, 1996); J. L. Casti, *Complexification: Understanding a Paradoxical World Through the Science of Surprise* (London: Abacus, 1994); Coveney and Highfield, *The Arrow of Time*; Hawking, *A Brief History of Time*; I. Prigogine, *From Being to Becoming: Time and Complexity in the Physical Sciences* (San Francisco: W. H . Freeman, 1980); I. Prigogine, *The End of Certainty: Time, Chaos, and the New Laws of Nature* (New York: Free Press, 1997).

time-space that must have occurred in order to generate the singular event that initially created the universe.

Quantum theory provides a further critique of orthodox notions of cause and effect. Quantum physicists describe a virtual state in which electrons seem to try out instantaneously all possible futures before settling into particular patterns. Quantum behavior is mysteriously instantaneous. The notion of cause and effect no longer applies within such a microscopic, indivisible whole. The position and momentum of any electron cannot be known with precision. Indeed, the interrelations and interactions between the parts are far more fundamental than the parts themselves.

Chronobiology shows that it is not only human societies that experience time or organize their lives through time. Rhythmicity is a crucial principle of nature, both within the organism and in the organism's relationships with the environment. And humans and other animals are not just affected by clock time but are themselves clocks. It seems that all plants and animals possess such a system of time that regulates the internal functions on a twenty-four-hour cycle. Biological time is thus not confined to aging but expresses the nature of biological beings as temporal, dynamic, and cyclical. Change in living nature involves the notions of becoming and rhythmicity.

More generally, thermodynamics shows that there is an irreversible flow of time. Rather than there being time symmetry and a reversibility of time as in classical physics, there is a clear distinction drawn between past and future. The arrow of time results from all systems showing a loss of organization and an increase in randomness or disorder over time. This accumulation of disorder, called positive entropy, results from the second law of thermodynamics. All energy transformations are irreversible and directional, and the clearest example of irreversibility can be seen in the process by which the universe has expanded—through the cosmological arrow of time following the singular historical event of the "Big Bang," which is like nothing else. Laws of nature are historical and imply pastness, presentness, and futureness. "The great thing about time is that it goes on."[12]

More recently, chaos and complexity theories have involved repudiating simple dichotomies of order and disorder, of being and becoming.[13] Physical

---

12. Eddington, quoted in Coveney and Highfield, *The Arrow of Time*.
13. See various sources, including Capra, *The Web of Life*; Casti, *Complexification*; Paul Cilliers, *Complexity and Postmodernism: Understanding Complex Systems* (London: Routledge, 1998); Raymond A. Eve, Sara Horsfall, and Mary E. Lee, eds., *Chaos, Complexity, and Sociology: Myths, Models, and Theories* (Thousand Oaks, Calif.: SAGE, 1997); N. Katherine Hayles, ed., *Chaos and Order: Complex Dynamics in Literature and Science* (Chicago: University of Chicago Press,

systems do not exhibit and sustain structural stability. The commonsense notion that small changes in causes produce small changes in effects is mistaken. Rather, we have deterministic chaos, dynamic becoming, and non-linear changes in the properties of systems as a whole rather than trans-formations within particular components. Time in such a perspective is highly discontinuous, and investigation takes place of many nonequilib-rium situations in which abrupt and unpredictable changes occur as param-eters change over time. Following a perfectly deterministic set of rules, unpredictable yet patterned results can be generated. The classic example is the famous butterfly effect, where minuscule changes at one location pro-duce, in very particular circumstances, massive weather effects elsewhere. Such complex systems are characterized by counterintuitive outcomes that occur temporally and spatially distant from where they appear to have orig-inated. Complexity theory emphasizes how complex feedback loops exac-erbate initial stresses in systems and render them unable to absorb shocks in a simple way that reestablishes the original equilibrium. Very strong inter-actions are seen to occur between the parts of a system, and a central hier-archical structure is lacking.

Such dissipative systems reach points of bifurcation when their behav-ior and future pathways become unpredictable. New structures of higher order and complexity then emerge. Dissipative structures thus involve non-linearity, a flowingness of time, no separation of systems and their envi-ronment, and a capacity for an autopoeitic reemergence of a new emergent order. Such notions of a self-making autopoeitic system have been em-ployed within the recent analyses of the World Wide Web. Plant argues that "no central hub or command structure has constructed it. . . . It has installed none of the hardware on which it works, simply hitching a largely free ride on existing computers, networks, switching systems, telephone lines. This was one of the first systems to present itself as a multiplicitous, bottom-up, piecemeal, self-organizing network which . . . could be seen to be emerging without any centralized control."[14]

Overall, then, the social sciences continue to employ incorrect models of how time is conceived of within the natural sciences, and they have neg-lected notions from within science that could well be relevant to a recon-figured sociology seeking to overcome the division between the physical

1991); Prigogine, *From Being to Becoming;* Prigogine, *The End of Certainty;* John Urry, *Global Complexity* (Cambridge: Polity Press, 2003).

14. Sadie Plant, *Zeros + Ones: Digital Women + the New Technoculture* (London: Fourth Estate, 1997), 61.

and social worlds. Comte, after all, described sociology as "social physics"; but if so, it is essential to incorporate twentieth- and twenty-first-century and not seventeenth-century physics.

In the next section I note that one particular time, clock time, has played a singularly powerful role within Western societies. Following this, I turn to the claim that a new time has more recently come powerfully into view— time as instantaneous or as pure speed. I consider some of the technologies and objects that have ushered in a time characterized by unpredictable change and quantum simultaneity. I then consider the metaphor of a slow-moving and sedimented glacial time that parallels the concept of dissipative systems embedded within its environment. In a brief conclusion I connects these time regimes to aspects of the events surrounding September 11.

Clock Time

The spread of clock time into almost all aspects of social life has been extraordinary. It has meant the general replacement of kairological time, which is the sense of time in which it is said that *now* is the time to do something irrespective of what any clock indicates. Kairological time is based upon using the experience of the past in order to develop the sense of when a particular event should take place in the future, of just when it is the right time for something to occur.[15]

Education is one context where kairological time has been almost entirely replaced by clock time. Lessons change, people move from room to room, French is spoken instead of German, maps are replaced with computers, and so on, because the minute hand has moved from what is signified as 9.59 A.M. to 10 A.M. Adam summarizes the awesome power of clock time within Western education: "The activities and interactions of all its participants are orchestrated to a symphony of buzzers, bells, timetables, schedules and deadlines. These time markers bind pupils and staff into a common schedule within which their respective activities are structured, paced, timed, sequenced and prioritized. They separate and section one activity from another and secure conformity to a regular, collective beat."[16]

The main characteristics of clock time are not only produced by the widespread use of clocks and watches; indeed, clocks of some sort had been in

15. See Richard Gault, "In and Out of Time," *Environmental Values* 4 (1995): 155.
16. Barbara Adam, *Timewatch: The Social Analysis of Time* (Cambridge: Polity Press, 1995), 61.

existence for some millennia. Rather, clock time is an appropriate meta-phor for "modern times." During the latter half of the nineteenth and for most of the twentieth century, many characteristics appeared more or less simultaneously and transformed the natural and social worlds. Adam notes that "neither the reckoning of time nor its measurement . . . constitutes the specific nature of industrial [or modern] time. Rather industrial time is a time that is abstracted from its natural source; an independent, decontex-tualized, rationalized time. It is a time that is almost infinitely divisible into equal spatial units . . . and related to as time *per se*."[17]

Lefebvre summarizes this march of clock time through society and nature. He argues that lived time experienced in and through nature has gradually disappeared. Time is no longer something visible and inscribed within space. It has been replaced by measuring instruments, clocks, that are separate from natural and social space. Time becomes a resource, differentiated off from social space, consumed, deployed, and exhausted. Lived (and kairo-logical) time are expelled as clock time dominates. Lefebvre describes this changing nature of time in terms of metaphor. In premodern societies lived time is inscripted into space as in a tree trunk and like a tree trunk shows the mark of those years that it has taken to grow, while in modern societies time is absorbed into the city such that lived time is invisible or reduced to its methods of measurement. Lived time "has been murdered by society."[18] Following are some of the main characteristics of clock time.

- The breaking down of time into a very large number of small, precisely measured, and invariant units
- The disembedding of time from meaningful social practices and from the apparently natural divisions of night and day, the seasons and movements of life toward death
- The widespread use of various means of measuring and indicating the passage of time: clocks, watches, timetables, calendars, schedules, clocking-on devices, bells, deadlines, diaries, alarm clocks, and so on
- The precise timetabling of most work and leisure activities

17. Ibid., 27. And see Barbara Adam, *Timescapes of Modernity: The Environment and Invisible Hazards* (London: Routledge, 1998); Manuel Castells, *The Rise of the Network Society* (Oxford: Blackwell, 1996); Paul Glennie and Nigel Thrift, "Reworking E. P. Thompson's 'Time, Work-Discipline, and Industrial Capitalism,'" *Time and Society* 5 (1994): 275–99; Scott Lash and John Urry, *Economies of Signs and Space* (London: SAGE, 1994); Niklas Luhmann, *The Differentiation of Society* (New York: Columbia University Press, 1982); Phil Macnaghten and John Urry, *Contested Natures* (London: SAGE, 1998); Jeremy Rifkin, *Time Wars: The Primary Conflict in Human History* (New York: Henry Holt, 1987); Urry, *Sociology Beyond Societies*.

18. Henri Lefebvre, *The Production of Space* (Oxford: Blackwell, 1991), 96.

- The widespread use of time as an independent resource that can be saved and consumed, deployed and exhausted
- The orientation to time as a resource to be managed rather than as activity or meaning
- The scientific transformation of time into mathematically precise and quantifiable measures in which time is reversible and possesses no single direction
- The synchronized time-disciplining of schoolchildren, travelers, employees, inmates, holiday-makers, and so on
- The synchronized measure of life stretching across national territories and across the globe
- The permeation of a discourse around the need for time to be saved, organized, monitored, regulated, and timetabled

Instantaneous Time

Quantum mechanics employs a notion of instantaneous (and simultaneous) time. How might this provide a productive metaphor for a social science of time? In premodern societies the predominant metaphors were those of various animals, as well as different kinds of agricultural work (many are still powerful today). In modern societies the predominant metaphors have been those of the clock, various types of machinery, and the photographic lens. For postmodern societies the hologram would be a productive metaphor. Holography is based upon nonsequentiality, the individual-whole relationship, and complexity. Information is not located in a particular part of the hologram. Rather, any part contains, implies, and resonates information of the whole. Thus, the focus here is not on individual particles in motion, crossing time and space in succession, but on all the information gathered up simultaneously. The language of cause and effect is inappropriate because connections are simultaneous and instantaneous. Everything implies everything else, and thus it makes no sense to conceive of the separate, if interdependent, "parts" of any such system. There is some similarity here to the views of Leibniz in that each monad in his monadological metaphysics is seen as mirroring the whole, albeit from each particular perspective.[19]

The hologram can be contrasted with the photographic lens, which provided a powerful metaphor for "modern" epistemology and aesthetics. With

19. See Adam, *Time and Social Theory*, 149; David Harvey, *Justice, Nature, and the Geography of Difference* (Oxford: Blackwell, 1996), 69–70.

a lens there is a one-to-one relationship between each point on the object and each point on the image that shows up on the plate or film. The metaphor of the lens implies sequentiality, the separation between parts and the whole, and a relatively extended process through clock time by which the image comes to be generated.

Various changes in the connections of time, space, and technology have produced a speeded up instantaneous time. Harvey shows how capitalism entails different "spatial fixes" within different historical periods.[20] In each capitalist epoch, space is organized in such a way as to facilitate the growth of production, the reproduction of labor power, and the maximization of profit. And it is through the reorganization of such time-space that capitalism overcomes its periods of crisis and lays the foundations for a new period of capital accumulation and the further transformation of space and nature through time. He particularly examines Marx's thesis of the annihilation of space by time and attempts to demonstrate how this explains the complex shift from "Fordism" to the flexible accumulation of "post-Fordism." Post-Fordism involves a new spatial fix and most significantly new ways in which time and space are represented. Central is the "time-space compression" of both human and physical experiences and processes.

This compression can be illustratively seen in relationship to mobility. The journey from the East to the West Coast of the United States would have taken two years by foot in the eighteenth century; four months by stagecoach in the nineteenth century; four days by rail at the beginning of the twentieth century; and less than four hours by air toward the end of the twentieth century. This generated a sense of foreboding, as when the railway first transformed the countryside. George Eliot, Dickens, Heine, Baudelaire, Flaubert, and others reflected some novel ways in which time and space were felt to be different, that there was a transformed and speeded up "structure of feeling" engendered by this rapidly transformed mobility. As a consequence, time and space appear literally *compressed:* "We are forced to alter . . . how we represent the world to ourselves. . . . Space appears to shrink to a 'global village' of telecommunications and a 'spaceship earth' of economic and ecological interdependencies . . . and as time horizons shorten to the point where the present is all there is . . . so we have to learn how to cope with an overwhelming sense of *compression* of our spatial and temporal worlds"[21] (emphasis in original).

---

20. David Harvey, *The Condition of Postmodernity: An Enquiry into the Origins of Cultural Change* (Oxford: Blackwell, 1989); and see Harvey, *Justice.*

21. Harvey, *The Condition of Postmodernity,* 240; and see N. J. Thrift, *Spatial Formations* (London: SAGE, 1996).

There is the accelerating turnover time in production and the increased pace of change and ephemerality of fashion. Products, places, and people go rapidly in and out of fashion at the same time that the same products become instantaneously available almost everywhere, at least in the West. The time horizons for decision making dramatically shrink—they are now in minutes in international financial markets. There is a hugely magnified speed of monetary and other transactions.[22] Products, relationships, and contracts are increasingly temporary because of short-termism and the decline of a "waiting culture." There is the production and transmission of rapidly changing media images and the increased availability of techniques of simulating buildings and physical landscapes from different periods or places. And new technologies of information and communication instantaneously transcend space at the speed of nanoseconds. Interestingly, Heidegger in 1950 foresaw much of this speeding up of social life. He talks of the "shrinking" of the distances of time and space, the importance of "instant information" on the radio, and the way that television is abolishing remoteness and thus "undistancing" humans and things.[23]

However, these dramatic ways in which time and space are compressed in order that a new round of capital accumulation can be realized does not mean that places decrease in importance. Some, of course, will decrease as a consequence of the "creatively destructive" power of capital. But more generally people appear to be more sensitized to what different places in the world contain or what they may signify. There is an insistent urge to seek for roots "in a world where image streams accelerate and become more and more placeless. Who are we and to what space/place to we belong? Am I a citizen of the world, the nation, the locality? Can I have a virtual existence in cyberspace . . . ?"[24] Thus, the more that time is speeded up, the greater the sensitivity of mobile capital, migrants, tourists, asylum seekers to the variations of place, and the greater the incentive for places to be differentiated in ways that attract the in-migration of most of the flows.

Castells elaborates some of the more precise connections of information and time in the network society. Key features of the "informational society," which developed within North America from the 1970s onwards, include the following: new technologies are pervasive since information is

22. Castells, *The Rise of the Network Society*, 434; Manuel Castells, *The Internet Galaxy: Reflections on the Internet, Business, and Society* (Oxford: Oxford University Press, 2001).

23. Michael E. Zimmerman, *Heidegger's Confrontation with Modernity: Technology, Politics, and Art* (Bloomington: Indiana University Press, 1990), 209.

24. Harvey, *Justice*, 246.

integral to more or less all forms of human practice; the building blocks are bits of electronically transmitted information; there are complex and temporally unpredictable patterns of informational development; such technologies are organized through loosely organized and flexibly changing networks; the different technologies gradually converge into integrated informational systems (especially the once separate biological and microelectronic technologies); these systems permit organizations to work in real time "on a planetary scale"; and such instantaneous electronic impulses provide material support for the space of flows.[25] Such electronic information generates a "timeless time." Capital's freedom from time and culture's escape from the clock are both decisively shaped by the new informational systems.

Thus, contemporary technologies and social practices are based upon accelerated time frames that lie beyond conscious human experience. While telex, telephones, and fax machines reduced the human response time from months, weeks, and days to seconds, the computer has contracted it into to event times of a billionth of a second. Computers make decisions in nanoseconds, and hence "events being processed in the computer world exist in a time realm that we will never be able to experience. The new 'computime' represents the final abstraction of time and its complete separation from human experience and rhythms of nature."[26] This instantaneous time stems from what Negroponte describes as the shift from the atom to the bit; the information-based digital age "is about the global movement of weightless bits at the speed of light."[27] The information can become instantaneously and simultaneously available more or less anywhere.

I thus use the term "instantaneous time" to characterize, first, new informational and communicational technologies based upon inconceivably brief instants, which are wholly beyond human consciousness; second, the simultaneous character of social and technical relationships, which replaces the linear logic of clock time, characterized by the temporal separation of cause and effect occurring over separate measurable instants; and third, a metaphor for the widespread significance of exceptionally short-term and fragmented time, even where it is not literally instantaneous and simultaneous.

I turn to the last of these characteristics, the instantaneous as metaphor. First, there is the *collage* effect, by which, once events have become more important than location, the presentation in the media takes the form of the juxtaposition of stories and items that share nothing in common except

25. Castells, *The Rise of the Network Society;* Castells, *The Internet Galaxy.*
26. Rifkin, *Time Wars,* 15.
27. Nicholas Negroponte, *Being Digital* (New York: Knopf, 1995), 12.

that they are "newsworthy." Stories from many different places and environments occur alongside each other in an often chaotic and arbitrary fashion, serving to abstract events from context and narrative. The experience of news is thus a temporally and spatially confused collage organized around instantaneously available stories simultaneously juxtaposed.

Second, such a mediated experience involves the "intrusion of distant events into everyday consciousness."[28] Events, often of a tragic character, are speedily and dramatically brought into people's everyday experience. Time-space compression thus takes place, as this collage of disconnected stories about famines, droughts, slaughters, nuclear accidents, terrorist attacks, scandals, and so on intrudes into and shapes everyday life. A "global present" has been produced in which, seemingly instantaneously, people are "transported" from one tragedy to another in ways that seem out of control. This can be characterized as a world of "instantaneous ubiquity," as particularly risky, and there is little likelihood of understanding the temporally organized processes that culminate in the newsworthy tragedies routinely represented. Such time-space compression magnifies the sense that we inhabit a world of intense and instantaneous speeded up risks.[29]

At the same time, those charged with decision making have to respond to this exceptionally risky world instantaneously. And as in the case of, say, the worldwide stock exchange crash in 1987, the effects of individual events upon the rest of the world are hugely magnified, as Wark elaborates in detail.[30] This increasingly accelerated pattern of responses has its roots in the early years of the twentieth century. Kern notes that new technologies emerging at that time played havoc with the established arts of diplomacy based upon customary times for "gentlemanly" reflection, consultation, and conciliation.[31]

These effects are connected to the accelerations of the three-minute culture. People watching TV/VCR hop from channel to channel and rarely spend time in following a lengthy program. Indeed, many programs mimic such a pattern, being comprised of a collage of visual and aural images, a stream of "soundbites," each one lasting a very short time and having no

28. Anthony Giddens, *Modernity and Self-Identity: Self and Society in the Late Modern Age* (Cambridge: Polity Press, 1991), 27.

29. See John Urry, "The Global Complexities of September 11th," *Theory, Culture, and Society* 19, no. 4 (2002): 57–70; Urry, *Global Complexity*; D. Morley and K. Robins, *Spaces of Identity: Global Media, Electronic Landscapes, and Cultural Boundaries* (London: Routledge, 1995).

30. McKenzie Wark, *Virtual Geography: Living with Global Media Events* (Bloomington: Indiana University Press), 1994.

31. Stephen Kern, *The Culture of Time and Space, 1880–1918* (London: Weidenfeld and Nicolson, 1983).

particular connection with those coming before and after. According to Cannon, there can be up to twenty-two separate images in a thirty-second commercial.[32] This acclerated conception of time could also be recharacterized as "video time," in which visual and aural images of the natural world are juxtaposed with multiple images of "culture." Williams describe this in terms of a "televisual flow" that replaces that of single and discrete events.[33] The speeding up of time may be generating new cognitive faculties, and "multimedia" skills based on the simultaneity of time may be more important in the future than conventional skills based upon linear notions of time.

Further, as a result of the need for instantaneous responses, particularly because of the speed implied by the telephone, telex, fax, electronic signals, and so on, the future dissolves into an extended present. It no longer functions as something in which people appear to trust. Qualitative research suggests that almost all groups of British citizens are pessimistic about what is happening in the future and feel that the accelerated pace of life and the development of new life cycles are increasing stress, pressure, and short-termism.[34]

There appears to be an increased sense of speed in social life that, according to Virilio, replaces the clear distances of time and space; there is a "violence of speed" of the military, the media, and cities that transcends and may destroy place. He asks rhetorically: "When we can go to the antipodes and back in an instant, what will become of us?"[35] Research by Cannon suggests that young people conceptualize the future as more or less instantaneous, and becoming even shorter. This generation does not seem to have long-term plans for or dreams of the future. It believes that "most organisations . . . [are] simply incapable of delivering future promises with any certainty. . . . Barings is just one more name on a long list which convinces young people that mortgaging one's life is a dangerous strategy."[36] Cannon suggests that the younger generation lives in "real time," seeing the day as having twenty-four hours in which to eat, sleep, work, relax, and play, a kind of student ordering of time writ into the rest of one's life! Bianchini describes the attempts to develop new and imaginative urban timetables

32. David Cannon, "Post-modern Work Ethic," *Demos Quarterly* 5 (1995): 32.

33. As shown in Stuart Allan, "Raymond Williams and the Culture of Televisual Flow," in *Raymond Williams Now: Knowledge, Limits, and the Future*, ed. Jeff Wallace, Rod Jones, and Sophie Nield (London: Macmillan, 1997), 115–77.

34. See data in Macnaghten and Urry, *Contested Natures;* and see R. E. Pahl, *After Success: Fin-de-Siècle Anxiety and Identity* (Cambridge: Polity Press, 1995).

35. Quoted Wark, *Virtual Geography,* 11; and see P. Virilio, *Speed and Politics: An Essay on Dromology* (New York: Columbia University Press, 1986).

36. Cannon, "Post-modern Work Ethic," 31.

that more closely reflect such patterns of social life.[37] The development of a rave culture on weekends involves the timing of activities and the use of illegal substances that enable the transcendence of the conventional divisions of night and day, work and play.[38]

Speeded up time also means that time-space paths are desynchronized. There is an increased variation in different people's times that spreads, if not over twenty-four hours, over much longer periods. People's activities are less collectively organized and structured as mass consumption patterns are replaced by more varied and segmented patterns. There are a number of indicators of time-space desynchronization: the increased significance of grazing, of not eating at fixed mealtimes in the same place in the company of one's family or workmates, and hence of fast-food consumption;[39] the growth of independent travelers who resist mass travel in a group where everyone has to engage in common activities at fixed times; the development of flextime, so that groups of employees no longer start and stop work at the same time; the growth of the VCR, which means that TV programs can be stored, repeated, and broken up, so that little sense remains of the authentic, shared watching of particular programs by the whole family; and the overwhelming use of the car for most journeys, which coerces everyone into desynchronized flexibility.[40]

Thus, the following list sets out the main characteristics of time as instantaneous, characteristics of a speeded up time particularly identifiable in north America and Europe:

- Informational and communication changes that allow information and ideas to be instantaneously transmitted and simultaneously accessed across the globe
- Technological and organizational changes that break down distinctions of night and day, working week and weekend, home and work, leisure and work
- Increasing disposability of products, places, and images in a "throwaway society"

37. Franco Bianchini, "The 24-Hour City," *Demos Quarterly* 5 (1995): 47–48; Juliet Schor, *The Overworked American: The Unexpected Decline of Leisure* (New York: Basic Books, 1992).

38. See George McKay, *Senseless Acts of Beauty: Culture of Resistance Since the Sixties* (London: Verso, 1996); George McKay, ed., *DiY Culture: Party and Protest in Nineties Britain* (London: Verso, 1998).

39. See George Ritzer, *The McDonaldization of Society* (London: Pine Forge Press, 1992), on the MacDonaldization of everyday life.

40. See Mimi Sheller and John Urry, "The City and the Car," *International Journal of Urban and Regional Research* 24 (2000): 737–57.

- Growing volatility and ephemerality in fashions, products, labor processes, ideas, and images
- Heightened "temporariness" of products, jobs, careers, natures, values, and personal relationships
- Proliferation of new products, flexible forms of technology, and huge amounts of waste often moving across national borders
- Growth of short-term labor contracts, what has been called the just-in-time workforce, and the tendency for people to develop "portfolios" of tasks
- Growth of twenty-four-hour trading so that investors and dealers never have to wait for the buying and selling of securities and foreign exchange from across the globe
- increased "modularization" of leisure, education, training, and work
- Extraordinary increases in the availability of products from different societies so that many styles and fashions can be consumed without one having to wait to travel to acquire them
- Increased rates of divorce and other forms of household dissolution
- Reduced sense of trust, loyalty, and commitment of families over generations
- Sense that the "pace of life" throughout the world has gotten too fast and is in contradiction with other aspects of human experience
- Increasingly volatile political preferences

Instantaneous time appears to transform the powers of nation-states. It played a significant role in what used to be called Eastern Europe. One set of processes activating the transformations that took place there more or less simultaneously was the inability of such countries to cope with the intense speeding up of time. Eastern Europe was stuck in modernist clock time and was unable to respond to the instantaneity of fashion, image and the microcomputer, and the parallel transformations of space. Such societies were caught in a time warp, in a forced modernization around clock time (note, of course, the appeal of scientific management to Lenin), while all around them, and increasingly criss-crossing their boundaries, were transformations of time that made such islands of modernist clock time unsustainable. Borneman suggests that time in the GDR was "petrified" compared with its "quickening" in the West.[41] With no incentive to speed it up, time appeared to stand still since "everything around them becomes

41. John Borneman, "Time-Space Compression and the Continental Divide in German Subjectivity," *New Formations* 21, no. 1 (1993): 105.

motionless, petrified and repetitious."[42] There was little or no chance of people acquiring status through instantaneous conspicuous consumption, let alone turning to the rapid growth of computing and its incessant doubling of capacity every few months.[43]

Moreover, German unification demonstrated that East Germany (the former GDR) was fundamentally behind in time. Two symbols of West Germany were the growth of travel abroad and the lack of speed limits on the autobahn. By contrast, East Germany appeared to be stuck in clock time, as the west moved into the intensely mobile "nanosecond [eighties and] nineties," characterized by what Keane calls "information blizzards."[44] Instantaneous time transforms contemporary modes of belonging and traveling. Current time is "like an ever-shrinking box, in which we race on a treadmill at increasingly frenetic speeds"; this allows us only "the very briefest experience of time."[45]

But all, we might say, is not lost. The very transformations that have speeded up social life are simultaneously bringing into being its very opposite, what I call glacial time.

Glacial Time

Glacial time resists instantaneous time and seeks to slow down time down to "nature's speed."[46] This metaphor of the glacier indicates a number of characteristics. First, glacial time is extremely slow-moving and ponderous, desynchronized from both clock and instantaneous times. Change therefore occurs over generations, and indeed can only be observed intergenerationally. Such change depends upon the glacier's context or environment. A glacier cannot be separated from the environment where it can be said to dwell. In that location it requires long-term care and monitoring. It is impossible to predict what will happen over such a long term because small changes in the glacier's environment can transform its viability. In turn, its condition significantly impacts upon this environment. The time of the

42. See John Keane, *The Media and Democracy* (Cambridge: Polity Press, 1991), 187.
43. See Manuel Castells, *The Power of Identity* (Oxford: Blackwell, 1997).
44. See Keane, *The Media and Democracy.*
45. Joanna Macy, *World as Lover, World as Self* (London: Rider, 1993), 206.
46. This is developed further in Macnaghten and Urry, *Contested Natures*; Adam, *Timescapes of Modernity*; Tim Ingold, "The Temporality of the Landscape," *World Archaeology* 25, no. 2 (1993): 24–174; Kathleen Sullivan, "This New Promethean Fire: Radioactive Monsters and Sustainable Nuclear Futures" (Ph.D. diss., Lancaster University, 1999).

glacier is part of its existence qua glacier and is not something to be imposed via particular measuring devices.

So glacial time is slow-moving, beyond assessment or monitoring within the present generation. It involves relating of processes within their context and imagining what will happen over many generations. It is a time intrinsic to its mode of dwelling, thus mimicking the enormously long "timescapes" of the physical world. Such timescapes include the thousands of years it takes for soil to regenerate, radioactive contamination to dissipate, or the impact of genetically modified organisms to be clearly evident.

Various writers and environmentalists have begun to articulate and perform such a time and to argue that humans should organize their lives in accordance with the glacial temporalities of the physical world. There is thus an increased performativity of glacial time.

Griffiths, for example, says that we should reject the obsession with speed and should walk and cycle rather than to drive or fly, to see how slowly nature works and to tailor actions to the slowness of time's nature.[47] Likewise, Macy argues that it is necessary to "break out of this temporal trap" caused by current instantaneous time. She advocates inhabitating "time in a healthier, saner fashion." She talks of opening up our experience of time in "organic, ecological or even geological terms and in revitalising relationships with other species."[48] Road protestors, according to McKay, seek to replace linear notions of time (clock time) with cyclical, cosmological, and bodily notions.[49] Adam shows how gardening involves knowing and caring about the future, where every action is marked by multiple, simultaneous time horizons. She argues for locally grown and seasonal foodstuffs to be a basic citizenship right that supermarkets should satisfy.[50] More generally, there is an increasing reflexive awareness of the long-term relationship between humans, animals, and the rest of "nature." It moves back out of immediate human history and forward into an unspecifiable and unknowable future.

Generally, it seems the more the future impinges on and predefines the present, the more intense becomes the concern about the past—in print, television, and electronic records, in museums and heritage parks, in collecting art and artifacts, through the dating of species, and so on. Huyssen describes the importance of memory as "an attempt to slow down

47. J. Griffiths, "Life of Strife in the Fast Lane," *Guardian*, August 23, 1995.
48. Macy, *World as Lover*, 206.
49. McKay, *Senseless Acts of Beauty*, 139.
50. Adam, *Timescapes of Modernity*, 95–96, 157.

information processing, to resist the dissolution of time . . . to claim some anchoring space in a world of puzzling and often threatening heterogeneity, non-synchronicity and information overload."[51]

Glacial time can be seen in various forms of resistance to the "placelessness" of instantaneous time. The UK organization Common Ground seeks to remake places as sites for "strolling" and "living in," and not just for passing through "instantaneously." It has developed the idea of community-based "parish maps." They believe, as Clifford writes, "that local people together know more and care more than they are ever credited with; that they can make brave decisions, guide change and keep the strands of history and richness of nature healthy and vibrant."[52] This slowing down of place, or the capturing of place by its "community," presupposes glacial time. People feel the weight of history, of those memories and practices within that very particular place, and believe that it can and will still be there in its essence in many generations' time. For Common Ground such places can be anywhere, not merely those places that have the right *look*. Clifford summarizes the determinants of local distinctiveness as "the patina and detail which make up ordinary places giving them identity and particularity" over the long term, stimulating our diverse senses.[53] Thus, the appreciation of the detail of certain localities presumes glacial time, as opposed to the clock time of the national state and the instantaneous time of much corporeal, imaginative, and virtual travel.

Glacial time can develop in relationship to where one was born or brought up, to one's place of current residence or work, or to where one has visited or even where one might visit corporeally or imaginatively. This can, however, produce conflicts over different glacial times. Lee shows such a conflict in her discussion of Yew Tree Tarn in the Lake District.[54] First there is the glacial time concerned with aesthetic beauty. The National Trust seeks to preserve the permanent look of the tarn for future generations. This preservation will be effected through a clear interference with nature. And second, there are the underlying geological and geomorphic processes that will naturally dry out the tarn and transform it into a meadow, and hence will not preserve it for viewing by future generations. In this second sense there are

51. Andreas Huyssen, *Twilight Memories: Marking Time in a Culture of Amnesia* (London: Routledge, 1995), 7.

52. Sue Clifford, "Pluralism, Power, and Passion," paper delivered at BANC Conference, St. Anne's College, Oxford, December 1994, 2.

53. Ibid., 3.

54. Keekok Lee, "Beauty for Ever," *Environmental Values* 4, no. 3 (1995): 213–25.

invisible long-term natural processes at work. Which glacial time wins out depends upon a struggle that is in part between different time regimes.

Women are often more able to perform glacial time. This is partly because they have had to develop shadow times, times that develop in the shadow of clock time but are partially distinguishable from it. Davies shows that the time of a "carer" is open-ended, outside commodified clock time, which is more men's time.[55] Women as carers are not only *in* time but also have to *give* time. But also because of women's role in the natural activities of childbirth and childrearing, they may develop alternatives to clock time, which "is clearly at odds with the rhythms of our body and the 'natural' environment where variations and the principle of temporality are a source of creativity and evolution."[56] Fox argues that a woman in labour is "forced by the intensity of the contractions to turn all her attention to them, loses her ordinary, intimate contact with clock time."[57] More generally, because of the role of many women in the activities of procreation, childbirth, and childrearing, women are often more likely to be tied into time as intergenerational and therefore "slowed down."

Conclusion

There are therefore a number of temporal regimes, what I call the clock, the instantaneous, and the glacial. There are multiple times, not a single time, let alone a single correct notion of time. Moreover, each of these times is a hybrid. They do not exist in some pure state. Each of these multiple times is simultaneously physical, technological and social. And they each get performed, just as Franklin, Lury, and Stacey have recently described the performativities involved in the making of the global.[58]

Thomas Friedman's *The Lexus and the Olive Tree* poignantly captures the contestation between the time regimes of the instantaneous and the glacial.[59] Half the world, he says, is intent on producing a better Lexus through

55. Karen Davies, *Women, Time, and the Weaving of the Strands of Everyday Life* (Aldershot: Gower, 1990); Adam, *Time and Social Theory*. Men can of course be carers and may thus also develop such a notion.

56. Adam, *Timewatch*, 52.

57. Meg Fox, "Unreliable Allies: Subjective and Objective Time in Childbirth," in *Taking Our Time: Feminist Perspectives on Temporality*, ed. Frieda Johles Forman and Caoran Sowton (Oxford: Pergamon Press, 1989), 127.

58. Sarah Franklin, Celia Lury, and Jackie Stacey, *Global Nature, Global Culture* (London: SAGE, 2000).

59. Thomas L. Friedman, *The Lexus and the Olive Tree* (London: HarperCollins, 2000).

modernizing, streamlining, and privatizing their economies so as to thrive within a global world. This is the "first modernity" of accelerating instantaneous time. And the other half is caught up in a fight to determine who owns which olive tree, the olive tree thus standing for roots, anchoring, identity, what Lash calls "another modernity"[60] or what I have characterized as glacial time. Olive trees also involve excluding others. So the struggle between the Lexus and the olive tree is taken by Friedman as a metaphor for the contested temporal regimes of the new global order.

In the 1990s it seemed as if the massive growth of global markets and the apparent success of neoliberal globalization would mean the Lexus would unambiguously win. It looked as though the accelerating instantaneous time regime was in the ascendancy, sweeping all before into a borderless nirvana. A world of speed and acceleration would drive onwards without challenge.

But although many might argue about the significance of September 11 to much of the world's six to seven billion population, it does seem that it marked that moment when the instantaneous time regime was brought to a shuddering, screeching halt. The strategy of liberal globalization, of the relatively unregulated growth of capitalist markets across the world, had produced extraordinarily heightened inequality. Among many effects was the generation of "wild zones" or "zones of turmoil."[61] And increasingly the time-space edges of the safe and the wild zones in the social world came into accelerating, dangerous new juxtapositions. Through money laundering, the drug trade, urban crime, asylum seeking, arms trading, people smuggling, slave trading, and urban terrorism, the spaces of the wild and the safe were chaotically juxtaposed, time-space was curved into new complex configurations in which those performing the glacial time of the Qur'an suddenly speak with a renewed voice, having an enemy not exactly on the run but no longer accelerating onwards and upwards. Glacial and instantaneous time came to mighty and bloody blows in the sky above New York on September 11, 2001.

60. See Scott Lash, *Another Modernity, a Different Rationality* (Oxford: Blackwell, 1999).
61. Michael Mann, "Globalization and September 11th," *New Left Review* 12 (2001): 51–72; Urry, "The Global Complexities of September 11th"; Urry, *Global Complexity*.

PART 3

HIGH-SPEED SOCIETY
POLITICAL CONSEQUENCES?

ELEVEN

THE STATE OF EMERGENCY

Paul Virilio

Speed is the essence of war.
> —Sun Tzu

.

The reduction of distances has become a strategic reality bearing incalculable economic and political consequences, since it corresponds to the negation of space.

The maneuver that once consisted in *giving up ground to gain Time* loses its meaning: at present, gaining Time is exclusively a matter of vectors. Territory has lost its significance in favor of the projectile. *In fact, the strategic value of the non-place of speed has definitively supplanted that of place,* and the question of possession of Time has revived that of territorial appropriation.

In this geographic contraction, which resembles the terrestrial movement described by Alfred Wegener, the binomial "fire-movement" takes on a new meaning: the distinction between fire's *power to destroy* and the *power to penetrate* of movement, of the vehicle, is losing its "validity."[1]

With the supersonic vector (airplane, rocket, airwaves), penetration and destruction become one. The instantaneousness of action at a distance corresponds to the defeat of the unprepared adversary, but also, and especially, to the defeat of the world as a field, as distance, as matter.

Immediate penetration, or penetration that is approaching immediacy, becomes identified with the instantaneous destruction of environmental conditions, since after *space-distance,* we now lack *time-distance* in the increasing acceleration of vehicular performances (precision, distance, speed).

From this point on, the binomial *fire-movement* exists only to designate a double movement of implosion and explosion; *the power of implosion* revives

---

1. Alfred Wegener, *Die Entstehung der Kontinente und Ozeane* [The Origin of Continents and Oceans], 5th ed. (Braunschweig: Friedrich Vieweg and Son, 1936), a theory of continental drift.

the old subsonic vehicles' (means of transportation, projectiles) power to penetrate, and *the power of explosion* revives the destructive power of classical molecular explosives. In this paradoxical object, *simultaneously explosive and implosive,* the new war machine combines a double disappearance: *the disappearance of matter in nuclear disintegration* and the *disappearance of places in vehicular extermination.*

Nonetheless, we should note that the disintegration of matter is constantly deferred in the deterrent equilibrium of peaceful coexistence, but not so the extermination of distances. In less than half a century, geographical spaces have kept shrinking as speed has increased. And if at the beginning of the 1940s we still had to count the speed of naval "strike power"—the major destructive power of the time—*in knots,* by the beginning of the 1960s this rapidity was measured *in machs,* in other words in thousands of kilometers per hour. And it is likely that current high-energy research will soon allow us to reach the speed of light with laser weapons.

If, as Lenin claimed, "strategy means choosing which points we apply force to," we must admit that these "points," today, are no longer *geostrategic strongpoints,* since from *any given spot* we can now reach any other, no matter where it may be, in record time and within several meters. . . .

We have to recognize that *geographic localization* seems to have definitively lost its strategic value and, inversely, that this same value is attributed *to the delocalization of the vector,* of a vector in permanent movement— no matter if this movement is aerial, spatial, underwater or underground. All that counts is the speed of the moving body and the undetectability of its path.

From the war of movement of mechanized forces, we reach the *strategy of Brownian movements,* a kind of chronological and pendular war that revives ancient popular and geographic warfare by a geostrategic homogenization of the globe. This homogenization was already announced in the nineteenth century, notably by the Englishman Mackinder in his theory of the "World-Island," in which Europe, Asia and Africa would compose a single continent to the detriment of the Americas—a theory that seems to have come to fruition today with the disqualification of localizations. But we should note that the indifferentiation of geostrategic positions is not the only effect of vectorial performances, for after the homogenization sought and finally acquired by naval and aerial imperialism, *strategic spatial miniaturization* is now the order of the day.

In 1955 General Chassin stated, "The fact that the earth is round has not been sufficiently studied from the military point of view." No sooner said than done. But in the ballistic progress of weapons, the curvature of the earth has not stopped shrinking. It is no longer the continents that become agglomerated, but the totality of the planet that is diminished, depending on the progress of the arms "race." The continental translation that, curiously enough, we find both in the geophysician Wegener, with the drift of land masses, and in Mackinder, with the geopolitical amalgam of lands, has given way to a world-wide phenomenon of terrestrial and technological contraction that today makes us penetrate into an artificial topological universe: *the direct encounter of every surface on the globe.*

The ancient inter-city duel, war between nations, the permanent conflict between naval empires and continental powers have all suddenly disappeared, giving way to an unheard-of opposition: *the juxtaposition of every locality, all matter.* The planetary mass becomes no more than a "critical mass," a precipitate resulting from the extreme reduction of contact time, a fearsome friction of places and elements that only yesterday were still distinct and separated by a buffer of distances, which have suddenly become anachronistic. In *The Origin of Continents and Oceans,* published in 1915, Alfred Wegener writes that in the beginning *the earth can only have had but one face,* which seems likely, given the capacities for interconnection. In the future the earth will have but one interface . . .

If speed thus appears as the essential fall-out of styles of conflicts and cataclysms, the current "arms race" is in fact only *"the arming of the race" toward the end of the world as distance, in other words as a field of action.*

The term "deterrence" points to the ambiguity of this situation, in which the weapon replaces the protection of armor, in which the possibilities of offense and offensive ensure in and of themselves the defense, the entire defensive against the "explosive" dimension of strategic arms, but not at all against the "implosive" dimension of the vectors' performances, since on the contrary the maintenance of a credible "strike power" requires the constant refining of the engines' power, in other words of their ability to reduce geographic space to nothing or almost nothing.

In fact, without the violence of speed, that of weapons would not be so fearsome. *In the current context, to disarm would thus mean first and foremost to decelerate,* to defuse the race toward the end. *Any treaty that does not limit the speed of this race* (the speed of means of communicating destruction) *will not limit strategic arms,* since from now on the essential object of strategy consists in maintaining the non-place of a general delocalization of means that alone still allows us to gain fractions of seconds, which gain is indispensable to any freedom of action. As General Fuller wrote, "When the combatants threw javelins at each other, the weapon's initial speed was such that one could see it on its trajectory and parry its effects with one's shield. But when the javelin was replaced by the bullet, the speed was so great that parry became impossible." Impossible to move one's body out of the way, but possible if one moved out of the weapon's range; possible as well through the shelter of the trench, greater than that of the shield—possible, in other words, through space and matter.

Today, the reduction of warning time that results from the supersonic speeds of assault leaves so little time for detection, identification and response that in the case of a surprise attack the supreme authority would have to risk abandoning his supremacy of decision by authorizing the lowest echelon of the defense system to immediately launch anti-missile missiles. The two political superpowers have thus far preferred to avoid this situation through negotiations, renouncing anti-missile defense at the same time.

Given the lack of space, an active defense requires at least the material time to intervene. But *these* are the "war materials" that disappear in the acceleration of the means of communicating destruction. There remains only a passive defense that consists less in reinforcing itself against the megaton powers of nuclear weapons than in a series of constant, unpredictable, aberrant movements, movements which are thus strategically effective—for at least a little while longer, we hope. In fact, war now rests entirely on the deregulation of time and space. This is why the *technical* maneuver that consists in complexifying the vector by constantly improving its performances has now totally supplanted *tactical* maneuvers on the terrain, as we have seen. General Ailleret points this out in his history of weapons by stating that *the definition of arms programs has become one of the essential elements of strategy.* If in ancient conventional warfare we could still talk about army maneuvers in the fields, in the current state of affairs, if this maneuver still exists, it no longer needs a "field." The invasion of the instant succeeds the invasion of the territory. The countdown becomes the scene of battle, the final frontier.

The opposing sides can easily ban bacteriological, geodesic or meteorological warfare. In reality, what is currently at stake with strategic arms limitation agreements (SALT I) is no longer the explosive but the vector, *the vector of nuclear deliverance,* or more precisely its performances. The reason for this is simple: where the molecular or nuclear explosive's blast made a given area unfit for existence, that of the implosive (vehicles and vectors) suddenly reduces reaction time, and the time for political decision, to nothing.

If over thirty years ago the nuclear explosive completed the cycle of *spatial wars,* at the end of this century the implosive (beyond politically and economically invaded territories) inaugurates *the war of time.* In full peaceful coexistence, without any declaration of hostilities, and more surely than by any other kind of conflict, rapidity delivers us from this world. We have to face the facts: today, speed is war, the last war.

But let's go back to 1962, to the crucial events of the Cuban missile crisis. At that time, the two superpowers had *fifteen minutes'* warning time for war. The installation of Russian rockets on Castro's island threatened to reduce the Americans' warning to *thirty seconds,* which was unacceptable for President Kennedy, whatever the risks of his categorical refusal. We all know what happened: the installation of a *direct line*—the "hot line"—and the interconnection of the two Heads of State!

Ten years later, in 1972, when the normal warning time was down to several minutes—ten for ballistic missiles, a mere two for satellite weapons— Nixon and Brezhnev signed the first strategic arms limitation agreement in Moscow. In fact, this agreement aims less at the quantitative limitation of weapons (as its adversary/partners claim) than at the preservation of a properly "human" political power, since the constant progress of rapidity threatens from one day to the next to reduce the warning time for nuclear war *to less than one fatal minute*—thus finally abolishing the Head of State's power of reflection and decision in favor of a pure and simple *automation* of defense systems. The decision for hostilities would then belong only to several strategic computer programs. *After having been* (because of its destructive capacities) *the equivalent of total war*—the nuclear missile launching submarine alone is able to destroy 500 cities—*the war machine suddenly becomes* (thanks to the reflexes of the strategic calculator) *the very decision for war.* What will remain, then, of the "political reasons" for deterrence? Let us recall that in 1962, among the reasons that made General de Gaulle decide to have the populations ratify the decision to elect the President of the Republic by universal suffrage, there was the credibility of deterrence, the legitimacy of the referendum being a fundamental element of this very deterrence. What will remain of all this in the automation of deterrence? in the automation of decision?

The transition *from the state of siege* of wars of space to *the state of emergency* of the war of time only took several decades, during which the political era of the statesman was replaced by the apolitical era of the State apparatus. Facing the advent of such a regime, we would do well to wonder about what is much more than a temporal phenomenon.

At the close of our century, *the time of the finite world is coming to an end;* we live in the beginnings of a paradoxical *miniaturization of action,* which others prefer to baptize *automation.* Andrew Stratton writes, "We commonly believe that automation suppresses the possibility of human error. In fact, it transfers that possibility from the action stage to the conception stage. We are now reaching the point where the possibilities of an accident during the critical minutes of a plane landing, if guided automatically, are fewer than if a pilot is controlling it. We might wonder if we will ever reach the stage of automatically controlled nuclear weapons, in which the margin of error would be less than with human decision. But the possibility of this progress threatens to reduce to little or nothing the time for human decision to intervene in the system."

This is brilliant. Contraction in time, the disappearance of the territorial space, after that of the fortified city and armor, leads to a situation in which the notions of "before" and "after" designate only the future and the past in a form of war that causes the "present" to disappear in the instantaneousness of decision.

The final power would thus be less one of imagination than of anticipation, so much so that to govern would be *no more than* to foresee, simulate, memorize the simulations; that the present "Research Institute" could appear to be the blueprint of this final power, the power of utopia.

The loss of material space leads to the government of nothing but time. *The Ministry of Time* sketched in each vector will finally be accomplished following the dimensions of the biggest vehicle there is, the *State-vector.* The whole geographic history of the distribution of land and countries would stop in favor of a single *regrouping of time,* power no longer being comparable to anything but a "meteorology." In this precarious fiction speed would suddenly become a destiny, a form of progress, in other words a "civilization" in which each speed would be something of a "region" of time.

As Mackinder said, forces of pressure are always exerted in the same direction. Now, this single direction of geopolitics is that which leads to the immediate *commutation* of things and places. War is not, as Foch claimed, harboring illusions on the future of chemical explosives, "a worksite of fire." War has always been a worksite of movement, a speed-factory. *The technological break-through,* the last form of the war of movement, ends up, with deterrence, at the dissolution of what *separated* but also *distinguished,* and this non-distinction corresponds for us to a political blindness.

We can verify it with General de Gaulle's decree of January 7, 1959, suppressing the distinction between peacetime and wartime. Furthermore, during this same period, and despite the Vietnamese exception that proves the rule, war has shrunk from several years to several days, even to several hours.

In the 1960s a mutation occurs: *the passage from wartime to the war of peacetime,* to that *total peace* that others still call "peaceful coexistence." The blindness of the speed of means of communicating destruction is not a liberation from geopolitical servitude, but the extermination of space as the field of freedom of political action. We only need refer to the necessary controls and constraints of the railway, airway or highway infrastructures to see the fatal impulse: the more speed increases, the faster freedom decreases.

The apparatus' self-propulsion finally entails the self-sufficiency of automation. What happens in the example of the racecar driver, who is no more than a worried lookout for the catastrophic probabilities of his movement, is reproduced on the political level as soon as conditions require an action in real time.[2]

Let us take, for example, a crisis situation: "From the very beginning of the Six Days' War in 1967, President Johnson took control of the White House, one hand guiding the Sixth Fleet, the other on the hot line. The necessity of the link between the two became clearly apparent as soon as an Israeli attack against the American reconnaissance ship *Liberty* provoked the intervention of one of the fleet's aircraft carriers. Moscow examined every blip on the radar screens as attentively as Washington did: would the Russians interpret the air planes' change of course and their convergence as an act of aggression? This is where the hot line came in: Washington immediately explained the reasons for this operation and Moscow was reassured" (Harvey Wheeler).

In this example of strategic political action in real time, the Chief of State is in fact a "Great Helmsman." But the prestigious nature of the people's historical guide gives way to the more prosaic and rather banal one of a "test pilot" trying to maneuver his machine in a very narrow margin. Ten years have passed since this "crisis state," and the arms race has caused the margin of political security to narrow still further, bringing us closer to the critical threshold where the possibilities for properly human political action will disappear in a "State of Emergency"; where telephone communication between statesmen will stop, probably in favor of an interconnection of computer systems, modern calculators of strategy and, consequently, of politics.

2. In terms of control, the meaning of this time is a function of the temporal field in which perception, decision, and action are involved.

(Let us recall that the computers' first task was to solve simultaneously a series of complex equations aimed at causing the trajectory of the anti-aircraft projectile and that of the airplane to meet.)

Here we have the fearsome telescoping of elements born of the "amphibi-ous generations"; the extreme proximity of parties *in which the immediacy of information immediately creates the crisis;* the frailty of reasoning power, which is but the effect of a miniaturization of action—the latter resulting from the miniaturization of space as a field of action.

An imperceptible movement on a computer keyboard, or one made by a "skyjacker" brandishing a cookie box covered with masking tape, can lead to a catastrophic chain of events that until recently was inconceivable. We are too willing to ignore the fact that, alongside the threat of proliferation resulting from the acquisition of nuclear explosives by irresponsible parties, there is a proliferation of the threat resulting from the vectors that cause those who own or borrow them to become just as irresponsible.

In the beginning of the 1940s, Paris was a six-days' walk from the bor-der, a three-hours' drive, and one hour by plane. Today the capital is only several minutes away from anywhere else, and anywhere else is only sev-eral minutes away from its end—so much so that the tendency, which still existed several years ago, *to advance* one's destructive means closer to the enemy territory (as in the Cuban missile crisis) is reversing. The present tendency is toward geographic disengagement, a movement of *retreat* that is due only to the progress of the vectors and to the extension of their reach (cf. the American submarine *Trident,* whose new missiles can travel 8,000 to 10,000 kilometers, as opposed to the *Poseidon's* 4,000 to 5,000).

Thus, the different strategic nuclear forces (American and Soviet) will no longer need to patrol the area in the target continents; they can hence-forth retreat within their territorial limits. This is confirmation that they are abandoning a form of geostrategic conflict. After the reciprocal renun-ciation of geodesic war, we will possibly see the abandonment of advanced bases, extending to America's extraordinary abandonment of its sovereignty over the Panama Canal. . . . A sign of the times, of the time of the war of time.

Nonetheless, we must note that this strategic retreat no longer has any-thing in common with *the retreat* that allowed conventional armies to "gain time by losing ground." In the retreat due to the extended reach of the bal-listic vectors, *we in fact gain time by losing the space of the (stationary or mobile) advanced bases, but this time is gained at the expense of our own forces,* of the performances of our own engines, and not at the enemy's expense, since, symmetrically, the latter accompanies this geostrategic disengagement. *Everything suddenly happens as if each protagonist's own arsenal became his (internal) enemy, by advancing too quickly.* Like the recoil of a firearm, the implosive movement of the ballistic performances diminishes the field of strategic forces. In fact, if the adversary/partners didn't pull back their means of communicating destruction while lengthening their reach, the higher speed of these means would already have reduced the time of decision about their use to nothing. Just as in 1972, in Moscow, the partners in this game abandoned plans for an anti-missile missile defense, so five years later they wasted the advantage of swiftness for the very temporary benefit of a greater extension of their intercontinental missiles. Both seem to fear—all the while seeking—the multiplying effect of speed, of that *speed activity* so dear to all armies since the Revolution.

In the face of this curious contemporary *regression* of strategic arms limitation agreements, it is wise to return to the very principle of deterrence. The essential aim of throwing ancient weapons or of shooting off new ones has never been to kill the enemy or destroy his means, but to deter him, in other words, to *force him to interrupt his movement.* Regardless of whether this physical movement is one that allows the assailed to contain the assailant or one of invasion, "the aptitude for war is the aptitude for movement," which a Chinese strategist expressed in these words: "An army is always strong enough when it can come and go, spread out and regroup, as it wishes and when it wishes."

For the last several years, however, this freedom of movement has been hindered not by the enemy's capacity for resistance or reaction, but by the refinement of the vectors used. Deterrence seems to have passed suddenly from the fire stage, in other words the explosive stage, to that of the movement of vectors, as if a final degree of nuclear deterrence had appeared, still poorly mastered by the actors in the global strategic game. Here again, we must return to the strategic and tactical realities of weaponry in order to grasp the present logistical reality. As Sun Tzu said, "Weapons are tools of ill omen." They are first feared and fearsome as *threats,* long before being used. Their "ominous" character can be split into three components:

The threat of their performance at the moment of their invention, of their production;
The threat of their use against the enemy;
The effect of their use, which is fatal for persons and destructive for their goods.

If these last two components are unfortunately known, and have long been experimented with, the first, on the other hand, *the (logistical) ill omen of the invention of their performance,* is less commonly recognized. Nonetheless, it is at this level that the question of deterrence is raised. *Can we deter an enemy from inventing new weapons, or from perfecting their performances?* Absolutely not.

We thus find ourselves facing this dilemma:

The threat of use (the second component) of the nuclear arm prohibits the terror of actual use (the third component). But for this threat to remain and allow the strategy of deterrence, we are forced to develop the threatening system that characterizes the first component: the *ill omen of the appearance of new performances for the means of communicating destruction.* Stated plainly, this is the perpetual sophistication of combat means and the replacement of the geostrategic breakthrough by the technological breakthrough, the great logistical maneuvers.

We must face the facts: if ancient weapons deterred us from interrupting movement, *the new weapons deter us from interrupting the arms race.* Moreover, they require in their technological (dromological) logic the exponential development, not of *the number* of destructive machines, since their power has increased (simply compare the millions of projectiles in the two World Wars to the several thousands of rockets in contemporary arsenals), but of their global *performances.* Destructive capabilities having reached the very limits of possibility with thermo-nuclear arms, the enemy's "logistical strategies" are once more oriented toward power of penetration and flexibility of use.

The balance of terror is thus a mere illusion in the industrial stage of war, in which reigns a perpetual imbalance, a constantly raised bid, able to invent new means of destruction without end. We have proven ourselves, on the other hand, not only quite incapable of destroying those we've already produced (the "waste products" of the military industry being as hard to recycle as those of the nuclear industry), but especially incapable of avoiding the threat of their appearance.

War has thus moved from the action stage to the conception stage that, as we know, characterizes *automation.* Unable to control the emergence of new means of destruction, deterrence, for us, is tantamount to setting in place a series of automatisms, reactionary industrial and scientific procedures from which all political choice is absent. By becoming "strategic," in other words, by combining offense and defense, the new weapons deter us from interrupting the movement of the arms race, and the "logistical strategy" of their production becomes the inevitable production of destructive means as an obligatory factor of non-war—a vicious circle in which the inevitability of production replaces that of destruction. The war machine is now not only all of war, *but also becomes the adversary/partners' principal enemy* by depriving them of their freedom of movement.[3] Dragged unwillingly into the "servitude without honor" of deterrence, the protagonists henceforth practice the "politics of the worst," or more precisely, the "apolitics of the worst," which necessarily leads to the war machine one day becoming the very decision for war—thus accomplishing the perfection of its self-sufficiency, *the automation of deterrence.*

The suggestive juxtaposition of the terms *deterrence* and *automation* allows us to understand better the structural axis of contemporary military-political events, as H. Wheeler specifies: "Technologically possible, centralization has become politically necessary." This shortcut recalls that of Saint-Just's famous dictum: "When a people can be oppressed, it will be"—the difference being that this techno-logistical oppression no longer concerns only the "people," but the "deciders" as well. If only yesterday the freedom of maneuver (that aptitude for movement which has been equated with the aptitude for war) occasionally required delegations of power up to the secondary echelons, the reduction of the margin of maneuver due to the progress of the means of communicating destruction causes an extreme concentration of responsibilities for the solitary decision-maker that the Chief of State has become. This contraction is, however, far from being complete; it continues according to the arms race, at the speed of the new capacities of the vectors, until one day it will dispossess this last man. In fact, the movement is the same that restrains the number of projectiles and that reduces to nothing or almost nothing the decision of an individual deprived of counsel. The maneuver is the same as the one that today leads us to abandon territories and advanced bases, and as the one that will one day lead us to renounce solitary human decision in favor of the absolute miniaturization of the political field which is *automation.*

If in Frederick the Great's time *to win was to advance,* for the supporters of deterrence it is *to retreat,* to leave places, peoples and the individual where they are—to the point where dromological progress closely resembles the jet engine's reaction propulsion, caused by the ejection of a certain quantity of movement (the product of a mass times a velocity) *in the direction opposite to the one we wish to take.*

3. The missile-carrying nuclear submarine has in itself the destructive power of all the explosives used in the Second World War.

In this *war of recession* between East and West—contemporary not with the illusory limitation of strategic arms, but with *the limitation of strategy itself*—the power of thermonuclear explosion serves as an artificial horizon for a race that is increasing the power of the vehicular implosion. The impossibility of interrupting the progress of the power of penetration, other than by an *act of faith* in the enemy, leads us to deny strategy as *prior knowledge*. The automatic nature not only of arms and means, but also of the command, is the same as denying our ability to reason: *Nicht raisonniren!* Frederick the Second's order is perfected by a deterrence that leads us to reduce our freedom not only of action and decision, but also of conception. The logic of arms systems is eluding the military framework more and more, and moving toward the engineer responsible for research and development—in expectation, of course, of the system's self-sufficiency. Two years ago Alexandre Sanguinetti wrote, "It is becoming less and less conceivable to build attack planes, which with their spare parts cost several million dollars each, to transport bombs able to destroy a country railroad station. *It is simply not cost effective.*" This logic of practical war, in which the operating costs of the (aerial) vector automatically entail the heightening of its destructive capability because of the requirements of transporting a tactical nuclear weapon, is not limited to attack planes; it is also becoming the logic of the State apparatus. This backwardness is the logistical consequence of producing means to communicate destruction. *The danger of the nuclear weapon, and of the arms system it implies, is thus not so much that it will explode, but that it exists and is imploding in our minds.*

Let us summarize this phenomenon:

—Two bombs interrupt the war in the Pacific, and several dozen nuclear submarines are enough to ensure peaceful coexistence. . . .

This is its *numerical* aspect.

—With the appearance of the multiple thermonuclear warhead and the rapid development of tactical nuclear arms, we see the miniaturization of explosive charges. . . .

This is its *volumetric* aspect.

—After having cleared the planet surface of a cumbersome defensive apparatus by reducing undersea and underground strategic arms, they renounce world expanse by reducing the trouble spots and advanced bases. . . .

This is its *geographical* aspect.

—Once responsible for the operations, the old chiefs of war, strategists and generals, find themselves demoted and restricted to simple maintenance operations, for the sole benefit of the Chief of State. . . .

This is its *political* aspect.

But this quantitative and qualitative scarcity doesn't stop. Time itself is no longer enough:

—Constantly heightened, the vectors' already quasisupersonic capacities are superseded by the high energies that enable us to approach the speed of light. . . .

This is its *spatiotemporal* aspect.

After the time of the State's political relativity as nonconducting medium, we are faced with the no-time of the politics of relativity. The *full discharge* feared by Clausewitz has come about with the State of Emergency. The violence of speed has become both the location and the law, the world's destiny and its destination.

TWELVE

THE NIHILISM OF SPEED:
ON THE WORK OF PAUL VIRILIO

Stefan Breuer

Faster cars, faster trains, faster planes . . . our age is obsessed with speed. The streets of the inner city have become dangerous racetracks; the suburbs, park-and-ride zones; the areas between cities, expressways, rail lines, runways. A high pace, hustle and bustle, and stress mark the work world, and even on vacation we know of nothing better to do than to continue the frenzy: as skiers on mountains reduced to inclined planes, as surfers on the smooth surfaces of rivers and lakes, as travelers who make themselves into projectiles and are fired to their destination. No doubt, speed is the idol of the day, and the number of victims it claims year after year in Europe alone is on the scale of a small city.

And yet how little we know about speed! Sociology concerns itself with meaning, economics with wealth (or poverty), political science with rule—phenomena that have little or nothing to do with speed. Only physicists talk about it in self-assured tones of having dissolved all its secrets into formulae. Can the equation $v = \Delta s/\Delta t$ be all there is to say about a phenomenon on which today, as the arms race for ever-faster delivery systems shows, nothing less that the continued existence of this planet depends?

Among the few authors who have posed this question, Paul Virilio is the most important. Virilio is the thinker of speed par excellence, the creator of "dromology," understood as the theory of the nature of speed, its conditions of emergence, its transformations, and it effects (*dromo* is Greek for race, and at the same time the designation of the entrance to the domed mausoleums of Mycenae). The findings of his research are devastating. The constant increase in acceleration, he argues, is leading to nothing other than the "liquidation of the world,"[1] to the realization of the one original idea the West has produced: nothingness, the being of nothing, the void.[2] Speed is nihilism in practice,[3] the "defeat of the world as field, as distance, as matter."[4] "Pollution, population growth, shortage of natural resources— more unsettling than all that is no doubt the constant rise of higher speeds; acceleration is literally *the end of the world!*"[5]

In the following I would like to present and examine some of the arguments developed by Virilio. I will begin with a sketch of preindustrial and thus pretechnological forms of speed and their basis, the "space-time *dispositif.*" I will then examine the concept of the "Dromocratic Revolution," and finally I will offer an analysis of "speed-space" and its implications. Because speed in its pretechnological as well as its technological forms is a relational quantity—the relation between a certain distance and a certain interval of time—it goes without saying that special attention must be given to the transformation of the relation between time and space.

I. Metabolic Speed and the Space-Time *Dispositif*

1. Speed is not witchcraft. It belongs to the human body, to the *conditio humana,* as metabolism belongs to nature: "to live, *to be alive,* means to be speed."[6] But during by far the greatest part of human history this speed was limited, since it was only "metabolic" speed, the speed of the human or animal body. Even the few artificial means of transportation that were discovered in preindustrial societies, like the sailing ship, were based on the use of natural speeds, like wind or ocean currents, and therefore remained relatively unchanged for long periods of time.[7] This "speed of the living" could be tamed by modest means.[8] Legal and political norms, police control, and military fortifications subjected movement in space to a regulation that, if not comprehensive or total, was nevertheless extremely effective

---

1. Paul Virilio, *L'horizon négatif* (Paris: Galilée, 1984), 59.

2. Ibid., 16.

3. Paul Virilio, *The Aesthetics of Disappearance,* trans. Philip Beitchman (New York: Semiotext(e), 1991).

4. Paul Virilio, *Speed and Politics,* trans. Mark Politizzotti (New York: Semiotext(e), 1986), 133.

5. Paul Virilio, *Fahren, fahren, fahren,* trans. Ulrich Raulff (Berlin: Merve, 1978), 30.

6. Ibid., 20.

7. Paul Virilio and Sylvère Lotringer, *Pure War,* trans. Mark Polizotti (New York: Semiotext(e), 1983), 44–45.

8. Ibid., 140.

and prevented such driving forces from becoming independent. Virilio therefore also calls the age of metabolic speed the "age of brakes,"[9] in which the powers of continuity dominated those of motion and change.

The primacy of continuity corresponded to a primacy of space—or, more precisely, of a particular kind of space that Virilio calls "geographical space."[10] This concept is connected to a wealth of associations. Geographical space is substantial and material.[11] It possesses volume, mass, density, and extension,[12] as well as gravity and weight.[13] It is opaque and nontransparent,[14] in direct opposition to the transparent and permeable space of the modern war of annihilation.[15] It does not connect, it divides, promoting separation and isolation. "I've always thought of space in terms of breaks."[16] Breaks divide space into noninterchangeable places, each with its particular here and now. They produce heterogeneity and multiplicity, but also distance and isolation. They put up obstacles to connection and relationality, and foster discontinuity and local fixity. "Space is that which keeps everything from occupying the same place."[17]

Geographical space is coupled with a particular form of time: "extensive, historical time."[18] Among its distinguishing features, the first is that it represents a dependent variable with respect to space—indeed, it must be thought directly in spatial concepts. Historical time is *longue durée* in Braudel's sense:[19] "extended time—time that lasts, is portioned out, organized, developed"[20] and so *eo ipso* acts as an "inertial limit" and a guarantor of "stability."[21] In order to emphasize the tight link of this concept of time with space, Virilio often speaks of "espace-temps" as well as the "space-time *dispositif*,"[22] already signaling by word order which of the two is to be accorded greater primacy.

9. Ibid., 45.

10. Ibid., 115 (translation modified).

11. Paul Virilio, *The Lost Dimension*, trans. Daniel Moshenberg (New York: Semiotext(e), 1991), 102; *Pure War*, 166.

12. Virilio, *Lost Dimension*, 102; *Pure War*, 174.

13. Virilio, *L'horizon négatif*, 199.

14. Virilio, *Lost Dimension*, 59.

15. Paul Virilio, *War and Cinema: The Logistics of Perception*, trans. Patrick Camillier (London: Verso, 1989), 72.

16. Virilio, *Pure War*, 117.

17. Virilio, *Lost Dimension*, 17.

18. Virilio, *Pure War*, 98.

19. Virilio, *L'horizon négatif*, 288.

20. Virilio, *Pure War*, 46 (translation modified).

21. Ibid., 72, 99.

22. Virilio, *Lost Dimension*, 128 (translation modified).

2. We must leave the space-time *dispositif* with this short sketch. It should have established that Virilio argues ontologically, and is thus vulnerable. Substance and material, space and time are spoken of *in intentio recto,* without reflection on the awareness, fundamental for modern scientific thinking, that there is no observer-independent objectivity, that the theoretical system of reference influences categories and ways of measuring the object, and that space and time are to be found on the side of the former rather than the latter.[23] The connection between space, extension, and material, typical of Aristotle and even of Descartes (to be sure, under the completely different presuppositions of a *mathesis universalis*), has not been tenable since Newton, and it can hardly be assumed that space before the Newtonian breakthrough obeys the same laws as thereafter.

The vulnerability of Virilio's conception could be reduced if it were grounded not ontologically but anthropologically. Virilio himself at times seems to be thinking in this direction when he speaks of the traditional structuring of appearances, of "the communal perception of sensible space,"[24] or when he defines geographical space primarily from sensual experience.[25] In fact, the criteria of the space-time *dispositif* correspond quite precisely to those that, according to Cassirer, are typical of the space of sensual perception. For an observer of this type, Euclidean space, with its basic features of continuity, infinity, and complete homogeneity, is alien.[26] This perspective can be more precisely defined with the help of developmental psychology. It has emerged from the research of Piaget and his students finding that formal-logical thinking (and with it the ability to grasp *geometrical* space and *operational* time) develops, first, relatively late ontogenetically (around age eleven) and, second, by no means automatically. Rather, it is promoted essentially by the individual's interaction with an environment that is, for its part, determined by formal-logical and technical structures. From this it can be concluded that, conversely, in a world in which such structures are lacking or only rudimentarily developed, ontogenetically earlier models of perception and thought dominate. In Piaget's schema these are sensory-motor intelligence, symbolic-preconceptual thought, intuitive thought, and concrete-operational thought.[27]

---

23. Cf., e.g., Peter Mittelstaedt, *Philosophical Problems of Modern Physics* (Dordrecht: D. Reidel, 1976), 23, 34.

24. Virilio, *The Lost Dimension,* 30.

25. Virilio, *Fahren, fahren, fahren,* 24.

26. Ernst Cassirer, *The Philosophy of Symbolic Forms,* vol. 2, *Mythical Thought,* trans. Ralph Manheim (New Haven: Yale University Press, 1955), 83.

27. Jean Piaget, *The Psychology of Intelligence,* trans. Malcolm Piercy and D. E. Berlyne (London: Routledge and Paul, 1950), 123.

Although these thinking models mark levels of development and are distinguished from one another above all by a progressive "decentering," they nevertheless present a certain commonality with respect to time and space that can be interpreted in Virilio's sense. Already on the first levels, a still-egocentric and elementary space of experience is constituted that results from the purely sensory coordination of form, distance, and dimensional movement by sight, hearing, and touch. Out of these visual, auditory, and tactile spaces, a space of perception is formed that is at once, as it were, a preconceptual and presymbolic system of orientation whose predominant relations are being adjacent, being separate, following in a series, being enclosed, and being continuous. Piaget also calls this elementary space "topological space."[28]

With the development of symbolic, graphic/concrete, and concrete-operational intelligence, this elementary topological space is increasingly structured and systematized, although in a way that remains closely coupled to the givenness of the space of perception. Spatial orderings are based on concrete physical features of the natural environment and/or the human body; they establish connections between experiences, but they do not seek to homogenize them and arrange them in an abstract system of coordination. Thus, writes Piaget, it is true that the whole of reality becomes accessible to thought. "But it is still only a *represented* reality; with formal operations there is even more than reality involved, since the world of the possible becomes available for construction and since thought becomes free from the real world."[29] We will return to the quality of this freedom.

But first it should be noted that the preformal model of perception and thought is distinguished by a primacy of (topological) space with respect to time. Not that the feeling of time and temporal coordination is entirely absent at the earliest stages. By the end of the sensory-motor stage, children are already in a position to assess the duration and consequences of events and actions and arrange them temporally.[30] However, these cognitive abilities refer to concrete-specific sequences, not to time thought of comprehensively as abstract and homogenous—a restriction clearly manifested, for example, in the inability to coordinate relative speeds with one another (that is, two or more sequences). That sequences and successions of events also

28. Jean Piaget and Bärbel Inhelder, *The Child's Conception of Space,* trans. F. J. Langdon and J. L. Lunzer (London: Routledge and Kegan Paul, 1963), 5.

29. Piaget, *Psychology of Intelligence,* 151 (emphasis added).

30. Jean Piaget, *The Child's Conception of Time,* trans. A. J. Pomerans (New York: Basic Books, 1969).

have a spatial dimension, however, means that the thinking tied to them cannot isolate the temporal component. The spatial and temporal vocabulary remain interchangeable; indeed, the understanding of time is itself to a large extent spatialized, such that usual and repeating successions are thought in an irreversible and static order, like the physical features of a landscape.[31] This corresponds quite exactly to Virilio's conception of historical, extensive time, so that topological space exhibits clear analogies to the conception of geographical space.

One can then go one step further and demonstrate, alongside its ontogenetic reality, the historical reality of the space-time *dispositif* as well. Here I will by no means speak of the parallel of ontogenesis and phylogenesis, an idea as beloved as it is untenable—first, because humanity is not a subject that proceeds through particular stages of development, and second, because, as will be shown, the transition from the space-time *dispositif* to the "speed-space" of modernity requires a much more complex explanation than those that cognitive psychology or learning theory can offer. Nevertheless, anthropological and historical research shows that most known societies moved within the space-time *dispositif*, and that even in modern, high-tech societies a not insignificant part of the population has not reached the stage of formal thinking. In his study, *The Basic Elements of Primitive Thought*, Hallpike establishes that in segmented societies individual thought processes as well as collective ideas are thoroughly determined by preoperational or concrete-operational models, which doubtless has nothing to do with a constitutional cognitive insufficiency but is rather determined by the internal makeup and construction of these societies.

In what Lévi-Strauss called "primitive thinking," ideas of space depend to a high degree on phenomenal appearances and contextual associations with the physical world, whereby the axis of the human body, the position of the sun, and the structure of the house play special roles. The most common dispositional principles, such as inside/outside, left/right, high/low, and open/closed, rest on these ideas of space—principles that on first glance appear very simple, yet allow the construction of more complex spatial orderings.[32] This is closely connected to an understanding of time that largely represents a far-reaching system of coordinating sequential spatial states of affairs. According to Hallpike, the basic feature of primitive time is that it is based on successions of qualitative events, such as those based on the

31. Christopher R. Hallpike, *Foundations of Primitive Thought* (Oxford: Clarendon Press, 1979), 348.
32. Ibid., 285.

seasons or everyday activities, that are typical only of a particular kind of society, so that duration, succession, and simultaneity cannot be coordinated from place to place. The effect of the cyclical and unchanging character of these events is that the time they structure is also irreversible and static, insofar as each event is connected only to the events that precede and follow it. "Such a sequence of events is closely comparable to a landscape, with each land-mark in a fixed relationship with every other, and relations of time can therefore be comprehended by spatial concepts such as near, far, beyond, behind, and so on. The spatialization of time, its incorporation in process and the lack of homogeneity, continuity, and uniformity are the principal characteristics of primitive time."[33]

This certainly does not hold to the same extent for more complex societies, especially not if, for example, spatial measurement and modes of quantification have developed in connection with land surveying and the subdivision of time is tied to astronomical observations. Nevertheless, the extent to which the rudiments of the space-time *dispositif* are a difficult obstacle to overcome even for politically organized early cultures is striking. Among the Inca, for instance, regularly recurring ritual functions were performed within the framework of the so-called *ceque* system, whereby the different stone shrines of Cuzco were organized in a row of sightlines (*ceques*) from which the sun radiated from the temple. Each of these sightlines was assigned to particular social groups, which had to perform particular rites, ceremonies, or public tasks, such as water control, at particular times; social organization was, as it were, projected into a space that, for its part, in turn structured the experience of time.[34] In similar ways, in ancient Mexico the magical organization of the world in four districts determined the division of the year.[35] In preimperial China, time was imagined as a liturgical order that was inseparably connected to a particular district and a particular order of domination. Through his regular round trip, the prince rhythmically renewed space as a hierarchically layered association of heterogeneous districts and assigned each place its appropriate emblems, which were at the same time based on the calendrical order. The idea of time as "a succession of closed

33. Ibid., 347.

34. Cf. R. Tom Zuidema, *The Ceque System of Cuzco: The Social Organization of the Capital of the Inca* (Leiden: E. J. Brill, 1964); Zuidema, "The Inca Calendar," in *Native American Astronomy,* ed. Anthony F. Aveni (Austin: University of Texas Press, 1977); and Zuidema, "Hierarchy and Space in Incaic Social Organization," *Ethnohistory* 30, no. 2 (1983): 49–75.

35. Anneliese Mönnich, "The 'Tonalpohualli' of Codex Tudela and the Four Quarters of the World," in *Space and Time in the Cosmovision of Mesoamerica,* ed. Franz Tichy, Lateinamerika-Studien 10 (Munich: Wilhelm Fink, 1982), 97–110.

eras, discontinuous, complete in themselves" thus corresponded to the idea of time as a manifold, labile whole, always renewed from the center.[36] Finally, in the European Middle Ages, as epics, travel reports, and pictures show, the qualitative, serial, empirical, and symbolic elements of the experience of space were connected to an "aggregate space."[37] Time, on the other hand, was "spatialized." In narratives, for example, moments did not follow successively, one after another, but rather developed as isolated events that were represented by the poet "flatly," as parts of a picture lying next to one another.[38] Insofar as there was an organization of time at all, it was theological, defined by a worldview that took all power over time away from people, since it was understood as the property of God and His trustee, the Church.

These remarks will suffice to show that the reality of the space-time *dispositif* can be demonstrated in other ways than those employed by Virilio. We can agree with Virilio when he stresses the significance of time for premodern societies and directly qualifies its ordering as "spatial order."[39] But this spatial order and its corresponding metabolic speed do not result, as many of his formulations seem to suggest, from a natural property of space and the body (however that may be understood), but rather from social conditions that privilege graphic/concrete and symbolic thinking—thinking that is not allowed to formalize space and time such that a rationalization of speed becomes possible. What processes, we must now ask, led to exploding these obstacles so that metabolic speed could be replaced with technological speed?

II. The Dromocratic Revolution

1. Virilio's answer to this question arises from his concept of the "Dromocratic Revolution." "Dromocracy," the fusion of power and speed, is not for him a specifically modern phenomenon. In most known societies, the position of the ruling classes was based not least on the fact that, compared with the ruled, they had greater speed at their disposal. (It is no accident that

---

36. Marcel Granet, *La pensée chinoise* (Paris: La renaissance du livre, 1934), 96.

37. Erwin Panofsky, "Die Perspektive als 'symbolischen Form,'" in *Aufsätze zu Grundfragen der Kunstwissenschaft* (Berlin: B. Hessling, 1964), 109; P. Czerwinski, "Das Ganze *ist* die Summe seiner Teile: Über nicht-systematische Räume in spätmittelalterlichen Texten und Bildern" (1987).

38. A. J. Gurjewitsch, *Das Weltbild des mittelalterlichen Menschen* (Dresden: Verlag der Kunst, 1978).

39. Virilio, *Pure War*, 115 (translation modified).

Ritter and *chevalier* [knight] come from "to ride" (*rîten* = *reiten*) and "man with a horse" [L. *caballarius*], respectively. The Dromocratic Revolution, on the other hand, is the birth of the modern age. With it, the transition occurs from metabolic to technological speed, from the "speed of the living" to the "speed of the dead," from "the age of brakes" to the "age of acceleration."[40]

In comparison to the Industrial Revolution, the key category of Marxist as well as liberal theories of modernization, the Dromocratic Revolution appears as a far more encompassing process. While the Industrial Revolution created the mass production of standardized objects by introducing new methods, the Dromocratic Revolution brought forth the means to produce speed—or, more precisely, to produce *artificial* speed that overcomes the possibilities of the human/animal body many times over: first the steam engine, then the internal combustion engine, and finally the modern technologies of telecommunication and televisualization. With new vehicles (railway, automobile, airplane), it became possible to aim at and overcome whatever space one liked. At the same time, the new communications technologies, from the telegraph to satellites, produced a comprehensive network in which "all the surfaces of the globe are directly present to one another."[41] Not the revolutionization of production but that of circulation was thus the decisive advance that began the "deterritorialization" basic to modernity, providing the conditions for a new "technological space" that is not geographical, but rather a "speed-space." "In fact, there is no 'industrial revolution,' but only 'dromocratic revolution'; there is no democracy, only dromocracy; there is no strategy, only dromology."[42]

But how did this revolution that has so far escaped the attention of historians and sociologists take place? For this, one must know that according to Virilio the decisive switch in the history of speed took place in the military sphere. This already holds for the first gain in the power of movement in prehistoric times, when the subjection of women put men in a position to specialize as hunters and warriors.[43] It holds even more for the development of an "aristocracy of speed" that resulted from the use of the metabolic power of the horse and the ship.[44] And it holds above all for the Dromocratic Revolution of the modern period, which began with the naval wars of the seventeenth and eighteenth centuries. By means of new maritime logistics

40. Ibid., 140, 45.
41. Virilio, *War and Cinema*, 46.
42. Virilio, *Speed and Politics*, 46.
43. Virilio, *Fahren, fahren, fahren*, 74.
44. Ibid., 20–21.

("fleet in being"), England managed with a single blow to unhinge the traditional system of fortresses and sieges, of direct struggles for territory, and to totalize war, which had previously been locally bounded. From this point on, not only single places were threatened, but entire countries and continents. Nations and states were cut off from their trade routes and sources of raw materials and driven to collapse without further need for a monumental decisive battle, which had hitherto constituted the nature of traditional war.

This new strategy was essentially facilitated by the natural condition of the sea, which presents far fewer obstacles to rapid movement than land, which is arranged into countless interruptions. Next to the air, the sea is the part of geographical space that best accommodates the requirements of the new, technological space. In a world of places and fixed positions, it embodies the "non-place,"[45] a field of organization independent of static arrangements, in which fast, linear movements in the form of vectors are possible. Certainly, the sea also has its dangers, as a glance at the *Odyssey* teaches. But since the beginning of sea travel, these dangers have at the same time worked as powerful stimuli for the development of astronomical, optical, chronometric, and magnetic orientation networks, which finally enabled movement to be largely independent of natural topography and the sea to be transformed into the first "machine landscape."[46] It was then just a small step to the development of further machine landscapes:

> We have not paid enough attention, in Western history, to the moment when this transfer from the natural vitalism of the maritime element . . . to an inevitable technological vitalism took place; the moment when the technical transport body left the sea like the unfinished living body of evolutionism, crawling out of its original environment and becoming amphibious. Speed as a pure idea without content come from the sea like Venus, and when Marinetti cries that the universe has been enriched by a new beauty, the beauty of speed, and opposes the racecar to the Winged Victory of Samothrace, he forgets that he is really talking about the esthetic: the esthetic of the transport engine. The coupling of the winged woman with the ancient war vessel and the coupling of Marinetti the fascist with his racecar . . . emerge from this technological

45. Ibid., 21.
46. Cf. Hans-Dieter Bahr, *Sätze ins Nichts: Versuch über den Schrecken* (Tübingen: Konkursbuchverlag, 1985), 105–6.

evolutionism whose realization is more important than that of the living world. The right to the sea creates the right to the road of modern states, which through this become totalitarian states.[47]

If Virilio, as above, speaks of technological evolutionism, we must of course remind ourselves that he means *military*-technological evolutionism, a development that thus involves not only the solution of some technical problems, but also and above all the solution of power problems—the increase of "movement-power," power's most fundamental and important manifestation.[48] For Virilio just as for historical materialism, technology is a dependent variable. But while historical materialism identifies the mode of production as "determining in the last instance," Virilio postulates that "war is the source of technology,"[49] that "the scientific and industrial mode of production is perhaps only a by-product or, as one says, a 'precipitate' of the development of the means of destruction."[50] As for Machiavelli, for Virilio science comes after weapons; the Dromocratic Revolution occurs under the a priori of war.[51] It was military engineers who were responsible for the decisive inventions in the field of mechanized transport,[52] and military leaders who forced the reshaping of national societies according to the imperatives of logistics. Under their dictate, the universe was rearranged by the military spirit:[53] the building of infrastructure, the "total mobilization" of the population, the harnessing of ever new sources of energy for the military economy of attrition. "Dromocratic intelligence is not exercised against a more or less determined military adversary," Virilio concludes, "but as a permanent assault on the world, and through it, on human nature."[54]

2. Virilio's thesis that it was above all the increase of movement-power through the Dromocratic Revolution that allowed the limits of the space-time dispositiv to be overcome can call upon a whole series of arguments. Already in 1910, Ernst Cassirer held that "*motion* and its laws remain the real problem" (emphasis added), about which modern thinking can achieve

---

47. Virilio, *Speed and Politics*, 60–61 (translation modified).
48. Virilio, *Pure War*, 55.
49. Ibid., 24.
50. Paul Virilio, "Der Urfall (Accidens originale)," *Tumult* 1 (1979): 78.
51. Virilio, *L'horizon négatif*, 87; cf. Herfried Münkler, *Machiavelli: Die Begründung des politischen Denkens der Neuzeit aus der Krise der Republik Florenz* (Frankfurt am Main: Europäische Verlagsanstalt, 1982), 339.
52. Virilio, *L'horizon négatif*, 74.
53. Virilio, *Speed and Politics*, 51.
54. Ibid., 64.

clarity about itself and its tasks.[55] One need only recall Kepler's work on the movements of the planets, Galileo's research on the causes of the speed of freely falling or constrained bodies, Huygens's dynamic theory of uniform rotation, or the laws of inertial motion developed by Newton to recognize that a precise grasp of movement was perhaps *the* central obsession of the dromocratic spirit of modernity. While the Aristotelian view was based on the primacy of rest, insofar as it assumed that a body removed from its natural place strove to return to it, modern thought was convinced that movement and not rest is a body's "natural inclination" (Galileo). Newton's law of inertia directly states that a body traveling in a straight line will continue to do so unless prevented by the effect of an external force. Perhaps most important was the virtual "self-perpetuation of movement" (Kondylis) thought by Hobbes, for whom rest no longer existed as the opposite of movement. According to Hobbes, rest can come about only through resistance. But resistance, for its part, is only thinkable as movement, so that movement now produces rest—in total opposition to the Aristotelian view, according to which the movement of the universe was caused by an unmoved mover.[56] Virilio's claim that Western societies are ruled by a "dictatorship of movement" here finds complete confirmation.[57]

Nor should it be overlooked that this absolutization of movement is achieved *pari passu* with a rapid rise of military technology. Above all, the use of firearms contributed like no other phenomenon to driving the mathematical understanding of projectile trajectories, the rise of scientific ballistics, and the construction of movement machines. The application of functions (*Funktionsbegriff*) to physical phenomena first appeared in a handbook for marksmen published by Tartaglia (1546); the first application of double-entry bookkeeping for public finances was by Simon Stevin, a Dutch expert on military engineering. One of Galileo's first publications, *Le operazioni del compasso geometrico et militare*, describes a measuring instrument he had invented for military purposes. His greatest achievement, the discovery of the laws of falling bodies, arose from a problem of contemporary artillery.[58] It is therefore by no means absurd when Leonhard Olschki suggests that the development of the law of falling objects is more intimately related to

55. Ernst Cassirer, *Substance and Function (with Einstein's Theory of Relativity)*, trans. William Curtis Swabey (Chicago: Open Court, 1923), 118.

56. Panagiotes Kondylis, *Die Aufklärung im Rahmen des neuzeitlichen Rationalismus* (Munich: Deutscher Taschenbuch, 1986), 110–11.

57. Virilio, *L'horizon négatif*, 94.

58. Edgar Zilsel, *Die sozialen Ursprünge der neuzeitlichen Wissenschaft* (Frankfurt am Main: Suhrkamp, 1976), 82, 60–61.

the war with the Turks than to the almost simultaneous discovery of these manuscripts.[59]

The deficiency of Virilio's conception emerges when he lays out these uncontestable relations such that knowledge-power (*pouvoir-savoir*) becomes a mere reflection of movement-power (*pouvoir-mouvoir*).[60] All of the evidence with which he explains this supposition indicates that he takes movement-power to have been historically and empirically the work principally of military practitioners, organizers, and engineers, so that the thesis of the primacy of movement-power at the same time implies a reductionist view of knowledge. Like Borkenau, Grossmann, or Bernal, Virilio seems to see modern knowledge only as an effect of certain empirical practices, except that for him these have to do with destruction rather than production.[61]

Koyré has opposed this view with the argument that classical physics, far from being a conception of craftsmen or engineers, embodies precisely its negation.[62] This is because, contrary to its own self-produced legend, it rests on a denial of all experience so radical that it can never be thought to have emerged from an experiential context, however it might be conceived. In order to think, for example, the inertial concept of movement, according to Koyré at least three presuppositions are necessary:

1. The possibility of isolating a body from its total physical environment, including its natural place, and thus at the same time abstracting from the whole natural order of the universe.
2. A view that takes movement, not, like Aristotle, as transformation (as a transition from potential to act), but as a *condition* that does not affect the moving body.
3. An understanding of space (and, one must immediately add, time) that divests it of all the qualitative-manifold properties that transform it into a continuum, so that it no longer has any center, no longer

---

59. Cited in Alfred Sohn-Rethel, "Das Geld, die bare Münze des Apriori," in *Beiträge zur Kritik des Geldes*, by Paul Mattick, Alfred Sohn-Rethel, and Hellmut G. Haasis (Frankfurt am Main: Suhrkamp, 1976), 116.

60. Virilio, *Pure War*, 55 (translation modified); *L'horizon négatif*, 184.

61. Franz Borkenau, *Der Übergang vom feudalen zum bürgerlichen Weltbild* (Paris: F. Alcan, 1934); Henryk Grossmann, "Die gesellschaftlichen Grundlagen der mechanistischen Philosophie und die Manufaktur," *Zeitschrift für Sozialforschung* 4, no. 2 (1935): 161–231; John Desmond Bernal, *Die Entstehung der Wissenschaft* (Reinbeck bei Hamburg: Rohwolt, 1970).

62. Alexandre Koyré, *Galileo Studies* (Atlantic Highlands, N.J.: Humanities Press, 1978), 2; cf. Bodo von Greiff, *Gesellschaftsform und Erkenntnisform: Zum Zusammenhang von wissenschaftlicher Erfahrung und gesellschaftlicher Entwicklung* (Frankfurt am Main: Campus, 1976).

knows up and down, and is everywhere of the same kind and uniform—the homogeneous space of Euclidean geometry.[63]

With Burtt, one could name as a fourth presupposition the valorization of
such abstract concepts as time and space, which elevate mere accidents of
the body to the level of basic coordinates of the inertial system and thus to
the rank of the highest metaphysical principles.[64] One correctly assesses the
full boldness of these presuppositions only if one considers that they "sub-
stitute for the real world a world of geometry made real, and . . . explain the
real by the impossible."[65]

The break with the Aristotelian tradition is too deep, the systematic character of the new episteme too pronounced, for this transformation to be
interpreted as the result of an accumulation of practical inventions or new
military strategies. Mechanistic philosophy is based on what Ernst Cassirer
fittingly called a "total project [*Entwurf*] of the 'nature of things,'"[66] a constitutive act in Kant's sense, by which the conditions of possibility of valid
experience were first of all established. Martin Heidegger expressed this
even more pointedly when he remarked that modern science and technology are "no mere handiwork of man . . . no mere human doing."[67] Science
and technology in the modern sense transcend the level of the empirical-
anthropological because they are a manifestation of metaphysics. But metaphysics cannot be derived from beings; it constitutes them in the first place
by making them into objects (of thinking, of research, of technical intervention). This happened in the "mathematical project," which laid the basis
for the modern experience of nature since Galileo and Newton. The mathematical project determines that only those observations that can be referred
to axioms of fundamental, ideally geometrical, schemata are scientifically
valid. It thereby draws the blueprint of how things and their relations with
one another are made up, and at the same time it specifies the conditions
under which alone nature can exist. "Now nature is no longer an inner

63. Alexandre Koyré, "Galileo and the Scientific Revolution of the Seventeenth Century,"
Philosophical Review 310 (1943): 337.

64. Edwin A. Burtt, *The Metaphysical Foundations of Modern Science* (London: Routledge
and Kegan Paul, 1967), 83–84.

65. Koyré, "Galileo," 336.

66. Ernst Cassirer, *Das Erkenntnisproblem in der Philosophie und Wissenschaft der neueren
Zeit*, vol. 1 (Darmstadt: Wissenschaftliche Buchgesellschaft, 1974), 346.

67. Martin Heidegger, "On the Question Concerning Technology," trans. William Lovitt,
in *Basic Writings*, ed. David Ferrell Krell (San Francisco: Harper San Francisco, 1977), 300;
cf. Günter Seubold, *Heideggers Analyse der neuzeitlichen Technik* (Freiburg: K. Alber, 1986),
19–20.

capacity of a body, determining its form of motion and place. Nature is now the realm of the uniform space-time context of motion, which is outlined in the axiomatic project and in which alone bodies can be bodies as a part of it and anchored in it."[68]

What distinguishes this spatial-temporal context of movement from the space-time *dispositif* sketched in the first section can be clarified by looking at Kant, to whom the characterization of modern scientific knowledge as a "plan" or "project" (*Entwurf*) goes back.[69] In his work, the break with the space-time *dispositif* first occurs very severely. Thus, in striking opposition to rationalistic speculation, Kant grants an outstanding place to sensual ex- perience, though not without at the same time insisting that certain, com- pelling judgments can only be expected from a priori knowledge. Thus, he notes the empirical reality of space and time, but not without at the same time referring to their transcendental ideality. And thus he attests to the ability of symbolic thinking to "present" the concept, only to announce in the same breath that it at best only amounts to an incomplete, because indirect and, by analogy, misleading, representation.[70] The true realization of the concept, in contrast, occurs in the system of pure reason through the "transcendental schematism," which bridges the gaping abyss between cat- egoriality and appearances by making pure understanding sensual. The detailed discussion of this procedure shows that time thereby takes on a constitutive role—indeed, time in its modern, operational sense, defined by the characteristics of homogeneity, universality, and uniformity. "The schemata," says Kant, "are thus nothing but *a priori* determinations of time in accordance with rules. These rules relate in the order of the categories to the *time-series*, the *time-content*, the *time-order*, and lastly to the *scope of time* in respect of all possible objects."[71] Kant here still restricts this state- ment to "inner sense." One also takes from this the "noteworthy fact" (*Merk- wurdigkeit*) he later stresses, "that in order to understand the possibility of things in conformity with the categories, and so to demonstrate the *objec- tive reality* of the latter, we need, not merely intuitions, but intuitions that are in all cases *outer intuitions*,"[72] so that when we, for example, falsely fig- ure time as a series, it becomes clear that we are not really dealing with

68. Martin Heidegger, *What Is a Thing?* trans. W. B. Barton Jr. and Vera Deutsch (South Bend: Gateway, 1967), 92.

69. Cf. Immanuel Kant, *Critique of Pure Reason*, trans. Norman Kemp Smith (New York: St. Martin's, 1965), Bxiii.

70. Kant, *Critique of Judgment*, trans. Werner S. Pluhar (Indianapolis: Hackett, 1987), §26.

71. Kant, *Critique of Pure Reason*, B184–85.

72. Ibid., B291–92.

a "space-time context of movement," as Heidegger says, but rather with a "time-space" order, in which the abstract and homogeneous time of formal-operational thought itself is spatialized.[73]

3. The mathematical project, says Heidegger, cannot be traced back to human doing. But to what, then? Heidegger's answer, that it is a matter of "sending," a "destining" of Being,[74] no longer satisfies anyone, since it is clear that the painstakingly established "ontological difference" between Being and beings is a Potemkin village.[75] Sohn-Rethel's approach, in contrast, continues to hold onto the concept of a project, but at the same time refers it to the "constitutive history" of "*social* Being,"[76] thus thinking autonomy and social determination together. Like Koyré, Cassirer, and Heidegger, Sohn-Rethel sees the *differentia specifica* of the Galilean method in the radicality with which it disregards the whole material and sensually perceivable reality of nature, how it also assumes "the non-empirical formal determination of the inertial concept of movement . . . as assured."[77] But while the philosophical interpretation of this finding remains and a social-historical unlocking of the phenomenon is taken to be ruled out, Sohn-Rethel sees here a hasty capitulation. On his view, a social-historical rearticulation of the mathematical design is only condemned to failure if one takes society in its superficial empirical manifestations as one's starting point. It can, in contrast, expect more success if it appropriates Marx's knowledge about the significance of the nonempirical, abstract form of exchange in capitalist society. According to Marx, the existence of empirical individuals who act instrumentally is only one, inessential side of this society. The other, essential side is the market, circulation, in which it is first shown what is socially acceptable and "valid." But social validity is achieved only at the price of abstraction. In order to be valorized on the market, the concrete, empirical properties of goods and their owners must be disregarded and they must appear as bearers of exchange value—which, as we know, is nothing other than abstract labor, labor in its "pure social form."

For Sohn-Rethel, the relation between the real abstractions of circulation

---

73. Klaus-Dieter Oetzel, *Wertabstraktion und Erfahrung: Über das Problem einer historisch-materialistischen Erkenntniskritik* (Frankfurt am Main: Campus, 1978), 152–53.

74. Heidegger, "On the Question Concerning Technology," 307.

75. Theodor Adorno, *Negative Dialectics*, trans. E. B. Ashton (New York: Continuum, 1973), 116.

76. Alfred Sohn-Rethel, *Warenform und Denkform* (Frankfurt am Main: Suhrkamp, 1978), 24 (emphasis added).

77. Sohn-Rethel, "Das Geld," 78.

and the mental abstractions of the mathematical design is obvious. Even simple circulation exhibits a striking parallel to the abstract concept of movement, insofar as, unlike production or consumption, it rules out any physical transformation of goods—and thus is a "condition," not a "process," in Koyré's sense. Appropriation takes place as an "abstract (uniform) movement through abstract (homogeneous, continuous, empty) space and equally abstract time, from abstract substances, by means of which they undergo no material transformations and admit of an exclusively quantitative differentiation."[78] According to Sohn-Rethel, this abstraction remains latent in prebourgeois society, since here circulation is only a means to ends lying outside itself and as a rule is of limited scope. Only with the transition to generalized circulation, in which money also allows labor power to be exchanged for goods, is this limit overcome, so that abstractions of exchange and money can find their way into theoretical consciousness. Insofar as thought "identifies itself" with the real abstraction of circulation, according to Sohn-Rethel, it comes to have the same "apparently transcendental power" that, according to Marx, capital has in the form of money. It constitutes itself as a transcendental subject in Kant's sense and projects nature so that it corresponds to its abstract categories. This is the true root of the mathematical project, the basis of modern mechanics' concept of motion, which now reveals itself as "the conceptual indication of the schema of movement of abstract exchange in a form that corresponds to the function of money for capital."[79]

The difference between this approach and Virilio's is obvious. It shifts the explanation of the Dromocratic Revolution from the contingent fact of war to the mathematical project, which it anchors in the concept of an abstract society. It is thus more convincing than Virilio's military metaphor, which can neither explain where the new formal-operational thought necessary for the Dromocratic Revolution comes from nor allow forceful and valid judgments of this thought. Nevertheless, we should not forget that this difference refers only to their grounding: the fact to be grounded itself, the Dromocratic Revolution and the "nihilism" that distinguishes it, are beyond question. For Marx and Sohn-Rethel, too, circulation is a "beyond,"[80] a "temporally and spatially measured vacuum of human material exchange

78. Ibid., 75.

79. Alfred Sohn-Rethel, "Die Formcharaktere der zweiten Natur," in G. Bezzel et al, eds., *Das Unvermögen der Realität* (Berlin: K. Wagenbach, 1974), 200.

80. Karl Marx, *Contribution to the Critique of Political Economy*, trans. S. W. Ryanzanskaya (New York: International, 1970), 90.

with nature";[81] for them, too, the sphere of movement is determined by a logic of disappearance: "One commodity is thrown out of it, another enters into it. But the same commodity is within it only fleetingly."[82]

What are the consequences when this sphere is generalized, when it seizes production and consumption and, by means of making it scientific, also revolutionizes thought, experience, and the social "lifeworld"? Does, as Virilio says, the "movement of our culture toward nothingness and disappearance"[83] become unstoppable? Must one think of this movement the way Virilio does, as absolute liquification, the "liquidation of the world"?[84] Or are there also other countervailing tendencies that make this seem one-sided? To answer these questions, we must look more closely at Virilio's presentation of the consequences of the Dromocratic Revolution.

III. Speed-Space

1. According to Virilio, a new configuration is being produced by the Dromocratic Revolution: speed-space (espace-vitesse) or "dromogeneous space."[85] What is to be understood by this? First of all, an order that is no longer defined, like the space-time dispositif, by metabolic speed. With the revolutionization of the nature of transport and communication, distances shrink; everything is equally "within reach"; the globe is transformed into a continuum in which everything is brutally pushed together, in which there are no more borders, no more distances, no more differences.[86] The substantiality of space Virilio assumes is finished as well. Technological speed requires not merely the absence of obstacles, but rather the absence of matter as such; its ideal space is, as Sohn-Rethel says, a vacuum.[87] Progressing technologies strive for complete transparency, an overcoming of gravity and weight.[88] Endoscopy penetrates living matter to the core; nuclear technology strives to release pure energy: "After the duration and extension of geo-physical space have been reduced to nothing or almost nothing by the acceleration

81. Alfred Sohn-Rethel, Geistige und körperliche Arbeit, rev. ed. (Frankfurt am Main: Suhrkamp, 1972), 80–81.

82. Karl Marx, Grundrisse: Foundations of the Critique of Political Economy, trans. Martin Nicolaus (New York: Random House, 1973), 620.

83. Virilio, L'horizon négatif, 31.

84. Ibid., 59.

85. Virilio, Lost Dimension, 102; L'horizon négatif, 210.

86. Virilio, Lost Dimension, 59; Speed and Politics, 141.

87. Virilio, L'horizon négatif, 90.

88. Ibid., 199.

of transport, it seems that the vivisection of speed now attacks the very density of mass itself, as if the aim of the pursuit had suddenly become the *durability* and *density* of the whole set of physical bodies. . . . Obsessed with *producing the void*, we no longer tolerate the density of the material"[89] (emphasis in original). With geographical space, the corresponding extensive time disappears. The *"longue durée"* is eliminated, and with it the time of chronology and history.[90] But while space clearly loses it structurally determining power along with the properties of extension and substantiality, this does not hold to the same extent for time. The more it sheds the characteristics it had in the time-space *dispositiv*, the more it becomes the decisive dimension in which the expansion of modern society occurs.[91] The population no longer lives in a particular territory, such as a city, but in the *"time* spent changing places" itself.[92] Cities become merely functional spaces for time-bounded activities, their residents become passengers, "displaced," "u-topic" citizens whose true homes are transport machines and waystations.[93] In place of settledness in space comes a new settledness in time, in place of societies of persistence comes a "society of disappearance."[94] Since the rise of telecommunications, social integration also increasingly occurs in time, such as the time of a program which gathers those who are physically absent into a "city of the instant."[95] The old depth of topological space is replaced by the depth of time, territoriality by temporality:[96] "Space is no longer in geography; it's in electronics. Unity is in the terminals. It's in the instantaneous time of command posts, control towers, etc. Politics is less in physical space than in the time systems administered by various technologies, from telecommunications to airplanes, passing by the TGV, etc. There is a movement from geo- to chrono-politics: the distribution of territory becomes the distribution of time. The distribution of territory is outmoded, minimal."[97]

How does Virilio define this new, technological time? He repeatedly names characteristics above all: technological time is dead time, it is intensive time, and it is scarce time. Dead time: for it has to do with the "travel

89. Ibid., 174–75.
90. Virilio, *Lost Dimension*, 14.
91. Virilio, *Pure War*, 72.
92. Ibid., 60 (translation modified).
93. Virilio, *Fahren, fahren, fahren*, 32.
94. Virilio, *Pure War*, 88, 75.
95. Ibid., 87.
96. Virilio, *Lost Dimension*, 31, 53.
97. Virilio, *Pure War*, 115.

time,"[98] thus with the time of circulation, in which the body is cut off from any interaction with its actual environment and is only, as it were, traded in for a life after arrival. Intensive time: for it is defined by immediate and abrupt presence, by the sudden entrance of what is absent, as manifested in the exchange of weapons of mass destruction as well as the exchange of information through the means of communication.[99] Scarce time: for the immense acceleration, which, for example, reaches the speed of light in laser weapons, leads everywhere to a shortening of time limits and time to think. In the age of cruise missiles and strategic "defense" initiatives, what is primarily at stake are warning times, the exploitation of the smallest possible intervals of time, of first-strike and preventative strike capacities—in a word, the "war for time."[100]

For individuals as well as society, this transformation in the space-time structures has fundamentally disruptive consequences. If the space-time *dispositif* was the basis and setting of manifold regulations, speed-space is defined by comprehensive deregulation. The animal body along with its sensory apparatus is devalued. The technologies of speed bring about a "disruption in the order of perception,"[101] a "derangement of the senses"[102] whereby individuals are catapulted into a space beyond, in which they can only maintain their position by means of a complex network of measuring instruments, of perceptual prosthetics. These prostheses in turn compel derealization, in which, as for example in film, old fields of perception are destroyed by the overproduction of movement. Cinema, writes Virilio, is based on a systematic psychotropic derangement, a destruction of chronology.[103] In place of the transcendental aesthetic, which brought sensory data into a spatiotemporal order and, in the categories of the understanding, also produced valid knowledge, we have the "aesthetic of speed,"[104] which only occasionally connects subject and object with blinding speed: "With speed, the world keeps on coming at us, to the detriment of the object, which is itself now assimilated to the sending of information. It is this intervention that destroys the world as we know it, technique finally reproducing permanently the violence of the accident."[105]

98. Ibid., 6.
99. Ibid., 46; *Lost Dimension*, 130.
100. Virilio, *Speed and Politics*, 45; *L'horizon négatif*, 64, 134, 137, 252, 282.
101. Virilio, *Fahren, fahren, fahren*, 22.
102. Virilio, *Aesthetics of Disappearance*, 92.
103. Virilio, *War and Cinema*, 27–28 (translation modified).
104. Virilio, *L'horizon négatif*.
105. Virilio, *Aesthetics of Disappearance*, 101.

So too in the field of social relations. The multitude and tempo of inter-actions increasingly turn a coming together into a colliding together—from which the breakdown of forms of social intercourse, the destruction of polite-ness, the brutality and aggressiveness of so-called open communication[106] make a work like that of Norbert Elias appear rather like the swansong of an already lost age. With the destruction of geographical space, civil rights, which were always bound to a particular territory, disappear. Places and cities become interchangeable, nations and states lose their identity.[107] The mobility of the population, now raised to an even higher level by telecom-munication, makes possible a breakdown of previous forms of urban con-centration, a movement to a new configuration that is "nodal" rather than "central"—junctions "in an unapparent morphological configuration, in which the *nodal* replaces the *central* in a preponderantly electronic envi-ronment, in which 'tele-siting' favors the deployment of a generalized ex-centricity, an unbounded periphery. This advance notice of the end of the rule of industrial urban life also announces the end of metropolitan seden-tariness"[108] (emphasis in original). Capital and labor leave the old centers in favor of a new, scattered settlement; whole metropolises turn into slums which house the superfluous and the unproductive: economic and social wastelands. Out of the welfare state, with its complex social-political regu-lations, emerges the "minimum-state" propagated by the monetarists, which withdraws to the traditional core of state activity, and, for the rest, leaves society to its own devices: "A minimum-state means pauperization, in my view, and more precisely endo-colonization. It would seem that societies have lost their capacity for self-regulation."[109]

Insofar as postindustrial society still possesses any unity at all, it exists alongside and over it: in the war machine, whose maintenance requires increasingly enormous resources. Here it has long since ceased to be a mat-ter of defending territorial integrity, national sovereignty, or any principle of collective life—goals that, in the age of absolute weapons, are in any case highly relativized (to put it mildly). According to Virilio, what is primarily at stake for the war machine as well as its military class is their own preser-vation. In order to secure the endless flow of resources they require, the civil-ian economy becomes ever more closely connected to arms production,

106. Virilio, *Fahren, fahren, fahren*, 35.
107. Virilio, *Lost Dimension*, 119.
108. Ibid., 120 (translation modified).
109. Virilio, *Pure War*, 99.

and society is subjected to an ever-thicker web of police control.[110] In this way economic and political decentralization goes along with a hypercon-centration of military power, already exemplified in the states of the Third World: "Third World Africa is not falling behind Europe, but is rather ahead of it: the army rules almost everywhere; postindustrial society is military society."[111]

2. This short sketch brings out the strengths but also the weaknesses of Vir-ilio's discourse. Among the strengths are the incredibly thick description of technological speed and its "nihilistic" effects on the space-time *dispositif,* the connection of such phenomena as deurbanization and denationaliza-tion with the new media, and the brilliant analysis of films and cinematic perception. In no other contemporary work is the effect of the "state of accel-eration" on individuals and their relations presented with such intensity and piercing acuteness.

But equally unmistakable are the weakness of its substantiation, by which Virilio leaves his diagnoses open to attack in ways that are often completely unnecessary. Among these is, first, the assertion that speed-space is by its nature a military space in which the laws of political economy no longer hold and in which the economy as a whole becomes a war economy.[112] Here Virilio—like Ernst Jünger, whom he often cites, before him—exhibits a fascination with the extreme, with the state of exception, which not infre-quently leads him to misrecognize that the manifestations he criticizes are anchored in "normality," that is, in the basic principles of society itself.

The distortions to which this procedure leads are evident not only in the thesis, cited above, that postindustrial society is military society, but above all in relation to the concept of fascism, which lacks any feeling for respon-sible thinking: "Whatever the case," says, for example, a key passage from *Speed and Politics,*

> since fascism never died, it doesn't need to be reborn. . . . It rep-resented one of the most accomplished cultural, political and social revolutions of the dromocratic West. . . . Fascism is alive because total war, then total peace, have engaged the headquarters of the great national bodies (the armies, the forces of production) in a new spatial and temporal process, and the historical universe in a Kantian

110. Ibid., 95.
111. Virilio, *Fahren, fahren, fahren,* 53.
112. Virilio, *Pure War,* 3.

world. The problem is no longer one of a historiality in (chrono-logical) time or (geographic) space, but in *what* space-time?[113]

Setting aside the noteworthy recollection of Kant for the moment, I do not believe any scientific value attaches to these assertions—not even to mention that a survivor of the concentration camps could quite rightly perceive such frivolous use of history as a mockery. Of course it is correct, to bring fascism and the war economy into relation, that the economic upturn under the Nazi regime was in fact a result of a state-led steering of investment and the profits of the arms industry. However, one must immediately add that this in no way set aside the laws of political economy, as Virilio supposes. The fascist increase in investment led to a deep distortion of the structure of the economy that sooner or later would have led to an outbreak of inflation; the war has thus been seen as the regime's desperate gambit to offload payment onto others.[114] The fascist project to eliminate the reg-ulative functions of the law of value within a single nation-state has so far remained an isolated enterprise that it was clear to end in catastrophe; it brought the ruin not only of the leadership circle, but also of the attempt to build a military society removed from the laws of the world market. No one can rule out that repetition of such an attempt; but to declare this *spe-cific* crisis solution, which can only be explained on the basis of the partic-ular conditions of the German economy, as a general, dominant principle of so-called postindustrial society is about as convincing a zoologist want-ing to determine the color characteristics of a species from an albino spec-imen. Beyond this, one need only cast a glance at the flourishing weapons export business to see that there can be no talk of an "end of economic rationality."[115]

Virilio's presentation of speed-space causes difficulties not only because of its over-emphasis of extra-economic factors, however. At least as prob-lematic is his tendency to absolutize processes of deregulation and dereal-ization, so that speed-space appears as the beyond not only of the space-time *dispositif,* but also of the mathematical project. Certainly, Virilio is not wrong to attest to some new technologies' tendency toward a "fragmentation [and]

---

113. Virilio, *Speed and Politics,* 117. That such sentences are not gaffes but reflect Virilio's firm conviction can be shown by his remark in *L'horizon négatif* that highways are not con-necting routes but concentration camps of speed (67).

114. Cf. Alfred Sohn-Rethel, *Economy and Class Structure of German Fascism,* trans. Mar-tin Sohn-Rethel (London: CSE, 1978).

115. Virilio, *Pure War,* 9 (translation modified).

disintegration of dimensions,"[116] or to stress that a consequence of Einstein's theory of relativity is to turn Kant's "temporal order" into a "speed order," an "order of exposition": "in the future, past and present become the mutually intertwined figures of underexposure, exposure, and overexposure."[117] The question, however, is whether one can totalize Einstein, whether there is sufficient reason to hypothesize a general "logic of disappearance" which, after topological space and chronological time, also explodes the homogeneous space and abstract time of the Kantian world, thus removing the foundations of formal-operational thinking.

With respect, for example, to the new information technologies, this assertion seems very hasty. Yes, a programmer simultaneously maintains several interlocking discourses with his computer, so that he constantly faces several different temporal orders. But operational time itself is by no means overcome; rather, it remains binding for each individual program as it does for the computer's mode of operation. The computer's binary procedure, the sequential although lightning-fast change between 0 and 1 states, almost seems like the mechanical realization of the Kantian schema, the technological expression of that "art concealed in the depths of the human soul," whose real modes of activity Kant still thought was hardly likely ever to be snatched from nature.[118]

In order to keep up with the complexity of information produced in this way and not to "crash," as computer jargon has it, requires such highly cultivated formal-operational intelligence, such extreme powers of concentration, that almost every second computer science student breaks down. The programmer, writes Johnson, must "not only possess a repertoire of logical-technical capabilities, he must also submit himself in many respects to a seemingly ascetic life discipline."[119] Even if behind the new "semantic technology" of information-processing machines appears the manipulation of external nature typical of classical mechanics, here we face a rise and acceleration of formal-operational thinking rather than its transcendence. Postmodernity? What an inappropriate concept for an age that is precisely the first to draw the consequences of the discourse of modernity.

---

116. Virilio, *Lost Dimension,* 96.

117. Paul Virilio, "Der Augenblick der beschleunigten Zeit," in *Die sterbende Zeit,* ed. Dietmar Kamper and Christoph Wulf (Darmstadt: Neuwied, 1987), 250–51.

118. Kant, *Critique of Pure Reason,* B180–81.

119. F. Grant Johnson, "Der Computer und die Technologisierung des Innern," *Psyche* 34 (1980): 793; Hermann Rosemann, *Computer: Faszination und Ängste bei Kindern und Jugendlichen* (Frankfurt am Main: Fischer-Taschenbuch, 1986), 57–58. I thank Holger Hogelücht for this reference.

3. If it is correct that in machinery the schematism of formal-operational thinking assumes technical-objective form, then Virilio's reflections must be corrected on a further point. Modern society is not only a "society of disappearance," but at the same time also a "society of appearance"—and in just this way defined as contradictory. According to Marx, whose theory is still appears convincing on this point, it is in the nature of capital that while on the one hand the immediate labor time of living labor is continually reduced, on the other an ever-greater share of production is taken over by a constantly growing system of machinery. But machinery is nothing other than *fixed* capital, *objectified* abstract labor, whose extent is determined by "the quantity of labor time that is put into and therefore absorbed in order to produce a new machine of the same kind."[120] Marx's remark that in machinery "the social spirit of labour obtains an objective existence separate from the individual workers"[121] cannot be taken seriously enough. It says nothing less than that the structures of formal-operational thinking based in circulation, the "general intellect," acquire an objective existence and take up ever more space. To speak of the "unleashing of the beyond," of the "annihilation of time,"[122] under these conditions is indeed a correct although one-sided observation that obscures the *objectification* of the beyond in the automatic system of machinery and the contradictions that arise from it:

> Capital itself is the moving contradiction, [in] that it presses to reduce labour time to a minimum, while it posits labour time, on the other side, as sole measure and source of wealth. Hence it diminishes labour time in the necessary form so as to increase it in the superfluous form; hence posits the superfluous in growing measure as a condition—question of life or death—for the necessary. On the one side, then, it calls to life all the powers of science and of nature, as of social combination and of social intercourse, in order to make the creation of wealth independent (relatively) of the labour time employed on it. On the other side, it wants to use labour time as the measuring rod for the giant social forces thereby created, and to confine them within the limits required to maintain the already created value as value. Force of production and

120. Karl Marx and Friedrich Engels, *Collected Works*, vol. 42 (New York: International, 1975).
121. Marx, *Grundrisse*, 529.
122. Virilio, *Fahren, Fahren, Fahren*, 88.

social relations—two different sides of the development of the social individual—appear to capital as mere means, and are merely means for it to produce on its limited foundation. In fact, however, they are the material conditions to blow this foundation sky-high.[123]

Marx's hope that the self-destruction of capital would at the same time create the conditions of possibility for a resurrection of labor proved to be a romantic dream. But this does not affect his analysis. Unlike those of the quick-thinking postmoderns, whom one often suspects make such a strong case for the end of "grand narratives" because they longer have the patience to read them, it still offers the advantage of being able to grasp and develop as contradictions phenomena that, from a postdialectical perspective, appear in the form of a temporal succession. For Marx, modernity is not first time-space and then speed-space, but rather both at once. It is time-space insofar as fixed capital is frozen, crystallized social time and variable capital is dominated by the meticulous rationing of time, reflected both on the individual level and on the level of the industrial organization of labor. And it is speed-space insofar as the rising organic composition of capital—"the diminution of the mass of labour in proportion to the mass of means of production moved by it"[124]—brings with it a permanent increase in the demands of synchronization, which, on the side of those whose labor is reduced to the level of a servo-apparatus, is experienced as constant pressure to intensify work, to raise the tempo of coordination—not infrequently with catastrophic consequences for subjective biographies and transsubjective chains of interdependence. What Virilio can only one-sidedly and on top of that for highly questionable reasons take as a destruction of space and time can be presented on this basis as a contradictory process in which formal operations, along with the disciplinary effects that belong to them, are both required and promoted, but also constantly negated.

The limited space available here forces me to break off the analysis. I hope that, despite all my criticism, something of the peculiar fascination exerted by Virilio's texts has become clear. At a time when, under the ubiquitous pressure to professionalize and distinguish oneself, the social sciences increasingly lose their capacity for a diagnosis of the times and simply threaten to become boring, one finds in Virilio's work an inexhaustible source of

123. Marx, *Grundrisse*, 706.
124. Marx, *Capital: A Critique of Political Economy*, vol. 1, trans. Ben Fowkes (New York: Vintage, 1977), 773.

insights, provocations, and suggestions, and not least a rare power to sharpen the point. As a crime writer might put it: it is impossible not to be caught by Paul Virilio. Of course, the greatest insight he affords comes *malgré lui:* that the first act of resistance against the terror of speed would consist in taking more time. Also, and especially, for thinking.

[Translated by James Ingram]

THIRTEEN

TEMPORAL RHYTHMS AND MILITARY FORCE: ACCELERATION, DECELERATION, AND WAR

Herfried Münkler

I.

He who can influence and alter time not only increases his chances of asserting his political will, he also acquires the possibility of transforming short-term power into long-term domination—at least when control over the rhythms of time is not merely the result of an accidental conjunction of factors, but instead derives from the possibility of a durable mastery of resources that can be employed at any time. Here control over temporal rhythms is understood chiefly as a capacity for acceleration unavailable to one's opponent. In fact, civilizational differentials and the gap between rich and poor nations can be interpreted in terms of a divergent ability to accelerate the course of events. It is in this sense that David Landes traces economic revolutions to the availability of energy:[1] the technological capacity to replace human labor power with energy is always connected not only to the stabilization of temporal rhythms, but also to their acceleration.

But the availability of and ability to use different kinds of energy is the key to stabilizing or accelerating temporal sequences not only economically, but also militarily. The conversion of the British navy from coal to oil in the early twentieth century, made possible by access to Arab oil, gave it a decisive advantage over its German counterpart: British oil-powered ships could operate much longer than German coal-fired ships since they could carry much more fuel and refuel at sea without coming into port, as coal ships could not. Oil-powered ships raised the operational rhythm of the

---

1. David Landes, *The Wealth and Poverty of Nations: Why Some Are So Rich and Some So Poor* (New York: W. W. Norton, 1998).

British navy, from which it gained additional advantages against the Germans. Similarly, as Michael Mann observes, the use and control of waterways greatly encourages empire building, if it does not make it possible in the first place, since only barges and ships can quickly transport large loads at reasonable cost.[2] This is particularly important for the transport of troops and supplies. The availability of waterways, be they rivers, lakes, or the open sea, enables acceleration and the maintenance of higher speeds, so that competitors who cannot keep up are left behind.

But the idea that acceleration is the only relevant factor in the creation of power by controlling temporal rhythms, as Paul Virilio's dromology suggests,[3] is too simple and fails to do justice to the complex interplay of acceleration and deceleration as generators of power. What may be correct from an economic point of view, namely that greater speed leads to greater effectiveness, is by no means generally the case in the political-military domain: defensive power, which Clausewitz defined as the stronger form with the weaker aims,[4] can be understood as systematically slowing down the course of military events; the basic idea is to extend the duration of an enemy's efforts so that they exceed his powers or eat up his resources. Thus, in the high and late Middle Ages the technology of building castles and the fortification of cities gave defenders such advantages that it was beyond the power of most conquerors to consolidate larger domains. Since castles and fortified cities could not be taken by storm, they had to be besieged and their inhabitants starved out; this quickly sapped the attacker's momentum as he wasted his time encircling them. The cost of besieging a castle or town far exceeded that of its defense; much more quickly than the defender's, the attacker's power drained away with the time it took to encircle and lay siege to a fortified position.[5] By defensively slowing down the course of military events, the weaker party stood a real chance of resisting far superior attackers and weakening them such that they lost their political will.

More powerful actors, in contrast, had a strong interest in expanding and improving their ability to accelerate war, since this was the most promising way of converting their superior resources into military success and

---

2. Michael Mann, *The Sources of Social Power* (Cambridge: Cambridge University Press, 1986).

3. Paul Virilio, *La vitesse de libération* (Paris: Galilée, 1995); *Un paysage d'événements* (Paris: Galilée, 1996).

4. Carl von Clausewitz, *Vom Kriege,* ed. Werner Hahlwege (Bonn, 1980), 617.

5. See Philippe Contamine, *War in the Middle Ages* (Oxford: Blackwell, 1984), 219; Norbert Ohler, *Krieg und Frieden im Mittelalter* (Munich: Beck, 1997), 87.

thereby extending their power. This possibility opened up toward the end of the fifteenth century, when large-caliber barrels and the technical improvement of carriages and mounts produced cannons that could quickly smash castles and fortified walls.[6] For a period of time this development provided acceleration with a strategic advantage over deceleration; the French King Henri VIII's string of victories through Italy in 1494 to the walls of Naples would have been impossible without the new heavy artillery. The temporary dominance of acceleration over deceleration came to an end when Italian architects developed new kinds of fortifications that better withstood heavy artillery.[7]

As a preliminary summary of these observations, we could say that in military conflicts the side with the greater *available* resources will try to speed up events, while the chances of success for the inferior side improve with its ability to slow them down. The potential of acceleration lies above all in military-organizational developments and innovations in weapons technology, while the ability to slow things down arises less from organization and technology than from political will, based first and foremost on the population's greater, or at least durably higher, readiness to sacrifice. This holds for waiting out a siege just as it does for conducting a guerrilla war, which Mao appropriately described as a "war that has to be borne for a long time."[8] The ability to speed things up essentially grows out of economic and especially technological superiority; the ability to slow things down out of the population's capacity for sacrifice and suffering. In this sense, the Vietnam War can be reconstructed as the paradigmatic collision of the acceleration and deceleration potentials of two powers, with the deceleration side prevailing in the end because its opponent's ability to accelerate could not make up for its own population's limited willingness to sacrifice over the long term.

If these considerations are correct, we can adduce some general laws concerning the relation between temporal rhythms and military force. First,

6. See John K. Nef, *Western Civilization Since the Renaissance: Peace, War, Industry, and the Arts* (New York: Harper and Row, 1963), 23.

7. See Simon Pepper and Nicholas Adams, *Firearms and Fortifications: Military Architecture and Siege Warfare in Sixteenth-Century Siena* (Chicago: University of Chicago Press, 1986), esp. 32.

8. That the number of casualties on the side conducting a partisan war is always higher than those of its opponent requires no demonstration. Things are somewhat different in the case of a siege, where the defender's capacity for suffering and sacrifice begins to exceed that of the attacker only when food begins to run out. Of course, the decision to maintain resistance and reject offers for surrender, including offers of escape, presupposes considerable willingness to sacrifice by the defenders. As a rule this is connected with the likely prospect that if the city falls, the men will be killed and the women raped.

the side that is better able both to speed up and slow down, and thus can either force or follow the rhythm according to its interests, will be advantaged. Since no power is equally able to accelerate and decelerate war, it will strive, second, to cultivate its abilities in that direction where economic or political costs are likely to be lower. In so doing it must be careful, however, third, that this compensatory development does not result in the complete loss of those abilities it possesses to a lesser degree, since it then loses options and, relative to its opponents, stands to lose more than it gains.

II.

This raises the question of the consequences of acceleration and deceleration not only on the rhythm *of* war, but also on the pace of socioeconomic development brought about *by* war. Clearly, wars have often acted as accelerators of social as well as political development, and they have been understood and occasionally even welcomed as such. In some respects, wars and revolutions (or at least a certain idea of revolution) are comparable: both speed up social and economic developments that are already taking place, though dramatically increased costs of course accompany such developmental takeoffs. Thus, for example, Ralf Dahrendorf takes the Second World War to be an accelerator of German development toward a stable, lasting democracy insofar as a good part of the male East Prussian nobility fell in battle or was executed after the Stauffenberg plot against Hitler, thereby eliminating a sociopolitical elite that was notoriously hostile to democracy and had played a significant part in the collapse of the Weimar Republic.[9] Dahrendorf describes the functional effects of the war as an acceleration of processes that may have taken place anyway, albeit much more slowly and hesitantly. Of course, in this imaginary alternative historical scenario, German social and political modernization would have been achieved, in terms of war casualties and ruined cities, at a much lower cost.

But it would be no less correct to see wars, in their middle- and long-term effects, as decelerators of socioeconomic development lacking in positive compensatory political results. In Germany this role has often been attributed to the Thirty Years War: it set the country back decades vis-à-vis its Western European neighbors, and Germany, with great effort, caught up

9. Ralf Dahrendorf, *Society and Democracy in Germany* (Garden City, N.Y.: Doubleday, 1967).

only during the nineteenth century.[10] A radical variant of this view goes so far as to interpret the First World War as the Germans' attempt, by violent means, to make up for the disadvantages and subsequent marginalization in the struggle for European hegemony that arose from the Thirty Years War. In this view, the consequences of the Thirty Years War as a decelerator of German political development supposedly was made up for by the First World War as an accelerator: the slowdown effects of one war are made good by the speedup effects of another.

War can thus be seen as both an accelerator and a decelerator of socio-economic and political development. This raises an immediate question: is the assessment of the temporal consequences of war generally dependent on one's political preferences and historical distance, or can objective criteria to be found that would allow us to speak of speedup effects and slowdown effects in another? A first criterion could lie in the difference between victor and vanquished. Our historical examples lead one to suspect that the winner-loser distinction has no significant overlap with acceleration and deceleration effects, especially since the war aims of some victors are precisely to slow down developments that would occur in the absence of war. Thus, Thucydides describes the Spartan war policy against Athens as an attempt to reverse Athenian hegemony, which was growing steadily in peacetime.[11] In other cases, the victor's aim is to overcome something blocking development—to hurry it up. Both Lenin's and Wilson's political goals in World War One might be interpreted in this way.[12]

A second possible criterion for sorting out the acceleratory or deceleratory quality of wars might be the difference between infrastate wars and

---

10. For a comprehensive treatment of the war's consequences, see Ernst Walter Zeeden, *Hegemonialkriege und Glaubenskämpfe, 1556–1648*, Propyläen Geschichte Europas 2 (Frankfurt am Main: Propyläen, 1975), 315–28. Zeeden's summary of the state of research strongly emphasizes the retardation of German development and resulting backwardness with regard to other European states. Heinz Schilling, by contrast, has found traces of the "productivity" of the war, which can be broadly understand as accelerating desirable development: "The most important change brought about the war concerned war itself. By cultivating [*züchtete*] man's wolfishness, it forced him to be self-conscious." And "Precisely out of the unmatchable fantasy and the brutalization of the war arose an unstoppable pressure to contain destructive power." Heinz Schilling, *Aufbruch und Krise: Deutschland, 1517–1648* (Berlin: Siedler, 1988), 441. For a refined weighing of the war's consequences through a critical appraisal of earlier views, see Geoffrey Parker, *The Thirty Years' War* (London: Routledge and Kegan Paul, 1984).

11. Thucydides, *The Peloponnesian War*, 8.23; cf. Herfried Münkler, *Über den Krieg: Stationen der Kriegsgeschichte im Spiegel ihrer theoretischen Reflexion* (Weilerswist: Velbrück, 2002), 19–33.

12. Cf. Gottfried Niedhart, "Der Erste Weltkrieg: Von der Gewalt im Krieg zu den Konflikten im Frieden," in *Wie Kriege enden: Wege zum Frieden von der Antike bis zur Gegenwart*, ed. Bernd Wegner (Paderborn: Schöning, 2002), 187–211, esp. 201.

wars between states,[13] the hypothesis being that wars between states work as accelerators, infrastate wars as decelerators. The bases of this hypothesis are that where war is conducted under the de jure and de facto monopoly of the state, military force remains subordinate to a system of control that functionalizes it as an instrument of political goals; under the conditions of a functioning state, war can be subjected to relatively precise cost-benefit calculations; and only states are in a position to mobilize and focus the energies of the whole society for war, clearly speeding up socioeconomic development.[14] Above all, the systematic use—if not the initiation—of technological progress for the purpose of war, unquestionably an important factor in speeding up social development, is only possible when the state appears as its organizer, since only the state can ensure a long-term mobilization of resources allowing for the close coupling of war and technological development. European state wars from the sixteenth and seventeenth to the twentieth centuries were accordingly marked by constant growth in the cost of armaments, while infrastate wars, which were almost always fought without heavy equipment and leading technology, remained cheap, at least when it came to the decision to unleash hostilities. These wars did not stimulate technological development. Instead, they destroyed existing potentials, and afterward societies were almost always kept busy for decades trying to retain their prewar condition.[15] Infrastate wars thus tend to slow down or completely block developmental processes. Accordingly, the "military revolutions" much discussed by researchers in recent decades[16] are only to be found where states are the masters of war.

Upon closer inspection, a number of objections can be made against this attempt to link wars between states to acceleration and infrastate wars to deceleration. Thus, for example, the 1980–88 Iran-Iraq War, unquestionably war between states, did not cause acceleration in the sense described above in either country. It left Iraq with debts in excess of U.S. $550 million—

13. Here I omit the mixed or intermediate form of so-called transnational wars, which combine elements of infrastate war and war between states.

14. On the rise of state war making in European history, as well as its preconditions and consequences, see Herfried Münkler, *Die neuen Kriege* (Beinbeck bei Hamburg: Rohwolt, 2002), 91. The different effects of state and non-state war making are discussed in detail in Mary Kaldor, *New and Old Wars: Organized Violence in a Global Era* (Cambridge: Polity Press, 1999).

15. On societies' social and economic self-destruction in infrastate as well as transnational wars, see Münkler, *Die neuen Kriege*, 131.

16. See Geoffrey Parker, *The Military Revolution: Military Innovation and the Rise of the West, 1500–1800* (Cambridge: Cambridge University Press, 1988), and Clifford J. Rogers, ed. *The Military Revolution Debate: Readings on the Military Transformation of Early Modern Europe* (Boulder: Westview, 1995).

which became one of the causes of its next war—and dramatically reduced the country's prewar level of development.[17] In Iran, the original élan of the Islamic Revolution collapsed during the course of the war, which, whatever one makes of it, did not have acceleratory effects on Iranian society. But in the same way, we can observe that infrastate wars can in principle have speedup effects on sociopolitical development. They certainly do not have these effects as stimuli of technological progress, but at least where they are connected to a revolutionary breakthrough in the old structure of domination, and can thus be understood as the violent rise of new political structures, they can very well have acceleratory qualities. The American War of Independence is the least controversial example of this possibility.

Clearly, it is not possible to offer an unambiguous answer to the question of whether war speeds things up or slows them down with reference to the objective properties of warfare without further clarifying the specific domain of acceleration or deceleration. Processes of political, social, economic, and technological acceleration or deceleration are neither co-originary nor coextensive, so wars can work as technological and economic accelerators but political decelerators. One way out of the confusing overlap of the acceleratory and deceleratory consequences of war could be offered by examining them in relation to learning processes. It is often noted in the literature that wars set off intensified, not to say accelerated, learning processes— especially for the losers.[18] What then would be decisive for the acceleration or deceleration of development is who learns, how these learning processes are organized, and which specific interests guide them. Thus, one could just as well learn that war does not pay as an instrument of policy because its costs are always higher than its returns, as one could learn how to fight future wars more effectively, at lower cost, and with greater chances of victory.[19] In either case, the learning process can nevertheless be understood

17. On this, see Herfried Münkler, *Der neue Golfkrieg* (Reinbeck bei Hamburg: Rohwolt, 2003), 69.

18. E.g., Karl Otto Hondrich, *Lehrmeister Krieg* (Reinbek bei Hamburg: Rohwolt, 1992); Wolfgang Schivelbusch, *Die Kultur der Niederlage* (Berlin: A. Fest, 2001). For a critical examination of modernization or learning-theory approaches, see esp. Hans Joas, *Kriege und Werte: Studien zur Gewaltgeschichte des 20. Jahrhunderts* (Weilerswist: Velbrück, 2000).

19. Both learning processes went on simultaneously in Germany after the First World War, though in the end only the process of learning increased military effectiveness proved to be important. After the Second World War, development went in precisely the opposite direction. Whether one or the other of these learning processes should be classified as pathological is a question of basic historical-theoretical assumptions or political preference. See Klaus Eder, *Geschichte als Lernprozess? Zur Pathogenese politischer Modernität in Deutschland* (Frankfurt am Main: Suhrkamp, 1985).

as speeding up established and above all sought-after forms of development. The possibility of contradictory lessons should not lead us to conclude that the results of learning are arbitrary, however. Rather, it should lead us to a meta-observation about which of the two processes is politically implemented or achieves social hegemony. The result of this conflict is then at the same time a decision about which preferences concerning acceleration or deceleration have the upper hand in society.

Which of the learning processes initiated during or after a war finally wins out depends both on the political framework—for example, the opportunities of the learners to articulate their perspective—and on how it is organized and the coherence of its results. This raises the suspicion that the military apparatus will, as a rule, organize learning processes more effectively than is possible by means of the diffused character of broadly based social consensus building (*Selbstverständigung*). Above all, the military can present the results of learning and transfer them into policy more quickly than social groups and political parties. However, social learning processes are generally much more comprehensive and fundamental than the instrumental learning of the military or the military-industrial complex.[20] While institutions typically learn in order to carry out their tasks more effectively, societies (also) learn by assessing the value of institutions and their goals. These learning processes become important when they lead societies to withdraw the resources that the institutions in question need to maintain themselves and pursue their aims. In the case of the military, this can extend from reduction of the armaments budget to massive refusals of military service. But the result of social learning can just as well be the conclusion that protecting society, its values, and its wealth requires more armaments and a greater willingness to sacrifice. Clearly, most European societies have passed through different learning processes than American society since 1989–90. The recently noted fissure in the so-called trans-Atlantic value community thus results not only from different interests, but also from different learning processes. In the political rhetoric of the protagonists, of course, these contrary learning processes are typically described as acceleration, not deceleration. This is because in modernity acceleration is cast

---

20. Certain reflections in Kant's *On Perpetual Peace* can be understood as a response to the asymmetrical, or at least differently timed, learning processes between different institutions or organizations and society as a whole. By the republican feedback-loop, which makes entrance into a war dependent on the agreement of the people, Kant seeks to counteract the notorious "learning advantage" of the government by giving the slower but more fundamental learning processes of the entire population additional political weight.

in a positive light, whereas deceleration has taken on negative connotations. In the present context, however, it makes sense to disregard these normative implications and use "acceleration" and "deceleration" neutrally to designate different learning processes.

III.

We are on surer ground when we ask about acceleration and deceleration *in* war. Here it is above all a matter of observable processes, like the duration of maneuvers, the velocity of projectiles, and the time it takes to move troops and equipment from one place to another. In this respect, the military history of the last centuries reveals a constant general acceleration, from Napoleon's systematic construction of tree-lined boulevards along which to march his troops, to the use of railways to deploy troops under the elder Möltke, to the motorization of entire divisions in the 1930s and '40s, leading to, among other things, greater mobility of troops in battle. Naval power also became much faster during this period, first through the transition from sail to steam, then with the replacement of coal by oil. The mere increase of speed of the navy relative to the army has perhaps seemed the least impressive instance of acceleration, yet the significance of a massive expansion of transport capacity and increased firepower of units cannot be overlooked. The speed of an aircraft carrier group may not differ as much from that of a squadron of sailing ships as the speed of a fully motorized division does from that of a classical infantry division. Nevertheless, the increase in fighting power of a carrier group over a sailing ship is many times greater than that of a motorized division over an infantry division. Never has a world power had such capacities to intervene on a global scale so quickly as the United States, thanks to its aircraft carriers.

But warfare has doubtless seen the greatest acceleration in the air, from its beginnings in the First World War to the Mach 2 fighter planes of the 1960s and '70s. Of course, here the latest developments, like the so-called stealth bomber, show that new military developments need not be toward further increases of speed, but instead can be devoted to reducing detectability, which may involve sacrifices of speed. These developments have increased again since the so-called militarization of space, with the stationing of satellites not only for reconnaissance, but also for targeting cruise missiles. No doubt the use of the air as well as space, together with the acceleration of information processing, has had dramatic speedup effects on the preparations for and conduct of war. Decisive here has been the decoupling of human capacities for movement and perception from the acceleration and steering of military equipment.[21] A number of war and military theorists, especially those who attach special importance to technological factors in determining the outcomes of wars, have concluded from this that wars are won by the side with the greatest acceleration capacities, meaning that in the coming decades, when the United States enters a war its victory will be assured. The consequence of this may be a greater political willingness to fight wars.

Highlighting technological acceleration as the single decisive factor in determining victory or defeat would, if true, render invalid the observations from all prior military history, and especially the principles of political and military strategy. Although it cannot be ruled out, it is unlikely that such a fundamental transformation, which has been repeatedly asserted in the past but has never occurred, finally has occurred. It is better to assume that the current invocation of technological factors is due to myopia, and could be sharply relativized by considering its larger context and embeddedness in broader historical trends. Essentially, suggesting the exclusive dominance of technological development assumes that the basic principle of all strategic action, the possibility of effective counteraction, no longer applies.

This assumption is probably based on a fatal underestimation of the creativity of potential adversaries, for whom a systematic deceleration of events and the resulting chances of success are of the utmost importance. In his major study of strategy, Edward Luttwak convincingly shows that the history of strategic thought and action in the nineteenth and twentieth centuries was always marked by creatively turning technological advantages against those who possessed them.[22] Even the overwhelming importance of technological factors, which is connected to the idea of the dominance of acceleration in war, is doubtful. In any case, the disappearance of classical interstate wars and their replacement by so-called low-intensity conflicts, noted by many recent military historians and theorists of war, speaks against any unidirectional development, since the new wars are without exception conducted with cheap, low-tech equipment and, contra assumptions about speed

21. See Goedart Palm, "Eine technologische Vorschau auf zukünftige Kriege," in *MedienTerrorKrieg: Zum neuen Kriegsparadigma des 21. Jahrhunderts*, ed. Goedart Palm and Florian Rötzer (Hannover: H. Heise, 2002), 279–91.

22. Edward Luttwak, *Strategy: The Logic of War and Peace*, rev. ed. (Cambridge, Mass.: Belknap Press, 2001).

and acceleration, often drag on for decades.[23] The "deceleration" of war clearly plays a central role in low-intensity conflicts and the so-called new wars, which suggests that they involve, among other things, a strategic response to the economically developed states' greater prospects of military success in wars based on speed and acceleration. This deceleration can be interpreted as a systematic turn to asymmetrical warfare in response to technological and organizational asymmetry. The opposing imperatives of acceleration and deceleration should thus be considered in terms of the distinction between symmetrical and asymmetrical warfare.

An abundance of examples from military history shows that a military apparatus that is technologically and organizationally superior to its opponent tends to accelerate warfare, since it can thus best bring its advantages to bear. To recall one early example, Marshall Murat's cavalry, which, by quickly overtaking the soldiers Napoleon pursued on the battlefield, turned their retreat into an uncoordinated flight, thereby forcing the enemy to abandon any heavy equipment and preventing them from reforming and mounting another battle. The reason Napoleon won all his wars in a single major battle is essentially this novel use of cavalry. The bulk of the cavalry would be held back during the battle in order to attack afterward, thereby taking full advantage of its speed relative to infantry in the space of the defeated enemy's path of retreat. Another example is the use of tank units associated with the name Guderian, by means of which the German army achieved its successes in the early years of the Second World War. Small breakthroughs in the enemy's frontlines were exploited by large armored units, which then moved rapidly behind enemy lines, wiping out supply units, spreading panic, and thereby contributing to a decisive breakthrough across the entire front. Finally, a third example is the use of American fighter-bombers and guided missiles by General Schwarzkopf in the 1991 Gulf War to paralyze the Iraqi command and supply structures before the ground war even began. After this, the resistance of Iraqi troops was uncoordinated and ill-supplied and quickly collapsed. What all three cases have in common is that one side's ability to accelerate the war, and thus to quickly expand the battlefield, was the decisive factor in victory.

This of course does not mean that one side's greater ability to accelerate

23. See Martin van Creveld, *The Transformation of War* (New York: Free Press, 1991); Klaus-Jürgen Gantzel, "Über die Kriege nach dem Zweiten Weltkrieg: Tendenzen, ursächliche Hintergründe, Perspektiven," in *Wie Kriege entstehen. Zum historischen Hintergrund von Staatenkonflikten*, ed. Bernd Wegner (Paderborn: Schöning, 2000), 299–318; Münkler, *Die neuen Kriege*, 13.

things *eo ipso* guarantees victory in war or even in a major battle. Stubborn resistance, like that mounted by the Russian infantry in the Battle of Eylau (1807) and again at Borodino, forced Napoleon to deploy the main body of his strategically withdrawn cavalry in the battlefield itself; although he won the battle, due to the exhaustion of his cavalry he could not make strategic use of the victory. He thus did not have the opportunity to exploit his battle-field victory to decide the war by destroying his opponent's fighting power. This, among other things, was a source of Napoleon's downfall in the campaign of 1812. His opponent at Borodino, the Russian general Kutuzov, was no military genius and could hardly approach the Emperor's tactical flexibility or strategic creativity. But his perseverance and strong nerves, not to speak of his stubbornness, deprived Napoleon of the chance to bring into play his ability to accelerate war, which in other contexts earlier proved decisive.[24]

But it was by no means only the Russian soldiers' stubborn resistance that slowed down Napoleon's 1812 Russian campaign; the size of Russia, its sheer physical expanse, also played a key role. The importance of speed and acceleration for the course of a war stands in relation to its spatial extent—what came in the eighteenth century to be called the "theater of war"—as well as the adjacent areas into which the defenders can shift the war. The larger these geographical spaces, the smaller the impact of acceleration. Or conversely, the smaller the theater, the more important differences of acceleration, which are in themselves insignificant, become for the course and outcome of military action. In the tight political and geographical confines of Western and Central Europe, the speed of Napoleon's troops was sufficient to guarantee victory. In the vastness of Russia, however, this advantage proved too small.[25] Clausewitz's famous, much-cited verdict on Napoleon's defeat in Russia pregnantly summarizes these observations: "His campaign was not ill-advised because he pushed too far too fast, as general opinion has it, but because the only tool of his success misfired. Russia is not a country one can formally conquer, i.e., occupy and hold—at least not with the power of today's European states, nor with the half-million men Napoleon led. Such a country can only be overcome by its own weakness and by the effect of its internal divisions."[26]

---

24. See in detail Herfried Münkler, "Clausewitz: Beschreibung und Analyse einer Schlacht: Borodino als Beispiel," in *Schlachtfelder: Codierung von Gewalt im medialen Wandel,* ed. Steffen Martus, Marina Münkler, and Werner Röcke (Berlin: Akademie, 2003), 67–92.

25. This consideration also applies in slightly modified form for the defeat of the German army in the summer and fall of 1941.

26. Clausewitz, *Vom Kriege,* 1024.

Greater speed and higher acceleration capacities are thus *eo ipso* no guarantor of victory, except given certain preconditions, like the spatial boundedness of the theater, the absence of markedly greater determination and stubbornness on the part of the defending troops, and the inability of the enemy to make the advantages of greater distance ("strategic depth") a factor in the war. Absent any of these preconditions, speed no longer improves one's chances; indeed, acceleration advantages can even turn into disadvantages, increasing the likelihood of defeat. Clausewitz discusses this kind of resistance, whereby a party is defeated by its own superiority, sometimes in speed, under the heading "Retreat Inside a Country":

> We have regarded voluntary retreat inside a country as a form of self-mediated resistance, by which the enemy is defeated not so much by the sword as by his own efforts. . . . He who is advancing in attack loses fighting power through the advance. . . . This weakening through action is increased when the opponent is not conquered, but freely pulls back with his fighting power unbroken, and through constant, measured resistance makes one pay in blood for every step into the country, so that the advance is a constant struggle and not a mere chase.[27]

Clausewitz compressed these thoughts into the theorem of the "culminating point of the attack," whereby the superiority of one side leads it to exceed the point of relative balance of forces, triggering a counterattack: The force of such a counterattack is usually much greater than the force of the attack was. We call this the culminating point of the attack."[28] That it is precisely the attacker's greater speed and acceleration capacities that lead it to cross the culminating point of the attack, setting off the counterstrike, requires no further explanation.[29]

Another way an opponent can compensate for the organizational or technological superiority that grows out of an opponent's acceleration advantages is by unleashing a guerrilla war, which can be defined in terms of the

---

27. Ibid., 784.
28. Ibid., 879.
29. Chalmers Johnson has recently translated Clausewitz's military concept of a counterstrike into political terms and, in connection with Paul Kennedy's anxious reflections on "imperial overstretch," see Paul Kennedy, *The Rise and Fall of the Great Powers: Economic Change and Military Conflict from 1500 to 2000* (London: Unwin Hyman, 1988). Johnson believes that the culmination point has been exceeded above all in the Pacific, and that clear evidence can be given of "blowback." Chalmers A. Johnson, *Blowback: The Costs and Consequences of the American Empire* (New York: Metropolitan, 2000).

rhythms of war as a comprehensive strategy for slowing war down. It is in this sense that Mao Zedong called partisan war the "long-lasting war." It begins by avoiding major battles in which the enemy can deploy his organizational and technological advantage by speeding up the war, and extends to the basic motto of all guerrilla wars: that in the end victory goes to the side with the greatest stamina, and not necessarily the greater capacity for acceleration. Raymond Aron expressed this with an idea that applies well to guerrilla war: not losing militarily in order to win politically;[31] while Henry Kissinger put it with the *aperçu* "The guerrilla wins if he does not lose. The conventional army loses if it does not win."[32]

At the same time, this calls attention to the fundamental asymmetry of guerrilla war, where the two sides have different amounts of time at their disposal: since one side has only a limited time budget, it is compelled to accelerate in order to achieve its political-military goals before this budget is exhausted. The other side, by contrast, which has only small reserves of acceleration, has a potentially inexhaustible time budget and is therefore always compelled to "decelerate" the war if it wants to prevail. If it gets involved in an acceleration race, it will lose very the war quickly; its chances of success increase to the extent that it manages to draw out the conflict, avoid decisive battles, and gradually wear down the enemy. Clausewitz accordingly understood the prospects of a guerrilla war, which he discussed under the headings "people's war" and "arming the people," as the product of spatial and temporal factors:

> That this kind of scattered resistance is not suited to the concentrated temporal and spatial effects of major strikes follows from the nature of things. Like evaporation, its effects are directed at the surface. The larger the surface, the more contact it can make with the enemy army, the greater the effects of arming the people. It destroys the basis of the enemy army like quietly burning embers. The fact that it takes time to succeed grows out of how the two elements work on one another in a state of tension, so that they either gradually dissolve, such as when a people's war gets stuck in some places and slowly burns out in others, or lead to a crisis, when the

---

30. Mao Zedong, *On Guerrilla Warfare*, trans. Samuel B. Griffith II (Urbana: University of Illinois Press, 2000).

31. Raymond Aron, *Peace and War: A Theory of International Relations* (Garden City, N.Y.: Doubleday, 1966), 30–36.

32. Henry Kissinger, "The Vietnam Negotiations," *Foreign Affairs* 47, no. 1 (1969): 214.

flames of this general fire crash over the enemy army, which must to leave the country to avoid total defeat.[33]

How, then, do these different time budgets, which compel one side to accelerate and enable the other to slow down, come about? Clearly, what is decisive here are the scale and kind of costs a society is prepared to pay to achieve its political goals. It is generally the case that the greater the available time budget, the more prepared the population is for suffering and sacrifice. Only societies with a very high capacity for suffering are thus in a position to carry off a guerrilla partisan war. Where this readiness is not available, if resistance is violently choked off in some places, it will quickly die out in the whole country and the guerrilla war will be lost. Thus, only "heroic" societies are able to conduct guerrilla wars—societies in which sacrifice and honor are accorded great importance. The more heroic values shape a society's self-understanding, the greater its time budget for mounting a successful war. Exactly the reverse is true of "postheroic" societies, which are integrated by work and exchange, tend to avoid sacrifice, and accord little importance to honor: they have only tight time budgets for war making, and their willingness to bear the cost of a war extends primarily to the financial burden and shies away from risking human life. Postheroic societies accordingly tend to be forced into a mode of war in which their own sacrifices are minimized by the use of ever more advanced technology. As a rule, this leads to a further increase of acceleration capacities, in part in order to remain within the framework of a tight time budget. Postheroic societies invest in military technology in order to save time and lives. This is their strength, for they are able to conduct wars with a previously unimaginable efficiency, as the most recent Gulf War showed. But it is also their weakness, for they are more vulnerable to opponents with greater staying power.

If symmetrical wars, which may well be historically out of date, were distinguished by a pronounced tendency to even out different temporal rhythms, asymmetrical conflicts are distinguished precisely by the fact that actors of different strength increase their chances of success by developing different temporal rhythms: the technologically and economically superior side speeds up, the inferior side slows down. War has thereby taken on a fundamentally different form from classical state wars: decisive battles, which are only made possible by relatively similar temporal rhythms, may be a thing of

---

33. Clausewitz, *Vom Kriege*, 800.

the past, their place taken by the struggle to impose one's own rhythm. This struggle is almost necessarily not restricted to a duel between combatants, but rather includes the whole society in all its aspects. The newest forms of terrorism give us a taste of this.

IV.

The political order of states that arose in Europe in the course of the six-teenth and seventeenth centuries was (and is) not only a spatial order, based on structural similarities, but also a temporal order, which fostered and occa-sionally even compelled similar rhythms. While space in the pluriverse of states was ordered by drawing borders, competition ensured that the tem-poral rhythms and acceleration capabilities of different states never grew all that far apart: when it briefly happened that one state had achieved a clear acceleration advantage over the others (which was almost always con-nected to an expansion of its spatial domination), due to the reciprocal rela-tions between them, they very soon endeavored to make it up.[34] This held for the temporal order and acceleration of economic production just as for the conduct of war. If one state had succeeded in maintaining its accelera-tion advantage over time, it would sooner or later have brought about the end of the pluriverse of European states and given rise to an imperial field of power. There were always developments in this direction, but none of them succeeded in the long run.[35]

Alongside economic competition, it was above all war and the threat of war that always led to the evening out of temporal rhythms and accelera-tion potentials in Europe, with the exception of the marked differences on its eastern and southeastern fringes, where the world of European states gave way to imperial order. Here the pressure to keep up and adapt dropped off, and the backwardness of these regions grew accordingly, also from a mili-tary perspective. In the center of Europe, by contrast, it entailed symmetrical wars and the reciprocal approximation of temporal rhythms. Here acceler-ation advantages were met with competitive acceleration, and an emerg-ing difference was offset by efforts to reassert symmetry before insuperable

34. Eric Liones Jones takes plurality and competition to be the factor that differentiates Europe from other continents. He explores its consequences in *The European Miracle: Envi-ronments, Economics, and Geopolitics in the History of Europe and Asia* (Cambridge: Cambridge University Press, 1981).

35. See Ludwig Dehio, *Gleichgewicht oder Hegemonie: Betrachtungen über ein Grundproblem der neueren Staatengeschichte* (Krefeld: Scherpe, 1958).

asymmetries could arise. Asymmetrical responses, by which acceleration advantages are met by systematic deceleration—described above as guerrilla war—thus remained limited to the European periphery, as for example in Spain and Russia in the time of the Napoleonic wars.

Symmetrical wars do not differ from asymmetrical wars in claiming fewer victims, but they are shorter and do not overthrow the basic structure of political order, instead limiting themselves to shifts in influence and power.[36] But above all they offer the prospect of being replaced by the rational balancing of interests and leading to an age of peaceful coexistence, as Kant described in his essay on perpetual peace. None of this is the case with asymmetrical war. Here actors follow different standards of rationality, often they have highly divergent values, and, as we have seen, the fact that they act according to different temporal rhythms and acceleration potentials reduces the chances of a peaceful balancing of interests. One of the great political hopes at the end of the Second World War and during the period of decolonization and its wars was that such an order of states could be established on a global scale, and that in time it might grow into a peaceful world order. None of this happened; to the contrary, states have increasingly lost their monopoly over the ability to make war.[37] While the symmetrical wars of European history, which led among other things to congruent temporal rhythms, are historically obsolete, the number of asymmetrical wars has grown dramatically. They are distinguished by a drifting apart of the different temporal rhythms of the parties to the conflict, and there is much to suggest that this will be a factor leading to uncontrollable escalation.

[Translated by James Ingram]

---

36. Christopher Daase, *Kleine Kriege, Große Wirkung: Wie unkonventionelle Kriegführung die internationale Politik verändert* (Baden-Baden: Nomos, 1999).

37. See Herfried Münkler, "Die Privatisierung des Krieges: Warlords, Terrornetzwerke und die Reaktion des Westens," *Zeitschrift für Politikwissenschaft* 13, no. 1 (2003): 1–11; "The Wars of the 21st Century," *International Review of the Red Cross* 85, no. 849 (2003): 7–22.

FOURTEEN

SPEED, CONCENTRIC CULTURES, AND COSMOPOLITANISM

William E. Connolly

The Ambiguity of Speed

It would be difficult to overstate the importance of Paul Virilio to comprehension of the effects of speed on the late modern condition. When speed
accelerates, space is compressed. And everything else changes too: the ability to deliberate before going to war, the priority of civilian control over the
military, the integrity of the territorial politics of place, the capacity to think
with concepts in relation to images, the ability to escape the eye of surveil-
lance, and so on and on. Not only does Virilio chart the multiple effects of
speed, he develops an arresting vocabulary to fix these effects in our minds:
the war machine, the unspecified enemy, the nonplace of speed, the negation of space, the perpetual state of emergency, the miniaturization of action,
the disappearance of the present, and the integral accident. These pithy
formulations encapsulate in their brevity the compression of time they represent, giving us a double dose of the phenomenon Virilio warns against.

And the danger is great. Little doubt about that. If you treat the war
machine as the paradigm of speed, as Virilio does, it seems that sometime
during the 1960s, the ability to deliberate democratically about military action
was jeopardized by the imperative to automatize split-second responses to
preemptive strikes a minute or less away from their targets. My concern,
nonetheless, is that Virilio allows the military paradigm to overwhelm all
other modalities and experiences of speed. Virilio remains transfixed by a
model of politics insufficiently attuned to the positive role of speed in intra-
state democracy and cross-state cosmopolitanism. He underplays the positive role speed can play in desanctifying closed and dogmatic identities in
the domains of religion, sensuality, ethnicity, gender, and nationality, and he

remains so committed to the memory of the nation as the place where democratic deliberation occurred that he dismisses the productive possibilities (I do not say probabilities) of cosmopolitanism in the late modern time.

Let us listen to some moves in Virilio's presentation of the correspondences between speed, temporality, territory, democratic deliberation, nationhood, and belonging.

> The speed of the political decision depends on the sophistication of the vectors: how to transport the bomb? how fast? The bomb is political . . . not because of an explosion that should never happen, but because it is the ultimate form of political surveillance.
>
> Social conflicts arise from rivalries between those who occupy and preserve an ecosystem as the place that specifies them as a family or group, and that therefore deserves every sacrifice, including sudden death. For "if to be is to inhabit" (in ancient German, buan), not to inhabit is no longer to exist. Sudden death is preferable to the slow death . . . of the man deprived of a specific place *and thus of his identity.*
>
> Contraction in time, the disappearance of the territorial space, after that of the fortified city and armor, leads to a situation in which the notions of "before" and "after" designate only the future and the past in a form of war that causes the "present" to disappear in the instantaneousness of decision.
>
> "Unlike cinema," Hitchcock said, "with television there is not time for *suspense,* you can only have *surprise.*" This is . . . the paradoxical logic of the videoframe which privileges the accident, the surprise, over the durable substance of the message.
>
> In the first instance, it [war] involves the elimination of the *appearance of the facts,* the continuation of what Kipling meant when he said: "Truth is the first casualty of war." Here again it is less a matter of introducing some maneuver . . . than with the obliteration of the very principle of truth. Moral relativism has always been offensive, from time immemorial.
>
> The more speed increases the faster freedom decreases.[1]

---

1. The first three quotations come from Paul Virilio, *Speed and Politics,* trans. Mark Polizzotti (New York: Semiotext(e), 1986), 100, 78, 140–41. The next two come from *The Virilio Reader,* ed. James Der Derian (Oxford: Blackwell, 1998), 140, 189. And the last comes from *Speed and Politics,* 142. I am indebted to the excellent introduction to Virilio offered by James Der Derian and to his interview of Virilio.

But what if the compression of distance through speed has effects Virilio records while some of those effects also improve the prospects for democratic pluralization within the state and a cosmopolitanism across states that speaks affirmatively to issues of ecology, peace, indigenous minorities, the legitimation of new identities and rights, and the protection of old rights? Then acceleration would carry positive possibilities as well as dangers. And a single-minded attack on its dangers would forfeit access to its positive possibilities. Thus, to summarize for now a few contentions: First, the contemporary accentuation of tempo in interterritorial communications, entertainment, tourism, trade, and population migration exposes numerous settled constituencies to the historical basis of what they are and the comparative contestability of faiths and identities they have taken to be universal or incontestable. Second, the acceleration of accident and surprise, listed by Virilio as effects of speed, can also function over time to disrupt closed models of nature, truth, and morality into which people so readily become encapsulated, doing so in ways that support new paradigms of natural science and careful reconsideration of the injuries to difference supported by dogmatic conceptions. Third, Virilio's identification of the territorial nation as repository of democratic unity and of slowness as the temporal condition of national deliberation depreciates the value of a more expansive practice of pluralism that speaks generously to the multidimensional diversity of life already operative on most territories today.

Speed can be dangerous. At a certain point of acceleration, it jeopardizes freedom and shortens the time in which to engage ecological issues. But the crawl of slow time contains injuries, dangers, and repressive tendencies too. It may be wise, therefore, to explore speed as an ambiguous medium that contains some positive possibilities. The positive possibilities are lost to those who experience its effects only through nostalgia for a pristine time governed by the compass of the centered nation, the security of stable truth, the idea of nature as a purposive organism or a set of timeless laws, and the stolidity of thick universals.

Today, ironically, the most virulent attempts to slow things down take the form of national and religious fundamentalisms that deploy media soundbites and military campaigns of ethnic cleansing to reinstate a slow, centered world. Indeed, the ambiguity of speed finds its most salient manifestation in the paradoxical contest taking place before our eyes between the pluralization and the fundamentalization of public cultures. The politics to pluralize culture along several dimensions and the politics to fundamentalize hegemonic identities form two contending responses to late modern speed.

Each propensity intensifies under the same temporal conditions. As this contest proceeds, it also becomes clear why democratic pluralists must embrace the positive potentialities of speed while working to attenuate its most dangerous effects.

Kant and Cosmopolitanism

When Kant penned his great essays on universal peace and cosmopolitanism in the 1780s and 1790s, clocks did not have a second hand; it took a week to set the print for a newspaper run, weeks to travel across Europe, more than a month to sail across the Atlantic, and close to a year to sail around the world. European engagements with people, religions, and languages in Asia and Africa were circumscribed by the slow media of travel and communication in which they occurred. Such a pace of life may show itself in Kant's racial hierarchy of civilizations, with Europe at the top and Africa at the bottom; it may also find expression in his judgment that only Christianity is truly a moral religion and that the morality applicable to the entire world finds its spiritual anchor in Christianity.[2] Kant's genius finds brilliant expression in his quest for a cosmopolitanism that rises above the particularity of a single nation; but the limits of that cosmopolitanism are bound to the temporal assumptions in which it is contained. That cosmopolitanism, as we shall see, can only gain a grip in his world because it flows from a transcendental imperative to act as if the world were filled with a providential direction that stretches beyond the reach of human agency. Kant's moral transcendentalism enables providential cosmopolitanism to function as a regulative ideal in his time, but it also folds an unconscious element of dogmatism into cosmopolitanism.

What, exactly, is the relation between Kant's conception of morality and his injunction to cosmopolitanism? Morality, according to the most famous Kantian dictum, takes the form of a categorical imperative that is applicable universally. He devises simple tests to help people decide when a candidate for the moral law passes muster. But prior to those tests, making them

---

2. "But in the moral religion (and of the public religions which have ever existed, The Christian alone is moral) it is a basic principle that each must do as much as lies in his power to become a better man, and that only when he has not buried his inborn talent (Luke XIX, 12–16), but has made us of his original predisposition to good in order to become a better man, can he hope that what is not within his power will be supplied through cooperation from above." *Kant, Religion Within the Limits of Reason Alone,* trans. Theodore Greene and Hoyt Hudson (New York: Harper Torchbooks, 1960), 48.

possible and necessary, is the idea that morality itself takes the form of a
law binding on everyone. How does Kant know that? How does he conclude so authoritatively that diverse theorists of ethics in Europe such as
Epicurus, Lucretius, Spinoza, Montaigne, and Hume, as well as vast numbers of people outside Europe, are mistaken in challenging this fundamental
dictum? He does not *know* it. He cannot, he agrees, prove this fundamental
dimension of his theory. Rather, he treats it as the fundamental *recognition*
that every ordinary person always already makes who has not been con-
founded by perversity or thrown astray by the dictates of an under-developed
civilization.

Kant's critique of pure reason in the domains of explanation and understanding does set limits within which understanding and "speculative" reason must remain. These are limits to which contemporary realists, neore-
alists, rational choice theorists, and empiricists would have to conform if
they abided by the Kantian dictates of modesty in explanation. But morality
as practical reason, that is, nontheoretical reason, is pure and unmediated.
Here is how Kant distinguishes the two:

> For whatever needs to draw the evidence of its reality from expe-
> rience must depend for the ground of its possibility on principles
> of experience; by its very notion, however, *pure practical reason can-
> not be held to be dependent in this way.* Moreover, the moral law is
> given, *as an apodictically certain fact, as it were, of pure reason.* . . .
> Thus the objective reality of the moral law can be proved through
> no deduction, through no exertion of the theoretical, speculative,
> or empirically supported reason; and even if one were willing to
> renounce its apodictic certainty, it could not be confirmed by any
> experience and thus proved a posteriori. Nevertheless, *it is firmly
> established of itself.*[3]

The fundamental character of morality is not known by conceptual reasoning; it is recognized apodictically. And all of Kant's strictures about the
moral effect of publicity, the proper role of philosophy in the university,
moral enlightenment, universal history, perpetual peace, and cosmopolitanism express the practical implications of the apodictic recognition that
precedes them. These strictures are not forms of knowledge but postulates

---

3. Kant, *Critique of Practical Reason*, trans. Lewis Beck (New York: Macmillan, 1993),
48–49 (emphasis added).

unavoidably adopted once you recognize morality to assume the form of law. And, as we shall see through Kant's encounter with Spinoza, they also function as shadow props to the very recognition that grounds them. For if the postulate/props were pulled away, the initial, apodictic recognition of morality as law would begin to unravel too. How solid is apodictic recognition?

The cultural security of Kantian recognition may depend in part on the tempo of life in which it is confessed. I want to suggest, at any rate, that the steadiness of Kantian recognition is even more difficult to support today than it was in Kant's time. As distance between cultures becomes abridged and plurality within them becomes enhanced, what appears in Kantian philosophy as the unavoidable moment of universal recognition increasingly becomes a critical site of cultural contestation. Today, the Kantian recognition of morality is endorsed fervently by some, rejected intensely by others, ignored by many, and strained through a vague sense of uncertainty by yet others. It can certainly be confessed as a contestable act of faith; it might even be imposed through cultural war as the official judgment of an entire country. But it cannot be shown without doubt to function, as Kant thought it must, as the apodictic and spontaneous basis of morality as such.

Moreover, it never was all that secure. The Kantian model of recognition—along with its translation of a God known immediately or "dogmatically" into a necessary subjective postulate of morality—was criticized in Kant's time by those who confessed a direct link to a loving/commanding God through prayer and, although in much smaller numbers, by those who supported a nontheistic ethic of cultivation over the command and teleological models set in the theological tradition. Kant got into trouble with ecclesiastical and state authorities for giving morality priority over ecclesiology. And anyone who did not confess either what every "ordinary man" was projected (by Kant) to recognize or what the Christian God was said (by ecclesiologists) to ordain was subjected to more decisive marginalization. Kant joined the ecclesiologists in repudiating the latter orientation to ethics.

If apodictic recognition—as the linchpin of Kantian morality—is even more contestable and contested today, this shift in its status throws into question the model of cosmopolitanism derived from it. It does so in a time when the need for cosmopolitanism is greater than ever. Let's look more closely, then, at the connection. Both "realism" and "idealism," as defined in contemporary international relations theory, find places within the Kantian system. If Kant had accepted "theoretical reason" and scrapped "pure practical reason," for instance, he would be a realist of the most uncompromising sort.[4] He would discern no sign of progress in history; he would counsel states to be governed by narrow self-interest; he would predict an endless series of wars and other catastrophes. History would appear to Kant as "an aimlessly playing nature" in which "hopeless chance" governs.[5] The integrity of practical reason, however, changes things. It demands that we act as if nature and history are intelligible. It suggests, further, that we act as if there is a guiding thread in history that pulls us, beyond the reach of effective human agency, toward a cosmopolitan world in which peace between nations might prevail. Practical reason tells us to "assume" that an "idea" of progress operates within the ugly empirical history of war and commerce; it tells us to "regard" history and nature as "providential"; it enables us to "hope" that the dictates of the moral will might be aided in the individual by grace and in collective life by a providence that exceeds the possible reach of human agency. The following is a formulation expressing that idea:

> I will thus *permit myself to assume* that since the human race's natural end is to make steady cultural progress, its moral end *is to be conceived* as progressing toward the better. And this progress may occasionally be *interrupted,* but it will never be *broken off.* It is not necessary for me to prove this assumption; the burden of proof is on its opponents. *For I rest my case on my innate duty . . .* —the duty so to affect posterity that it will become continually better (something that must be assumed to be possible).[6]

The "innate duty" to cosmopolitanism, the practical assumption of its possibility, and the idea of providence in nature and history all flow from

4. Indeed, if Kant rejected practical reason and the "idealism" it sanctions, that would place his conception of theoretical reason under pressure, with corollary effects on the "realist" side of this thinking. For practical reason provides the "purest" expression of reason, and it therefore provides the best index of the regulative idea of reason governing theoretical reason, practical reason, and aesthetic judgment alike. For a thoughtful account of the central role that the regulative idea of reason plays in the Kantian system, see Susan Nieman, *The Unity of Reason: Rereading Kant* (New York: Oxford University Press, 1994).

5. "Idea for a Universal History with a Cosmopolitan Intent," in *Immanuel Kant: Perpetual Peace and Other Essays,* ed. Ted Humphrey (Indianapolis: Hackett, 1983), 30. The larger quotation brings out how Kant's practical presumption of the possibility of cosmopolitanism constrains the empirical judgment he would otherwise make about the course of the world. "If we stray from that fundamental principle [that "all of a creature's natural capacities are destined to develop completely and in conformity with their end"] we no longer have a lawful but an aimlessly playing nature and hopeless chance takes the place of reason's guiding thread."

6. "On the Proverb: That May be True in Theory but Is of No Practical Use," *Immanuel Kant: Perpetual Peace,* 86 (emphasis added).

the same slender, apodictic recognition that morality takes the form of universal laws we are obligated to obey. That is why Kant says—to the realist in himself and others—that "empirical arguments against the success of these resolutions, which are based on hope, fail here."[7] And that is why decades of refutations by IR theorists of Kant's cosmopolitanism on empirical grounds remain beside the point. For they speak to the historical probability of cosmopolitanism, not to the moral necessity to act as if it were possible.

It is clear to Kant that human agency by itself is radically insufficient to realize the cosmopolitan idea in his time. The slow pace of history helps Kant to adopt a subjective postulate of providence to supersede the reach of human agency. So the Kantian trust in providence in the otherwise ugly flow of commerce, wars, migrations, and natural disasters speak to "what human nature does in and with us so as to compel us to a path that we ourselves would not readily follow." But the assumption of providence itself flows in part from a disjunction between the historical fact that "while men's ideas (Ideen) can extend to the whole as such, *their influence cannot,* not just because it is too vast for them, but primarily because it would be difficult for them to freely unify their conflicting plans into a single purpose."[8]

Kant projected dramatic changes into the future. He projected an "unbroken" historical progress promoted by the beneficent effects of "pathological" wars, the extension of gentleness in commerce, and the gradual cultivation of a higher moral culture by these and other pathological means. But he did not anticipate—nor could he be expected to have done so—the late modern compression of global distance, the accentuation of global interdependencies, and the multiplication of global dangers through the acceleration of speed in military delivery systems, communication networks, production processes, commercial activity, cross-territorial migrations, refugee movements, tourism, disease transmission, criminal networks, ecological effects, drug trade, interstate social movements, nuclear danger, and climatic change. Had he done so, he might have sensed how the apodictic recognition of morality he took to be implicit in every culture could be challenged through the intensification of intraterritorial pluralization and cross-territorial compression. And he might have seen how the gap between the scope of agency and the aspiration to cosmopolitanism could close somewhat through the effect of speed.

7. Ibid., 87.
8. Ibid.

Today the specific terms of that cosmopolitanism have not only become even more contestable, they carry within them elements of a dogmatic Western imperialism still in need of reconstruction. One key, in my judgment, is to relinquish the demand that all reasonable people in all cultures must actually or implicitly recognize the logic of morality in the same way Kant did. Or even as neo-Kantians do.[9] Once this pivot of Kantian morality is treated as a contestable act of faith, it becomes possible to engage a late modern world of speed and dense interdependencies in which cosmopolitanism involves the difficult task of coming to terms receptively and reciprocally with multiple and contending universals. Kantianism can provide one faith within such a pluralized matrix. But it can no longer pretend to embody the universal matrix of cosmopolitanism.

The Concentric Image of Political Culture

Today, when speed compresses distance and intercultural action transcends state boundaries, cosmopolitanism becomes both unavoidable and diverse. There are military, corporate, Christian, Islamic, ecological, aboriginal, and feminist modes of cosmopolitanism for starters, with each type containing considerable variety in itself and involved in a series of alliances and struggles with the others. Even fervent nationalists of a decade ago are hopping onto the bumper of the cosmopolitan bandwagon. Thus, Samuel Huntington, recently a devotee of the nation-state and the provincial citizen, now invokes what might be called "civilizopolism." This is Huntington's implicit concession to the compression of territory: The territorial nation, he concludes, is no longer large enough to secure the political unity essential to military security and civilian governance. It must be secured by a more encompassing civilization.[10]

9. I explore the tangled relations between the Kantian two-world metaphysic of morality and attempts by Rawls and Habermas to replicate significant aspects of it without adopting that metaphysic in *Why I Am Not a Secularist* (Minneapolis: University of Minnesota Press, 1999).

10. The relation between the typical image of the nation and Huntington's image of Western civilization is brought out by considering both in relation to David Campbell's *National Deconstruction: Violence, Identity, and Justice in Bosnia* (Minneapolis: University of Minnesota Press, 1998). Campbell shows how contending demands to create a nation out of the plurality of Yugoslavia engendered ethnic cleansing, population deportations, and massacres. Huntington, on the other hand, contends that the attempt to foster such plurality is the problem because you cannot mix "civilizations" in the same state. The implications this has for aboriginal peoples and ethnic minorities in a large variety of territorial states are incredibly pernicious. See in particular chapters 6 and 7 of the Campbell study.

Unlike Kant, Huntington does not project a (Western) universal that non-Western cultures might someday hope to realize. Rather, he now defines "Western civilization" as a unique formation that must be protected from migration and other assaults from foreign "civilizations." But even as he cuts the Kantian universal down to civilizational size, he shares with Kant a concentric model of political culture. For Kant, every nation is surrounded by a universal that encompasses them all. But Western civilization now provides the outer circle of allegiance and identification for Huntington. Identity in "the West," Huntington thinks, flows from the family to the neighborhood to the community to the nation to Western civilization and back again, with each band in this expanding web resonating with identities, mores, customs, values, and interests in the others.

But in a fast-paced world, "the West" is not self-sustaining. So Huntington gives primary responsibility to "the core state" within Western civilization. Its job is to protect the larger complex from multiculturalism on the inside and diplomatic, trade, and military threats from the outside. To sustain this model of civilizational governance, however, Huntington must anticipate citizens whose identifications and allegiances do not stop at the boundaries of the state within which they reside. Some dimensions of citizenship, such as identification, allegiance to a way of life, and support for cross-state, intracivilizational action, now extend to the edges of Western civilization as such. As he puts it in a formulation expressing succinctly the concentric image of political culture, "a civilization is an extended family."[11] Huntington has become a civilizopolite.

The need today is to challenge the closures of nationalism and civilizopolism with a more rhizomatic or network conception of political culture. The idea is not to delegitimize concentric identifications as such, for you need to participate in the family that nourishes you and the state that governs you. It is to appreciate how concentric circles of political culture are complicated and compromised by numerous crosscutting allegiances, connections, and modes of collaboration. Even more, it is to take advantage of the possibilities created by the compression of distance to enact a more vibrant plurality of connections exceeding the concentric model. For existing patterns of identification, allegiance, and collaboration already exceed

---

11. Samuel Huntington, *The Clash of Civilizations and the Remaking of World Order* (New York: Simon and Schuster, 1996), 156. A comparison between Kant and Huntington that speaks to other issues can be found in William E. Connolly, "The New Cult of Civilizational Superiority," *Theory and Event* http://muse.jhu.edu/journals/theory_&_event/toc/archive/.html#2.4 The essays by Michael Shapiro and Sandra Buckley in the symposium in which this piece occurs are also very relevant to the relation between speed and the politics of civilization.

the concentric image of them. You might cultivate ties to ecologists or feminists in South America that are more significant than those you share on these two issues with some neighbors, in-laws, or corporate leaders in your own state. You might support cross-country citizen networks designed to protect rainforests in several countries (including your own) or to reduce toxic emissions in the world, doing so to nourish the future of life anywhere and everywhere on the planet.[12] You might cultivate extra-state lines of identification with aboriginal peoples, targets of state torture, refugees, or boat people, partly because you extrapolate from experiences of minority standing in your own state to these more radical conditions, partly because your state may have helped to produce the injuries involved, and partly because you realize that cross-state citizen pressure is often needed to modify oppressive state, interstate, and international corporate practices. In these cases, and numerous others, your participation may involve creative political tactics, such as the formation of e-mail networks to protect the rain forests, or a cross-country citizen divestment movement to end apartheid, or the organization of cross-country boycotts against corporate use of child labor, or the introduction of cross-country labor negotiations with international auto corporations, or the creation of global tribunals to try tyrants.[13]

The question is inevitably posed, if Kantian universalism does not provide the universal ground and guidance for cosmopolitan movements, what does or could? Are such efforts necessarily devoid of universal inspiration and guidance? If so, must they not fall into some form of relativism, subjectivism, provincialism, or amoral narcissism? Martha Nussbaum thinks so. She thinks that unless "we" reach a general consensus on a thick, vague experience of the universal, there will not be enough to draw on to inspire

12. For an excellent account of ecological "terrapolitanism," see Daniel Deudney, "Global Village Sovereignty: Intergenerational Sovereign Publics, Federal-Republican Earth Constitutions, and Planetary Identities," in *The Greening of Sovereignty in World Politics*, ed. Karen Liftin (Cambridge, Mass.: MIT Press, 1998).

13. Huntington loves to reduce cosmopolitan connections above the intracivilizational level to snobbish gatherings of effete intellectuals and journalists. But, to cite just one example, the conference organized in Australia in 1996 by Paul Patton and Duncan Ivison on aboriginal rights in the United States, Australia, New Zealand, and Canada drew aboriginal leaders from all four countries, as well as an assortment of scholars from each. And it quickly became clear to the rest of us that the aboriginal leaders are in close cross-country contact with each other. For two books that cross and compromise lines Huntington draws so thickly, see Saskia Sassen, *Losing Control? Sovereignty in an Age of Globalization* (New York: Columbia University Press, 1996); and Michael Shapiro, *Violent Cartographies: Mapping Cultures of War* (Minneapolis: University of Minnesota Press, 1997). An essay by Stacie Goddard of Columbia University, "Of Boundaries and Societies: Population and International Relations Theory," also speaks to these issues very effectively.

and inform citizen actions when they reach the circumference of the "nation-state." Nussbaum is a cosmopolite who resists the moral enclosures of nationalism. She says,

> We should *recognize humanity wherever it occurs,* and give its fundamental ingredients, *reason and moral capacity,* our first allegiance and respect. . . .
>
> We should give our first allegiance to no mere form of government, no temporal power, but to *the moral community made up by the humanity of all human beings.* The idea of the world citizen is in this way the ancestor and source of Kant's idea of the "kingdom of ends.". . . One should always behave so as to treat with equal respect *the dignity of reason and moral choice in every human being.*
>
> They must learn enough about the different to recognize common aims, aspirations, and values, and enough about these common ends to see how variously they are instantiated in many cultures and their histories.
>
> If one begins life as a child who loves and trusts his or her parents it is tempting to want . . . an idealized image of a nation (as) a surrogate parent. . . . Cosmopolitanism offers no such refuge; it offers *only reason and the love of humanity,* which may seem at times less colorful than other sources of belonging.[14]

There is much to admire in Nussbaum's position—particularly by comparison to that of Huntington. She refuses to cut all connections and obligations to others once you reach the boundaries either of your territorial state or your "civilization." In *Love of Country,* Nussbaum's case for extending such commitments beyond the states we inhabit derives primarily from Kantianism, as these quotations so amply indicate. She does not, however, evince appreciation of the dicey role that apodictic recognition plays in supporting Kantian morality or in the difficulties that conception of morality encounters as intracultural migrations bring people into close contact with many who do not honor the claims to universality of the Kantian faith. These omissions are perhaps due to her failure to identify how the acceleration of pace from the time of Stoicism to today affects the texture of intercultural relations. In another essay, however, Kant gives ground to a

---

14. Martha Nussbaum, *For Love of Country: Debating the Limits of Patriotism* (Boston: Beacon Press, 1996), 7–9, 13, 15.

version of Aristotelianism issuing in a set of thick universals that inform ethical relations across cultures. I do not know how Nussbaum herself squares her Aristotle with her Kant. But I imagine she could proceed by saying that Kantianism provides the authoritative basis for moral obligation to people in other cultures (must they accept this basis too?), while her modified Aristotelianism fills out more than Kant did (or would) the character of the functional universals to which we can appeal when cross-cultural engagement occurs.

Nussbaum calls her list of universals "thick and vague." I like that characterization, as a first approximation. These formulations rise, she says further, above differences in metaphysical or religious orientation; and they are to be *filled out* in particular ways in each "locality." Their thickness gives "us" resources to draw on in expressing and informing our compassion for people suffering in other places. And their vagueness allows them to be particularized. So Nussbaum appreciates both the "universal" and "the particular." Sounds pretty good. But not, on reflection, good enough. This single-entry orientation to the universal needs to be complicated. I call it a single-entry orientation (in contrast to the double-entry orientation I will propose in the last section) because while the universal is to be filled out in various ways in "local" settings, and while there is a modest sense that the details of the universal might change over time, both her proclivities and the dictates of her model require that its basic character rise above metaphysical differences so that different faiths can participate in it. There is thus too little appreciation in this account of how much each formulation of the universal itself is apt to be shaped and conditioned by the specific, metaphysically inflected experiences from which it is crafted. Consider the first two items on her list of ten universal goods:

1. Being able to live to the end of a complete human life, as far as is possible; not dying prematurely, or before one's life is so reduced as to be not worth living.
2. Being able to have good health; to be adequately nourished; to have adequate shelter; having opportunities for sexual satisfaction; being able to move from place to place.[15]

Yes, these generalities make a claim on us. I endorse them. But as soon as three people discuss them, a series of intense debates are apt to arise as

15. Martha Nussbaum, "Human Functioning and Social Justice: In Defense of Aristotelian Essentialism," *Political Theory* 20 (May 1992): 222.

to how the injunctions are to be interpreted and applied. And yet the universals are supposed to regulate those debates. Consider, for instance, the situation today with respect to the relation between sensuality and chastity, the relation between marriage and sexuality, the issue of the right to doctor-assisted suicide, the legitimacy of homosexuality, and the legitimacy of abortion. Epicurus, Augustine, and Nietzsche, to take just three exemplary perspectives, disagree profoundly on the question of when and how to die. Augustine insists that we are obligated to wait until God takes us. Kant pretty much agrees. Nietzsche, however, recommends that you prepare yourself at the peak of life to end life when it falls below a minimal threshold of consciousness and vitality. The former would resist doctor-assisted suicide to the death, while the latter would support it. The first out of respect for the grace and wisdom of the universal God, the second to encourage more people to fend off existential resentment against finitude and the absence of an intrinsic purpose in being to tap into the fund of compassion and generosity blocked by those orientations. Epicurus is closer to Nietzsche than to Augustine, but he is not entirely reducible to either. These sharp disagreements also find ample expression in contemporary life, as do similar disagreements with respect to the other questions listed above. These disputes, in turn, are connected to persisting differences over the legitimate diversity of identities, the best account of how to prolong life or reduce income inequality, and the proper shape of public policy. All these debates find expression within and across cultures. When you fold Buddhism and Hinduism into the picture, the plurality increases. Differences in the metaphysical or religious picture of the world you honor profoundly affect the organization of the list.

This suggests to me that every formulation of such a list contains highly contestable elements. Nussbaum's inflection of its terms is neo-Aristotelian in character (dropping out his orientation to women and slaves). An Augustinian Christian, a Nietzschean, an Epicurean, a Kantian, and a Buddhist might constitute priorities and limits on it differently. Each might also have different ideas about how to regulate, resolve, or bypass such debates in political life. Key issues to be resolved thus reside inside the list that is supposed to govern their resolution.

Nussbaum wants a general, nonmetaphysical list of thick, vague universals because she finds it impossible to imagine how compassion across cultures could be mobilized or informed unless you find such a consensus. She thus regularly describes those who contest the sufficiency of thick universalism as "relativists" or "subjectivists" who lack "compassion" for people who are suffering. These types are figured as cold, amoral, playful, uncompassionate beings. The way she throws these terms around sounds to me a lot like the representations Augustine gave of pagans who did not endorse his universal God.

I contend that there are actually few relativists running around these days and that compassion plays a significant role in most of the orientations Nussbaum disparages. As Nietzsche makes the point in *Beyond Good and Evil*, it is "compassion, in other words, against compassion,"[16] a compassion toward the "creator" in us that resists giving hegemony to the "creature" in us. Nor do most theorists who resist Nussbaum's single-entry model of the universal represent themselves to be relativists. Nietzsche, for instance, claims that the tendency to ressentiment is present in every culture, and he seeks to inspire people to resist its ugly and punitive orientation to life wherever it arises. Derrida thinks deconstruction is an important strategy to apply to every text and every culture because of the unethical tendency built into the infrastructure of cultural life per se to cover up points of rational undecidability in its practices and to make concentric habits of judgment look, well, more generous and compassionate than they are.

So I dissent from Nussbaum's representation of many of her opponents. But why does she do this? It may be pertinent to note that her texts disclose a perhaps unconscious tendency to identify territorial cultures as if they were concentric, national cultures surrounded by a set of thick, vague universals. It seems to me, however, that most politically organized territories today contain rhizomatic tendencies that exceed and compromise the hegemony of this web of circles.[17]

16. Nietzsche, *Beyond Good and Evil*, trans. Marianne Cowan (Chicago: Henry Regnery, 1955), 151–52. In the paragraph from which this formulation is taken, Nietzsche expresses a hardness toward those who respect only the "creature" in humanity (as opposed to the "creator") that I do not endorse in the way he articulates it. My relation to Nietzsche is something like Nussbaum's relation to Aristotle. She draws extensively from the latter while resisting his orientation to slaves and women. I trust that it is not unreasonable to ask thick universalists to respect selective indebtedness to Nietzsche in a way that parallels Nussbaum's selective debt to Aristotle. The point of the quote is to show that Nussbaum's "binary" distinction (Nussbaum hates that word) between the exercise of compassion and its lack thereof is overdrawn.

17. I will shortly consider a quotation that reflects this presumption. There are others. And there are also some that pull Nussbaum away from such a focus. The following is one that both opens up the possibility of learning from other cultures and encloses that learning in a conception of culture too unambiguously concentric for me: "For we want to allow the possibility that we will learn from our encounters with other human societies to recognize things about ourselves that we had not seen before, or even to change in certain ways, according more importance to something we had considered peripheral" ("Human Functioning," 216).

Yes, but if you start with a reading that plays up the interdependence and tension between the concentric and the rhizomatic in the life of a state (more than do "we," "our encounters,"

Would Nussbaum's compulsion to define her opponents as relativists lacking compassion (or inconsistently attached to it) relax if her own conception of territorial culture were less concentric? I think so. For if relativism means accepting whatever norms are adopted in a particular nation or locality, it makes most sense to be one if you picture politically organized territories of the world to be divided into concentric cultures. And it makes the most sense to charge others with that sin if you implicitly assume that they too adopt a concentric image of territorial cultures. So the charge of relativism reveals more about the presumptions and ideals of those throwing it around than about those against whom it is leveled. Hence, Nussbaum, Virilio, and many others for whom they stand. This connection also helps to explain the rage against deconstruction and genealogy. For if you have a concentric image of culture, you see little reason why such strategies are needed to bring into the fore rhizomatic dimensions of life obscured by the hegemony of that image; it is also tempting to conclude that those who practice such arts lack compassion rather than practicing a version of it.[18]

These charges find their most colorful expression in Nussbaum's imagination of a place called "Textualité," a nonearthly world in which those in love with French deconstructionism, as Nussbaum understands it, have won the battle over thick universalists:

> There are on Textualité many nations. Some are rich and some are very poor. Within most of the nations, there are also large inequalities that have perceptible effects on the health and mobility and educational level of the inhabitants. The people of Textualité do

---

"ourselves," and "other human societies"), you are in a better position to appreciate how minorities in one state might forge significant connections with minorities or majorities in other states commanding the attention of authorities in both. A rhizome is a form of plant life stabilized by a dense network of connections close to the ground. Potatoes and grasses are rhizomatic. Oak trees are "arboreal." Nussbaum is not attentive enough either to the rhizomatic dimension of culture or to how new identities, rights, and possibilities, previously unanticipated, come into being out of a background of difference and injury.

18. This may help to explain the crude summary of Judith Butler's perspective offered by the defender of compassion and sensitivity to the particularity of others in the *New Republic*. See "The Professor of Parody: The Hip Defeatism of Judith Butler," February 22, 1999, 37–45, in which Nussbaum, among other things, announces that Butler's philosophy "collaborates with evil." From reading Nussbaum's piece, you would never suspect that Butler had previously responded politely and critically to Nussbaum's thick universalism with a double-entry orientation to the universal that has some affinities to the perspective defended here. The main difference is that Butler does not there endorse a regulative idea against which to test thick universals under new and unexpected conditions. See Butler, "Universality in Culture," in *For Love of Country*, 45–53.

not see things as we see them. For they have really discarded—not just in theory but in the fabric of their daily lives—the Earthly tendencies of thought that link the perception of one's neighbor's pain to the memory of one's own and the perception of a stranger's pain to the experience of a neighbor's, all this through the general idea of the human being and human flourishing. To these people, strangers simply look very strange. They are seen as other forms of life who have nothing in common with their own lives.[19]

Nussbaum shows how empty and cruel such a world would be, even as she misrepresents many philosophies on the planet Earth today held to embody such a perspective. But her imagination of that world also expresses the concentric image of culture she invests in this one. That investment finds expression in the interdeterminations between terms such as a world of "many nations," "the people of Textualité'" (who have all lost the human capacity for compassion), "they," "strangers," and "forms of life."

Nussbaum must place the universals she elaborates above the reach of metaphysical contestation if they are to perform their regulative function. But this demand supports powerful tendencies at work in most states to translate dominant models of gender, family life, sexual affiliation, religion, reason, sovereignty and morality into thick, concentric universals against which people inside and outside that state are to be measured.[20] Nussbaum does advise cosmopolites to pay attention to the "particularities" of other cultures. You compare your cultural assumptions to theirs to locate the element of commonality between them. Not a bad recommendation, but insufficient. For often enough, dominant commonalities across cultures themselves need to be subjected to critical scrutiny. Previous conceptions of women, sexuality, race, and the necessity to ground a nation in one religion have carried considerable weight across several cultures at one time or another, only to be called into question at a later date by new movements within and across those cultures. It is apt to happen again. Because we are defined, to some uncertain degree, by the concentric circles in which we move, we need periodically to work on ourselves to deuniversalize selective

19. Nussbaum, "Human Functioning," 241.
20. I will not rehearse here the pressures regularly at work to give hegemony to the concentric image. Close attention to the work of genealogists and deconstructionists, however, brings this out. It is because they feel the discrepancy between the concentric image and that in life which exceeds it that they find these arts to be so virtuous. When Nietzsche says "the chamber of consciousness is small," he takes the first big step toward such an appreciation.

particularities that have become universalized in or by us. So, again, it is not that the concentric image misrepresents territorial culture entirely or that thick universals must be scrapped. Far from it. But when insufficiently complicated by dense, rhizomatic connections that cross and exceed its circles, the concentric image points you either to the ugly particularism of the nation/civilization (Huntington) or toward single-entry universalism in a putative world of territorial nations (Nussbaum).

The insufficiency of both the concentric image and thick universals must be challenged together. It is appropriate to put some ethical money on the thick universals in your world that have acquired cultural density, as you weigh the desire of people to be judged according to standards already in circulation. But if you put too much money on them, you will not have much to go on when new, unexpected movements induce a sense of anxiety or panic into a chunk of your faith, your identity, or one of your operative universals. You will not have enough to go on as the acceleration of pace throws into doubt this or that aspect of the universal insinuated into your operative unconscious.

Nussbaum weaves the images of concentric culture, thick universals, the eclipse of metaphysics, consensus, compassion, and respect for particularities inside the universal into the picture of a world in which the acceleration of pace is not acknowledged. While respecting the extra-national aspiration that governs Nussbaum's work, I invoke creative tension between concentric and rhizomatic forces in cultural life, a double-entry orientation to the universal, an element of contestability in any specific rendering of the universal, and a mode of compassion that includes critical responsiveness to new movements of identity and rights challenging the previous sense of sufficiency invested in concentric renderings of the universal.[21]

21. For an essay that explores the strengths and weaknesses of my conception of "critical responsiveness" in relation to two other notions, see Stephen K. White, "Three Conceptions of the Political: The Real World of Late-Modern Democracy," in *Democracy and Vision: Sheldon Wolin and the Vicissitudes of the Political*, ed. Aryeh Botwinick and William E. Connolly (Princeton: Princeton University Press, 2001), 173–92. A relativist, Nussbaum says, is someone who thinks that "the only available standard to value is some local group or individual" ("Human Functioning," 242). I agree. That is why I resist the idea that Nietzsche, Derrida, Foucault, Butler, or I am a relativist. But what does it mean to say a perspective might be "contestable" or "essentially contestable"? Is that another word for the same thing? Far from it. To say that a basic perspective is contestable is to say that it advances presumptions and claims that can be supported but have not yet received, and are not likely to receive in the foreseeable future, such definitive support that they rule out of court every other possible perspective. To be a relativist is to discourage dialogue and debate across cultures, theories, and perspectives. To adopt the theme of essential contestability is to encourage it. For the alternative perspective might make surprising claims on you or bring out elements in your perspective that you

Toward a New Matrix of Cosmopolitanism

Speed is not the only solvent of thick universals. Surprising events can shock cultural sedimentations when things move at a fairly slow pace. Thus, Bartolome de Las Casas, the sixteenth-century Spanish priest, shifted from a campaign to convert "the pagans" in the New World to Christianity to a quest to roll back the destruction of Amerindian life engendered by the conversion imperative. An agonizing reappraisal of the Christian universalism he brought to the New World enabled him to accomplish this amazing feat of self-redefinition.[22] One side of his faith, Christian love, moved him to modify the universal doctrine of Christianity under new and surprising circumstances. For he and the explorer/conquerors he accompanied encountered a shock to their faith when they landed in a New World populated by millions of people who did not recognize the universal God. The acceleration of pace increases the number of such shocks and surprises. Sometimes it numbs its recipients. That is one of its dangers. But when joined to a double-entry orientation to thick universals, speed can inspire generous possibilities of thought, judgment, and human connection otherwise unlikely to emerge.[23]

---

now see need reformulation or revision and so on. To affirm the contestability of the interpretation you honor the most without existential resentment is to seek to find ways to promote agonistic respect across these differences while engaging the challenges the other positions pose to your faith or perspective. The latter promotes intra-and cross-cultural exchanges; the former discourages it. Too radical a commitment to thick universals exerts the same sort of pressure that relativism does, although Nussbaum, to her credit, seeks to soften these tendencies to some degree. She could do so even more if she further compromises the concentric model of culture.

22. An excellent account of the struggle of Las Casas occurs in Tzevetan Todorov, *The Conquest of America: The Question of the Other,* trans. Richard Howard (New York: Harper and Row, 1985). I explore the implications of the Las Casas conversion for contemporary global politics in "Global Political Discourse," in *Identity/Difference: Democratic Negotiations of Political Paradox,* chap. 2 (Ithaca: Cornell University Press, 1991).

23. I say possibilities, not probabilities. A key role of theory is to probe positive possibilities that might otherwise be overlooked and that, indeed, may be unrecognized because they have been generated by new circumstances of being. The next thing to do is to inspire the pursuit of those possibilities that are most desirable. Paying too much attention to "probabilities" undercuts these two efforts. For, most of the time, the recognized register of probabilities consists of things that are already part of established practice. Those who pursued Christianity, secularism, feminism, gay rights, and so forth at the key moments of their emergence from below the register of established practice were not probabilists of the sort anointed by most social scientists. They were acting to bring something new into the world even more than they were watching to see what was already there. And each time such a project succeeds, in a large or small way, it provides another piece of evidence, for those who will look, against the ontology of much of contemporary social science. Possibilities are for visionaries and activists; probabilities are for spectators and consultants.

Today, for instance, the speed and global scope of communication make it difficult to avoid the question of indigenous peoples in "settler societies." Vigorous movements by indigenous peoples in the United States, Canada, Australia, and New Zealand are magnified by the ability of these constituencies to combine their efforts through Internet connections and international conferences and to reach audiences and agencies stretching beyond the states in which they are contained. Responsiveness to such movements involves agonizing reconsideration by dominant constituencies of the practices of sovereignty, territoriality, and nationhood that have informed their political identities.[24] A similar set of cross-country pressures is discernible with respect to homosexuality. The activation of cross-country gay rights movements puts inside and outside pressure on a variety of states to reconsider the universalization and naturalization of heterosexuality. And since the naturalization of heterosexuality has been inscribed on several interdependent layers of being, including the visceral level, to cultivate responsiveness to these movements is to work on these intersubjective layers by multimedia means such as films, speeches, marches, and demonstrations.[25] You reenact some of the ways in which heterosexuality became naturalized to deuniversalize it as a layered norm.

Perhaps some theorists of morality ignore the ambiguity and layered character of constitutive universals because they want morality to function smoothly without the agents of morality having to work critically on the shape of their own identities. They wish ethics were less disruptive to the stability of identity than it must be. But the most fundamental obstacle to ethical mobilization is not, as Kantians and neo-Kantians tend to assume, mustering the collective will to enact a thick universal already adopted. That is difficult enough. The most fateful ethical issues arise, however, when we encounter through the politics of becoming conflict over the shape of thick universals themselves in ways that disturb the visceral identities of some of the parties involved.

While genealogy, deconstruction, and political disturbance can help to call selective elements of a thick universal into question during such moments, before productive work proceeds far you may need a regulative universal to

---

24. For an account that takes several valuable steps in the needed direction, see James Tully, *Strange Multiplicity: Constitutionalism in an Age of Diversity* (Cambridge: Cambridge University Press, 1995).

25. I have explored tactics by which the visceral sensibility may be modified elsewhere, namely, chaps. 6 and 7 of *Why I Am Not a Secularist* and "Brain-Waves, Transcendental Fields, and Techniques of Thought," *Radical Philosophy* 94 (March/April 1999): 19–28.

offer positive inspiration and guidance. This is the point at which Kant's notion of a regulative idea can do productive work for non-Kantians. The distinction between a thick, constitutive universal and a regulative universal may already find some expression in Nussbaum's phrase "reason and the love of humanity," if the latter feeling is understood to be in conflict sometimes with the putative dictates of reason.

I support a double-entry orientation to the universal, then. If constitutive universals tend to become consolidated in our habits and institutions, the very vagueness and diffuseness of a regulative idea now becomes a compensatory virtue.[26] In Kantian philosophy, regulative reason functions as a diffuse background idea, guiding, in different ways, speculative reason, practical reason, and aesthetic judgment. Regulative reason is unified, even as it manifests itself differently in each domain and even though we are incapable of formulating this idea in clear concepts. But the Kantian regulative idea presupposes a two-world metaphysic of the supersensible and the sensible. It thus reflects a profoundly contestable metaphysic during a time in which the global variety of religious/metaphysical perspectives is both visible and palpable.

Perhaps today we can act as if this diversity itself is both ineliminable and replete with promise. There are multiple regulative ideas in play, but, against the Kantian expectation, it now seems unlikely that any single one will emerge as the diffuse source that all thoughtful pluropolites must draw on. For some, a regulative idea might be responsibility to difference grounded in a monotheism of the Book; for others, contact with the nothingness of being that may inspire participants in Buddhism; and for still yet others, the Kantian idea of reason. Each variant of cosmopolitanism invokes distinctive regulative ideas, then. If a general matrix is to become consolidated, several of these variations must find ways to enter into receptive negotiation. The task today is not to articulate one regulative idea that encompasses all others— the goal of Kantianism, religious ecumenicism, and single-entry universalism. It is to inspire participants in each religious and metaphysical perspective to come to terms with its comparative contestability and to explore creative lines of connection to other orientations. That order, while tall

---

26. To pursue this point further, one would need to explore in detail how fragments of citizen connection across countries can launch the needed political connections and help give concrete specificity to the regulative ideas you draw on to inform and expand those connections. This is an important issue to Nussbaum as well. On this issue, see the introduction by Bruce Robbins in Pheng Cheah and Bruce Robbins, eds., *Cosmopolis: Thinking and Feeling Beyond the Nation* (Minneapolis: University of Minnesota Press, 1998); and Peter Euben, "The Polis, Globalization, and the Citizenship of Place," in Botwinick and Connolly, *Democracy and Vision*.

enough, is no taller today than the call to diversify Christianity within European states was at the inception of secularism. It sets a horizon toward which to move as time flies by.

The term *idea* in this context means a thought-imbued effect that enters into an ethical sensibility. A regulative idea is not something you invoke every time judgment is needed. It comes into play most actively when the necessity or sufficiency of a thick universal already in play has been called into question in a surprising way. Let me, then, identify two regulative ideas that inspire nontheists such as me, to the extent I can. They are attachment to the Earth and care for a protean diversity of being that is never actualized completely in any particular cultural setting. These thought-imbued sources of inspiration are grounded in visceral gratitude for the abundance of being that precedes them. Such attachments and ideas do not transcend the interests, desires, and identities of those moved by them; they enter into these modalities, stretching them a little here and ennobling them a bit there. Such ideas are capable of inspiring many ethically; they are susceptible to further cultivation by artistic means; and they are invaluable to draw on periodically when a constitutive universal heretofore occupying you has been called into question. Moreover, these two regulative ideas allow nontheists to enter into productive engagements with less earthy ethical orientations.

The consolidation of such idea-feelings into a thought-imbued sensibility is susceptible to some degree of cultivation only if the initial disposition is already there incipiently; and there is no cosmic guarantee that it must be there in everyone. An element of good fortune in your childhood helps. The sense of the significance and fragility of these ideas connects this ethical perspective to the tragic Greek tradition. But once they acquire existential weight, the ideas can be activated and mobilized by particular events. You might, for instance, encounter unexpected suffering in others engendered by the operation of a thick universal you had heretofore accepted as part of the furniture of being. This has happened to millions of people several times over the past few decades in the domains of faith, sensuality, and gender roles. Or you might find yourself gazing one day at a surprising image of the planet Earth. In 1968, Apollo 8 sent back to earthlings a picture of a vivid azure planet suspended in the middle of the solar system, a stunning, bright sphere unlike any planet so far observed from the ground of the Earth. This image, received as if from nowhere, underlines the fragility and uniqueness of the Earth, as well as its richness as a source of sustenance. Distributed to diverse places in the world, it provides a bountiful source of energy for cross-country ecological movements. A new perspective on the world enabled by speed. We have still not plumbed the limit of its effects.

By contrast to the Kantian postulate of a world intelligible in the last instance—even if humans themselves are incapable of grasping that instance—the regulative ideas advanced here project a world containing incorrigible elements of opacity, unintelligibility, and unpredictability because it was not designed by a higher being. Such a regulative idea requires neither a "dogmatic" (as Kant would say) conception of God nor the "necessary" postulate of a moral God, although there are versions of both compatible with it. It is grounded, let us say, in the earthy experience of groundless being in a world of abundance without higher design. These regulative ideas move you closer to sources prospected by Epicurus, Lucretius, Spinoza, Hume, Nietzsche, and Deleuze than to those invoked by Augustine, Newton, and Kant.

It still remains perplexing to many Kantians, neo-Kantians, and orthodox Christians how some could be moved by such an earthy idea. And, it must be said, some of us remain perplexed why so many adults still require either a transcendental command or the self-sufficiency of thick universals to energize and guide ethical life. The probable persistence of such reciprocal perplexity is a key issue to address in the new matrix of cosmopolitanism.

Kant gives vent to such perplexity when he asks how Spinoza, who seemed moral to him, could consistently be so. Spinoza is a pivotal figure. This two-time heretic inside Europe lived outside the protection of Christianity and Judaism. Spinoza, Kant says, is righteous but is "persuaded there is no God" and "no future life." He is

> unselfish and wants only to bring about the good. . . . Yet his effort encounters limits: For while he can expect that nature will now and then cooperate contingently with the purpose of his that he feels so obligated and impelled to receive, he can never expect nature to harmonize with it in a way governed by laws and permanent rules (such as his inner maxims are and must be). Deceit, violence, and envy will always be rife around him, even though he himself is honest, peaceable and benevolent. Moreover . . . the other righteous people he meets . . . will stay subjected to these evils, always, until one vast tomb engulfs them . . . and hurls them, who managed to believe there were no final purpose in creation, back into the abyss of the purposeless chaos of matter from which they were taken.[27]

27. Immanuel Kant, *Critique of Judgment,* trans. Werner S. Pluhar (Indianapolis: Hackett, 1987), pt. 2, no. 87, 342.

Kant resists the temptation to convict Spinoza of a "lack of compassion." But it does sound like Spinoza, already convicted of heresy by the Jewish community in his home town, is now doomed to hell on earth by Kant because he does not endorse the Kantian postulate of a moral God. Let us set aside whether Kant correctly attributes to Spinoza the idea of nature as a "purposeless chaos of matter." The point is Kant's failure to explore how some might be inspired ethically by visceral and intellectual participation in a rich world ungoverned by moral law. Kant convicts such an orientation of a pragmatic self-contradiction because he cannot imagine how the adventures, trials, and creative possibilities rendered vivid by such an immanent orientation could inspire a sense of responsibility to the world and the future by those participating in it. He thus demoralizes an immanent source of ethical inspiration in others to curtail the pluralization of final moral sources. At the close of the paragraph in question, he insists that Spinoza "must, from a practical point of view . . . assume the existence of a moral author of the world, i.e., the existence of a God; and he can indeed make this assumption, since it is at least not intrinsically contradictory."[28] Let's call the universalizat on of this "practical point of view" transcendental blackmail. It amounts to saying, "Either you confess the apodictic recognition or thick universal I take to be essential or I must convict you of inconsistency or a lack of compassion." Such a strategy fosters dogmatic cosmopolitanism.

It may forever be impossible for parties on either side of the transcendental/immanent divide to appreciate fully the force of regulative ideas adopted by those on the other. Why so? Well, my ability to assess the inspirational power in the faith of the other is limited by the fact that I am not myself inhabited by it. In a world marked by the persistence of mystery and a plurality of interpretations, there is not enough time for any mortal to inhabit experimentally every challenging possibility. If we lived forever, such difficulties could be attenuated. But we do not. Where freedom is honored, then, mortals might come to terms ethically with an irreducible plurality of regulative ideas. They might practice agonistic respect toward opaque faiths that do not move them. Kant walks to the edge of this horizon when he confesses that his idea of morality rests in the last instance on recognition rather than argument. But he converts that acknowledgment into the demand that every reasonable person must recognize things as he does, and he secures that demand by leveling harsh charges against those inside and outside "the West" who do not do so.

28. Ibid., 342.

But the jig is up. As the hope to secure a single perspective is shaken by the experience of a world spinning faster than heretofore, a window of opportunity opens to negotiate a plural matrix of cosmopolitanism. The possibilities of affirmative negotiation depend on several parties relaxing the demand that all others subscribe to the transcendental, universal, or immanent basis of ethics they themselves confess. That ain't easy. Still, a start can be made if Kantians, neo-Kantians, and Nussbaumites acknowledge the profound contestability of the conception of morality they endorse fervently and as they adopt a modest stance toward those who do not confess it. By affirming without existential resentment the element of contestability in regulative ideas that move us, we contribute to a plural matrix appropriate to the late-modern world. The possible consolidation of such a matrix involves cultivation of agonistic respect between parties who proceed from diverse, overlapping sources. Indeed, the pursuit of agonistic respect across such lines of difference sets a threshold through which to measure the element of compassion in each perspective. Unless, of course, one party dissolves the mysteries of being by proving that its thick universals, transcendental arguments, or apodictic recognition sets the frame in which everyone must participate. Do not hold your breath waiting. To do so is to forfeit the time available to pursue a plural matrix grounded in respect for diverse responses to persisting mysteries of being. And time is short.

The indispensability and contestability of multiple regulative ideas set two conditions of possibility for a new matrix of cosmopolitanism in a fast-paced world. To the extent a variety of Christians, Jews, secularists, neo-Aristotelians, Islamists, Kantians, deep ecologists, Buddhists, and atheists cultivate such modest orientations, the late-modern world becomes populated by more citizens coming to terms thoughtfully with contemporary issues unsusceptible to resolution by one country, one faith, or one philosophy.

FIFTEEN

CITIZENSHIP AND SPEED

William E. Scheuerman

Let's face it: most of us feel far too busy to devote attention to the basic activities of democratic citizenship—getting informed about the issues, deliberating with our peers about matters of common concern, attending a political meeting, or even voting. My hunch is that for most of us, this sense of busyness means that we relegate political activities to the bottom of a long and sometimes tedious laundry list of "things to get done." In fact, many of us no longer even bother to include citizenship on the list in the first place. Like this author, many of you probably feel somewhat guilty about this as well, and thus try to compensate in some way or another. Rather than volunteering for a presidential campaign, for example, I spend a few minutes writing out a check to the candidate or campaign of my choice. Even better (because it's less time consuming), I go online and provide my credit card number and make a donation transmitted in a matter of nanoseconds. I make up for the fact that my day is already crammed full with time-consuming activities by privileging forms of political activity that can be engaged in rapidly and even instantaneously. At worst, busyness generates political disinterest and apathy: many of our fellow citizens openly describe the most fundamental form of democratic participation, the vote, as "a waste of time." At best, it seems to privilege an acceleration of political activity: we seek speedy and rapidly consummated types of involvement that do not unduly add to the enormous time pressures we already feel.

Unfortunately, it remains unclear whether even such high-speed forms of citizen involvement are normatively satisfactory. Can liberal democracy flourish when a growing number of us avoid the responsibilities of citizenship altogether, while even those of us who try to remain politically involved insist that they be dealt with quickly and painlessly?

In this chapter I hope at the very least to deepen our understanding of this quagmire. If I am not mistaken, it provides a useful starting point for examining one of the core challenges of contemporary political life: how can we make sure that social acceleration and citizenship coexist in a potentially fruitful, though by no means necessarily harmonious, relationship? I start by linking the ubiquitous experience of busyness to one of the core structural trends of modern society, social acceleration. According to an impressive body of recent research, ours is a high-speed society in which core social processes are undergoing dramatic rates of acceleration. Social acceleration not only represents a fundamental source of busyness, but it also helps explain why contemporary society tends to favor high-speed over slow-going activities. I then take a closer look at the nexus between social acceleration and citizenship, arguing that the temporality of active citizenship meshes poorly with the imperatives of high-speed society. Finally, I consider ways by which the apparent tension between citizenship and social speed might be minimized. Although no easy solutions are available, we need to acknowledge some virtues to speed while doing a better job of making sure that citizens can take advantage of new political possibilities offered by it. Can accelerated citizenship take normatively more satisfying forms than our example of the harried citizen who goes on-line to make a quick campaign donation?

Social Acceleration: Why Are We So Busy?

The fact that many of us feel rushed and tired by day's end does not merely result from inefficient personal time budgeting. John Robinson and Geoffrey Godbey are undoubtedly right to note that the immediate source of the shortage of time experienced by most Americans, for example, rests on our decision to watch virtually endless hours of television everyday and thereby reduce the time available for other potentially more enriching activities.[1] But the dilemmas at hand go deeper, and they are unlikely to be solved by moralistic pleas for Americans to turn off their television sets and instead engage in some ostensibly more virtuous set of civic activities. The speedup of contemporary society rests on structural roots, and as long as analysts fail to acknowledge them, such entreaties are just as likely to exacerbate the problems at hand as resolve them. Extreme busyness is endemic to modern

---

1. See John Robinson and Geoffrey Godbey, *Time for Life: The Surprising Ways Americans Use Their Time* (University Park: Pennsylvania State University Press, 1997).

society, and not simply a product of irrational or even morally deplorable individual choices.

The widespread sense of being rushed rests on empirically verifiable roots: many of us in fact now do undertake to fit an increased range of activities into ever-shorter spans of time.[2] Substantial survey data confirm that a large majority of our contemporaries are plagued by experiences of hurriedness and a sense of not being able to "keep up."[3] As Hartmut Rosa argues in chapter 6 of this volume, these subjective experiences rest on objective social processes, which we can plausibly group into three distinct forms. First, we find significant evidence in modernity of *technological acceleration*, meaning that key technical processes (especially in transportation, communication, and production) operate at a vastly more rapid pace than in earlier epochs. Travel times have been dramatically reduced, communication operates at an ever-faster pace, and the time it takes to produce even complex commodities is constantly slashed. Second, *social transformation* itself undergoes acceleration, meaning that social structures and basic patterns of social activity now change at an ever more rapid rate. In many instances this second facet of acceleration appears directly linked to technological acceleration: new high-speed computer technologies, for example, play a crucial role in fundamental changes presently at work in production and consumption. Nonetheless, it makes sense to separate them analytically, since the connections between technological acceleration and the pace of social change sometimes prove complex. Third, the *tempo of everyday life* undergoes rapid-fire alterations, as evinced by the increasingly high-speed character of many familiar forms of both social and individual activity. We find substantial empirical evidence of an objectively ascertainable intensification of activities and experiences that typically takes place during any given unit of time. This facet of temporal speedup is most immediately linked to the experience of *busyness*. We are able to load up our daily calendars with a mind-boggling set of activities in part because their accelerated tempo allows us to do so: I can drive my daughter to daycare because my car chugs along at a rapid pace despite its advanced age, then check correspondence from far-off locations via e-mail within a few minutes, teach my classes, and then quickly finish a range of once time-consuming household activities in a relatively quick span of time with the aid of labor-saving technology.

2. See Manfred Garhammer, *Wie Europär ihre Zeit nutzen: Zeitstrukturen and Zeitkulturen im Zeichen der Globalisierung* (Berlin: Edition Sigma, 2001); Robinson and Godbey, *Time for Life*.
3. For example, see Robert Levine, *A Geography of Time* (New York: Basic Books, 1997), 145–46.

Rosa makes two additional crucial points. First, he points out that the three basic forms of acceleration work together to generate a self-propelling feedback loop. High-speed technology (new computer technology, for example) may contribute to new patterns of social organization (e.g., novel workplace organization); in turn, we respond to accelerated technology and social change by accelerating everyday life. As the social world around us seems ever less stable and predictable, we pursue life strategies that provide at least a glimmer of hope that we can keep up with it and thereby successfully navigate its rapidly shifting waters. Thus, we quite reasonably fill up our already busy days with as many activities as possible since it becomes ever more difficult beforehand to determine which activities are likely to prove useful or advantageous. We also gain an immediate psychological incentive for starting the whole process anew since an understandable response to heightened everyday busyness is to turn to new high-speed technologies that hold out the promise of catching up with the fast-paced course of everyday life. The paradox, however, is that resulting forms of technological acceleration tend to generate subsequent accelerations of social change and everyday life. Notwithstanding our intentions, they inadvertently function to deepen our sense of lagging behind since they again unsettle social experience. Timesaving technology may provide a *temporary* relief from the pressures of time, but it tends to generate further changes that simply reinforce our sense of living in a "runaway world" where events appear to occur far too quickly.[4]

Second, Rosa also shows that this feedback cycle is unleashed by more fundamental social mechanisms. A lively debate has erupted about the specific nature of those mechanisms, but no serious analyst of social acceleration disputes the central role played by modern capitalism in buttressing social acceleration. Cutting the time necessary to produce a specific product, decreasing the turnover time essential to profit making, speeding up the pace of technological innovation, accelerating production in order to exploit labor power, getting goods to distant markets as rapidly as possible, making sure that production adjusts to constantly changing fluctuations in consumer demand—many familiar economic phenomenon contribute to social acceleration. As David Harvey has correctly observed, capitalism generates

---

4. Anthony Giddens, *Runaway World: How Globalization Is Reshaping Our Lives* (New York: Routledge, 2000).

new organizational forms, new technologies, new lifestyles, new modalities of production and exploitation and, therefore, new objective social definitions of time and space. . . . The turnpikes and canals, the railways, steamships and telegraph, the radio and automobile, containerization, jet cargo transport, television and telecommunications, have altered space and time relations and forced new material practices. . . . The capacity to measure and divide time has been [constantly] revolutionized, first through the production and diffusion of increasingly accurate time pieces and subsequently through close attention to the speed and coordinating mechanisms of production (automation, robotization) and the speed of movement of goods, people, information, messages, and the like.[5]

No greater empirical confirmation of Max Weber's famous description of capitalism as "the most fateful force in our modern life" can be found than the myriad ways in which the high-speed temporality of capitalism directly contributes to social acceleration.[6]

The intimate nexus between capitalism and social acceleration also helps explain why in modern society "when fast and slow time meet, fast time wins" on most occasions.[7] Social acceleration not only renders busyness an endemic feature of modern social existence; it also means that we become increasingly busy or preoccupied with fast rather than slow activities. Of course, medieval peasants were "busy" to the extent that during bad economic times, they were forced to engage in exhausting forms of tedious backbreaking agricultural labor. Yet busyness in contemporary society takes a fundamentally distinct form: social acceleration drives us to pack an ever more intense range of *accelerated* activities into shorter periods of time. Those institutional mechanisms which constitute the main sites for power and privilege in society also possess a special status in the hierarchy of social temporalities: the enormous impact of capitalism over countless arenas of social life means that its high-speed temporality tends to become pervasive as well. Just one example: childbirth is often a time-consuming as well as temporally unpredictable and irregular, yet the business-oriented imperatives of U.S. medical care drive our hospitals to synchronize the biological

5. David Harvey, *Justice, Nature and the Geography of Difference* (Oxford: Blackwell, 1996), 240–41.

6. Max Weber, *The Protestant Ethic and Spirit of Capitalism*, trans. Talcott Parsons (New York: Routledge, 1992), 17.

7. Thomas Hylland Eriksen, *Tyranny of the Moment: Fast and Slow Time in the Information Age* (London: Pluto Press, 2001), 130.

(and psychological) rhythms of childbirth with its own high-speed dynamics. Irresponsible efforts to rush women and their newborn babies out of hospital rooms a mere twenty-four hours after childbirth result. The pervasive influence of capitalism on the social texture of present-day human existence is by no means the only way in which social speed is privileged, however. Political and bureaucratic actors advance their power position and heighten their prestige by means of high-speed weapons and rapid-fire communication and transportation technology making it "possible for them to exert more effective control over distant territories, tributaries, and markets."[8] Speed is essential to successful military competition in the existing system of states, and to those political actors who best employ it accrue innumerable advantages.[9] To be sure, no automatism guarantees that new forms of acceleration will necessarily stabilize existing power inequalities. Yet acceleration often serves existing relations of power and inequality, and they consequently impact countless facets of human experience: "A fragmented and rushed temporality is typical of a growing majority of the population in the rich countries."[10]

No wonder that prominent social analysts, including most of the authors represented in this volume, have advanced different versions of the basic thesis that the temporal horizons of contemporary society have experienced far-reaching acceleration vis-à-vis earlier forms of social organization. Everywhere we turn—from the fifteen-second "soundbites" of television news, our high-speed capitalist workplace, to our culture's eroticization of fast automobiles and fascination with high-speed sports—contemporary society exhibits an obsession with speed.

No Time for Citizenship?

Much of modern democratic theory could be appropriately compared to the high school civics or social studies teacher who periodically extorts his politically apathetic students to "get involved" in public affairs. Like the high school teacher, most democratic theorists no longer really expect much to result from their sermons: they have abandoned ambitious normative ideals

---

8. Lewis Mumford, *The Pentagon of Power* (New York: Harcourt Brace Jovanovich, 1970), 148.

9. William E. Scheuerman, *Liberal Democracy and the Social Acceleration of Time* (Baltimore: Johns Hopkins University Press, 2004), 19–21.

10. Eriksen, *Tyranny of the Moment,* 148.

of active citizenship. Some of them have even made a science of their resignation. The Realist theory of democracy, inspired by the conservative econ-
omist Joseph Schumpeter and recently reformulated by free-market jurist
Richard Posner, underscores the alleged virtues of mass political apathy.[11]
Other students of democracy refuse to give up on the dream of active citizenship, in which citizens would be relatively well-informed, speak their
minds, attend political events, join civic organizations, vote in elections,
serve on juries, and may even consider the possibility of running for office
themselves. They tirelessly point out that a thriving liberal democracy requires a relatively significant dose of such virtues. Like the high school
teacher, they acknowledge the improbability of their ideals being realized
in the foreseeable future. But this fact merely suggests evidence of the "fallen"
nature of contemporary politics and the necessity of more-or-less ambitious institutional reforms. In this spirit, participatory, republican, communitarian—and most recently, deliberative—democrats periodically extol
the virtues of democratic citizenship while typically linking its realization
to various proposals for new forms of decision making.[12] Library shelves
devoted to political science books are littered with their proposals.

Of course, the Realists appear to have the facts on their side.[13] Even in
the most robust liberal democracies, Schumpeter famously observed, "the
great political questions take their place in the psychic economy of the typical citizen with those leisure-hour interests that have not yet attained the
rank of hobbies, and with the subjects of irresponsible conversation."[14]
Recent time-budget studies confirm the accuracy of this claim. We are
indeed intensely busy, but few hours are devoted to political activities. Americans typically spend three times as much time on their hobbies as on
"nonreligious organizational activity," which the surveys hardly define as
exclusively political in character anyhow. Even if we were to expand the

---

11. Joseph Schumpeter, *Capitalism, Socialism, and Democracy* (New York: Harper, 1950),
250–83; Richard A. Posner, *Law, Pragmatism, and Democracy* (Cambridge: Harvard University
Press, 2003), 130–249.

12. See Ronald Beiner, ed. *Theorizing Citizenship* (Albany: State University of New York
Press, 1995); Engin F. Isin and Bryan S. Turner, eds., *Handbook of Citizenship Studies* (London:
SAGE, 2002); Carole Pateman, *Participation and Democratic Theory* (Cambridge: Cambridge
University Press, 1970); Michael J. Sandel, *Democracy's Discontent: America in Search of a Public
Philosophy* (Cambridge, Mass.: Belknap Press, 1996).

13. Not always, however, as Dennis Thompson presciently demonstrated in an early attempt
to overcome crude juxtapositions of "empirical" against "normative" democratic theory. *The
Democratic Citizen: Social Science and Democratic Theory in the Twentieth Century* (New York:
Cambridge University Press, 1970).

14. Schumpeter, *Capitalism, Socialism, and Democracy*, 261.

definition of citizenship and add religious activity to the equation, the total still would still amount to less than two hours per week. And the measly portion of our time devoted to activities that we might group under a broad definition of "active citizenship" continues to decline: in 1965 Americans spent 2.3 hours weekly on overall organizational activity; by the mid-1980s the figure had fallen to well under two hours, with the biggest decreases occurring in the sphere of non-religious activity. Newspaper readership has also declined.[15] Voting turnout has suffered dramatically as well in the United States and in many other liberal democracies as well. To be sure, the amount of time devoted to watching television has increased substantially over the same period of time (from 10.4 to 15.1 hours weekly), and one might easily point to the rise of "around-the-clock" news networks like CNN and Fox as evidence of increased political interest. Yet even "hard news" tends to be presented in terms of an unceasing series of dire emergencies, and "abrupt developments are regarded as more newsworthy than chronic conditions."[16] The time devoted on television to uninterrupted political speech fell from 42.3 seconds in 1968 to a mere nine seconds in the 1990s.[17] As the Norwegian anthropologist Thomas Eriksen presciently observed, "acceleration affects both the production of knowledge and the very mode of thought in contemporary culture."[18] If we ignore the minute group of citizens intensely involved in political affairs on a regular basis, "active citizenship" in the United States means little more than catching wind of the latest "headline news" buzzwords, consuming some tidbits from a daily newspaper, paying haphazard attention to major political campaigns (which increasingly consist of little more than TV ad slugfests), and perhaps voting in a national election. For a significant number of present-day U.S. citizens, however, significantly less political involvement represents the norm.

Social acceleration helps explain the origins of such trends, which appear especially intense in the United States but are obviously found elsewhere as well. The mistake of Realist theory is to ascribe the sources of political apathy to human nature or insufficiently specific claims about social complexity. Realists reify the most problematic political consequences of the process of social acceleration while obscuring the fundamental social roots

15. Robinson and Godbey, *Time for Life*, 143, 176.

16. Thomas Patterson, "Time and News: The Media's Limitations as an Instrument of Democracy," *International Political Science Review* 19 (1998): 57. See also Herbert J. Gans, *Democracy and the News* (Oxford: Oxford University Press, 2003).

17. Cass R. Sunstein, *Democracy and the Problem of Free Speech* (New York: Free Press, 1993), 61.

18. Eriksen, *Tyranny of the Moment*, 148.

of political disengagement. Proponents of more ambitious visions of democratic citizenship also typically ignore the implications of social acceleration. Unless they pay attention to the ways in which social acceleration potentially clashes with even a relatively modest vision of liberal democratic citizenship, however, their oftentimes sensible proposals for political reform are doomed to fail.

At first glance, social acceleration and citizenship seem mutually supportive. Social acceleration lies at the root of the dynamic and experimental character of modernity, in which "uninterrupted disturbance, everlasting uncertainty and agitation" characterize social relations, and prejudices and opinions "become antiquated before they can ossify."[19] Where everyday experience rests on constant change, and even relatively fundamental features of social life undergo rapid-fire alteration, the relatively contingent character of social life becomes increasingly self-evident. Social acceleration is a fundamental source of the characteristically modern insight that individual "purposes, roles, occupations, and lifestyles are not given and never fixed."[20] It helps breed an awareness of novel possibilities for self-realization, as well as a particularly modern unease and vulnerability as we grapple with the hard truth that tradition and custom may be irrelevant in the face of novel experience. Cultural conservatives have relied on the more disruptive facets of this feature of social acceleration to lament the loss of simpler (and typically mythical) forms of static community life. By doing so they obscure not only the fundamentally desirable normative core of a process that finally begins to liberate humanity from centuries of stupidity, poverty, and tyranny, but also the immediate ways in which it prepares the ground for the most attractive features of modern liberal democracy. If liberal democratic societies can be characterized as relatively "open, diverse, critical, experimental, uncertain, and ever-changing," social acceleration represents their indispensable structural presupposition.[21]

For example, liberal democratic societies need to acknowledge the virtues of pluralism rather than squelch them. Liberal democratic citizens should practice tolerance and show a willingness to treat with respect even those whose conceptions of the good may be fundamentally opposed to their own. Social acceleration helps make this essential feature of citizenship possible.

19. Karl Marx, *The Communist Manifesto,* in *The Marx-Engels Reader,* ed. Robert Tucker (New York: W. W. Norton, 1979), 476.

20. Stephen Macedo, *Liberal Virtues: Citizenship, Virtue, and Community in Liberal Constitutionalism* (New York: Oxford University Press, 1991), 267.

21. Ibid., 279.

One concrete manifestation of social acceleration is the unprecedented possibilities it provides for us to pursue a rich variety of alternative life choices: in some contrast to our historical predecessors, we often pursue self-chosen careers, for example, which we then alter, with increasing frequency, during the life course. Possibilities for novelty in human experience increase at ever more rapid rate, and our lives become correspondingly busy. Only when we "acquire a range of 'live options' and become open to change," however, can we be reasonably expected to "sympathize with widely divergent ways of life."[22] By rapidly multiplying the variety of experiences available to us, social acceleration allows to sympathize with a rich diversity of otherwise alien commitments and values. In part because of social acceleration, the "fact of pluralism" becomes something we can embrace rather than fear because the "value conflict playing itself out in" pluralistic society becomes internalized.[23]

Yet social acceleration simultaneously conflicts with core features of modern liberal democratic citizenship. Even as it meshes with constitutive components of modern liberal society, it clashes fundamentally with the temporality of citizenship.

Rudimentary features of liberal democratic citizenship are typically perceived as unnecessarily time-consuming and temporally inefficient in high-speed society. Deliberation and debate in anything but the smallest of groups taxes our patience. It requires a willingness to hear others out, carefully consider their views, and then formulate a thoughtful response. Even hard-core political enthusiasts often leave such meetings overwhelmed with a sense of both ennui and impatience, and political newcomers often never bother to return because "the whole thing seems like a waste of time." Acquiring sufficient political competence to speak with even limited familiarity about the main issues of the day appears no less time-consuming. In light of the enormous time-pressures we face, how many of us are even able to wade conscientiously through the pages of a daily newspaper? Most of us recoil from the horror of potentially time-consuming jury duty, and ever-increasing numbers of citizens fail to engage in the simple behavior of pulling a lever on a voting machine every couple of years. Here as well the reason typically given is revealing: the mere act of voting, like so many other features of citizenship, is supposedly a "waste of time."

To be sure, political apathy rests on numerous sources. But one of them is undoubtedly the growing misfit between the increasingly high-speed

22. Ibid., 267.
23. Ibid.

structural dynamics of modern society and the slow-going pace of traditional forms of liberal democratic citizenship. As social acceleration generates intense busyness in our lives, we face hard choices. Is it any surprise that we tend to neglect slow-going activities resting on temporal horizons fundamentally out of sync with the social imperatives of speed? Public life rests on the citizen's ability to pursue relatively long-term goals as well as a basic capacity for undertaking mutual commitments; effective action in concert with our peers may be impossible otherwise. How are the requisite character traits to emerge in a high-speed social context privileging episodic personal and institutional ties, adaptation to constantly changing situations, and short-term temporal perspectives? A capacity to make long-term temporal commitments is necessary "if one is to play Chopin, grow outstanding orchids, or learn to craft furniture," let alone regularly attend tedious political meetings, get properly informed, engage intelligently in political argumentation, remain active in a civic organizations, participate in juries, or run for office.[24] Researchers report that one of the most immediate offshoots of social acceleration, however, is that we "are becoming more likely to avoid activities that require patience, learning, and total commitment."[25] Citizenship is cultivated outside the political sphere (such as in the workplace or school) at least as much as within it. Yet in a society where the capacity for speed is directly associated with efficiency and progress, the temporal presuppositions of "slow" liberal democratic citizenship increasingly are robbed of their necessary social foundations. The "new economy," for example, favors speed and flexibility over loyalty and long-term temporal commitments.[26]

Of course, citizenship has always been a time-consuming activity. Thomas Jefferson surely suppressed a yawn or two on hot summer afternoons in Philadelphia in 1776, and the historical record reveals many examples of his impatience with his revolutionary interlocutors. The fundamental dilemma is that in a society obsessed at all levels with speed, even the basic rudiments of citizenship are likely to seem temporally wasteful and even self-indulgent. In a society where "fast time wins," democratic citizenship will not typically belong among our favorite pastimes. Jefferson and his peers may have found the temporal restraints of citizenship annoying or frustrating, but for the inhabitants of a social universe accustomed to speed and

24. Robinson and Godbey, *Time for Life,* 47.

25. Ibid.

26. See Richard Sennett, *The Corrosion of Character: The Personal Consequences of Work in the New Capitalism* (New York: W. W. Norton, 1998).

obsessed with temporal efficiency, they are likely to seem suffocating and probably intolerable.

The tension between citizenship and speed is more than a matter of individual or group perception, however. Its ramifications also take a "hard" institutional form. Citizen activity is ultimately supposed to culminate in binding legal norms, promulgated by an elected legislature. The whole purpose of liberal democratic citizenship is self-government, but self-government is only realized when citizens participate, typically via their representatives, in the creation of enforceable norms that govern the ruled as well as rulers. A large body of legal scholarship devoted to the problem of "statutory obsolescence" clearly suggests, however, that social acceleration tends to render this pivotal and seemingly straightforward institutional aspiration ever more problematic.[27] In a high-speed society subject to constant change, the half-life of even the most well conceived legislative norms suffer from dramatic decline, as statutes become ever more outmoded at increasing rates. Forced to regulate our dynamic, fast-moving capitalist economy, for example, relatively slow-moving citizens and their elected representatives may finally manage to agree on some set of legal rules, only to learn that the social and economic preconditions of legislation have dramatically shifted in the meantime. This, too, is a familiar problem from the annals of legislative history, but social acceleration means that it takes on ever-greater significance. No wonder that so many of our peers consider rudimentary forms of citizenship a "waste of time." If even the most farsighted lawmakers have a hard time keeping up with the fast pace of social events, the sad realities of legislative rulemaking too often provide a ready empirical justification for their apathy. Nor is it surprising that impatient citizens used to getting quick answers to their questions and concerns often fail to appreciate the formalities and legal niceties of time-consuming legislative procedure and debate. They may instead prefer an actor—typically the executive—who promises quick and decisive action.[28]

The tension between citizenship and speed also helps us make sense of the disoriented and even amnesiac characteristic of so much of contemporary political activity. In chapter 9 Hermann Lübbe uses the term *Gegenwartsschrumpfung* (contraction of the present) to describe the process by which past experience seems decreasingly reliable at an ever more rapid pace. In

---

27. See Carl Schmitt, chapter 5 of this volume; as well as Guido Calabresi, *A Common Law for the Age of Statutes* (Cambridge, Mass.: Harvard University Press, 1982); also, Scheuerman, *Liberal Democracy*, 105–43.

28. This is developed at greater length in Scheuerman, *Liberal Democracy*.

a rapidly changing society, even relatively recent historical experience proves ever less dependable as a basis for orienting social action: as the pace of social change undergoes acceleration, the decay rate of the reliability of past experiences increases correspondingly.

Little imagination is required to discern the likely impact of this trend on political activity. To an ever-decreasing extent, citizens will be able to rely successfully on past political experience in order to orient themselves effectively to act in the present. As novelty becomes ubiquitous, we are likely to find it ever more difficult to provide our political activities with a coherent structure or narrative. Consequently, a general sense of political disorientation—as well as the apathy it often breeds—tends to result. As Schumpeter prophesied, "the sense of reality is . . . completely lost" among political actors who suddenly lack any basis in their lived experience for making sense of fast-moving events.[29] In addition, the ever more toilsome task of gaining some useful set of political guideposts in a constantly chang-ing universe is likely to engender an understandable but ultimately prob-lematic disregard for the past. If even recent political experience seems irrelevant to an ever-increasing range of present and future experiences, why should it really interest us? If citizenship involves acting and deliber-ating so as to contribute to some commonly created political narrative (the realization of freedom and equality, for example) in which we necessarily build on the achievements of our historical predecessors, however, one might legitimately worry about the possible dangers of such amnesia. Republican theorists delight in celebrating the immortality allegedly generated by the heroic deeds of glorious citizen-warriors. We need not endorse their in-flated aspirations to recognize the dangers at hand. The historical amnesia engendered by a speed-obsessed society invites propagandistic and fictional retellings of the past, where political history is simply recounted to the direct advantage of presently dominant political and economic groups. If ordinary citizens can no longer be expected to possess even a residual his-torical memory capable of putting up some resistance to such retellings, do they possess sufficient cognitive tools to counter the ever-present danger of ideologically manufactured history?[30]

29. Schumpeter, *Capitalism, Socialism, and Democracy*, 261.

30. These dangers are most evident in totalitarian and post-totalitarian societies where the "loss of reality" in the populace is most obvious. But such trends can be found in long-standing liberal democracies as well. Think, for example, of the nostalgic portrayal of the Reagan years that characterized most press coverage of his funeral. The realities of economic disloca-tion, illegal wars, the failure to tackle AIDS, budget deficits, and his mediocre approval ratings were all but extinguished from the historical record.

Yet perhaps this argument still exaggerates the amount of political involvement required by liberal democracy. To be sure, liberalism should not force "on its citizens a conception of the good life with a very large political component," and we need to be willing to acknowledge that liberal democratic citizens will often favor nonpolitical and even selfish activities. By the same token, as Stephen Macedo correctly notes, inevitably there is "a participatory element in liberal practice, and ample opportunity for participation in the liberal ideal."[31] What that necessary minimum of political involvement specifically requires remains an open question, but it exists nonetheless. When liberal democratic citizens are no longer able or willing to meet the requirements of that minimum the legitimacy of the political order suffers. Liberal democracy without *some* relatively significant dose of active citizenship remains normatively implausible.[32] Although I cannot demonstrate this point conclusively here, legitimacy and stability *are* closely related, and deep losses in legitimacy ultimately undermine the basic preconditions of political order as well. For now I leave it to others to consider the possibility that liberal democracies such as the United States are already failing to meet these minimal conditions. More important here is noting that unless we figure out how we might counter the deleterious impact of acceleration on citizenship, liberal democracy may be forced to pay a high price. Busyness has many advantages, but busy lives without time for citizenship bode poorly for the future of constitutional self-government.

Macedo plausibly argues that liberal society needs a set of basic citizen virtues corresponding to its notion of the separation of powers in which legislative, executive, and judicial authority are distinguished. Without a citizenry possessing "virtues connected fairly closely with active support for and participation" in each of the core institutions of liberal democracy, it is difficult to see how it can perform its proper functions. Each form of virtue is realized most fully in the institutional actors found in the respective

---

31. Macedo, *Liberal Virtues*, 273.

32. Some recent theorists of deliberative democracy suggest that their approach, in contrast to earlier models of participatory democracy, reduces unrealistic demands for political involvement on citizens. See James Bohman, *Public Deliberation: Pluralism, Complexity, and Democracy* (Cambridge, Mass.: MIT Press, 1996). By implication, deliberative democracy might require less active citizenship and consequently minimize the dilemmas I am describing here. This is a complicated issue, but let me just say for now that I think that arguments of this type risk underestimating the high demands placed on citizens in deliberative conceptions of democratic legitimacy. As Emily Hauptmann has noted in a thoughtful critique, deliberative democrats tend to overstate some of the differences between their views and those of earlier radical or participatory democrats. See "Can Less Be More? Leftist Deliberative Democrats' Critique of Participatory Democracy," *Polity* 33 (2001): 397–421.

(judicial, legislative, and executive) branches of government, but a healthy mix of them must be found in the citizenry as well. Thus, liberal democratic citizens need a good dose of what Macedo describes as judicial virtues, which allow us to stand back from our personal preferences and try to judge impersonally according to basic principles. At least as important are the legislative virtues, which share the impersonality of judicial virtues but require a more inclusive outlook. Legislators typically are asked not only to apply principles to individual cases, but also to deliberate and debate with peers while taking a broader range of interests into consideration. In accordance with the relatively compromise-oriented character of the lawmaking process, the legislative virtues are also characterized by willingness to bargain when faced with otherwise intractable conflicts. Finally, the executive virtues require us to act decisively or expeditiously at the completion of the complex processes of adjudication, deliberation, and negotiation.[33] Unless we act energetically to realize the results of judicial and legislative resolutions, they necessarily remain ineffective. In this account, each virtue also possesses an extreme or degenerate form. For example, "an excess of the executive virtues would lead to the headstrong pursuit of one's own projects without appreciation or proper regard for others."[34]

Even if we acknowledge the improbability of extensive active participatory citizenship, a striking imbalance in the virtues described by Macedo is likely to occur in the context of social acceleration: judicial and legislative virtues will be neglected in favor of an impatient and oftentimes obstinate preference for resolute action or *getting things done*. Although Macedo neglects this side of the story, judicial, legislative, and executive virtues rest on distinct temporal presuppositions. In classical models of the separation of powers, judicial and legislative activities were typically conceived as necessarily slow-going, whereas the executive was envisioned as expeditious or fast.[35] Not surprisingly, Macedo's description of the judicial and legislative virtues implicitly reproduces this traditional picture. The careful consideration of individual cases according to impersonal principles constitutive of the judicial virtues, as well the open-minded willingness to deliberate with others whose views and interests differ deeply from our own crucial to the legislative virtues—these clearly require the temporally oriented virtues of

33. One should have no illusions about the far-reaching implications of this proposal: it would entail significant alterations to the economic (e.g., capitalism) and political (e.g., competitive state system) motors pivotal to the process of social acceleration.

34. Macedo, *Liberal Virtues*, 275.

35. Ibid., 277; Scheuerman, *Liberal Democracy*, 26–70.

patience and even forbearance, both of which are in short supply in high-speed society. In striking contrast, a preference for rushed and hectic action appears to mesh well with its basic ethos. Not surprisingly, headstrong-ness and obstinate impatience increasingly seem to represent the apex of virtuous citizenship. Citizens tend to internalize an excessive dose of the executive capacity for rapid-fire resolute action, but no longer are able to judge patiently according to general principle or deliberate cautiously with peers. Correspondingly, ours is a political culture in which soundbites and televised political advertisements replace meaningful deliberation, TV and radio broadcasters shout at their listeners, bestselling books are little more than collections of easily consumable slogans, and prominent political lead-ers brag about ignoring the views of their opponents in order to provide evidence of their strength and capacity for "getting things done."

What Is to Be Done?

How, then, might we reduce the tension between social acceleration and cit-izenship? The most obvious way out of the quagmires described in the pre-vious section would be to decelerate fundamental social processes. If the process of social acceleration is intrinsically linked to busyness, and if the practices of citizenship undergo decay in high-speed society, why not reject contemporary society's accelerated dynamics altogether?[36] If citizenship ap-pears to rest on many relatively time-consuming activities, might it not flour-ish more effectively in a society whose temporal motor operated at a slower pace than our own? If our everyday lives were significantly less busy, would we not then have more time for political deliberation and participation?

The appeal of this approach is obvious enough. Who among us can fail to appreciate the potential virtues of a significantly less harried pace of life? Many facets of social acceleration are unattractive and perhaps even destruc-tive. In particular, the fast-paced texture of contemporary economic life leaves many of us exhausted by day's end, with little time remaining not only for citizenship, but also for intimate partners, family, and friends. In light of striking evidence that speed and busyness are overtaxing our basic physiological and psychic capacities, social deceleration might appear to represent nothing less than a biological necessity.[37] Not surprisingly, social

---

36. Scheuerman, *Liberal Democracy*, 26–70.
37. Jeremy Rifkin, *Time Wars: The Primary Conflict in Human History* (New York: Henry Holt, 1987).

scientists who have analyzed the high-speed tempo of contemporary society often conclude that social deceleration represents the only suitable anti-
dote to speed.[38] What better way to reform social life as well as open up new
possibilities for democratic political involvement than by slowing down the
pace of life and substantially reducing existing temporal pressures?

Despite its understandable appeal, this approach remains flawed: social
acceleration constitutes an essential presupposition of open, critical, experimental, and pluralistic political and social orders. As William Connolly
aptly notes in chapter 14 of this volume, speed can jeopardize freedom, yet
"the crawl of slow time contains injuries, dangers, and repressive tendencies too. It may be wise, therefore, to explore speed as an ambiguous medium
that contains some positive possibilities." A radical program of social deceleration risks unduly reducing the impressive array of choices for advancing the self-chosen life plans many of us now enjoy. We might minimize
busyness, but only at the cost of losing too many of our liberties. To be sure,
we need to think hard about how we can make social acceleration consistent
with a decent social order, and we need to strive to discard its least attractive
features. Nonetheless, we need to start from the assumption that elements
of social speed constitute indispensable components of modernity, rather
than unambiguously negative pathologies to be discarded at will. A slow-
paced society might reduce busyness and thereby provide greater time for
active citizenship, but citizenship in such a society would likely reproduce
the worst elements of every static and unchanging social order: it too would
prove parochial and perhaps even suffocating from the perspective of those
of us accustomed to the liberties of modern liberal democracy.

If full-scale deceleration provides neither an attractive nor probably realis-
tic response to the political pathologies of social acceleration, how then might
we synthesize speed and citizenship? Can high-speed society generate adequate possibilities for citizenship? Might our busy lives still leave sufficient
room for effectively undertaking the responsibilities of self-government?

At the outset of this chapter I suggested that we are already witness to
familiar ways by which citizen activity is undergoing acceleration in response
to the pressures of social temporality: I decide that I am too busy to get
actively involved in the presidential campaign, and thus instead go on-line
and make a quick donation. One could easily interpret many other facets
of contemporary political experience along similar lines. In order to become
informed about the issues and candidates, for example, I may lack the time

38. Eriksen, *Tyranny of the Moment*, 147–64.

necessary to wade through a daily newspaper, but instead turn on the television or the computer and economize my time by turning to those programs or Internet Web sites providing me with the specific information I seek. Or perhaps I join an online organization such as MoveOn.org and allow my name to be added to electronically transmitted petitions and letters that flood the offices of my elected representatives. On a more ambitious institutional note, many political theorists have begun considering how new technologically based possibilities for speed, instantaneousness, and interactivity could be more effectively integrated into the actual process of political decision making. Their oftentimes innovative and sophisticated proposals can now legitimately claim to have transcended the realm of science fiction.[39]

As also intimated at the outset of the essay, however, such accelerated forms of citizenship often seem ambivalent. Any claim that high-speed information and telecommunications technologies offer an easy answer to the pathologies of contemporary liberal democracy should be greeted with deep skepticism. Meaningful cyber-citizenship remains an aspiration more than reality, and the Internet has hardly morphed into a site for idealized models of deliberative democracy. Internet information and news "surfing" is generally undertaken in a highly selective manner, with users tending to seek out those news and information sources that simply reinforce existing biases and prejudices.[40] Extensive evidence suggests that new forms of interactive technology are subject to strong commercial pressures, usage tends to be highly stratified, and they often seem to offer greater possibilities for both public and private bodies to monitor the activities and behavior of users than for increasing the accountability of power-holders to citizens.[41] The unfortunate truth is that too many examples of accelerated citizenship entail political experiences that remain fragmentary, episodic, and disjointed in character. Can they be expected to provide citizens with adequate opportunities for political self-education along the lines of the town meeting or active membership in a political party or organization? Or do they simply reproduce the worst features of social acceleration and thereby threaten to deplete the already scarce resource of active citizenship?

It would be easy to offer a pessimistic portrayal of contemporary trends

---

39. Ian Budge, *The New Challenge of Direct Democracy* (Cambridge: Polity Press, 1996).

40. See Cass R. Sunstein, *Republic.com* (Princeton: Princeton University Press, 2001), for a useful discussion.

41. Hubertus Buchstein, "Bytes That Bite: The Internet and Deliberative Democracy," *Constellations* 4 (1997): 250.

in order to insist that the crisis of citizenship is irreversible. Rather than a priori exclude the possibility of potentially satisfactory forms of accelerated citizenship, let me instead conclude by cautiously suggesting that we should see the political and institutional tasks at hand as an unavoidable challenge. Speed and its cousin busyness are here to stay; the real question is how we can preserve the indispensable normative kernel of liberal democratic citizenship while some of its forms inevitably undergo acceleration.

Of course, there are many reasons why "fast is often bad, [and] slow sometimes good" in democratic citizenship.[43] As I have tried to argue, the temporality of many forms of citizen activity appears slow-going and thus inconsistent with the basic dictates of high-speed society. When engaged in by anything but tiny groups, meaningful popular deliberation, for example, seems to require a time-consuming process of debate and discussion as well as complicated forms of interest mediation. Since "two speakers at an assembly [or political meeting] cannot both be heard by everyone if they try to speak simultaneously," even a deliberative exchange involving anything more than a handful of participants is likely to prove time consuming.[43] Necessary preconditions of sequentiality and reciprocity in deliberative exchange set temporal limits to its normatively satisfying forms: deliberative politics always necessarily requires a process of reciprocal give-and-take, and some indispensable element of (time-consuming) sequentiality remains basic to it. Yet the question of exactly where those temporal limits should be drawn in real-life terms remains historically contingent. Early modern political theorists, for example, repeatedly insisted that popular deliberation was necessarily a slow-going and even sluggish matter, and they did so in part because they implicitly presupposed relatively underdeveloped forms of transportation and communication: well into the nineteenth century, elected representatives engaged in time-consuming travel when trying to meet their peers, and news or information might take weeks or even months to reach its target.[44]

Although deliberation requires normatively satisfactory forms of sequentiality and reciprocity, there is no necessary reason for dogmatically excluding the possibility that they might manifest themselves in novel and normatively satisfactory ways. Geographical distance—as famously noted by

42. Benjamin Barber, "Three Scenarios for the Future of Technology and Strong Democracy," *Political Science Quarterly* 113 (1998): 585.
43. Robert Allan Dahl and Edward R. Tufte, *Size and Democracy* (Stanford: Stanford University Press, 1973), 72.
44. Scheuerman, *Liberal Democracy*, 102–3.

James Madison in Federalist No. 10—has traditionally been a crucial source of the time-consuming character of popular deliberation. Yet "the existence of electronic communication means that physical proximity is no longer necessary" for relatively unmediated forms of interaction.[45] Since new technologies "can enhance lateral communication among citizens, can open access to information to all, and can furnish communication links across distances that once precluded direct democracy," many traditional temporal and spatial restraints on popular deliberation no longer necessarily obtain.[46] By implication, it now at least seems possible that we might successfully reduce unnecessary and historically contingent sources of slowness in popular deliberative exchange. By doing so, we would also succeed in at least reducing the seemingly insurmountable gap between slow-going citizenship and high-speed society.

Of course, these concluding reflections raise numerous questions, not the least of which concerns the appropriate role of new high-speed technologies in the decision-making process. But they at least suggest the possibility that social acceleration contains potentially fruitful possibilities for citizenship presently untapped by the liberal democratic status quo. If we are to refurbish liberal democracy, we will need to think hard about how social acceleration not only threatens citizenship but might rejuvenate it as well. Instead of a political community in which busyness typically serves as an excuse for *neglecting* citizenship, we might then finally establish one in which citizens were busy in part because enough of them had freely chosen to *embrace* citizenship.

45. Budge, *New Challenge*, 1
46. Barber, "Three Scenarios," 584.

Henry Adams (1838–1918) was a prominent American historian, journalist, and novelist.

Stefan Breuer is Professor of Sociology at the University of Hamburg.

William E. Connolly is Krieger-Eisenhower Professor of Political Science at Johns Hopkins University.

John Dewey (1859–1952) was probably twentieth-century America's most important philosopher and educational reformer.

Bob Jessop is Distinguished Professor of Sociology at the University of Lancaster.

Reinhart Koselleck (1923–2006) was a leading German intellectual who taught history for many years at the University of Bielefeld.

Hermann Lübbe is a prominent German philosopher who has taught at the Erlangen, Hamburg, Münster, Cologne, Bielefeld, and Zurich universities.

Filippo Tommaso Marinetti (1876–1944) was an Italian literary figure and the leading voice in the Futurist movement.

Herfried Münkler is Professor of Political Theory at the Humboldt University (Berlin).

Hartmut Rosa teaches sociology and social theory at the University of Jena.

William E. Scheuerman teaches political theory at Indiana University (Bloomington).

Carl Schmitt (1888–1985) was twentieth-century Germany's most prominent right-wing authoritarian legal thinker.

Georg Simmel (1858–1918) was a sociologist and social theorist whose work has garnered worldwide renown.

John Urry is Professor of Sociology at Lancaster University.

Paul Virilio is one of France's most significant contemporary cultural critics and philosophers. He taught for much of his career at the École Spéciale d'Architecture.

Made in the USA
Lexington, KY
04 July 2013